THE big book OF REAL ESTATE ADS

third edition

1001 ADS THAT SELL

WILLIAM H. PIVAR | BRADLEY A. PIVAR

Dearborn™
Real Estate Education

This publication is designed to provide accurate and authoritative information in regard to the subject matter covered. It is sold with the understanding that the publisher is not engaged in rendering legal, accounting or other professional service. If legal advice or other expert assistance is required, the services of a competent professional person should be sought.

President: Roy Lipner
Publisher: Evan Butterfield
Development Editor: Tony Peregrin
Production Coordinator: Daniel Frey
Typesetter: Todd Bowman
Creative Art Director: Lucy Jenkins
Cover Design: Gail Chandler

04 05 06   10 9 8 7 6 5 4 3 2 1

Contents

Preface

Every day each of us is bombarded by thousands of ads. Billboards and signs seem to occupy every vertical space that can hold a nail. Most newspapers, magazines, radio, and television depend on advertising revenues. While most ads are thrust upon our eyes or ears, classified real estate advertising is different. Real estate ads are purposely sought out by readers who either seek to purchase or lease property or who desire knowledge of the real estate marketplace.

While classified ads are not the only effective advertising medium for real estate, the average real estate broker budgets the greater part of his or her advertising dollar on newspaper classified ads. Classified ads are relatively simple to prepare, are time-efficient from the moment of preparation until viewed by the reader, and bring in responses that can be converted to sales. Surveys reveal that the majority of homebuyers have used classified ads during their search for a new home. We also know that better ads can mean more sales without increasing the advertising budget.

The purpose of this book is to help you in maximizing the effectiveness of your real estate classified ads.

A SPECIAL THANKS

I would like to thank two real estate professionals who have done a great deal to improve the quality of real estate advertising—Ian L. Price, Advertising Book Publishers, Brisbane, Australia, and Gordon Wearing Smith, Philip Webb Real Estate, Doncaster East, Victoria, Australia.

Ian L. Price inspired ad numbers 3, 367, 388, 585, 671, 717, 759, 889, 912, 988, and alternative ad heading 725.

Gordon Wearing Smith provided ideas for ad numbers 5, 297, 372, 504, 647, 783, 850, and 967.

WANT TO HELP?

If you have an idea for a real estate ad that you feel should be in the next edition of this book, I would like to hear from you. Contact: William Pivar at *pivarfish@webtv.net*

Understanding Classified Advertising

Classified real estate ads differ from other forms of advertising in that they are actually sought out by prospective buyers. They are not thrust upon the reader without permission.

Almost every broker feels that he or she writes pretty good classified ads because in "seller markets," where there is strong seller demand for a limited product, virtually every ad a broker writes will generate a response. However, when the market is less favorable to sellers, responses to mediocre ads will dwindle, while responses to poor ads may all but disappear. In this kind of market an ad has to compete with other ads to generate responses, and competition means it is important for an ad to noticeably stand out among its competitors. A better ad can sometimes mean the difference between the success and failure of a real estate business.

PURPOSE OF CLASSIFIED ADS

The purpose of real estate classified ads is to get reader response that will result in a personal encounter and will provide the advertiser an opportunity to sell property. Ads don't sell property; people do. No matter how enticing you make a property appear in an ad, you probably won't sell that property if it isn't a marketable one.

You may remember the character "Joe Isuzu," from the award-winning automobile advertising campaign in the 1980s. While most everyone loved the ads and identified them with the product, the ads failed because they didn't fulfill their purpose: to sell more vehicles. The reason the ad campaign failed is that at that time the public did not consider the Isuzu product to be competitive with other Japanese automobiles and trucks on the market. The lesson those of us in the real estate profession can derive from the Isuzu experience is that it is not cost-effective to advertise a noncompetitive product. The first step in marketing real estate is to obtain a listing at a fair market price. While advertising can go a long way to assist a salesperson in marketing property, by itself it will fail to meet the needs of the client and the broker.

Every piece of real estate is good in that it has worth. Every home has had an owner and will eventually have another owner. It will be attractive to someone, for some purpose at some price. If a property is overpriced in relationship to what is available on the marketplace, however, it is not a good product to advertise. Not only will advertising dollars be wasted, the prospective buyers who do respond will be "turned off" by what they regard as your attempt to obtain an unrealistic price.

AIDA

In advertising, we use the acronym *AIDA*:

- Attention
- Interest
- Desire
- Action

We want the ad to catch the reader's *attention,* create an *interest,* then a *desire* to know more about the property, and *action,* which is the telephone call or visit to your office, project, or open house. If your ads fail to achieve that last *A, ACTION,* they merely serve as institutional advertisements. While institutional advertising makes a reader feel good about a firm, it does not help sell a product.

ANATOMY OF AN AD

Ad Heading

The ad heading is what gets a reader's attention. To develop a heading, ask yourself what feature or features of a house are likely to be of greatest importance to the type of buyers who will purchase the property. You will find that there are many important features that appeal to different categories of buyers. As an example, 4BR is a very important feature for larger families, so if you want to appeal to a larger family, then the fact that the property has four bedrooms should be emphasized in the heading. Please note: If the strongest feature of the property is its "location" and the *location* is *already* clearly indicated in some way by the newspaper, repetition of that feature in your ad does not serve your needs.

You don't have to rely on only one feature in your heading. Features can be combined in a heading such as an area and a price, for example, "Shorewood Hills—$187,500."

Quite often, the more desirable a feature is, the easier it is to prepare the ad heading. As an example, assume a seller has little equity in a property and a no-qualifying, assumable mortgage in place. Examples of headings would be:

**Low-Down,
No-Qualifying**

Almost Nothing Down

and assume a no-qualifying loan for this . . .

Bad Credit OK— Assume Loan

after a low down payment.

The first and second headings primarily appeal to buyers with limited down payment resources, while the third heading appeals to buyers who have had credit problems.

It is possible to use two-line headings, although a better approach would be a split heading, where another heading breaks up the text, or body, of the ad. You will see a number of split headings in this book.

When a property does not have a particularly strong feature to generate a creative heading, you should consider using an attention-getting heading, one that leads into the ad, as in the following examples:

It's Sold!

or it will be as soon as you've seen this . . .

Undressed

and waiting for you to choose the colors in this new . . .

Ringo Starr

didn't stay here, but Beatle records were constantly played in the separate teen suite of this . . .

Body

Your ad body should state a limited amount of information, just enough, so that the reader will want to know more about the property.

When designing your ad, keep in mind that potential buyers normally respond to ads that are within a specific price range or are priced slightly higher than they wish to pay.

The closing portion of the ad can be a simple statement reflecting the property's price, but a more effective closing is a call for action, such as the following:

- "Call now, because at [$189,500] it's unlikely to be available tomorrow."

- "At [$247,900], it's call now or be sorry."

- "First one to call will be the winner at [$234,900]."

GENERAL DO'S AND DON'TS

Here are some general guidelines for preparing classified ads.

Do's

- Be honest in your ad (a notable exception: By describing a "fixer-upper" property or problem property worse than it actually is, you're likely to increase the response to the ad and offer a pleasant surprise to property viewers).

- Designate one person in the office to write the ads. It's an unfortunate truth that many salespeople will not take the time to write good ads, which can lead to a listings portfolio comprised of mediocre ads. Mediocre ads will result in mediocre responses.

- Try to differentiate your ads from those of other firms. This is of extreme importance when there are a great many ads. (There is a "sameness" to most real estate ads. When there are multiple columns of ads, you want your ad to stand out and grab the reader's attention. An ad that isn't read is a wasted opportunity.)

- The ad writer must always see the property prior to writing the ads. By viewing the property, the ad writer will gain a perspective of the benefits offered that would not be fully understood from a few photos and a basic description of the property.

- The heading should highlight the most desirable and sought after feature of the property. If such a distinguishing feature doesn't exist, use an attention getting heading. (Note: attention getting headings can be combined with desirable features.)

- Concentrate your advertising dollars on properties that *will* probably sell rather than properties that *might* sell.

- Place greater emphasis on advertising properties when you have similar property listings available (substitute properties). In this way, the ad will attract buyers for more than just the property advertised.

- Advertise in various price ranges with a focus on a variety of property types. Properties advertised in this manner will bring responses that can potentially be substituted for other properties. A few ads could actually cover your entire inventory.

- Use adjectives to enhance the ad.

- Change your ads so a property does not appear *shopworn*. The longer an ad appears, the fewer "hits" it receives per insertion. Ads are most effective the first time they run. Consider no more than three insertions of the same ad. The next step would involve rewriting the ad using a different approach. Consider appealing to different readers in various ads.

- Always include your firm's name in your ads.

- Include an Internet address. If the property is featured on your office Internet site, include a designation so the property can be found.

- Include the number of bedrooms and baths, as well as locations of the properties (if not mentioned in the ad heading). Buyers want to know these kinds of basics.

- Include the price in the ad or indicate the price range.

- Use curiosity to gain readers' responses. The ad should make readers want to know more.

- Consider negative ads—while most advertising books tell us to avoid negative ads, this general rule does not hold true for real estate. In fact, the worse you make a fixer-upper appear to be, the greater the response appears to be. To many property seekers, problems appear to spell *b-a-r-g-a-i-n!*

- Track ad response. You want to know what type of ads and type of properties advertised are bringing better or less than average responses.

Don'ts

- Never include information about an owner or an owner's motivation to sell without express permission from the owner. Such permission should be in writing.

- Never include any indication that an owner might accept less than the advertised price without express permission of the owner. Permission should be in writing.

- Never set advertising limits per property or stop advertising a property because you're not getting responses. Ads from one property can create sales of other properties. Also, you agreed to use your best efforts to locate a buyer. Discontinuing advertising may constitute a breach of your fiduciary duty to the owner.

- Don't use abbreviations in ads or terms that the majority or readers may not understand.

- Never place ads for the purpose of pleasing owners or salespeople. (Once you start letting other people decide how your advertising dollars will be spent, you will have pressure from other salespeople and/or owners. The focus of your advertising must be on anticipated sales.)

- Never advertise properties you do not control with an exclusive-right-to-sell listing.

- Never repeat in the *ad heading* what is in the newspaper *category heading*. (If the newspaper has a *Middleton* ad column heading you would not head the ad "Middleton.")

- Don't just give laundry lists of properties without descriptions. The exception would be multiple units available in a desirable development. Such an ad would show that you have a large inventory to select from.

- Don't put multiple properties in a single classified ad unless all those properties would be properly located under the same classified ad heading.

- Don't advertise the obvious. In most markets people would expect a half-million-dollar home to have a large kitchen, a living room, a dining area, and an attached garage. You should advertise features that add *zing* such as "a private home office," "solarium," or "English rose garden."

- Don't advertise the unimportant. Most readers are not influenced because you advertised the basement as "10-course" or the lot as ".237 acres."

- Don't include words that won't benefit the ad. (For example, if a solarium is unheated, words such as "unheated" or "could be easily heated" don't benefit the ad. In fact they detract from the ad. On the other hand, "window-wrapped" solarium creates a positive image and benefits the ad.)

- Don't insert ads for lengthy time periods in order to obtain lower ad rates.

- Never advertise an overpriced property. If you feel it is overpriced, give the listing back or get the price adjusted. (Overpriced property costs money to advertise, takes salespersons' time, and has little likelihood of being sold. The belief of some agents that "any listing is better than no listing" is untrue. In fact, it is just the opposite.)

- Don't say too much. Paint a picture with details to be filled in by the readers' imagination.

> The final rule in advertising is that there is no hard-and-fast rule. We always seem to find exceptions. Doing what others are not doing or doing something in a completely different fashion can, at times, be highly effective. Keep an open mind and be willing to experiment.

Because of the high cost of classified ads in some large metropolitan newspapers, your financial resources and your advertising budget may determine when and how you advertise in these papers. While ad prices vary by the insert day, the number of insertions, and the lines contracted for, several newspapers have rates over $40 per line for a single insertion. You can readily see that several 10-line ads in such a newspaper can eat up your firm's advertising budget in just a few days. On the other hand, there are many community newspapers that have classified advertising rates of a dollar or two per line.

When a newspaper has a large circulation over a vast area, you will be paying for circulation in areas unlikely to produce buyers. Consider using lower circulation papers where distribution is more closely aligned with your buyer base. As an example, because of high advertising costs, the *Los Angeles Times* has a relatively small classified section for Homes For Sale. Instead of using the *Los Angeles Times* for the majority of their ads, most brokers use more regional newspapers such as the *Orange County Register*, which covers a more limited area. The newspapers that provide the most ads for your area are the papers that will be sought by persons interested in buying within that area.

Nevertheless, large papers with expensive classified sections can be valuable. Less expensive short ads can be effectively used as teasers with references to an Internet site for more information. You will see a number of ads of this type within this book.

As an example, ad number 56 on page 38 (ad heading: "Taurus? No Bull") paints a desirable picture of a property, but the cost of running such an ad in a major newspaper might be a budget buster. The alternate ad directing the reader to the Internet significantly reduces the cost of the ad.

EVALUATING CLASSIFIED ADS

Despite the dollars involved, many brokers tend to write their ads in a matter of minutes, and if they are too busy, they often recycle old ads. When there is a seller's market with more buyers than sellers, even the weakest ad will generate inquiries and, eventually, sales.

When the market changes and competition for buyers gets tough, telephones ring less often. Real estate salespersons will often pressure their brokers to increase their advertising budgets to regain their sales volume. Increasing advertising expense in a declining market as the primary corrective measure towards generating sales is generally a formula that turns a once-successful broker into a salesperson for a wiser broker.

Very few brokers have been able to successfully increase sales in a declining market by increasing advertising. Those that have expanded in such a market generally owe their success to a reallocation of advertising dollars or a change in advertising approach.

Before you even consider altering your advertising budget, first find out where you are now.

You should determine three things:

1. The source of advertising inquiries:
    ■ Newspaper or other medium that resulted in the inquiry
    ■ Type of ad that brought inquiries
    ■ Day of the week that the ad appeared

2. Cost per inquiry:
    ■ By different media
    ■ By different days
    ■ By type of property

3. Sales of advertised or substitute property:
    ■ By different media
    ■ By property type
    ■ By type of ad

Your three-part analysis could indicate ad categories that appeared effective but in fact resulted in a great deal of wasted energy and wasted dollars. You may also determine that some categories of ads are more effective in eventual sales than the number of responses would indicate.

Your research might indicate greater effectiveness in particular papers, marginal effectiveness in others, and even papers where ad costs resulted in a negative cash flow. You might decide from the responses that your office should concentrate on particular geographical areas, types of properties, price ranges, or buyer groups for more effective operations rather than trying to advertise a wider range of properties to more diverse buyers. Your ad analysis might reveal most effective days for the bulk of your advertising and even indicate effectiveness based on ad size.

You also might wish to modify your advertising budget or relocate advertising dollars for a more effective response. In this way, your advertising can become more effective without improving ad quality.

But ad quality does affect ad response. Ads of identical size written for the same property can result either in general reader apathy or a deluge of calls. The dollar savings in ads that work to maximize response can be tremendous. As an example, assume a $4,000 per month advertising budget brings in 100 inquiries per month. The direct advertising cost per inquiry is $40. If the same $4,000 could be spent on ads that bring in 200 calls, the cost per inquiry would be reduced to $20. Professional copywriters have doubled, tripled, and even quadrupled ad response by enhancing ad quality. You can do the same by following our advice. It is important to note that what is or is not considered to be a good ad will vary by geographical area, your particular market, and the type of property. A type of ad or even a specific ad that is effective in a small midwestern community may experience far different results in a large eastern city or even a southern community of similar size. You must continue to evaluate your ads to find out what does and does not work in your market area for the inventory that you are marketing. In this way, you can learn from both successful and unsuccessful ads.

FAIR HOUSING

The federal *Fair Housing Act* states that it is unlawful "to make, print, or publish any notice, statement, or advertisement with respect to the sale or rental of a dwelling that indicates any preference, limitation, or discrimination because of race, color, religion, sex, handicap, familial status, or national origin..." Violation of the federal act can result in fines. State laws also provide for disciplinary action against licensees who discriminate in advertising. The federal Fair Housing Act is enforced by the Department of Housing and Urban Development (HUD). You may review the federal Fair Housing Act at *www4.law.cornell.edu/uscode/42/ch45.html*.

For an overview of the various federal housing laws and executive orders, check: *www.hud.gov/offices/theo/fhlaws/index.cfm*.

This Act specifies that the following phrases, if used in real estate ads, violate the law:

Blacks Only	Able-Bodied Man	Singles Preferred
Adults Only	No Hispanics	Married Couples
No AIDS or HIV	Single Working Male	Christian
Muslims Only	Ladies Only	Gentlemen Only

There are, however, other discriminatory words and phrases that are not readily recognized as discriminatory language. To complicate matters, words have different connotations among different social, ethnic, and economic groups. A location (a particular neighborhood, etc.) can also contribute to how a word or phrase is used and understood.

A number of human rights commissions, real estate organizations, and newspaper groups have generated lists of words that should be excluded from real estate ads because the words are regarded as discriminatory. The lists differ significantly and the Department of Housing and Urban Development (HUD), which enforces the Fair Housing Act, has been reluctant to clarify which terms are classified as discriminatory. This has placed real estate brokers in a vulnerable position.

There was a partial clarification on January 9, 1995, when HUD sent a memo to its staff as to guidelines for investigation of discrimination allegations. The memo addressed a number of points:

1. ***Race, Color, National Origin.*** Complaints should not be filed for use of "master bedroom," "rare find," or "desirable neighborhood." Some groups had felt that "master" indicated slavery and "rare find" and "desirable neighborhood" indicated areas without minorities.

2. ***Religion.*** Statements such as "apartment complex with chapel" or services such as "kosher meals available" do not, on their face, state a preference for persons who might use such facilities. Prior to HUD's memo, groups were advising that any reference in an ad to religion would violate the federal Fair Housing Act.

3. ***Sex.*** Use of the term "master bedroom," "mother-in-law suite," and "bachelor apartment" do not violate the act, as they are commonly used physical descriptions.

4. ***Handicap.*** Descriptions of properties such as "great view," "fourth-floor walk-up," and "walk-in closets" do not violate the Act. Services or facilities such as "jogging trails" or references to neighborhoods, such as "walk to bus stop," do not violate the Act.

   Because many handicapped individuals cannot perform these activities, it was formerly thought that references to walking, biking, jogging, and so on would violate the law. It also is acceptable to describe the conduct required of residents such as "nonsmoking," or "sober." You can't however, say "nonsmokers" or "no alcoholics," as these describe persons, not barred activities. You can advertise accessibility features such as "wheelchair ramp."

5. ***Familial Status.*** While advertisements may not contain a limitation on the number or ages of children or state a preference for adults, couples, or singles, you are not "facially discriminatory" by advertising the properties as "2-BR, cozy, family room," services and facilities with "no bicycles allowed," or neighborhoods with "quiet streets."

The HUD memorandum leaves a great deal of unanswered questions regarding which words and phrases are considered to be a violation of the law when used in real estate advertising.

The authors have discussed the problem of what is or is not discriminatory advertising with several HUD officials. The rule *appears* to be one of reasonableness. If an ordinary person would feel that an ad favored or showed disfavor for a protected group, it would be discriminatory.

In deciding whether a word or phrase is appropriate for use in an ad, you should use a Golden Rule approach. Put yourself in the shoes of the individual reading your ad. Ask yourself if you, as such an individual, would feel comfortable responding to the ad. This in itself might not be enough, as you might not be aware of a word or phrase connotation used by particular groups. You might also check with your local Board of REALTORS® and/or state licensing agencies as well as state human rights commissions as to advertising guidelines that may reflect state laws.

FIGURE 1.1 Fair Housing Advertising Word and Phrase List (Revised 11/05/02)

This word and phrase list is intended as a guideline to assist in complying with state and federal fair housing laws. It is not intended as a complete list of every word or phrase that could violate any local, state, or federal statutes.

This list is intended to educate and provide general guidance to the many businesses in the Miami Valley that create and publish real estate advertising. This list is not intended to provide legal advice. By its nature, a general list cannot cover particular persons' situations or questions. The list is intended to make you aware of and sensitive to the important legal obligations concerning discriminatory real estate advertising.

Bold = Acceptable	*Italic* = Caution	~~Cross-Through~~ = Not acceptable

A
~~able-bodied~~
Active
~~adult community~~
~~adult living~~
~~adult park~~
~~adults only~~
~~African~~
Agile
~~AIDS, no~~
~~Alcoholics, no~~
~~Appalachian, no~~
~~American Indians~~
Asian
Assistance animal(s)
Assistance animal(s) only

B
Bachelor
~~Bachelor pad~~
~~Blacks, no~~
~~blind, no~~
board approval required

C
Catholic
~~Caucasian~~
~~Chicano, no~~
~~children, no~~
~~Chinese~~
Christian
~~Churches, near~~
Close to
college students, no

~~Colored~~
~~Congregation~~
Convalescent home
Convenient to
~~Couple~~
~~couples only~~
Credit check required
~~crippled, no~~
Curfew

D
~~Deaf, no~~
Den
~~disabled, no~~
domestics, quarters
Drug users, no
Drugs, no

E
~~employed, must be~~
~~empty nesters~~
~~English only~~
Equal Housing Opportunity
~~ethnic references~~
Exclusive
Executive

F
~~families, no~~
families welcome
family room
family, great for
*female roommate ***
*female(s) only ***

*55 and older community ***
fixer-upper
gated community

G
Gays, no
Gender
~~golden-agers only~~
golf course, near
~~group home(s) no~~
guest house

H
handicap accessible
~~handicap parking, no~~
~~Handicapped, not for~~
~~healthy only~~
~~Hindu, no~~
~~Hispanic~~
~~HIV, no~~
~~housing for older persons/seniors ***
~~Hungarian, no~~

I
Ideal for ... (should not describe people)
~~impaired, no~~
~~Indian~~
Integrated
~~Irish, no~~
~~Italian, no~~

J
Jewish

K
kids welcome

L
Landmark reference
~~Latino~~
Lesbians, no

M
*male roommate ***
~~male(s) only ***
*man (men) only ***
Mature
~~mature complex~~
~~mature couple~~
~~mature individuals~~
~~mature person(s)~~
membership available
Membership approval required
~~Mentally handicapped, no~~
~~Mentally ill, no~~
~~Mexican~~
~~Mexican-American~~
~~Migrant workers, no~~
~~Mormon Temple~~
Mosque
Mother in law apartment
Muslim

FAIR HOUSING ADVERTISING WORD AND PHRASE LIST

Of the many lists of nonacceptable terms, cautionary terms, and acceptable terms, we were impressed by the Fair Housing Advertising Word and Phrase List developed by the Miami Valley Fair Housing Center, Inc., Dayton, Ohio: *www.mvfairhousing.com;* The center has granted us permission to reprint its list in Figure 1.1. We feel that this list is the most reasonable. You might note that many of the terms shown as "Cautionary" are listed by others as being "Not Acceptable." How the caution term is used in the ad determines if it is discriminatory or not.

Note: The list is not intended as legal advice but to provide general guidance.

All cautionary words are unacceptable if utilized in a context that states an unlawful preference or limitation. Furthermore, all cautionary words are "red flags" to fair housing enforcement agencies. Use of these words will only serve to invite further investigation and/or testing.

N
Nanny's room
Nationality
Near
Negro, no
Neighborhood name
Newlyweds
Nice
nonsmokers
# of bedrooms
# of children
# of persons
# of sleeping areas
Nursery
nursing home

O
Older person(s)
one child
one person
Oriental

P
Parish
perfect for . . . (should not describe people)
pets limited to assistance animals
pets, no
Philippine or Filipinos, no
physically fit
play area, no
preferred community
Prestigious
Privacy

Private
Private driveway
Private entrance
Private property
Private setting
Public transportation (near)
Puerto Rican

Q
Quality construction
quality neighborhood
Quiet
Quiet neighborhood

R
references required
religious references
Responsible
Restricted
retarded, no
Retirees
Retirement home

S
safe neighborhood
school name or school district
se habla espanol
seasonal rates
seasonal worker(s), no
Secluded
section 8 accepted/ welcome
section 8, no

Secure
security provided
senior adult community *
senior citizen(s) *
senior discount
senior housing *
senior(s) *
sex or gender **
Shrine
single family home
single person
single woman, man **
singles only
sixty-two and older community *
Smoker(s), no
Smoking, no
Snowbirds*
sober
Sophisticated
Spanish speaking
Spanish speaking, no
Square feet
Straight only
student(s)
Students, no
Supplemental Security Income (SSI), no

Synagogue, near

T
temple, near
tenant (description of)
Townhouse
traditional neighborhood
traditional style
tranquil setting
two people

U
Unemployed, no

V
Verifiable Income

W
walking distance of, within
Wheelchairs, no
White
White(s) only
winter rental rates
winter/summer visitors *
woman (women) only **

* Permitted to be used only when complex or development qualifies as housing for older persons.

** Permitted to be used only when describing shared living areas or dwelling units used exclusively as dormitory facilities by educational institutions.

TRUTH IN LENDING

The *Truth-in-Lending Act* is part of the *Consumer Credit Protection Act*. It is a disclosure Act that applies where there will be more than four installment payments for an owner-occupied residence. Therefore, most home sales are covered by the Act. The Truth-in-Lending Act applies to real estate advertising because full disclosure of the finance terms must be made if an ad includes any of the following "trigger" terms:

■ The specific amount or percentage of down payment

- The amount of any installment payment

- The amount of finance charges or a statement that there shall be no finance charges

- The number of installments

- The period of repayment

The use of the interest rate of a loan by itself does not trigger full disclosure. If an ad includes the interest rate, however, it must indicate it as annual percentage rate or use the abbreviation APR.

If any of the "trigger" terms are included in an ad, then the ad must include all of the following:

- Down payment (amount or percentage)

- The terms of repayment of the loan

- The annual percentage rate of the loan and if there is any possibility of an increase in the interest rate

The law does not apply to creditors who have not extended credit more than five times in the prior year for dwellings. Therefore, an ad indicating seller financing would generally be exempt from the advertising disclosure requirements of the Truth in Lending Act. The Truth In Lending Act is enforced by the Federal Trade Commission (*www.FTC.gov*).

USING THIS BOOK

This book was prepared to serve two purposes: (1) to give you a variety of high-quality, readily adaptable ads and (2) to enable you to quickly prepare original ads for a property.

When you are ready to prepare an ad, check the category or categories that best appear to relate to your property, then review specific ads within those categories. You will see that ads can be quickly modified to serve specific properties.

The Ad Generator, beginning on page 289, helps to achieve these two purposes:

1. It allows ads included in this book to be readily modified for specific properties.

2. It allows completely new ads to be readily prepared based upon specific features likely to be of importance to prospective buyers.

The ads included in this book have material in parentheses. The parentheses indicate that the material is specific for the particular property and that the material within the parentheses will need to be modified for any property for which you wish to use the ad. The Ad Generator is arranged alphabetically by property features and types. By looking up features that you wish to emphasize, you will find a choice of language. Select wording that sells the benefit of your particular features or property type. In this way, in just a few minutes, you can modify ads for a property you wish to advertise.

To prepare a new ad, first consider which feature or features will be of most interest to the type of person or family that likely will be the eventual buyer. Then turn to the "Ad Generator." The Ad Generator features items set in boldface type, which indicates that items are suitable for ad headings. By choosing several of these headings, you can prepare multiple ads for a property within minutes. In using other features or benefits likely to be of interest to a buyer, you will find appropriate language to highlight the property's features or benefits in an appealing manner. A great many ad closings that include the price can be found in the ad generator under "Price Closings." For the completed ad, you will now only need to add your firm name and logo, if appropriate, and phone number and Web site address.

You will discover that the more ads you prepare or modify, the easier the ad preparation process becomes. Chances are you will also discover that ad writing can be fun.

The Internet and Other Multimedia Approaches to Classified Ads

You can use the classified ads included in this book and the material in the Ad Generator in *more media than* the classified pages of your local newspaper. Ads originally prepared and intended for use as classified ads can be used, with or without modification, in a variety of media. A significant benefit of featuring real estate classifieds in multiple media formats is that they reinforce the effectiveness of your print advertising efforts.

Alternative media include the following:

■ The Internet

■ Television bulletin boards

■ Radio

■ E-Brochures

■ Business CD cards

In addition to the above, classified ad copy and references to the Internet can be included in display ads, property sale magazines, displays, property flyers, and direct mail pieces.

THE INTERNET

The Internet is at the center of all advertising media—all advertising points to it. Besides media mentioned in this chapter, the Internet address would be included on For Sale signs, office signs, billboards, etc. Even talking signs, the short-range radio messages received by persons viewing the exterior of a property, should mention the Internet site for interior pictures and further information.

There is a good reason why the Internet should be at the center of your advertising program. In many markets, it is believed that over half the home-buyers use the Internet as part of their house hunting efforts—and those numbers are increasing every year.

Besides being a wonderful tool for a homebuyer to begin his or her housing search, the Internet is almost too good to be true for the broker. Once the broker establishes a site, the broker is not limited as to size of copy or even number of photos that can be included on a broker's own Internet site.

When prospective buyers find a property that interests them on your Internet site, they feel that they found the property and it gives them a sense of empowerment. They are more likely to be half-sold on the property before they have physically viewed it, perhaps even more than if a broker had introduced them to it.

However, it might be challenging for prospective buyers to locate your Internet site on their own, especially considering the millions of sites currently residing on the Web. You can direct interested parties to your site by including your Web address in all of your advertising and promotional materials.

Classified Ads Lead to the Internet

By including your Internet address in your ads, readers will know how to access detailed information and pictures of properties advertised. We have included Internet addresses in all of our ads. If your Internet site, among all the listings, allows the viewer to zero in on certain advertised properties, your ads should indicate with a number or key how to locate each one on your site. We have also done this in a number of ads.

Multiagent Sites

Your multiple-listing service (MLS) might have its own Internet site or be combined with other MLS offices. Chambers of Commerce representing various cities set up some sites. Many franchise Internet sites include many offices. Many brokers place their listings on a dozen or more sites. One agent currently advertises that he will place properties listed with his firm on 42 sites. For a listing of many of these cyberspace sites, you can check *www.recenter.tamu.edu/links*.

While these sites customarily charge for member users, the fees are relatively small. Brokers should utilize these sites, but realize they have limitations. Brokers are limited on many sites as to the size of photos displayed, number of words, and even the format used. These sites tend to be factual with little room to distinguish one ad from another.

Because these group sites include homes presented by many brokers, you wouldn't want to advertise the sites in ads you pay for directly. Otherwise, you could be paying to direct a prospect to another broker. You don't want to present the prospective buyer you attracted as a gift to another agent.

Single-Agent Site

You want your ads to stand out on a site that is wholly yours. You don't want visitors to your Web site directed to properties controlled by anyone other than yourself.

The descriptions on your Web site should mirror what you would use in classified ads. Keep in mind that there are no budgetary restraints on your own Web site.

Contents of Your Site

To help you decide what to put on your Internet site, a good starting point is to review the Internet sites of larger brokers in your area, as well as a number of national sites such as *www.Realtor.com.*

Site Features

Features you should consider include the following:

- An "About Us" feature that displays information on the firm and its personnel. This might include success comparisons with averages from MLS records.

- A viewer option to zero in on property based on parameters entered by the viewer such as price, area, number of bedrooms, etc.

- Ability to immediately go to a property advertised by number.

- Map showing location of a property or properties.

- Ability to increase size of photos and to view additional photos.

- An offer to provide e-mails about new listings (before they are advertised). This offer should be on every page of your site. The viewer would fill in blanks to determine features of homes that would be featured in the e-mails. For developments and large properties, you might want an e-mail that will appear to the recipient like a TV commercial. It's an extremely effective approach and can be embedded right in your e-mail. For information and examples about this feature, check out *www.ilpostino-mail.com.*

- Ability to scroll down listings and photos by price.

- Loan qualifying or prequalifying. Viewers would fill in information requested and you would then get back to them with qualifying limits.

- An "800" telephone number.

- A back to home page feature from any page.

- Virtual Reality Tours (discussed under the next heading).

- Motion and/or sound. These site features will make your site stand out from other sites. Consider a voice narrative.

- A contact-us feature so the viewer can send an e-mail to the agent. (It is essential that someone check the e-mails several times per day, answer them, or take action. Otherwise, much of your effort will be wasted.)

You don't want visitors to your Web page to be linked to any other page that includes links to other brokers. Again, you want to avoid sharing your prospects with others.

Virtual Reality Tours

A Virtual Reality (VR) Tour on the Internet allows a visitor to view a home with VR 360-degree room-view vision on your Web site, to zoom in on areas or back away, to move right or left, up or down, and to move from room to room. The tour can be combined with text and/or audio description of the property. The description should be similar to a classified ad as to the use of adjectives. Mentioning the architect's name and/or the architectural style, such as Mediterranean Revival, can enhance the property's desirability.

Many professional photographers using special cameras will shoot photos for you. Firms are available that will even place the finished tour on your Web site. These services are not inexpensive.

Software programs are also available that allow you to prepare any number of tours for an initial cost of around $300. You use the software to build your own tours using the photos you take with a digital camera. Some of the programs allow you to use film as well as digital photos. If you're interested in preparing your own virtual reality tours, you might want to check *www.visualtour.com* as well as Photo Vista Virtual Tour available through *www.Z-LawSoftwareInfo@Z-Law.com*.

Although it is estimated that currently less than 5 percent of listings can be seen as a Virtual Tour, they are an excellent selling tool and well worth the preparation time required. Before you prepare a Virtual Tour, obtain the owner's permission in writing to do so. There is a danger that the Virtual Tour will be used by predators interested in what's in the house rather than in buying the house itself. The owners should be advised to review their insurance coverage, especially if the home contains valuable art and/or antiques.

Internet Site Design

Plenty of people are eager to help you create a Web site for a fee. A number of these consultants and firms specialize in sites for real estate brokers. Some brokers have created their own Web sites. There are a number of books available to help you get you started, but you will likely need professional help in creating a Web site offering many of the features we have suggested.

No matter who designs your Web site, you are going to need a domain name for your dotcom. *Cedant.com* will register your domain name for two years for only $39.95, which is significantly less than the fees charged by other registers. They will also inform you if the domain name you want is available and charge you nothing for this service. We suggest a domain name that is or abbreviates your firm name and indicates that it is a real estate firm, by using *re, real, realt, realty*, etc. You also want a domain name that will fit on a single line in a classified ad.

TELEVISION BULLETIN BOARDS

Some cable company channels display bulletin board notices of community events and ads. These notices are usually accompanied by graphics and music and are often repeated a number of times daily. The language and creative themes used in your classified ad headings and in the ad copy will work well in this format, as will your pictures. Use one good high contrast color photo that will showcase the property in a positive manner.

Costs for a 15-second bulletin board ad repeated four times daily for one week can vary between $25 to about $60, which includes the production cost of the ad. (Some stations use 30 seconds per ad, but the exposure time would be the same for all their ads.) Because the length of the ad copy is based upon the exposure time, make certain the viewer can absorb your message, your firm name, and contact information in the time allotted for the ad. Include your firm logo in the same color used for your "For Sale" signs. Also, include your telephone number and Internet address for further details.

RADIO

While relatively few brokers utilize radio as an advertising medium, many brokers in smaller markets have used radio for years. Some brokers have regular weekly programs, usually on a Saturday or Sunday morning, in which they broadcast classified type ads featuring their open houses for that day. Other brokers use 30-second or 60-second spot ads to feature a single property.

For non-Open House ads for single properties, consider running your ads during drive-time hours, which are between 6 A.M. and 10 A.M. and 3 P.M. and 7 P.M. These times are considered prime time because they reach listeners traveling to and from work. Classified ad type attention-getting headings are important, often accompanied by sound effects. A bell, a horn, or a shout in your message will alert viewers that a radio classified ad is about to broadcast.

Some radio advertisers have had excellent results by using a distinctive voice for their radio ads. Examples would be use of an accent or a celebrity sound-alike voice. An unusual voice will be identified with your ads and will help to gain listeners' attention. Your local radio stations can arrange for celebrity sound-alike voices. No matter what sound effect or vocal style you select for your ad, attention-getting headlines are critical if you wish to get listeners' attention.

For spot ads, consider the technique known as *flashing* or *pulsing*. This technique uses a short burst of an intensive radio presence followed by a much weaker presence. As an example, a firm might have 12 or more spot ads per day for 10 days followed by 20 days with only 3 spot ads per day. The effect of flashing is to give the listener the impression that your firm occupies a dominant market presence in addition to selling benefits of particular properties.

A variance of the flashing technique is to rotate your slots either horizontally or vertically. In horizontal rotation, you would buy your time for a 30-day period but use the majority of your spots on a single day such as a Monday. The next month, you would rotate to Tuesday, etc. Vertical rotation refers to changing the time of day of your spots.

For radio spot ads, repeat the company name at least twice as well as the telephone number and Internet address for more information. (But remember, you want to avoid compressing too much copy into the time allowed.)

Selecting the radio station that will feature your ad is important because you want programming that appeals to the age group that matches the prospective buyers you have in mind for a particular listing. Arbitron is one example of a rating service that provides radio stations with information about audience numbers, market shares, and demographics. The demographics of the listeners will vary based on time of day and station programming. Local radio stations will have Arbitron information for you and/or information compiled about other services.

E-BROCHURES

Generally, properties featured in property magazines are formatted into a single column of about four inches, with a property picture followed by ad copy similar to classified ad copy. It is possible to have your own version of a property magazine in electronic form for display on your Web site, which may be used as e-mail attachments or included in CD business cards.

Software is available to prepare e-brochures. An e-brochure is essentially the Internet version of the property brochure or magazine prepared by many brokerage firms. The software also makes it relatively easy to prepare a print copy of brochures prepared for the Internet. For information on e-brochures, we recommend: *www.inprev.net.*

BUSINESS CD CARDS

While it is a good idea for paper business cards to reference an Internet site for information about properties, a better multimedia approach is a business CD card.

The business CD card is a standard CD usually cut to the exact size of a standard business card. It is possible to have the cards in any shape you want, such as the shape of a house. The card can also be printed, and it is usually given in a vinyl sleeve that usually has a label that can be printed. The printing can contain information normally found on an ordinary paper business card.

A business CD card stands out from other cards and it practically begs to be inserted in a CD-ROM drive (playable in any computer with a CD-ROM drive).

The CD card can present property descriptions, maps, photos, e-brochures, virtual tours, and even movies. A point and click interface can take a prospect to where he or she wants to be on your Web site (no additional software required). With the CD business card, you really carry your Web site in your pocket. It is possible to have CD cards keyed so that you will know the number of Web site hits that are linked through your business CD cards. Besides links to your Web site, you will want a hyperlink to your e-mail address for viewers to readily contact you.

Business CD cards accommodate from 30mb to over 190mb so the possibilities of what you can present on them are extensive. We suggest that you check some of the video and audio presentations shown on *www.ilpostino-mail.com.* Consider a high-impact introduction, such as those shown, for your business CD card.

There are many suppliers of business CD cards, including large office supply stores. By exploring the Internet, you will find suppliers who provide special shapes and printing for your cards and sleeves. There are also many firms selling kits to burn your own CD cards. Some of these kits are geared for the real estate business. An example is found on *www.impactbuilder.com.* They have a system of templates to produce material to use as a business CD card, to create a Web site, or as an e-mail.

An advantage of a business CD card is that you can easily update it as your inventory changes just as you update your Web site. Another advantage is the novelty design of the business CD card, which makes it more difficult to throw away than a paper business card.

Business CD card costs vary based on the quantity ordered, the special shapes, and the supplier used. Prices for blank cards range from about $.75 each to approximately $1 each in quantities of 100. Large quantities are significantly lower in price.

If a business CD card is not used as intended, inserted in a computer CD-ROM drive, it serves no better purpose than a regular paper business card, which costs far less. One real estate firm has reportedly received excellent results by numbering each business CD card. If the number on the CD card matches a number on the firm's Web site, the cardholder wins a prize that can be claimed at the broker's office. Information on the sleeve of the CD card announces the contest as well as the fact that the firm's Web site can be accessed by using that card.

Acreage (Undeveloped)

Undeveloped acreage parcels appeal to different groups of potential buyers:

■ "Wanna-be" farmers or ranchers

■ Homesite buyers for family, retirement, or vacation homes (motivations for homesite buyers could be to escape city problems, to find a better life for children, to enjoy lower taxes, to commune with nature, etc.)

■ Campers and hunters who desire to have their own land

■ Speculators who hope for a profit on resale

■ Subdividers and developers who will prepare land for development or develop it

Ads can be targeted toward the interests of likely buyers. For additional ad ideas, please see Chapters 12 (Gardens, Landscaping, and Trees), 14 (Homes, Acreage), 36 (Vacation Homes), 37 (View), and 38 (Water-Related Property).

3

Nudist Camp Site?
[5 Acres]

[$49,500] for your future, [close yet remote]. See it all at #47, *www.ur-home.net*.

UR

HOME REALTY

555-8200
www.ur-home.net

5

Question

Is it possible to find a [2½-acre wooded homesite, zoned for horses in a family-oriented community within 45 minutes of the city] for less than [$50,000]?

Answer

We found one, and it also comes with [a natural spring] [views you only dreamed of]. It's a rare find, so the second caller will likely be sorry.

UR

HOME REALTY

555-8200
www.ur-home.net

➡ This question and answer split-heading approach can be used for all types of property.

4

[40] Acres Zoned [R-1]

There is room for [160 homes] [a shopping center] and [all utilities are available] [engineering work has been completed] [percolation tests have been completed] [a feasibility study has been completed] for this [highway frontage] [fully accessible] site in an area that will excite any investor or developer. Priced for immediate sale at [$1,000,000] [with seller financing available].

UR

HOME REALTY

555-8200
www.ur-home.net

ALTERNATIVE HEADINGS

Future City [40] Acres

Subdivision Ready [40] Acres

Path of Progress [40] Acres

Future [RV Park]?

6

[10] Lost Acres

The directions to it read like a pirate's map, but if you follow them you will be delighted by the tranquil beauty, [a gentle brook, ancient hardwoods, soaring pines, sun-drenched glen, a natural spring,] and incomparable vistas. Your treasure chest for [a low down payment and] a price of only [$30,000].

UR

HOME REALTY

555-8200
www.ur-home.net

ALTERNATIVE HEADINGS

Private Preserve [10] Acres

A Private World [10] Acres

An Hour To Nowhere

7

Cowboys and Desperados

probably camped [beneath the stars] [under the huge cottonwood] on this very special [20] acres. See the vistas at #67 at *www.ur-home.net* and then experience your future. [$74,500].

UR

H O M E   R E A L T Y

555-8200
www.ur-home.net

ALTERNATIVE HEADING

Black Bart

➤ Note: If you have pictures that convey a positive image, you should use the Web to presell buyers.

8

Arrowheads and Pottery Shards

have been reported found on this [10-acre, mostly wooded] site, which is only [45] minutes from [the Civic Center]. While the former residents didn't commute, they must have enjoyed the clean, crisp air; the chatter of squirrels in the [hickory trees]; magnificent vistas; and [cold, clean water flowing year-round from a natural spring]. The old ways are surely the good ways, and they can be yours at [$79,900].

UR

H O M E   R E A L T Y

555-8200
www.ur-home.net

➤ This ad appeals to people looking for a homesite. Native American artifacts are a very positive feature for many buyers.

9

Fabulous [5]

Acres near [Oakridge] with [trees, view, and utilities available]. It's a site for your future at only [$89,500].

UR

H O M E   R E A L T Y

555-8200
www.ur-home.net

➤ The same heading can be used for a five-room condominium or cooperative.

10

Happy Camper [5 Acres]

[Woods with trees that are yours] and [giant boulders] plus [squirrels, chipmunks, raccoons, and deer] as your neighbors. Located [less than two hours from Detroit], this exceptional site is a great place for weekend camping until you build your special home [in the sun drenched glen] [beneath giant oaks] [on a glorious hillside] with a view that must be experienced. Priced to put a smile on your face at [$89,500 with terms available].

UR

H O M E   R E A L T Y

555-8200
www.ur-home.net

ALTERNATIVE HEADINGS

Ah! Wilderness!

Creatures Cavort

Feed the Deer

Roam for Miles

East of the Sun— West of the Moon

Back to the Country

11

[$4,000] Per Lot

That's the total land cost for these [40 West Side] acres that could mean [120] lots worth [$40,000] each and likely a great deal more. Definitely worth your immediate investigation.

UR
HOME REALTY

555-8200
www.ur-home.net

→ Price does not need to be stated. It is clear what the price is.

12

[40] Acres = [160] Lots?

Less than [20 minutes from the city], with [utilities available], this [West Side] parcel [on a paved road] stands in the natural path of progress. Tremendous appreciation potential. A very special opportunity at [$400,000] with only [$40,000 down].

UR
HOME REALTY

555-8200
www.ur-home.net

13

[10] Quiet Acres

No buildings, no phones. The loudest neighbor will be a chattering chipmunk. This is your escape from the city [only 40 minutes away]. Magnificently landscaped by Mother Nature, with a perfect site for your home. Yours for the price of a city lot [$87,500].

UR
HOME REALTY

555-8200
www.ur-home.net

14

Jurassic Park [10] Acres

Do you have the courage to explore the [hidden valley] or enter the [silent glen] on this time-forgotten [wooded] site that might have been home to marauding dinosaurs? While only [60 minutes] from the [city], it's another world but only a phone call away at [$87,500].

UR
HOME REALTY

555-8200
www.ur-home.net

15

[40] Acres of Happiness

[Ancient hardwoods and sun drenched meadows coupled with wild flowers] grace this natural preserve that's presently home to [deer, chipmunks, and a very curious raccoon]. Only [2 hours from Chicago], this can be the site of future happiness. Yours for the taking at [$98,000].

UR
HOME REALTY

555-8200
www.ur-home.net

ALTERNATIVE HEADING

[40] Acres of Love

16

Run Naked

in the sunshine in the privacy of your own **[20]**-acre **[woods and meadows]**. It can all be yours including **[deer, raccoons, a curious fox]** plus other assorted 4-legged friends. This private place, just **[20 minutes]** from **[the city]**, is a perfect site for a perfect future at **[$37,500]**.

UR
HOME REALTY

555-8200
www.ur-home.net

17

A New World To Conquer [10] Acres

of pristine beauty with **[massive oaks, huge boulders, postcard views,]** and a perfect setting for your future home. Just **[40 minutes away]**, it's priced to sell at **[$30,000]**.

UR
HOME REALTY

555-8200
www.ur-home.net

18

The Forest Primeval

Ancient arrowheads have been found **[near the gentle brook flowing through this 10-acre tract of pristine beauty]**. Interspersed among the hardwoods are **[soaring pines]**. The current tenants are **[deer, raccoons, squirrels, and a curious fox family]**. It's a place to go to commune with nature or to spend a lifetime. A **[sun-drenched glen]** will make an ideal homesite. Priced for you at **[$120,500]**.

UR
HOME REALTY

555-8200
www.ur-home.net

19

Wyatt Earp

would have felt right at home on these **[10]** acres in a land he knew so well. He may have camped under **[an ancient oak]** and savored the natural beauty of this special place. With several superb home sites **[and just 40 minutes away]**, it can be your future for **[$39,500]**.

UR
HOME REALTY

555-8200
www.ur-home.net

➤ You can use names of legendary outlaws, lawmen, or pioneers, such as The Dalton Gang, Black Bart, Doc Holliday, Bill Hickock, Daniel Boone, etc., who once operated within the area. They create a romantic image.

20

The Blue and the Gray

Civil War troops once bivouacked in the quiet meadow on this **[20-acre]**, mostly **[wooded]** site. They are long gone, but on a quiet summer night it is said you can still hear young voices raised in song by ancient campfires. This is a very special place for a special buyer. Offered at **[$49,500]**. **[Terms available]**.

UR
HOME REALTY

555-8200
www.ur-home.net

This type of description can be applied to many areas in our country. Point out that troops passed through the land by using a phrase such as "Union cavalry galloped through this quiet meadow on the way to . . ." or indicate that troops camped on the land. (Do not say that troops died there.)

ALTERNATIVE HEADINGS

The Army of the Potomac

For the Revolutionary War, consider:

The Continental Army

The Green River Rangers

The 4th Connecticut Infantry

The Virginia Light Dragoons

The Third New York Regiment

The First Pennsylvania Battalion

once bivouacked in . . . (use names of local units)

CHAPTER FOUR

Architecture

Emphasizing architectural style allows the reader to form a visual image of your listing and increases the property's desirability in the mind of the reader. If you attach importance to the architect and/or architectural style, the buyer will probably feel that the home is very special and will likely repeat your ad language when describing the home to others.

Please see Chapters 20 (Homes, Luxury) and 22 (Homes, Old) for architectural styles and descriptions used to enhance the desirability of luxury homes and older homes.

21

Architect [R.J. Fox]

Space and elegance take on a whole new meaning in this stunningly conceived and elegantly executed [Colorado Contemporary] that exemplifies the best of American architecture. [3,500 square feet] in a prestigious [Westbrook view setting], the [3BR and den, 3½-bath masterpiece] features [sky-soaring ceilings, walls of stone and glass, cantilevered decks that seem suspended in space, tons of tile,] and every amenity you could want and a whole lot more. A bold statement that can be your own, offered at [$595,000].

UR
HOME REALTY
555-8200
www.ur-home.net

➤ Even if not well known, mentioning the architect's name will add prestige to the property.

22

Not a Cookie Cutter

version of every other house. A one-of-a-kind [Arizona Contemporary] on a spectacular site in [Walden Hills]. Designed by [Thomas Mitchell], this [3BR, 2½-bath, 2,400-square-foot residence] features [soaring ceilings, spectacular vistas, wraparound decks,] and so much more. A home with its own fun-loving personality can be yours for [$249,500].

UR
HOME REALTY
555-8200
www.ur-home.net

ALTERNATIVE HEADING

Odd Ball!

If you follow your own drummer, you will appreciate this one-of-a-kind . . .

23

Architectural Digest

did not feature this [Carolina Colonial] embraced by a [columned portico], but it should have. This fine [3BR, 2½-bath, 3-car garage] residence is a striking statement of design with its authentic detailing and [multipaneled windows that begin at the knee and seem to go on forever]. There's a feeling of happy spaciousness making this the perfect home for family living or entertaining on a grand scale. Set amid dream land-scaping in a [Brentwood] estate setting, this home features [baths sheathed in marble and a private cherry-paneled den]. Elegance beyond words can be yours for [$385,000].

UR

H O M E   R E A L T Y

555-8200
www.ur-home.net

24

Don't Throw Stones

in this [window-wrapped, 3BR, 2½-bath Colorado Contemporary] on [its hillside setting overlooking Sherman Park]. With [soaring ceilings, huge trees, BBQ deck, master suite right out of the Arabian nights, private home office, expansive family areas, and 2½-car garage], it's a very special place at a price that won't break you: [$264,500].

UR

H O M E   R E A L T Y

555-8200
www.ur-home.net

ALTERNATIVE HEADING

Captain Kirk

would love to explore the vast space...

25

[Massive Oak Beams]

[An orchard stone fireplace, random-plank hardwood floors, and soaring ceilings] make this spacious [cedar and glass, 3BR, 2-bath hillside chalet] in [Westmoreland] a home that will touch your heart. This is a place you'll love coming home to at [$339,500].

UR

H O M E   R E A L T Y

555-8200
www.ur-home.net

ALTERNATIVE HEADINGS

Turreted Entry

Soaring Ceiling

Walls of Glass

 An architectural feature can be used to make an effective heading, as the examples above show.

26

Frank Lloyd Wright Eat Your Heart Out

This is the home you wished you designed. A [3BR, 2½-bath New Mexico Contemporary] that blends with its [hillside] setting. [Sky-reaching ceilings, sun-drenched rooms, sweeping decks, and forever-views] make it [2,500] square feet of perfection at [$247,500].

UR

H O M E   R E A L T Y

555-8200

27

Don't Do Windows?

Then hope your spouse loves Windex. This [3BR, 2-bath Arizona-style Contemporary] has [walls of glass] that seem to join the natural surrounding with the sunlit living areas. With [soaring ceilings, magnificent beams, state-of-the-art kitchen, master suite right out of the movies, 2-plus car garage, dining patio, magnificent trees, and colorful plantings,] it's an exceptional offering at only [$197,500].

UR
HOME REALTY
555-8200
www.ur-home.net

28

"Rare"

means "uncommon" or "unique." This one-of-a-kind [Contemporary] has been stunningly designed and exquisitely executed to create a home that will always be fresh and new. Amenities include [two master suites, a great room with a massive river rock fireplace, ceilings that seem to reach to the sky, walls of glass that meld the living area with the world of nature, forever views,] the choicest [Westport] location, and a great deal more. In years to come there may be copies, but the original can be yours now for [$329,500].

UR
HOME REALTY
555-8200
www.ur-home.net

29

Wrapped in Glass

This happy and bright [stone and glass New Mexico Contemporary] has sunlight overflowing every room. Offering [3BR, 2½ baths, private office or study, 14-foot ceilings in huge living area, monumental fireplace,] and so much more. It's sited [on a hillside so you will enjoy sunrise to sunset on the open deck]. Your very own place in the sun for [$310,000].

UR
HOME REALTY
555-8200
www.ur-home.net

ALTERNATIVE HEADINGS

Definitely Not a Tract Home

Not Ordinary

Not for the Ordinary

Dramatic—Yes! Expensive—No!

Tomorrow is Today

Stone and Glass

Exuberant Contemporary

30

Hercule Poirot

would have loved this Art Deco [3BR, 1¾-bath] residence on a [wooded site in Morningside]. He would have delighted in the graceful curves and openness of space [as well as the creative use of glass block]. A living reminder of the gracious life of the [late 1920s], it has been preserved for you in all its splendor. Available at a fraction of reproduction cost, [$149,500].

UR
HOME REALTY
555-8200
www.ur-home.net

ALTERNATIVE AD

Hercule Poirot

would have loved this Art Deco [3BR, 1¾-bath] residence on a [wooded site in Morningside]. See what gracious living is all about. #44 *www.ur-home.net*

UR
HOME REALTY
555-8200
www.ur-home.net

➤ An ad can be effectively shortened if tied in with the Internet.

31

Prairie Style Craftsman [$269,000]

[2,500 sq. ft.] of simple elegance, unadorned charm, clean and joyous design in sought-after [Westwood.] View it now: #38 *www.ur-home.net*

UR
HOME REALTY
555-8200
www.ur-home.net

ALTERNATIVE HEADINGS

American Craftsman

Stickley Craftsman

Gustav Stickley

would have loved this . . . [California] Bungalow, [American] Bungalow

32

Amish Inspired

This [3BR, 1½-bath, white, American Traditional] on [almost ½ acre] in [Clintonville] looks as if it had been transported from an Amish farm with its pure, clean design and attention to every detail. With [glorious sun-filled rooms, harvest-crew-sized kitchen, formal dining room, woodwork and hardwood flooring of a quality seldom seen, simple stone fireplace with massive beamed mantle, 2-car garage, full basement plus a storage attic], there's a feeling of fulfillment in its simplicity. Proudly offered for your future at [$145,000].

UR
HOME REALTY
555-8200
www.ur-home.net

33

Brownstone Magic [$179,500]

In [Georgetown] this [12-room, 3-bath] Brownstone would sell for [6] times the price. See this impressive residence. #28 *www.ur-home.net*

UR
HOME REALTY
555-8200
www.ur-home.net

ALTERNATIVE HEADINGS

Brownstone Classic

Front-Stoop Brownstone

Brownstone Townhouse

Sophisticated Brownstone

Brownstone Opulence

34

Southern Comfort

A [3BR, 2-bath Carolina Colonial] on [a wooded half-acre] in [Clifton Hills]. There's [a screened porch, BBQ patio, light, bright rooms, mantled fireplace, and 2-plus car garage]. Even the price is relaxing at [$119,500].

UR
HOME REALTY
555-8200
www.ur-home.net

35

Welcome Home, Scarlett!

[A circle drive leads to this] white-columned Colonial set amidst magnificent [willows and flowering shrubs] in a [Williams Point] estate setting. Offering [3BR, 3½ baths, expansive family areas, sweeping staircase,] and so much more, it can be your own Tara for a very affordable [$379,500].

UR
HOME REALTY
555-8200
www.ur-home.net

36

Scarlett and Rhett

would feel right at home in this Virginia Colonial with its [soaring white columns and covered portico]. There are [3BR, 2 baths, a very private home office, glassed conservatory/studio, full basement, and a 3-car garage]. In impeccable condition, this fine residence is impressive but not expensive at [$249,500].

UR
HOME REALTY
555-8200
www.ur-home.net

ALTERNATIVE HEADINGS

George Washington

Thomas Jefferson

37

Crown Moldings

and all the intricate detailing you expect in a pure [New England] Colonial are here to delight you. This exceptional [Westchester] residence, [guarded by ancient oaks], is tucked away on [almost a full acre of] beautiful grounds. Offering [3BR, study or home office, 3½ baths, 3 fireplaces, a large screened porch, 3-car garage, and circle drive,] it is [almost new but it appears to have been here for ages]. A home to reflect your SUCCESS offered at [$597,000].

UR
HOME REALTY
555-8200
www.ur-home.net

38

[Quaker Village] Colonial

Magnificent detailing and classic lines exemplify all that is great in [American] architecture. This [like-new] [fine] residence boasts [3BR, 2½ baths, an oversized double garage,] and all of the amenities one could wish for carefully integrated into the design so as not to break the mood of a happier, gentler time. This home exudes the very best amidst [landscaping that would be the envy of any garden club]. A rare offering at [$239,500].

UR
HOME REALTY
555-8200
www.ur-home.net

ALTERNATIVE HEADINGS

Dutch Village Colonial

Dutch Colonial

Gambrel Roof Colonial

Federal Colonial

39

Havana Wrapper

[Tile, balconies, intricate wrought iron, and trellises covered with flowers] are reminiscent of the charm of old Cuba present in this [7-year old, 3BR, 2½-bath Spanish Colonial] in [Wilshire Estates]. With [Saltillo tile floors, courtyard fountain, beehive fireplace, private home office, huge family area, dining terrace, pool, spa, 3-car garage,] and all the amenities expected in a world-class residence, this showplace must be experienced. Offered to the family who won't accept second best at [$325,500].

UR
HOME REALTY
555-8200
www.ur-home.net

ALTERNATIVE HEADINGS

Spanish Renaissance

Spanish Revival

40

Tons of Tile

[Flowing Saltillo tile floors, red tile roofs, and tiled fountain courtyard] add to the peaceful ambiance of this old-world hacienda [nestled against the Anaheim foothills]. [Three exquisite suites, 3½ tiled baths, 2 massive fireplaces, huge beams, and flower-bedecked balconies] have been integrated into this masterful plan of Spanish charm. Any caballero or señorita would love to call it home at [$425,000].

UR
HOME REALTY
555-8200
www.ur-home.net

41

Mariachi Music

Your own Hacienda in [Newport Heights] with [2BR, 2 baths, 2-car garage, tons of tile, huge beams, magnificent fireplace, family room opening to the colorful garden patio, master suite with whirlpool,] and a spacious open feeling that's fiesta-ready at [$184,500].

UR
HOME REALTY
555-8200
www.ur-home.net

ALTERNATIVE HEADINGS

Spanish Omelet

Spanish Eyes

Presidio Spanish

Old World Spain

42

Your Own Mariachi Band

would have the perfect place to practice [next to the bubbling fountain] in [the red-tiled courtyard of this arched and beamed] Spanish Colonial. The authentic design of this [3BR, 2½-bath] masterpiece has a warmth seldom achieved in a home. This home offers generously proportioned rooms, [a richly paneled den or quiet place, soaring ceilings, massive beams, delicate balconies with intricate ironwork, tons of tile,] and everything a fine hacienda should have. Bring your castanets, and a fiesta lifestyle can be yours at [$349,500].

UR
HOME REALTY
555-8200
www.ur-home.net

43

Salsa the Border

[Massive red tile roof, flowing tile floors, bubbling fountain and a setting amidst colorful plantings and flowering shrubs] create an ambiance of life and joy for this [3BR, 3½-bath Monterey hacienda] with an enviable [Westhills] address. Offering [intricate ironwork, warm-paneled library, expansive family areas, massive beams, carved woodwork] and so much more, this premier residence [,while only 7 years old,] captures a mood of long ago. Offered to the buyer who appreciates the beauty of a casual lifestyle at [$324,500].

UR
HOME REALTY
555-8200
www.ur-home.net

44

A True Hacienda

[One hundred and fifty years] of living have not diminished the classic beauty of this Spanish colonial hacienda. The [ancient tile, intricately hand-carved beams, and colonnaded, enclosed courtyard with its fountains] still echo the happy sounds of fiestas long ago. Situated on a prestigious [20+ acre ocean view site], the home has been thoughtfully updated to combine the best of the old with the new. Offering [6+ bedrooms, 6 full baths, 2 half-baths, and a dramatic but modern kitchen with tons of Mexican tile.] Far more than just a grand and beautiful home, it is a part of our history. Proudly offered at [$2,800,000].

UR
HOME REALTY
555-8200
www.ur-home.net

45

A Proper English Garden

comes with this handsome [brick and stone Yorkshire Tudor] in the [estate area of Westchester]. The [11]-room manor house features [3 royal-sized bedrooms, 2½ baths, paneled library, drawing room, 2 fireplaces mantled with ancient beams, leaded glass, slate, and even heated parking for motor-cars]. An uncommonly civilized home offered at an uncommonly reasonable price of [$395,000].

UR
HOME REALTY
555-8200
www.ur-home.net

46

Proper English Brick

An [Edwardian] residence offering [9 rooms and 3 baths] [that has been flawlessly maintained] for gracious living. If you could choose the most prestigious block of the most prestigious street in [Westlake] for your dream home, this would be your choice. This home is as solid as the [giant oaks] that guard it. At [$349,500] we strongly recommend you contact the estate agent at once.

UR
HOME REALTY
555-8200
www.ur-home.net

ALTERNATIVE HEADINGS

Belgravia in [Akron]

British Brownstone

Edwardian Gentility

Smashing!

47

The British Are Coming!

At last, a proper British [Town House!] This [red brick, 3BR, 2-bath] residence reflects the subdued quality of fine craftsmanship. The proper English garden [is enclosed by a high wall], and there's a garage for [2] motor cars. Offered to you at [$93,500], it's strongly recommended you contact the estate agent at once.

UR
HOME REALTY
555-8200
www.ur-home.net

48

Charles Dickens

would feel right at home in this proper [English Manor House] in prestigious [Southaven]. Of course he would be amazed at the dazzling array of modern amenities this [3BR, 2-bath] residence has to offer. Whatever you desire, plus [manicured hedges, a rose garden,] and all the charm you associate with old England are waiting for you. Proudly offered for the discerning buyer at [$311,000].

UR
HOME REALTY
555-8200
www.ur-home.net

ALTERNATIVE HEADING

To the Manor Born

Charles Dickens . . .

49

"I Say, Old Chap"

Would you like a frightfully civilized, **[9-room, 3BR, 2-bath]** residence with every conceivable option an anglophile could possibly want? Patterned after the fine estates in York, this English **[brick]** masterpiece was built not for the years but for the centuries. It's your opportunity to be lord or lady of the manor at **[$219,500]**.

UR
HOME REALTY
555-8200
www.ur-home.net

ALTERNATIVE HEADINGS

Civilized British

Tudor Magic

Flawless Tudor

Tiffany Tudor

50

Irish Manor House

No blarney. This handsome **[3BR, 2-bath]** estate appears to have been transported from County Cork. Old-world craftsmanship is evident in the **[intricate detailing and exceptional woodwork]**. On **[almost 2 rolling acres]**, this is a heritage for your family that we proudly present at **[$379,500]**.

UR
HOME REALTY
555-8200
www.ur-home.net

51

A British Accent

This **[stone and brick]** Manor House, patterned after the fine estates in York, is set on **[over ½ acre]** in the most sought-after area of **[Westchester]**. Offering **[3BR, 3½ baths, paneled drawing room, huge dining room, estate office, cavernous cellar for your fine wines, and a rose garden]**, the home includes every conceivable option an anglophile could hope for. Offered for those who desire an extremely civilized way of life at **[$398,000]**.

UR
HOME REALTY
555-8200
www.ur-home.net

ALTERNATIVE HEADINGS

Elizabethan Manor

English Country Home

Proper English

English Brick

52

Italian Renaissance

Reminiscent of the grand Mediterranean villas, this architectural masterpiece is set on **[over an acre]** of resplendent grounds in the choicest section of **[Tuscany Estates]**. The property boasts **[3 magnificent bedroom suites, 3½ baths, library, 3 fireplaces, rooms of expansive proportions, 50-foot flower-bedecked veranda, circle drive, garages for 4 vehicles, pool, spa, cabana,]** and every amenity one would expect in a world-class estate. For those who refuse to compromise on quality, this very civilized residence is available at **[$950,000]**.

UR
HOME REALTY
555-8200
www.ur-home.net

ALTERNATIVE HEADINGS

Lavish Villa

Brick Italianate

Venetian Gothic

Old World Mediterranean

53

Sassy French Provincial

Reminiscent of the country homes near Lyon, this **[12-room Bellwood]** Estate is available for **[under $1,000,000]**. See what success is all about. #82 at *www.ur-home.net*

UR
HOME REALTY
555-8200
www.ur-home.net

ALTERNATIVE HEADINGS

Provence Revisited

Flemish Country

French Country House

French Norman

Exquisite Chateau

French Regency

Astrological Signs

A great many people read their daily astrological forecasts in their newspapers. Even though they may not be true horoscope devotees, readers typically have at least a casual fascination with these forecasts—even if the ad's headline doesn't happen to feature their own birth sign. The ads that we have included are based on general characteristics attributed to astrological signs.

54

Aries Are High

above the ordinary and demand homes to match. We've found the perfect home for a fortunate Aries, a [3BR, 2½-bath proud Colonial masterpiece] set amidst resplendent grounds in prestigious [Shorewood Estates]. The home offers a [3-car garage, a very private den or home office, formal and informal dining areas, a sun terrace,] and all the amenities normally seen only in home magazines. It's your sign of the future at [$379,500].

UR
HOME REALTY
555-8200
www.ur-home.net

55

Are You an Aries?

If so, you want much more than the ordinary. You've worked hard for what you have, and you want a house that reflects your success. In [Oakton Heights] we have just such a home. A flawless [Edwardian brick town house] with [3BR including a master suite with sitting room, 2½ baths sheathed in Italian tile, garage space for three vehicles, gleaming hardwood paneling, a private walled garden] plus every amenity you would expect in a fine residence. As an Aries, you will appreciate the value at [$219,500].

UR
HOME REALTY
555-8200
www.ur-home.net

56

Taurus? No Bull

when we say we have that special house for you. You're a steady and solid person who wants a home to match. You value your family and friends and seek a quiet, secure, and comfortable lifestyle. You will take pride in this **[3BR, 2-bath, brick Traditional]** on [its tranquil one-half acre site] in a much sought-after area of **[Newport Heights]**. [The mature landscaping rivals any you have seen.] The spacious and sunlit home features **[a paneled den, elegant dining room as well as a breakfast room, heartwarming brick fireplace,]** and a host of features that will delight you. At **[$214,500]**, you should call now or some Gemini will get here first.

UR
HOME REALTY
555-8200
www.ur-home.net

ALTERNATIVE AD

Taurus? No Bull

when we say this is the positively best **[3BR, 2½-bath]** home in Newport Heights for **[$214,500]**, we can prove it. See #24 at *www.ur-home.net*

UR
HOME REALTY
555-8200
www.ur-home.net

57

Are You a Taurus?

If so, you value a quiet comfortable lifestyle centered on family and close friends. We have your future home in this **[American Colonial]** on a quiet street in **[Midland Heights]**. This **[3BR, 2½-bath residence]** offers the warmth and charm of **[two mantled brick fireplaces, gleaming hardwood floors, intimate dining room, glassed conservatory, country-sized kitchen,]** and a host of features and amenities any Taurus would love. Comfortably priced for you at **[$214,500]**.

UR
HOME REALTY
555-8200
www.ur-home.net

58

Are You a Gemini?

If so, you are a special person whose individuality is reflected in a wide range of interests. This one-of-a-kind **[3BR, 2-bath, 2-car garage]** home in **[Orchard Ridge]** is as individual as yourself. You will love the **[panoramic views from the breakfast patio and the Jacuzzi in the master suite]**. Spacious and gracious with many features normally only found in fine estates, it's twice as nice as anything you have seen at **[$219,500]**.

UR
HOME REALTY
555-8200
www.ur-home.net

59

Gemini Special

A double-story, [like-new Cranberry Cove Contemporary] that will double your pleasure and fun. Offering [double baths, double north/south views, double-car garage and almost a double-sized lot] without doubling the price [$124,900].

UR
HOME REALTY
555-8200
www.ur-home.net

60

Hey! Gemini!

Double your pleasure, double your fun with this [3BR, 2½-bath, French Provincial] on [almost ½ acre of manicured lawn in Williamstown]. There is [a huge terraced patio for dining and entertaining, a pool and bubbling hot spa for fun and relaxation, formal dining room, and a den that would make a great home office plus an oversized double garage to hold your cars and toys]. One look and you will know that at [$249,500] it is the house that the stars ordained for you.

UR
HOME REALTY
555-8200
www.ur-home.net

ALTERNATIVE HEADING

Gemini!
Double Your Pleasure . . . double your fun . . .

61

If You're a Cancer

you want substance, not pretense. We have such a home in this [3BR, 2½-bath, stone-front colonial] with [hardwood floors, triple-glazed windows, and full poured basement]. The home features [a huge living area with 10-foot ceilings, mantled fireplace, greenhouse kitchen, formal dining room, baronial size master suite, 2½-car garage,] and a long list of extras. Sited [amidst giant oaks] on the choicest lot in [Westburg], it's been ordained to show you a delightful future at [$237,500].

UR
HOME REALTY
555-8200
www.ur-home.net

62

Are You a Cancer?

If so, you enjoy the pleasures of home. We have that very special home for you to love and enjoy [a 3BR, 2-bath sprawling California Ranch with a screened-in patio/breezeway and double garage] on [an estate-sized site in West Highlands]. [There is a great family room with fireplace that's just perfect for watching Sunday afternoon football, hardwood floors, a fenced yard for Rover and the kids,] and all the extras to spell COMFORT. It's your future at [$189,500].

UR
HOME REALTY
555-8200
www.ur-home.net

63

Are You a Leo?

If so, you are a hard worker who loves people. You are not afraid to express your individuality and prefer comfort over pretense. We've found your home, a solid [3BR, 2-bath, double garage, brick ranch with over 2,000 square feet for living] in the friendly community of [West Lawn]. There's a [lion-sized den, a family room with an orchard stone fireplace for casual entertaining, a patio that would be great for a neighborhood barbecue,] and it's set [amidst tall trees and flowering shrubs]. We're not "LION" when we say that at [$219,500] any Leo would own it with "PRIDE."

UR
H O M E   R E A L T Y
555-8200
www.ur-home.net

64

Leos Are Nice

friendly people who enjoy the company of others. The perfect house for a Leo is this [3BR American Traditional] in the friendliest [West Side] neighborhood where neighbors greet each other by name and stop to talk on their evening strolls. The home has [rose bushes that are a neighborhood landmark, a rocking-chair front porch, three apple trees, a large garage, full basement, and spacious sun-filled rooms that are decorator-perfect]. We are not "LION" when we say it's the friendliest house in town at a very friendly [$129,500].

UR
H O M E   R E A L T Y
555-8200
www.ur-home.net

65

Leos Have More Fun

That's why so many Leos live in [Capri Gardens], where every amenity of a first-class resort is theirs. Join them in this [2BR, bright and spacious end unit] with [a private deck overlooking the pool and court areas. Decorated in soft hues], it will turn a roar into a purr at [$93,500].

UR
H O M E   R E A L T Y
555-8200
www.ur-home.net

ALTERNATIVE HEADING

Leos Dominate

66

Perfect Virgo?

You want to control your future down to the last detail. You are not content with a home that's "almost" perfect. We offer perfection in this [3BR, 2-bath, West-wood Colonial] with its [two-plus car garage, woodburning fireplace, family room, huge oak trees, and financing that will seem too good to be true]. Even the price is perfect at [$189,500].

UR
H O M E   R E A L T Y
555-8200
www.ur-home.net

67

Are You a Virgo?

If so, you are not about to settle for anything less than the perfect house in perfect condition in the perfect location. We've found your home in this **[3BR, 2-bath, Cape Cod]** on the nicest street in **[Westhaven]**. From its **[gleaming matched hard-oak floors to the cut-stone fireplace]**, you will agree that the home is "just right." Other features include **[baths sheathed in ceramic tile, a kitchen any chef would envy, flagstone dining terrace, oversized garage,]** and a whole lot more. It's a home as perfect as you are at **[$239,500]**.

UR
HOME REALTY
555-8200
www.ur-home.net

ALTERNATIVE AD

Are You a Virgo?

If so, you are not about to settle for less than perfect. See the perfect 3BR, 2-bath Cape Cod in Westhaven for just **[$239,500]**. See #52 at *www.ur-home.net*

UR
HOME REALTY
555-8200
www.ur-home.net

68

Libra!

You know how to balance quality, location, and price. You know a value when you see one. One look and you will be convinced that this **[3BR, 2-bath, double garage, light and bright American Traditional]** was built with care, that it's in a very desirable **[West Side]** location, and that the price is far less than would be imagined, not even considering **[the delightful barbecue deck and family orchard]**. The scales are in your favor at **[$229,500]**.

UR
HOME REALTY
555-8200
www.ur-home.net

ALTERNATIVE HEADING

Libras Are Free

thinkers and know . . .

69

Are You a Libra?

If so, you want quality, beauty, and balance. While you love the past, you plan for the future. We have the home destined to fill your needs in this **[3BR, white clapboard Traditional with its simple classic lines, high ceilings, and intricate detailing set amidst stately oaks on an emerald lawn.]** There also is **[a 2-car garage, family garden, 2 apple trees]**, and it's located in the friendliest **[West Side]** neighborhood, where pride of ownership is evident in the well-kept homes and lawns. At **[$139,500]**, it's the perfect balance.

UR
HOME REALTY
555-8200
www.ur-home.net

70

Passionate Scorpio!

Scorpios are persons of great passion. They want the best and will not settle for less. We think we have found the home any Scorpio would love. A [3BR, 2½-bath, almost new 2,200-square-foot Spanish Colonial with red tile roof, graceful arches, fountain courtyard entry, vaulted ceilings, garden kitchen, Saltillo tile floors, Jacuzzi tub, three-car garage,] and a whole lot more. It's a home to excite any Scorpio at [$279,500].

UR
HOME REALTY
555-8200
www.ur-home.net

71

Are You a Scorpio?

If so, no amount of selling will get you to buy a home that doesn't meet your standards. When you see that perfect home, you will know it. We want you to look at this light and bright [3BR, 2-bath American Mediterranean with its attached 2-car garage] on a [wooded estate sized lot in Westover]. You will be impressed by its [proportions, pristine condition, quiet den, high ceilings, whitewashed oak cabinetry, ceramic tile, heartwarming fireplace,] and so much more. We think it's Scorpio perfect at [$249,500].

UR
HOME REALTY
555-8200
www.ur-home.net

72

Attention Sagittarius

You appreciate quality and recognize the best when you see it and act decisively to make it your own. You will be enthralled by this better than new [3BR, 2½-bath, New Mexico Contemporary with incomparable Wasatch Mountain views]. The home features [a cantilevered deck that seems suspended in space, a living room almost big enough for an archer, soaring ceilings, walls of glass,] and every amenity on your wish list. It hits the mark at [$327,500].

UR
HOME REALTY
555-8200
www.ur-home.net

ALTERNATIVE HEADING

Sagittarius Score

because you know your target. You appreciate . . .

73

Are You a Sagittarius?

If so, you love activity and the sheer joy of living. You're also competitive and don't want to take second place to anyone. Well, we found your perfect home, [a 3BR, 2-bath Westside Rambler] with [a 2-car garage plus a workshop you will love]. There's [a blue-ribbon quality garden, manicured lawns, and sculptured hedges that take second place to none, walnut paneled den, formal dining room, sun-drenched country kitchen, mantled fireplace, enormous master suite,] and a whole lot more. One look and you will see it's a definite bull's-eye at [$247,500].

UR
HOME REALTY
555-8200
www.ur-home.net

74

Capricorns Won't Compromise

They expect the best, and we have it in this [3BR, 3½-bath Tudor estate] that makes other fine homes seem plain by comparison. The understated elegance whispers "quality." In an incomparable [Westbrook] setting, this [brick and stone masterpiece] features [leaded glass windows, French doors to the 60-foot terrace, library/estate office, and music alcove] as well as all the usual and most of the unusual luxuries. Offered to the qualified Capricorn at [$930,000].

UR
HOME REALTY
555-8200
www.ur-home.net

ALTERNATIVE HEADING

Capricorns Star

75

If You're a Capricorn

Your star is ascending and it's time to see this upscale [3BR, 2½-bath, 3,000 square foot Tuscany-inspired villa] set [behind the gates in Brentwood Estates]. This fine residence features sun-filled rooms [of dramatic proportion, baths sheathed in Carrara marble, giant-high ceilings, a kitchen that is best described as incomparable, a starship den, delightful dining patio, landscaping to be envied,] and a vast array of quality appointments. The stars portend a great future for the lucky Capricorn buyer at [$347,500].

UR
HOME REALTY
555-8200
www.ur-home.net

76

Pisces

While the 12th sign of the zodiac, you won't accept second best in anything. This [magnificent 2,700-plus square foot Mediterranean] in [Newhaven Estates] with [3BR, 2½ baths, 12-foot ceilings, 3-car garage, walls of glass opening onto the dining patio, pool-spa, and colorful garden], plus every amenity you could wish for makes it Pisces-perfect at [$387,500].

UR
HOME REALTY
555-8200
www.ur-home.net

77

Pisces Swim

against the current. They're leaders rather than followers and value substance over fads. This [7-year-old, 3BR, 2-bath Georgian Colonial] set [among giant oaks] in [Westwood Acres] offers [fine detailing, open, bright rooms, antique brick fireplace, gleaming hardwood floors, formal and family dining areas, 2-plus car garage, and colorful flowers]; it would delight any Pisces at [$184,500].

UR
HOME REALTY
555-8200
www.ur-home.net

Birds, Pets, and Other Animals

Most people enjoy the presence of animals and birds, even if they are merely viewing them through a window. The fact that they have been observed on a property presents a positive image for the reader and will likely entice them to read the entire classified ad.

Many pet owners tend to regard their dogs and cats as members of their families. These readers value features of a home that are favorable to their pets and will naturally be attracted to an ad heading indicating the home's unique, pet-friendly qualities.

While these ad headings feature birds, pets, and other animals, favorable language can be inserted in other categories of ads to increase the interest in a property.

78

Awaken Each Day

to the sound of birds, [your very private garden view,] and sun-drenched rooms in this [practically new, 3BR, 2½-bath Virginia-inspired Colonial] in [the garden community of Westlake Village]. [Soaring ceilings, incomparable master suite, formal and family dining, entertainment-size family area, magnificent dining patio, and 3-car garage] are just a few of the features you will love. It's a whole new day at [$219,500].

UR

H O M E   R E A L T Y

555-8200
www.ur-home.net

79

A [Goldfinch] and a [Hummingbird]

were at the feeders when we visited this [3BR, 1½-bath Cape Cod] set amidst colorful plantings on the nicest street in [Vista]. Bright rooms, [huge country kitchen, gleaming hardwood, rose-brick fireplace, full basement, garage,] and birdwatcher's [patio] make this a special delight at [$179,500].

UR

H O M E   R E A L T Y

555-8200
www.ur-home.net

80

For the Birds

The backyard of this [American Gothic, 3BR home] is host to everything from hummingbirds to [quail], and a [red-tailed hawk] is a frequent visitor in [the ancient beech tree(s)]. The home is delightful, with [sun-filled high-ceilinged rooms, a country kitchen with huge walk-in pantry, and a separate garage that could be a great studio or work-room]; and it's set on [an oversized lot] on a [tree-canopied street] in the friendliest [Eastside] neighborhood. One look and you will chirp with delight. At [$169,500], the early bird who calls first will get this prize.

UR
HOME REALTY
555-8200
www.ur-home.net

ALTERNATIVE HEADING

Bird Sanctuary

81

Robins and Roses

share the [huge fenced] yard of this [3BR, 1½-bath traditional Cape Cod] on a quiet street in [Cloverdale]. This happy residence features [an old-fashioned mantled fireplace, gleaming wood trim, rich, neutral carpeting, country-sized kitchen, screened summer porch, double garage,] and just about everything you would want for your family. It's cheep-cheep at [$127,500]

UR
HOME REALTY
555-8200
www.ur-home.net

82

[Robins] Perch

on the [balcony] of this [3BR, 2-bath Monterey Colonial] in [Hacienda Heights]. This [7-year-old residence] has [large family areas, a magnificent fireplace, massive beams, flowing tile floors, flower-bedecked garden patio, 2-plus car garage, landscaping better than anything you have seen,] and it's birdseed-priced at [$264,500].

UR
HOME REALTY
555-8200
www.ur-home.net

83

A Curious Raccoon

watched as we put up the For Sale sign on this [3BR, 2-bath sprawling brick ranch home] just [20 minutes] from [the city]. The home features [big-city conveniences; large, bright rooms; central air; a quiet den; and a rose-brick fireplace] with the added charm of rural America. Your children will love the [miles of trails, trees, wild animals,] and friendly neighbors (both 2-legged and 4-legged). Set on [3 acres] all your own, this is the chance to make all your labors worthwhile at [$187,500].

UR
HOME REALTY
555-8200
www.ur-home.net

ALTERNATIVE HEADING

A Shy Fox

A Friendly Roadrunner

84

Gone to the Dogs

Seven trees and [a chain-link dog run] come with this [3BR, 2-bath Cape Cod] set on [a wooded hillside acre] in [Bayberry Heights]. This fine home offers a [2½-car garage, a full basement, a Great Dane-sized family room, and a kitchen to delight any chef]. Bring Rover along to check out the accommodations. Definitely not a dog, this home is priced to sell at [$179,500].

UR
HOME REALTY
555-8200
www.ur-home.net

ALTERNATIVE HEADINGS

Lucky Dog

K-9 Heaven

A Dog's Life

A Dog House ... plus ...

85

Attention Charlie Brown

Snoopy would love the [8] trees in the backyard of this [3BR, 1½-bath Carolina Cape Cod] on a friendly street in [Westward Hills]. There's [a colorful flower bed perfect for burying things, a lemonade-sipping patio,] and even a really great house with [curl-up fireplace and 2-car garage]. With practically no bones down, it's your kind of place at [$149,500].

UR
HOME REALTY
555-8200
www.ur-home.net

86

Puppy Paradise

The owners of this [3BR, 2½-bath Executive Ranch] in [Orchard Ridge] have [a Cocker Spaniel and a Beagle]. They love the [huge fenced yard with 7 trees]. There are lots of [squirrels] to chase and birds to bark at among the flowering shrubs and colorful plantings. There's [a huge kitchen with bleached oak cabinets to hold treats, a family room with a curl-up fireplace], plus lots of stuff to please the humans. This is your chance for a real dog's life at [$178,500].

UR
HOME REALTY
555-8200
www.ur-home.net

ALTERNATIVE AD

The [Collie] Next Door

hopes the new owner of this [3BR, 2½-bath Orchard Ridge ranch] has a friendly dog to share her trees and gossip. Let your dog see your new home. #44 at *www.ur-home.net*. It's people-priced at [$178,500].

UR
HOME REALTY
555-8200
www.ur-home.net

87

A [Cocker Spaniel]

enjoyed the [huge fenced] back yard of this [3BR Cape Cod] in much sought-after [Brentwood Estates]. The home comes with [14 large] trees for sniffing, flower beds to bury 100s of bones, [a playful poodle next door,] and [a bashful Dalmatian across the street]. Your dog will love it here as will your children. It is walking-close [to grade school and park]. Incidentally, the house [which is in near-perfect condition and even comes with a warranty] has large [bright rooms, antique brick fireplace, new soft beige carpeting that Fido can't stain, a full basement with a hobby room, a delightful dining patio, and a 2-car garage]. Definitely a Best Buy at [$169,500].

UR
HOME REALTY
555-8200
www.ur-home.net

88

A Dog Door

leads to the fenced yard and [massive, leaded glass entry doors] to [the dramatic soaring foyer] of this [almost-new Tuscany Mediterranean] in [Whitehall Estates]. With [3BR, 2 baths, 2-plus car garage, 12-foot ceilings, expansive family room, white rock fireplace, walls of glass, dramatic master suite, breakfast patio, and landscaping to be envied], it's a special place for 2-legged and 4-legged folks at [$219,500].

UR
HOME REALTY
555-8200
www.ur-home.net

89

Picture a Hound-Dog

on the lazy-day [front porch] of this [3BR, farmhouse-styled, white clapboard bungalow near Williams Corners] on [a tree-sprinkled, 1/3-acre] site. With [high ceilings, sun-drenched rooms, gleaming hardwoods, updated systems, basement/workshop and 2-car garage], it has a simple charm that makes it a special place much nicer than the price would indicate, [$214,500].

UR
HOME REALTY
555-8200
www.ur-home.net

ALTERNATIVE AD

Picture a Hound-Dog

on the lazy-day [front porch] of this [3BR farmhouse-styled white clapboard bungalow near Williams Corners] that's kibble-priced at [$214,500]. Better yet, take a tour: *www.ur-home.net*

UR
HOME REALTY
555-8200
www.ur-home.net

90

Dog Gone

So owner is selling this [3BR, 2-bath, 2-plus car garage, American Traditional] on [a choice wooded site near Weston Estates]. With [chain-link fencing and dog run, screened porch, garden patio, cut stone fireplace, French doors, a view to be envied,] and more, it's practically kibble-priced at [$149,500].

UR
HOME REALTY
555-8200
www.ur-home.net

91

Scratch and Sniff

Your dog will love the [large fenced] yard complete with [7] great trees that come with this [3BR, 2-bath, stunning Mediterranean] in [Washburn Heights]. With [formal and family dining areas, 11-foot ceilings, family room with river rock fireplace, delightful patio, colorful garden views,] and a very happy feeling, it deserves a woof [$179,500].

UR
HOME REALTY
555-8200
www.ur-home.net

ALTERNATIVE HEADINGS

Definitely Three Woofs

Friendly Dog

not included but . . .

The ad could be modified for cats with:

Definitely Deserves 3 Meows

Cat People Special!

Your felines will love this . . .

92

[3] Dogs, [2] Cats,

and a family of [6] have left for [California], leaving behind this empty [3BR, 2½-bath Mediterranean] in [Clement Woods Estates]. There's [a sparkling pool and spa, home office, flower-bedecked breakfast patio, walled garden, magnificent master suite, 3-car garage,] and so much more. Bound to please 2-legged and 4-legged folks at [$197,500].

UR
HOME REALTY
555-8200
www.ur-home.net

93

A Squirrel Lives

in the [oak tree] in the backyard of this [3BR American Traditional] in [Westward Acres]. You will need a bird guide to identify all the colorful birds that frequent the feeders. The home offers [large] sun-drenched rooms, [all the modern built-ins, and a double garage] in the most delightful setting imaginable. You will call it home at [$119,500].

UR
HOME REALTY
555-8200
www.ur-home.net

→ The ad could be modified as follows:

ALTERNATIVE HEADING

A Friendly [Tortoise]

comes with the fenced backyard of this . . .

Condominiums and Cooperatives

Condominiums, cooperatives, community apartment projects, and planned-unit developments share the following features: They each may contain shared areas that are owned in common with other owners; they are all governed by boards of directors; and they are each typically multiunit structures. Generally, these types of properties offer an attractive alternative to renting, in that the owner is protected against rent increases and obtains the tax benefits of ownership as well as possible equity appreciation. An advantage over normal single-family dwellings is that condominium-style property usually can be purchased for a significantly lower price than a single-family dwelling of the same size and quality. This makes condominiums the choice by necessity of some buyers who would prefer a single-family dwelling.

Condominium ownership, however, is sought by many buyers for reasons other than costs, such as convenient central location, security, recreational amenities, and the fact that others handle the maintenance duties of single-family ownership. Retirement community living projects offer the added benefit of fostering a happy, active, carefree environment for people of a similar age who enjoy sharing similar interests.

Ads can be tailored to appeal to specific types of potential buyers. For additional ad ideas, please see Chapters 33 (Sports), 36 (Vacation Homes), and 38 (Water-Related Property).

94

Designing Women

and men too, will enjoy this [2BR, 2½-bath, 24th-floor corner unit] with [a power address]. Featuring [high, sun-filled rooms, dining balcony, views of everything, and decorating that will knock your socks off], it's a place above the rest at [$345,000].

UR

H O M E   R E A L T Y

555-8200
www.ur-home.net

95

For The Wild Life

Enjoy the two-legged kind around the [pool, courts, and health club] with this [2BR, 2-bath end unit] in [Westlake] at [$147,900]. Don't miss the tour. #68 at *www.ur-home.net*

UR

H O M E   R E A L T Y

555-8200
www.ur-home.net

96

Feels Like a House

[End unit] privacy in delightful gate-guarded [Chambray Woods]. A spacious [2BR plus den, 2-bath, window-wrapped home with fireplace, soaring ceilings, walk-in closets, dining terrace, and garage] coupled with the amenities of a fine resort can be yours at a fraction of what you would expect to pay. Available right now at [$214,500].

UR
HOME REALTY
555-8200
www.ur-home.net

ALTERNATIVE HEADINGS

Condo or Castle

Big as a House

97

Sun-Lover Terrace

for a full body tan comes with this [oversized 2BR, double-bath, view unit] in [Westshore Towers]. The living area with its [high ceiling and open concept] flooded with natural light makes this a happy place to live and entertain. Onsite amenities include [indoor parking plus pool, spa, health club, and tennis court]. Don't miss out on this Malibu-like lifestyle when it can be yours for only [$247,500].

UR
HOME REALTY
555-8200
www.ur-home.net

ALTERNATIVE HEADING

Nudists!

A full body tan is possible on the private terrace that comes with this . . .

98

Lock the Doors

and travel the world knowing the maintenance will be taken care of when you live in [Mariner's Walk]. This lovely [2BR, 2-bath end unit] with its [private patio] offers the seclusion and amenities of a fine single-family residence with none of the responsibilities. Tastefully decorated with [just about every upgrade offered], this sought-after [Barcelona] model with [a double garage] is priced to sell quickly at [$189,500].

UR
HOME REALTY
555-8200
www.ur-home.net

99

Sell the Lawn Mower

but you will want plenty of flower pots for the sunny [balcony] of this light and bright [2BR and den, 2-bath corner unit that has been upgraded with almost everything] and [is within walking distance of the Harbor Mall]. Everything on your wish list is waiting for you, including [vaulted ceilings, huge walk-in closets, security parking] plus a recreational ambiance that rivals the world's most prestigious resorts. You can enjoy the best that life has to offer for [$279,500].

UR
HOME REALTY
555-8200
www.ur-home.net

ALTERNATIVE HEADING

We Mow the Lawn!

100

Let It Snow

Others will shovel snow, mow the lawn, and even paint the outside of your home while you enjoy all the amenities that go with this [oversized, 1BR, 1½-bath, end unit in Clifton Estates]. You will love the [dining balcony, mantled fireplace, gourmet kitchen, marble-sheathed baths, walk-in closets,] and the sophisticated ambiance of the lifestyle you deserve. Call now at [$98,000,] it's too nice to last.

UR
HOME REALTY
555-8200
www.ur-home.net

ALTERNATIVE AD

Lazy Owner Condo [$98,000]

Not a thing to do but "enjoy" in this [oversize 1BR, 1½-bath Clifton Estates end unit]. See why. #62 at *www.ur-home.net*

UR
HOME REALTY
555-8200
www.ur-home.net

ALTERNATIVE HEADING

Bone Idle

101

All You Have To Do

is move into this immaculate, entertainment size [2BR, 2-bath end unit] in [Mariner's Village] with its [soaring ceilings, wood-burning fireplace, sun-lover's patio, and double garage]. All the amenities of country-club living are yours to command and enjoy. Only those who live here can play here: [$239,500].

UR
HOME REALTY
555-8200
www.ur-home.net

102

Big-City Blues

Doomed to another night in front of the TV? Would you like an exciting alternative to apartment living? This huge, [1BR condominium only minutes from the heart of the city] offers you the opportunity for the lifestyle you have dreamed about. [Take the elevator to your own health club with its heated pool, relaxing spa and sauna, or relax with your friends on the roof garden]. All the amenities of a fine resort can be yours. You won't believe the financing available, and the price is right at [$159,500].

UR
HOME REALTY
555-8200
www.ur-home.net

ALTERNATIVE HEADING

Never Be Lonely

 This is a different way to promote a high-rise condo. It's designed to appeal to singles and couples working in the central city.

103

[Mariner's Walk]

is a planned, recreationally oriented community with a balanced environment where you and your family will enjoy the best life has to offer. This **[3BR, 2½-bath garden unit]** exudes an aura of style, comfort, and sophistication with a dazzling array of exquisite features to delight the senses. At **[$197,500]**, this is a unique opportunity deserving your immediate attention.

UR
HOME REALTY
555-8200
www.ur-home.net

➡ This ad communicates a mood without giving many details. If the project is considered very desirable or the name conveys a favorable image, the name can make an effective heading.

104

A Gorgeous Hunk

of a very desirable **[Westside]** address. This **[2BR, 2½-bath]** unit offers **[views of the city lights from all 12 windows]**. There is a **[28-foot living room with woodburning fireplace, dining terrace, baths sheathed in marble, and closets to get lost in]**. It's paradise in the city for **[$595,000]**.

UR
HOME REALTY
555-8200
www.ur-home.net

105

Party Time

is every day as the owner of this **[garden unit]** in **[Sunset Vista]** with **[twin master suites, soaring ceilings, magnificent views of the greenbelt, Corian and whitewashed oak kitchen, fireplace, dining patio,]** and so much more; plus you are part owner of the **[pools, spas, courts, and fitness center]**. You'll meet fun people in a fun place for a pleasant **[$147,500]**.

UR
HOME REALTY
555-8200
www.ur-home.net

106

Like To Entertain?

You will love this **[23rd-floor, spacious Clifton Tower home with an open concept living area, river view, sumptuous master suite, delightful dining terrace,]** and so much more. Everything about it will exceed your expectations, except the price **[$339,500]**.

UR
HOME REALTY
555-8200
www.ur-home.net

107

Isn't It Romantic

[1BR plus music room decorated in soft tones with a view of the city lights, privacy veranda for intimate dining, woodburning fireplace for cool evenings, sumptuous marble bath, and a short walk to fine dining and shops]. Perfect for you and your special someone(s) at **[$169,500]**.

UR
HOME REALTY
555-8200
www.ur-home.net

108

Hate To Share?

This [newer brick, 2BR, 1½-bath town house] features its own [separate basement, its own private patio, its own fenced yard, and its own 2-car garage]. It can be yours alone with low and likely no down payment and a price of just [$127,500].

UR
H O M E   R E A L T Y

555-8200
www.ur-home.net

➤ This ad could be used for row housing, as well as some condominium and co-op units.

109

Willing To Share?

There are two magnificent master suites in this sun-drenched [garden villa behind the gates] in [Capri Gardens]. With [11-foot ceilings, open concept living areas, white marble fireplace, washed oak cabinetry, private garden patio] plus the amenities of a luxury resort, it's "circle me" priced at [$237,500].

UR
H O M E   R E A L T Y

555-8200
www.ur-home.net

➤ This ad could be used whenever there are two master suites (bedrooms having private baths).

110

Junk The Car!

Everything is walking close to this [huge 1 BR, 1½ bath classic]. See what can be yours for [$289,000]. #112 at *www.ur-home.net*

UR
H O M E   R E A L T Y

555-8200
www.ur-home.net

ALTERNATIVE HEADINGS

Car Free

Kiss Your Car Goodbye

111

Celebrate Living

[Cliftwood Estates], a fun place to live with [community pools, spas, courts, health club, and recreation building] available to only the property owners as part of their low homeowner fees. See this [free-standing, seldom-available 2BR, 2½-bath, sun-drenched Mediterranean on the greenbelt] with its [tile and marble, 10-foot ceilings, fireplace, garden patio, and sumptuous whirlpool tubs]. Add a new dimension to your life at [$269,500].

UR
H O M E   R E A L T Y

555-8200
www.ur-home.net

112

No Board Approval

Bright [2BR, park-view] unit with [entertainment-sized living areas, dining terrace, underground parking, electronic security, low association fees]; and it's action priced at [$279,500].

UR
HOME REALTY
555-8200
www.ur-home.net

→ This heading can be effective for a condominium unit in an area where many cooperatives require board approvals.

113

X-Rated Condo
[$189,500]

- Intimate hot spa for 2
- Private terrace for a full body tan
- Sensuous double-size shower
- Cuddle-up fireplace

Tour this sophisticated [2BR, 2-bath Westside unit]. #44 at *www.ur-home.net*

UR
HOME REALTY
555-8200
www.ur-home.net

114

Condo in a Crunch

Must sell this [2BR, 2-bath] choice, [Winston Club end unit] with [10-foot ceilings, sun-drenched rooms, dining veranda, fireplace, therapeutic whirlpool tub, garage plus resort amenities] at the lowest price we've seen: [$179,500].

UR
HOME REALTY
555-8200
www.ur-home.net

115

Indulge Yourself

Every conceivable luxury is included with this [2BR, 2½-bath corner unit] in prestigious [Northrup Towers]. [Roman marble hot spa, closets to get lost in, private study, double-high ceilings, fireplace, delightful dining terrace, views to be envied,] and a great deal more. If the best isn't quite good enough for you, your dream is now possible at [$349,500].

UR
HOME REALTY
555-8200
www.ur-home.net

116

It's Loaded

with upgrades. This [2BR plus music room, 1¾-bath end unit] in [Briarwood] comes with [floor-to-ceiling fireplace, wet bar, built-in vacuum, upgraded appliances, Corian counters,] and a lot more, yet it's priced like an ordinary unit at [$209,000].

UR
HOME REALTY
555-8200
www.ur-home.net

117

Your Children's Inheritance

need not be spent. [This Westwood 2BR, 2-bath corner unit with its spectacular greenbelt view, Corian kitchen, 11-foot ceilings, private dining balcony, and underground parking] just looks like a million dollars. It can be yours for [$219,500].

UR
HOME REALTY
555-8200
www.ur-home.net

118

Life at the Top

Look down at the world spread at your feet from this [22nd-floor, window-wrapped, 1BR-plus office/guest room]. With [high ceilings, expansive living area, wet bar, state-of-the-art gallery kitchen, and private dining terrace], it's the pinnacle of living at [$207,500].

UR
HOME REALTY
555-8200
www.ur-home.net

ALTERNATIVE HEADING

Halfway to Heaven

119

Love in the Air

[Twenty-two stories] above the world is a [2BR, 2-bath] private place made for you. There are [two balconies— one ideal for dining and entertaining above the lights and the other for soaking in the sun]. [Rooms of generous proportions and amenities include a woodburning fireplace, a state-of-the-art kitchen, Jacuzzi baths sheathed in marble, and an incomparable river view.] An opportunity unlikely to be repeated at [$309,500].

UR
HOME REALTY
555-8200
www.ur-home.net

ALTERNATIVE HEADINGS

Batman View

Spiderman Special

120

Get in on the Ground Floor

A seldom available [2BR, 2-bath Cherokee] garden unit at [gate-guarded Williams Point] with [garage, 12-foot ceilings, fireplace, breakfast patio, kitchen to fry for plus pool, spa, courts, and fitness center] at a fast-sell price of [$134,500].

UR
HOME REALTY
555-8200
www.ur-home.net

ALTERNATIVE HEADING

Shlepp No More

121

Work Harder Play Less

If that's your philosophy, forget about this [2BR, 2½-bath, garden unit] at [the Links]. You won't want to go to work with [pools, spas, tennis, golf, and magnificent clubhouse] practically at your doorstep. There's [a home office that would be great as a game room, high ceilings, sun-drenched rooms, breakfast patio plus a 2-car garage], all included at a lazy [$249,900].

UR
HOME REALTY
555-8200
www.ur-home.net

122

OK! Don't Believe Me!

You know darn well it isn't possible to find a spacious [2BR, 2-bath unit] in a quality building in a desirable [West Side] location for only [$149,500]. Check it now or be too late. #44 at *www.ur-home.net*

UR
HOME REALTY
555-8200
www.ur-home.net

➤ This also is an attention-getting, negative heading. It is an appropriate type of ad when the price seems low.

123

Condominiums

Location	BR/Bath	Price
[Deepwell]	[1/1]	[$79,000]
[Mariner's Walk]	[2/2]	[$97,500]
[Ridgecrest]	[2/2]	[$127,800]
[Skyhaven]	[3/2]	[$139,500]
[Westview]	[2/2]	[$205,000]
[Mountainback]	[2/2]	[$219,000]
[The Lakes]	[3/2]	[$247,800]
[Horizons]	[3/3]	[$364,500]

UR
HOME REALTY
555-8200
www.ur-home.net

➤ This simple listing of units by location, size, BR/bath, and price indicates that you have many units available. This will increase your calls. If the ad category is Condominiums, consider the following.

ALTERNATIVE HEADINGS

Pick of the Litter

Choices-Choices

124

Northern Exposure

A [2BR, 2-bath garden unit] in [Cypress Grove] with [shaded patio overlooking a pond and wide expanse of lawn and trees]. With [walls of glass, Corian and tile kitchen, sumptuous whirlpool tub, delightful fireplace, and walk-in closets] it's sheer luxury living. Offered for your future at [$119,500].

UR
HOME REALTY
555-8200
www.ur-home.net

125

Lie about Your Age

and dye your hair gray, because only those over 55 can qualify to own this [2BR, 2½-bath garden unit] in [Summerset]. It will be worth it once you see the [spacious, bright rooms decorated in soft hues, 10-foot ceilings, garden patio, kitchen that's sheer ecstasy, twin sumptuous master suites with whirlpool tubs, dramatic fireplaces, 2-car garage,] and so much more. Plus you get all the amenities of a fine resort at less than the price of a plain little house at [$249,500].

UR
HOME REALTY
555-8200
www.ur-home.net

126

Unretire

Life will just begin at 55 living in this [2BR, 2-bath garden unit] in [Cambridge Gardens] with its [spacious sun-drenched rooms, soaring ceilings, massive fireplace, delightful dining patio,] and all of the resort facilities you can imagine are yours. Your future is in your grasp at [$119,500].

UR
_____
H O M E   R E A L T Y

555-8200
www.ur-home.net

127

55? You're Lucky!

You qualify to live in [Westport Village], a fun place with all the amenities of a fine resort. You're lucky because we have a much sought-after [2BR, 1½-bath, corner unit with soaring ceiling, private patio, great view of the greenbelt,] and everything you would expect in a luxury unit. It's even lucky priced at [$147,500].

UR
_____
H O M E   R E A L T Y

555-8200
www.ur-home.net

128

Gray Around the Edges?

If you or your spouse are 55, you can own a fabulous [2BR, 2-bath] unit with the finest resort facilities in [Westhaven]. If you like [gate-guarded privacy,] friendly neighbors, [huge, sun-drenched rooms, walk-in closets, your own whirl-pool tub, private dining patio, soft neutral tones, and the finest Maytag appliances,] you'll call this home at [$94,500].

UR
_____
H O M E   R E A L T Y

555-8200
www.ur-home.net

129

For Grown Ups

Over 55? You're in luck! A [2BR, 2½-bath plus private study/music room, end unit] in desirable [Hampton Village] has just come on the market. Perfect in every way with its [high ceilings, wet bar, large, bright family area, tiled fireplace, and dining veranda]; your ownership includes resort amenities that are unparalleled, [in a gate-guarded community]. For the young at heart, it's your chance at [$169,500].

UR
_____
H O M E   R E A L T Y

555-8200
www.ur-home.net

130

The Golden Girls

and boys too, will enjoy living in this 55+ community of [Edgemont Hills]. Set [on a quiet street behind gates] is a [semi-detached, 2BR-plus den, 2-bath, 4-year-old Mediterranean]. Offering [sun-filled rooms, a light, bright decor, limestone fireplace, high ceilings, greenbelt view, fountain atrium, and 2-car garage], it's a very happy place at [$112,500].

UR
_____
H O M E   R E A L T Y

555-8200
www.ur-home.net

131

Joe Millionaire Condo

Impressive [2 BR, end unit in Chesterfield] that shouts RICH but is plain-Joe priced at [$197,500]. See it first. #128 at *www.ur-home.net*

UR
_____
H O M E   R E A L T Y

555-8200
www.ur-home.net

132

Loft Lovers

[900 square feet, 14-foot ceilings, and a wall of glass] all awaiting your imagination. The [modern kitchen and bath are in, but the rest is up to you. Centrally located with a key elevator and low association fees]. It's a rare opportunity at [$187,500].

UR

H O M E   R E A L T Y

555-8200
www.ur-home.net

ALTERNATIVE AD

Hedonist

Indulge your every desire with this everything loft. Yours alone at [$189,500]. #24 at *www.ur-home.net*

UR

H O M E   R E A L T Y

555-8200
www.ur-home.net

133

A [14-Foot] Sculpture

would fit in this [1,200]-square-foot loft with seemingly sky-high ceilings and great [west] light through [the wall of glass]. [A brand new fully applianced kitchen and tile bath] make this a delightful place to live and work. With [security elevator, inside parking, and low association fees], it's an exceptional value at [$139,500].

UR

H O M E   R E A L T Y

555-8200
www.ur-home.net

134

[Sailmaker] Loft

[2,000 square feet, 14-foot ceilings, floor-to-ceiling windows, tiled kitchen and bath plus protected parking] in [an elevator building just a short walk from virtually everything] available with [below market seller financing] and a price of only [$189,500].

UR

H O M E   R E A L T Y

555-8200
www.ur-home.net

→ A former tenant or owner occupation can be an effective heading, such as the following.

ALTERNATIVE HEADINGS

Bicycle Factory Loft

Sculptor's Loft

135

Sky Loft [1,200] Sq. Ft.

[16-foot ceilings, exposed brick walls, separate meters, west exposure with knee-to-ceiling glass, new kitchen and bath], and it's [less than 2 blocks from the Civic Center]. Starving-artist priced at [$147,500].

UR

H O M E   R E A L T Y

555-8200
www.ur-home.net

ALTERNATIVE HEADINGS

Loft With Light

Loft in Space

James Bond Loft

Failed Sales

When a sale fails to close and the property is put back on the market, the fact that the sale failed is a fact worth advertising.

Logically, a failed sale could be viewed as a negative factor, but readers tend to react to "failed sales" in a positive manner. Potential buyers often sense a frustrated owner, which they hope will increase the likelihood of a bargain. And remember the phrase "failed sale" also sends a subliminal message that another hopeful buyer once considered the property desirable.

136

Blown Sale [$249,500]

As soon as we offered this [almost-new 3BR, 2-bath Mediterranean villa] in [Clydesdown Estates] we had a buyer. With [neighbor-envied landscaping, giant high ceilings, castle-sized living areas, twin fireplaces, tons of tile, and a three-car garage] it's no wonder it sold so fast. Opportunity is knocking twice. Respond or be sorry.

UR

H O M E   R E A L T Y

555-8200
www.ur-home.net

ALTERNATIVE HEADINGS

Failed Sale

Failed to Close

Encore Opportunity

Whoops! It's Back!

137

It's Back Again

When this [3BR, 1½-bath, Weston Hills Cape Cod] came on the market, we had it sold [in just a few days] but, because of unusual circumstances, it's available again. With its [finished basement fitness center, new state-of-the-art kitchen, antique fireplace, and attached garage], it should be gone for good in just a few days, because it's priced at only [$137,500].

UR

H O M E   R E A L T Y

555-8200
www.ur-home.net

ALTERNATIVE HEADINGS

A Second Chance

Play It Again Sam

Unsold

138

A Second Chance

[Several months ago] we offered this fine [West Side Ranch home] and in a matter of days, we thought it was sold. The sale was unable to be completed so we have again placed it on the market. This [like-new, 3BR, spacious home has 2½ luxurious baths, formal dining area, breakfast room, family room, and everything you would expect in a quality home in an estate setting.] When you see the home and consider the price, you will understand why it sold so quickly. Only [$219,500].

UR
HOME REALTY

555-8200
www.ur-home.net

ALTERNATIVE HEADINGS

Opportunity Knocks Twice

It's Back!

Second Time Around

139

What a Kick

Sale fell through so this [3-year old New England Colonial] is

Available Again

with [3BR, 1½ baths] in a great [Westhampton] location; it's going to sell this week, because it's priced at just [$189,500].

UR
HOME REALTY

555-8200
www.ur-home.net

140

We Lied to You

when we said that the first one to see this [3BR, 2-bath, tiled, Mediterranean] in [Shorewood] would be the owner. Actually, the second one to see it put in the offer. Because of unusual circumstances,

It's Available Again

with its [soaring ceilings, private home office, flowing family areas, dramatic fireplace, 2-plus car garage, and landscaping to knock your socks off], it should be quickly sold again at [$219,500].

UR
HOME REALTY

555-8200
www.ur-home.net

CHAPTER **NINE**

Financing

Financing a home is a vital concern for virtually every homebuyer. Many buyers do not realize that there are purchase opportunities featuring very low and, sometimes, no required down payment.

Other approaches to financing can be found in Chapter 19 (Homes, Low Price) where down payments, as well as monthly payments, are used to sell ownership over renting.

141

No Down Payment?

Then you will want to see this [3BR, 2-bath American Traditional] in a friendly neighborhood in the [Finchey] School District. The home offers [a fenced yard for your children and their dogs, full basement, kitchen with lots of built-ins that will hold the biggest family, sun-filled rooms, double garage that will also hold wagons, bikes and trikes, and it's walking-close to park and grade school]. Priced for the family at [$149,500]. Call and ask about the financing.

UR
HOME REALTY

555-8200
www.ur-home.net

ALTERNATIVE HEADING

Zilch Down

142

A Little Dough Will Do Ya

Less than [$5,000] down will make you the proud owner of a [better-than-new, 3BR, 1½-bath Cape Cod with double garage, fireplace, and a huge family garden] in [Oakhill Estates]. It's not going to last at just [$137,500.]

UR
HOME REALTY

555-8200
www.ur-home.net

143

Herman Doesn't Know

He can buy a great [3BR bungalow on the west side] with only [$2,000] down and a full price of [$122,900]. Check it out before Herman does. *www.ur-home.net*

UR
HOME REALTY

555-8200
www.ur-home.net

144

Not a Vet?

The U.S. Department of Veterans Affairs will sell you a **[3BR, 1½-bath Cape Cod]** VA foreclosure in a delightful family area with

Almost Nothing Down

and payments that are likely less than your rent. Call now or be sorry.

UR
HOME REALTY

555-8200
www.ur-home.net

→ Price is not really important for callers on this ad. It is the selling terms offered by VA foreclosures.

145

Can't Afford [$229,500]

for a **[7-year-old, 3BR, 2-bath, 2-car garage, Santa Fe Ranch]** on **[a ¼-acre estate setting]** in desirable **[Wilson Grove]**? Because of low-interest financing, we think you can. After a really low-low down payment, your monthly payments will likely be less than your current rent. Own a much nicer home than you thought possible. Only one like this so call NOW!

UR
HOME REALTY

555-8200
www.ur-home.net

146

Seller Wants [$5,000]

and you can assume the no qualifying **[low-interest loan]** on this **[2BR and den, expandable Cape Cod]** in a prime **[West Side]** neighborhood. With **[1½ baths, fireplace, huge kitchen with all appliances, fenced yard, and garage]**, it's an opportunity that's not going to last long at **[$139,500]**, call.

UR
HOME REALTY

555-8200
www.ur-home.net

147

Yes You Can

own a **[3BR, 2-bath, newer Colonial in the Freemont School District]** because it's likely available with

[NO] Down Payment

[and no qualifying.] Call now for details as it's not going to last at **[$129,500]**.

UR
HOME REALTY

555-8200
www.ur-home.net

148

Rent Now Buy Later

The owner will give the renter an option to buy on this **[3BR, 1½-bath, brick and cedar Contemporary with a Thunderbird Heights address]** and **[over one-half]** of the rent will apply to the down payment. Call for details and find how **[$1,100/mo]** can lead to ownership.

UR
HOME REALTY

555-8200
www.ur-home.net

149

Earn the Down Payment while You Rent

The owners of this [3BR, 3-bath Thunderbird Heights Mediterranean Villa] have indicated that they will give a renter an option to buy with [most of the rent] applying to the purchase. Call for details on this [$2,200/month] lease/option opportunity.

UR
HOME REALTY

555-8200
www.ur-home.net

→ The option price is not as important as the rent.

150

Rejected For a Loan?

Not to worry, a [3BR, 1½-bath Cape Cod] in a prime [West Side] neighborhood with a

NO-QUALIFYING ASSUMABLE LOAN

With [bright, light rooms, formal dining plus country kitchen, double garage, fenced yard] and so much more, it's not going to be around long at [$139,500].

UR
HOME REALTY

555-8200
www.ur-home.net

151

Worthless

That's what rent receipts are. You can't deduct them from taxes, they provide no equity, and they certainly don't appreciate in value. You don't have to remain a renter because with less than

[$3,000] Down

we can make you the owner of your own [3BR, 2-bath home] in the sought-after community of [Washburn]. Sorry, we only have 1 home available. It's first-come, first-served at [$157,500].

UR
HOME REALTY

555-8200
www.ur-home.net

152

Owner Willing To Rent

this [3BR, 1½-bath Westside Cape Cod] for [$1,200] per month but you can buy it for almost identical payments with very little down. Check #194 at *www.ur-home.net*

UR
HOME REALTY

555-8200
www.ur-home.net

→ The above ad could be placed in a Homes For Rent ad category that might lead to prospects who didn't think they could be buyers.

153

Move in Free!

That's right: [If you qualify] no down payment is necessary to become the owner of this [3BR, brick rambler with double garage] in a choice [West Side] family neighborhood. Payments will likely be less than rent and full price, only [$109,500]. It's first-come first-served.

UR
HOME REALTY
555-8200
www.ur-home.net

155

Let Us Walk You

through the financing. If you have good credit but are short on cash, you can still become the owner of this [3BR, 1½-bath, 2-car garage, 7-year-old, brick splitlevel, 3 blocks from Jefferson School]. Don't just circle this ad, call now as the price is just [$84,500].

UR
HOME REALTY
555-8200
www.ur-home.net

154

Short on Green

Not to worry, this [3BR, 1½-bath Cape Cod] in a friendly neighborhood might be purchased with

No Down Payment

and it has everything you want: [formal and family dining areas, fireplace, hardwood floors, basement, fenced yard, and double garage]. The price just [$147,500].

UR
HOME REALTY
555-8200
www.ur-home.net

156

UFOs

Unusual Financing Options with low and even no down payment are available for this [4-year-old, 3BR, 1¾-bath Tennessee stone ranch] on [a quiet cul de sac just 2 short blocks to Washington School]. There's [a large family room/kitchen, puppy-safe fenced yard with a great tree for a swing, full dry basement that offers limitless possibilities, 2-car garage], friendly neighbors, and a friendly price [$139,500].

UR
HOME REALTY
555-8200
www.ur-home.net

157

Stingy Relatives?

No need to borrow the down payment when you can own a [3BR, 1½-bath, brick split ranch with double garage] for less than

[$1,000] Down

It's a great house in a great [Cherrywood] neighborhood. Call now for details. At [$129,500], it's not going to be available very long.

UR
_____
HOME REALTY

555-8200
www.ur-home.net

ALTERNATIVE HEADING

Mean In-Laws?

158

No More Excuses

For very low or even no down payment, you can be the owner of this [3BR plus family room, Cape Cod] in desirable [Westhaven]. There's a [fenced yard, delightful patio, full basement, garage, and it's in move-in condition]. No need to procrastinate with a price of only [$137,500].

UR
_____
HOME REALTY

555-8200
www.ur-home.net

159

No Cash Dreamer?

Dream of owning a home but can't raise the down payment? We have a great [3BR, West Side] home immaculately maintained that comes with a homebuyer warranty, and we can move you in with [either owner, FHA, or VA financing] and monthly payments so low you won't believe it. Priced at only [$132,900].

UR
_____
HOME REALTY

555-8200
www.ur-home.net

160

All for Nothing

A [3BR, 2-bath Southern Traditional] with every modern amenity plus [2½-car garage and landscaping to make a gardener jealous], [No] down payment possible to a qualified buyer. It's see-worthy at [$139,500].

UR
_____
HOME REALTY

555-8200
www.ur-home.net

ALTERNATIVE HEADING

**A Penny Down . . .
or Nothing At All**

CHAPTER TEN

Fixer-Uppers

Fixer-upper ads are a form of negative ads where you emphasize the properties' problems. You can expect more responses from fixer-upper ads than from any other type of property ads because this category implies a bargain—and "bargains" are virtually guaranteed to make the phones ring!

If there are a great many ads in a newspaper, your heading must make it clear that you are advertising a fixer-upper property. However, when there are fewer properties listed in the paper, your heading can be more inventive. In either case, there should be no doubt in the reader's mind that you are offering a fixer-up type of property.

Never advertise a property as a fixer-upper without an owner's prior written approval. An owner's view of the property may be far different than yours and could potentially result in an angry owner who finds what he or she regards as a beautiful home advertised as "el dumpo."

Please see Chapter 29 (Negative Ads) for additional ad ideas.

161

The Roof Leaks

the [paint is peeling and the plumbing is not well] in this [3BR, 2-bath Westhaven Hills ranch]. Even at [$139,500], it isn't much. See if you agree #49C
www.ur-home.net

UR
HOME REALTY

555-8200
www.ur-home.net

162

The Basement's Damp

probably because of the leak in the roof. And those are the good points about this [2BR, Cape Cod in Westlake] that's a disgrace to an otherwise beautiful neighborhood. See if you can do something with it at [$137,500].

UR
HOME REALTY

555-8200
www.ur-home.net

163

See the Disaster

Click on to #131 at *www.ur-home.net* and see what can happen to a [3BR, 2-bath Arlington] home and why the price of [$149,500] is not a misprint.

UR
HOME REALTY
555-8200
www.ur-home.net

164

A $98,000 Problem

[3BR, 2-bath Westhaven] with some unusual problems. Check them out. #68B *www.ur-home.net*

UR
HOME REALTY
555-8200
www.ur-home.net

165

Fixer-Upper [$149,500]

Why would a [spacious, 3BR brick home] in [Northgate] with a [large fenced yard, full basement, two-car garage, and built-in appliances] be offered at such a ridiculous price [and with low-low down financing]? Frankly, it needs a buyer who is not afraid to put in some hard work. Call if you think it's you.

UR
HOME REALTY
555-8200
www.ur-home.net

➤ "Fixer-upper" implies a financial opportunity either as a bargain to own or a profit to be made.

166

It Will Never Sell

said Ms. Higgins when she put the For Sale sign on the lawn of this [3BR, 2½-bath West Hills Contemporary] despite the fact that it's just about the lowest priced home in the area at [$174,900]. See if Ms. Higgins is right #42C *www.ur-home.net*

UR
HOME REALTY
555-8200
www.ur-home.net

167

Older than Dirt

and just as pretty. But with a price of just [$169,500] this [3BR, 2-bath Westside Traditional] is worth a tour. Check #131 *www.ur-home.net*

UR
HOME REALTY
555-8200
www.ur-home.net

168

Pack Rat Special

This [3BR, 2-bath West Side Colonial] comes with [double garage; basement; and an attic full of boxes, parts,] and we don't know what all. For someone who loves to save things rather than throw them away, the saving's been done for you, and it's all included at [$187,500].

UR
HOME REALTY
555-8200
www.ur-home.net

➤ This ad turns the fact that owners or renters have left an accumulation of junk on the property into a tongue-in-cheek asset.

169

Depressing Fixer-Upper

[The shrubs haven't been trimmed in ages, there's more bare earth than lawn, and the landscaping is the best feature.] This [3BR, 1½-bath Traditional] while on a nice street in [Westport] has been neglected and abused. It will take more than paint to solve its problems. Sure, there's [a nice 2-car garage and fenced yard, the basic systems work, and the roof doesn't leak], but make no mistake, this is one miserable house and it's priced to reflect misery at [$69,500].

UR
HOME REALTY
555-8200
www.ur-home.net

ALTERNATIVE HEADINGS

Yuk! It Ain't Much!

Restorable?

Almost Livable-Fixer

Faded Glory

Wrecking-Ball Special!

The Bottom of the Barrel

AS IS Fixer
and it isn't very good . . .

You Get What You Pay For
and the price isn't much . . .

Better Than A Cave
but just barely . . .

170

Home Improvement

badly needed as this [3BR, 1½-bath Colonial] on a quiet street in [Westhaven] is truly a

Fixer-Upper

While the house appears basically sound and has [a 2-car garage, full basement, screened summer porch, and lovely trees], it's going to take a lot of work to make it as presentable as the neighbors'. Priced to reflect its pathetic condition at [$119,500].

UR
HOME REALTY
555-8200
www.ur-home.net

ALTERNATIVE HEADINGS

Not For Miss Muffet
If you're afraid of spiders avoid this . . .

Henry Higgins
would have a hard time turning this into My Fair Lady. It truly is a . . .

171

It Could Be Worse

The roof doesn't appear to leak, but just about everything else in this [3BR, 2-bath, brick English Tudor] in [Westwood] is in need of mending. While it has [expansive lawns, hedges, and flower beds], you'll have to imagine how it will look trimmed without the weeds and bare spots, and with flowers blooming. If you love to tinker, you have enough work for a lifetime. The only redeeming feature is the price: [$124,500].

UR
HOME REALTY
555-8200
www.ur-home.net

172

Old Dingy Cheap

Sure, the neighborhood's great and this [3-bedroom Traditional] may be structurally sound, but it all ends there. This is a fixer-upper that makes every other fixer-upper look like a palace. Don't take our word for it. Check out the mess at [$69,000]. #42 www.ur-home.net

UR
_____
H O M E   R E A L T Y

555-8200
www.ur-home.net

➤ A true buyer of fixer-uppers will be captivated by this ad. Because the property has a low price, is in a good area, and is structurally sound, it has the three features this type of buyer looks for. While the word "cheap" ordinarily shouldn't be used in an ad, this is an exception.

173

Doesn't Look So Good

Needs [paint, weed killer, grass, and hard work].

[3BR, 2-bath] Fixer

[Great location, 2 plus-car garage,] and a lot of other good things, but it definitely is not move-in ready, and it's priced to reflect this at [$119,500].

UR
_____
H O M E   R E A L T Y

555-8200
www.ur-home.net

ALTERNATIVE HEADINGS

Less Than Perfect

Filthy Old House

174

Paint Won't Do It

This [3BR, 1½-bath English Tudor] needs a plumber, electrician, heating and cooling contractor, and a gardener; and that's just for starters. This is the ultimate

Fixer-Upper

Besides the price, [Westhaven] address, and [some rather nice trees], the only redeeming feature is the price: [$87,500].

UR
_____
H O M E   R E A L T Y

555-8200
www.ur-home.net

175

Minor Problems?

[The air conditioner hasn't worked for 2 years, the roof leaks, and when you slam the front door, the living room lights go on]. Other than that, if you [paint inside and out and replace the carpet], this [3BR, 2-bath, split level] in [Weston Acres] would be almost respectable. We hope the price encourages someone [$99,500].

UR
_____
H O M E   R E A L T Y

555-8200
www.ur-home.net

➤ This ad was written to make the property appear worse than it is. Get ready for lots of calls.

176

Terminal Case?

Major surgery might save this [classic, 3BR Cape Cod] in [Westchester]. While there are many nice things such as [the neighborhood, the 2½-car garage, stone fireplace, hardwood floors, and new furnace/central air], it's definitely a Fixer and basket-case priced at just [$79,500].

UR
HOME REALTY
555-8200
www.ur-home.net

177

It's a Miserable House

This [3 BR, 2-bath Cape Cod] in [Lucerne Valley] appears to need everything. It's been abused and abandoned, so the [lender] says "SELL IT!" It's priced it to go away at [$89,500].

UR
HOME REALTY
555-8200
www.ur-home.net

ALTERNATIVE HEADING

An Ugly American Colonial
that appears . . .

178

Kiss The Frog

and it will turn into a handsome prince. Well, not exactly, but if you have that decorator touch and a few buckets of paint and rolls of wallpaper, you can turn this neglected [3BR, 2-bath Tennessee stone ranch] into one of the nicest homes in a desirable [West Side] neighborhood. Incidentally, the home comes with a [2-car garage, full basement, central air, and is on an oversized corner lot]. Magic-wand priced at [$132,500].

UR
HOME REALTY
555-8200
www.ur-home.net

179

Ghosts!

If you are easily frightened, don't come near this [3BR, 2-bath Pennsylvania Colonial] on a [large wooded lot] in [Westbury]. The home has [been boarded up for years while tied up in legal procedures], so we don't know what you'll find inside. [Miss Clancy], from our office, claims she definitely heard chains clanking when she put up the For Sale sign. The price, however, is a haunting surprise at only [$132,500].

UR
HOME REALTY
555-8200
www.ur-home.net

→ The above heading will really attract attention to a home that has been vacant for some time. This could also be used as a Halloween ad.

180

Almost Livable

if you don't mind [a lawn that looks like a jungle, walls that are begging for paint, carpeting that has seen better days, torn screens, and even a few cracked windows]. Actually, this [3BR, 1½-bath Cape Cod] is quite impressive, if you stand back far enough. It has [some nice trees and a 2-car garage], but it is the blight of an otherwise pristine community where neighbors take pride in their homes and lawns. If you're not allergic to work, we can offer [unbelievable financing] and a price of only [$69,500].

UR
HOME REALTY
555-8200
www.ur-home.net

181

Livable Barely!

But if you love to paint and fix, this [classic 3BR, 1½-bath Colonial] in [Westchester] will definitely excite you. The basics are all here, [hardwood floors, fireplace, French doors, 2-plus car garage], etc. If you have confidence in yourself, it could be an exceptional opportunity at just [$147,900].

UR
HOME REALTY
555-8200
www.ur-home.net

182

[Seven] Generations of Grime

have been lovingly preserved in this [3BR West Side Victorian] that looks as if it hasn't been cleaned since [the War]. It appears solid, but perhaps the grime is just holding it together. If you're looking for "original," this is certainly the place. Anyway, it's priced far less than a clean house at [$92,500].

UR
HOME REALTY
555-8200
www.ur-home.net

→ This is an unusual ad for an older, "dirty" home where the primary problem is decorating.

183

Easy Money

A little landscaping and cosmetic work should significantly increase the value of this neglected [3BR, 1½-bath English Tudor] in a desirable [West Side] area of [quality homes]. Featuring [leaded glass entry, massive oak doors, hardwood floors, paneled home office/study and bright kitchen leading to a breakfast patio], it has all the basics and more; but make no mistake, it's a fixer-upper and priced accordingly at [$149,500].

UR
HOME REALTY
555-8200
www.ur-home.net

ALTERNATIVE HEADING

Want to Make [$50,000]?

184

The Worst Home in Southport

We have the winner in the ugly-house contest with this **[3BR, 2-bath, brick Italianate traditional]** set on a **[huge South Side]** lot. It needs everything, starting with soap and water.

The Best Buy in Southport

Because of its horrendous condition, you have the opportunity for the buy of a lifetime at **[$219,500]**.

UR
HOME REALTY
555-8200
www.ur-home.net

→ An ad with a split heading is very effective in this case.

185

If I Had A Hammer

And a ton of nails I might be able to fix this **[3BR Westlake]** Fixer. See what you get for **[$129,500]**. #84 *www.ur-home.net*

UR
HOME REALTY
555-8200
www.ur-home.net

186

Teenager in Trouble [$147,500]

This **[16]** year old **[3BR, 2-bath Colonial]** needs help. See this ultimate fixer-upper. #124 *www.ur-home.net*

UR
HOME REALTY
555-8200
www.ur-home.net

187

A Fallen Woman

She was once a stately **[10-room Victorian]** lady. Now they call her a

Fixer-Upper

See if she is worth saving, #22 *www.ur-home.net*

UR
HOME REALTY
555-8200
www.ur-home.net

CHAPTER ELEVEN

Furnished Homes

Most buyers are not seeking a furnished home. However, if furnishings are included either as a fully furnished or partially furnished home, they are an especially important feature in the following situations:

- Mobile homes where buyers are likely to be young persons or families who may not have much in furnishings

- Vacation homes where included furnishings save the buyer the time and money of purchasing new furniture

- Luxury homes where the furnishings and decorator items are included, especially when the decorator is well known

It is also important to note that in the aftermath of floods and other natural disasters, furnished property becomes an important feature for buyers.

The ads in this section emphasize the fact that the property is furnished.

188

Have Nothing?
Have It All!

We have a [3BR, West Side Cape Cod] available NOW with [almost nothing down] and it's

FULLY FURNISHED
[$189,500]

One look and you'll be delighted, but the second one to call will be sorry.

UR
H O M E   R E A L T Y

555-8200
www.ur-home.net

ALTERNATIVE HEADING

Just Bring Yourself

189

Exquisitely Furnished

and accessorized [by Rozanne Ramon], this [3BR, 3½-bath Beverly Glen Contemporary] puts the ordinary to shame with its feeling of life and spaciousness. There is [a music room, chef-envy kitchen, whirlpool tubs, three-car garage, and it's set amidst manicured lawns and sculptured hedges]. Best of all, it's priced to give you a fortune in furnishings practically for free. [$379,500].

UR
H O M E   R E A L T Y

555-8200
www.ur-home.net

→ Mentioning the name of the decorator, even if not well known, increases the attraction.

190

Have Nothing?

We have a [fully furnished] [3BR, 1½-bath Middlebury Cape Cod with garage] available with [a down payment that's so low you won't believe it]. Payments will likely be less than you are paying in rent because the full price is only [$169,500]. If you call NOW, you can have it all.

UR
HOME REALTY
555-8200
www.ur-home.net

ALTERNATIVE HEADINGS

Everything but a Toothbrush

Forks and Salt Shakers
are about all you need . . .

Furnished—Furnished—Furnished
Even the pots and pans are included . . .

The Furniture is Free!

Everything comes with this . . .

191

Decorated by [Jon Chase]

All you need bring are pajamas and toothbrush, as this [Canyon Club Estates Mediterranean Villa] has been exquisitely and thoughtfully appointed. With [3 master suites and over 3,500 square feet] for living, it is perhaps the finest residence we have seen on the market this year. It's all waiting for you at [$695,000].

UR
HOME REALTY
555-8200
www.ur-home.net

192

You Better Like [Colonial]!

Because this [3BR, 2-bath Bayside Traditional] comes

Completely Furnished

at just [$279,500]. Take a tour #14 at *www.ur-home.net*.

UR
HOME REALTY
555-8200
www.ur-home.net

➡ When the furnishings leave something to be desired, you might consider a negative-ad approach such as the following.

ALTERNATIVE HEADINGS

Salvation Army Modern...
that's how [Mrs. Kelly] of our office described this fully furnished . . .

The Salvation Army
would love the furniture in this . . . and you can get a great tax deduction.

➡ Obtain the owner's permission in writing before you use any negative approach.

Gardens, Landscaping, and Trees

Gardens, both flower and vegetable, are regarded favorably by readers of ads. Even if the reader has never worked in a garden, it creates a positive image of a relaxed and pleasant lifestyle.

Landscaping is very important to most buyers. It showcases how others view the home and contributes to pride of ownership. Describing the landscaping gives the reader a positive mental image that distinguishes an ad from many others.

Trees are a particularly important element of landscaping. Trees not only help to frame the visual appearance of a home, they also project a sense of permanence. Mentioning tree types, and including details such as the varieties of birds that inhabit them, helps to reader to paint a positive mental image of a property.

The ads in this chapter feature gardens, landscaping, and trees in headings to capture the reader's interest. For ads related to these topics, please see Chapter 6 (Birds, Pets, and Other Animals).

193

Fire and Flowers

An [antique brick] fireplace and a garden ablaze with color go with this [3BR, 2-bath Pennsylvania Dutch Colonial] in a [Wilford Heights] estate setting. With [2-plus car garage, expansive family areas, formal and intimate dining, gleaming hardwoods, and breakfast patio], it's a hot deal on a colorful home at just [$187,500].

UR

H O M E   R E A L T Y

555-8200
www.ur-home.net

194

Don't Eat the Rabbit

Eat like one instead with the family-size garden [and fruit trees] that come with this [3BR Traditional] in [Millwood Heights]. You will love the [gleaming hardwood detailing, large front porch, oversize garage, neighbor friendly corner site,] and even the price: [$82,900].

UR

H O M E   R E A L T Y

555-8200
www.ur-home.net

195

A Garden Gnome

comes with a [3BR, 1½-bath Cape Cod on a huge lot] in [Westhaven]. A rainbow of flowers and colorful plantings [plus a vegetable garden that would be the envy of any farmer] will make your green thumb itch. The home has [bright and spacious rooms, formal dining room, country sized kitchen, beautiful hardwood trim and cabinetry as well as a 2-car garage]. It's blue-jean priced at only [$169,500].

UR
_____
HOME REALTY

555-8200
www.ur-home.net

ALTERNATIVE HEADINGS

Gherkins and Gnomes

Rhubarb Pie

A rhubarb patch comes with …

Strawberry Shortcake

A strawberry patch comes with …

ALTERNATIVE AD

An abbreviated alternate ad that ties in with the Internet could be:

A Garden Gnome

Plus a garden that is the envy of [Westhaven] comes with a [3BR, 1½-bath Cape Cod] for just [$169,500]. Tour it on the Internet, #47 *www.ur-home.net*, then call

UR
_____
HOME REALTY

555-8200
www.ur-home.net

196

A Secret Garden

[behind high walls] with [a delightful patio and bubbling fountain] is just one of the features that makes this [3BR, 2-bath English Townhouse] an exceptional property. It also offers [fine hardwood detailing, mantled fireplace, expansive living areas, 2-car garage, and a much sought after East Side location]. It's attention-priced at just [$168,500].

UR
_____
HOME REALTY

555-8200
www.ur-home.net

ALTERNATIVE HEADING

A Rose Garden

197

Green Is For Garden

It's practically planting-time for the family-size garden and flowerbeds on this [estate] setting in [Woodland Hills] that comes with this [3BR, 1¾-bath, 2-car garage, charming English Country Home]. With [expansive sun-filled rooms, extensive use of hardwoods, rich detailing, mantled fireplace,] and so much more; you can sow your seeds with an extremely low down payment and a price of just [$213,500].

UR
_____
HOME REALTY

555-8200
www.ur-home.net

ALTERNATIVE HEADING

Seed-Catalog Special!

198

Ramblin' Rose

bushes and colorful plantings surround this [immaculately maintained 3BR, American Bungalow] on a quiet [tree-lined] street in [Westchester]. There's [a rocking-chair-ready front porch, fenced yard with room for a vegetable garden, and garage plus RV parking]. Available now with [a LOW down payment], priced less than imagined at [$94,500].

UR
HOME REALTY
555-8200
www.ur-home.net

ALTERNATIVE HEADING

Promise Her A Rose Garden
Fulfill that promise with roses and colorful plantings that surround this . . .

199

The War of the Roses

Other gardens will come in second best to the colorful garden and plantings of this [3BR, white American Traditional] on [Hovely Lane]. With [gleaming hardwood floors, built-in china cabinets, sun-drenched rooms, country-size kitchen, formal dining, columned front porch plus garage], it's a home that radiates happiness. Available with low-down financing at a surprisingly affordable [$112,500].

UR
HOME REALTY
555-8200
www.ur-home.net

ALTERNATIVE HEADING

Moonlight and Roses

200

Wine and Roses

Grapevines and rosebushes can be found in the [large] garden of this [3BR, Traditional] in a quiet [West Side] neighborhood where families take pride in their homes and lawns. With [covered front porch, mature landscaping, large, bright rooms, full basement, and 2-plus car garage], it's family-ready with low and possibly no-down financing at a price of just [$179,500].

UR
HOME REALTY
555-8200
www.ur-home.net

201

Smell the Roses

and dozens of other flowers [surrounding the covered patio of this 3BR, 2½-bath Arizona Contemporary] on the nicest street in [Casa Grande]. This [2,400-square foot] home was built for an informal, relaxed lifestyle with [flowing floor plan, Mexican tile, walls of glass, magnificent fireplace, huge family area, 3-car garage, and walled yard]. An extraordinary offering at [$197,500].

UR
HOME REALTY
555-8200
www.ur-home.net

202

A Neglected Garden

But with your green thumb, it could again be ablaze with color and the envy of the neighborhood. It comes with a [3BR, 2½-bath, center-hall Colonial, flanked by towering maples] on an estate-sized [Middleton] site. The [beyond-perfect] home offers sun-filled rooms, [soft Berber carpeting, twin fireplaces, home office/music room, oversized garage, garden patio, and full, dry basement perfect for potting and storage of bulbs]. Definitely your place to grow at [$219,500].

UR
HOME REALTY
555-8200
www.ur-home.net

➤ This ad turns nondescript or neglected plantings into a very positive feature.

ALTERNATIVE HEADING

Weeds In The Garden

203

Grow Your Own

Vegetables, children, or both. This [West Side, 3BR, 1½-bath Traditional] has [a country-sized garden plus 6 assorted fruit trees, light, bright rooms, gleaming hardwoods, huge eat-in kitchen plus dining room, 2-car garage,] and more. With low down financing, it's the place to put down your roots at [$264,900].

UR
HOME REALTY
555-8200
www.ur-home.net

204

A Greenhouse

sits along the [quaint] garden path behind this [3BR, 1½-bath, split level Colonial] in [Washburn Heights]. If rare and exotic plantings excite you, you'll be ecstatic. Offering [a formal dining room, sun-drenched kitchen, garden patio, full basement ideal for potting and bulb storage plus a 2-car garage and RV parking], it's green-thumb priced at [$239,900].

UR
HOME REALTY
555-8200
www.ur-home.net

ALTERNATIVE HEADING

Orchids and Daisies

will flourish in the green house that . . .

205

Luther Burbank

would have loved the virtual rainbow of colorful plantings in the botanical wonderland surrounding this [3BR, 2½-bath, proper English Tudor] in [Windward Estates]. Features of this very proper residence include [leaded and beveled glass, intricately carved woodwork, brick fireplace, paneled home office/music room, garden patio, full dry basement, double garage, and garden patio]. The only thing modest is the price [$219,500].

UR
HOME REALTY
555-8200
www.ur-home.net

ALTERNATIVE HEADING

Botanical Wonderland

You will love the . . .

206

Vegetarian?

You may never have to go to a grocery store again. This [3BR, West Side, brick split-level] comes with a huge family garden, [plus there are 3 apple trees and raspberry bushes]. [Seven years old,] it offers [a tiled family room with fireplace, whitewashed oak cabinetry, double garage, flower-bedecked patio, and an acre of happiness] for a peanut-price of [$194,500].

UR
HOME REALTY
555-8200
www.ur-home.net

ALTERNATIVE HEADING

Harvest The Benefits

207

Vegetarian's Delight

The garden of this [3BR, 1½-bath, West Side Colonial] produces enough vegetables to fill [a dozen] freezers. There's even [a strawberry patch and 2 apple trees]. The home features [spacious sun-filled rooms, formal dining, country-sized kitchen with plenty of counter and storage space for canning, and a 2-car garage plus room for an RV]. A green-thumb home available for very little green: [$139,500].

UR
HOME REALTY
555-8200
www.ur-home.net

ALTERNATIVE HEADINGS

An Organic Garden

Cholesterol Free!

208

Tomato People

will love the family-size garden that comes with this [3BR, 2-bath California-style Ranch] in [Washburn Estates]. There's also a [2-car garage, full basement ready for finishing, and 3 fruit trees], plus we'll throw in some friendly neighbors and all for just [$219,500].

UR
HOME REALTY
555-8200
www.ur-home.net

ALTERNATIVE HEADINGS

Broccoli People

Carrot People

Radish People

Cabbage People

209

It's Sitting Pretty

on [¼-acre of tree studded lawns]. A [3BR, white Cape Cod] right out of a picture book with [shutters, fireplace, gleaming woodwork, fenced yard, finished basement, garage plus RV parking], and it's priced at just [$89,500].

UR
HOME REALTY
555-8200
www.ur-home.net

210

Neighbor Jealous Landscaping

comes with this [young, 3BR, 1¾-bath American Victorian] in the nicest area of [Westlawn]. Offering [bright spacious rooms, 10-foot ceilings, mantled fireplace, greenhouse windows, private home office/music room, a kitchen that any chef would fry for, double sized garage,] and more. A [one-of-a-kind] masterpiece that you will take pride in, priced no more than an ordinary home at [$239,500].

UR
HOME REALTY
555-8200
www.ur-home.net

ALTERNATIVE HEADING

Knock Your Socks Off

landscaping . . .

211

Green Grass of Home

Expansive park-like lawns [majestic trees] and colorful plantings surround this [3BR, 2-bath American Classic] on [almost an acre] in [Hillendale School District]. With [family and formal dining areas, magnificent woodwork, basement hobby shop plus fitness center, a 2-plus car garage, and a welcome-home front porch], it's a home to cherish at a very affordable [$284,500].

UR
HOME REALTY
555-8200
www.ur-home.net

ALTERNATIVE HEADING

Yard Sale

212

Gardener Needed

or a riding mower, because this [3BR, 2-bath Colonial Ranch] in [Saddleback Estates] has [almost a full acre] of park-like grounds. The home offers [a sumptuous master suite, large family areas, finished recreation/fitness center, window-wall views, river-rock fireplace, breakfast patio, 2-car garage,] and more. Look and you'll agree it's a lot for very little green: [$164,500].

UR
HOME REALTY
555-8200
www.ur-home.net

213

Horse Manure Needed

The lawn, [family garden, and flower beds] have been neglected but this [3BR, 1½-bath Cape Cod with 2-car garage] in desirable [Walnut Estates] just needs [dusting and perhaps a dab of paint]. With [near-new Berber carpeting, stone fireplace, finished basement recreation-fitness center] and more, it's fixer-upper priced without the work at [$180,000].

UR
HOME REALTY
555-8200
www.ur-home.net

214

Wild and Untamed!

Garden and lawn haven't seen a hoe or mower in ages! This **[3BR, 1½-bath, 2-car garage, Cape Cod]** is in remarkably good condition **[although a bit dusty]**. It has **[large sunlit rooms, orchard rock fireplace, magnificent woodwork, a full basement, and formal and family dining areas]**. Not a fixer, but it's fixer-priced at **[$147,900]**.

UR
HOME REALTY
555-8200
www.ur-home.net

215

Bring Your Squirrels

[7 Oak trees loaded with acorns] come with this **[3BR, 1½-bath, 7-year-old American Traditional]** in **[Walnut Grove]**. There's **[an oversized 2-car garage, family garden, intimate and formal dining areas, and a front porch like Grandma used to have]**. With a down payment that's practically peanuts, it's your future at **[$329,500]**.

UR
HOME REALTY
555-8200
www.ur-home.net

ALTERNATIVE HEADING

NUTS

and fruit trees surround this . . .

216

Tall Trees

furnish a screen of privacy, and soft cascades of light provide a timelessness where yesterday, today, and tomorrow become one. Sited in the midst of this serenity is a **[white clapboard Norman Rockwell Traditional]** that enjoys nature's vistas from every room. The **[3BR, 2-bath]** home was built for comfortable living and has all the amenities one could wish for, including **[a quiet home office, a full basement that awaits your imagination, a double garage, and a storage building perfect for an artist's studio]**. This home for many happy tomorrows can be yours today for **[$249,500]**.

UR
HOME REALTY
555-8200
www.ur-home.net

217

[40 Oak] Trees

and flowering shrubs come with this **[7-year-old stone and glass Arizona Traditional]** in friendly **[New Castle Heights]**. With **[3BRS, 2 baths, 10-foot ceilings, glass-wrapped family room, river-rock fireplace, and a master suite that will knock your socks off]**, it's a very special home available now at a very special price: **[$279,500]**.

UR
HOME REALTY
555-8200
www.ur-home.net

218

In the [Oaks]

A wooded grove is the home of this [3BR, 2½-bath, 7-year-old Carolina Colonial]. In an area of similar fine homes, it features [a home office/music room, spacious family room, sumptuous master suite, delightful dining patio, colorful plantings, 3-car garage,] and a lot more. We think it's an exceptional opportunity at [$247,500].

UR
HOME REALTY
555-8200
www.ur-home.net

219

Tarzan and Jane

would love swinging in the trees surrounding this [3BR, 2½-bath Southwest Colonial] in [Taos Heights]. They could [bathe their elephant in the sparkling pool, relax in a bubbling hot spa, and BBQ on the 40-foot patio surrounded by colorful plantings]. If they checked the house, they would find [2,700 square feet of luxury including a lion-sized den, tribe-sized kitchen, giraffe-high ceilings,] and more. It's priced for the civilized savage at [$279,500].

UR
HOME REALTY
555-8200
www.ur-home.net

220

Made in the Shade

of [giant oaks], this [3BR, 2-bath Chesapeake Colonial is only 7 years old]. A [huge family room with fireplace, formal and intimate dining areas, breathtaking master suite with therapy spa, dining patio, and 2½-car garage] are just some of the many features that will delight you. Priced to sell today at [$239,500].

UR
HOME REALTY
555-8200
www.ur-home.net

ALTERNATIVE HEADING

Something On The Side

In this case it's a [giant oak] . . .

221

$1,000,000 Trees

That's about what it would cost to have a landscaper supply just the many magnificent [oak, maple, and pine trees] on this estate-sized lot in [Clifton Hills], but we only want

[$240,000]

and this includes a delightful [3BR, 2-bath Pennsylvania Quaker Colonial] with [hardwood floors, two magnificent fireplaces, garden kitchen, 2-car garage,] and so much more. Call now for an immediate showing.

UR
HOME REALTY
555-8200
www.ur-home.net

→ This heading could be used wherever a property is on a natural setting; a variation would be "$1,000,000 landscaping."

222

A Cathedral

of tall trees guards this [3BR, 2-bath, brick and timber French Norman masterpiece] on [a hillside setting] in [Shorewood Estates]. Special features include [leaded glass, gleaming wood-work, dramatic staircase, paneled home office/music room, sun-filled garden kitchen, breakfast veranda, rose garden,] and so much more. A home to be experienced and priced at far less than you would imagine: [$319,500].

UR
HOME REALTY
555-8200
www.ur-home.net

223

[Dogwood Trees] Are Blooming

and flowers are pushing through the earth as nature renews itself. You'll feel it's a whole new life in this [almost-new 2,400 square foot, 3BR, 2½-bath, 3-car garage Mediterranean] in [Westwood] with [light hues, sun-drenched rooms, soaring ceilings, walls of glass that join the living area with the magnificent garden setting, 40-foot dining veranda, and a master suite fit for a movie idol]. It's your chance to blossom at [$237,500].

UR
HOME REALTY
555-8200
www.ur-home.net

224

[Apple] and [Peach] Blossoms

will bloom in the spring, and there will be pie, cobbler, and preserves in the fall for the owner of this [3BR, brick Ranch and mini-orchard] on a private [½-acre in Weston]. There's a happy feeling in the [country-sized kitchen and bright rooms]. Offering [a garage, a full base-ment that's great for the hobbyist, and an oak tree with a perfect branch to hang a swing], it's [just minutes from shopping, schools, and park]. It's a place you'll want to call "home," offered to you at [$159,500].

UR
HOME REALTY
555-8200
www.ur-home.net

ALTERNATIVE HEADINGS

Birds Bees and Apple Trees

[Apple] [Pear] [Plum]

Apple Pie
on Sunday from your own trees . . .

Johnny Appleseed
must have come this way. [6] apple trees come with this . . .

An Apple a Day
from your own trees . . .

Maple Syrup
possible from your own trees . . .

Little Jack Horner
would have loved the [6] plum trees that . . .

Holidays

While these ads do not highlight a property's feature, a holiday-related heading can be an unusual and creative lead-in to an ad, and in some cases, may even relate to a specific feature of the property. These ads are intended for use in the week or weeks preceding a holiday, but they are not necessarily more effective than other attention-grabbing ads.

MARTIN LUTHER KING, JR. DAY

225

Martin Luther King, Jr.

had a dream that we share of all people living together as equals with equal rights and opportunities. We want the world to know we subscribe to and practice Equal Housing Opportunity.

UR
H O M E   R E A L T Y

555-8200
www.ur-home.net

→ While not an ad for a special property, it is an appropriate ad for Martin Luther King Day. It lets readers know they can expect fair and equal treatment in their housing needs.

ALTERNATIVE HEADING

He Had A Dream
that we share . . .

226

Enjoy the Dream

of friendly neighbors, quiet streets, good schools, and homes that reflect the pride of their owners. You can live that dream in this [3BR, 1½-bath American Traditional] in [New Glarus]. With [a sun porch/studio, hardwood floors, river-rock fireplace, child-safe fenced yard, 2-car garage plus RV space], it can be realized now with a low or possibly no down payment and a full price of only [$169,500].

UR
H O M E   R E A L T Y

555-8200
www.ur-home.net

ALTERNATIVE HEADING

Don't Dream
about owning the perfect house with friendly neighbors and good schools. It can be a reality with this . . .

GROUNDHOG DAY

227

Groundhog Special

Don't hide from the world. Winter's almost over, and summer can't be far behind. Get ready with this [**3BR, 1½-bath Cape Cod**] complete with [**a rose garden**] that's the pride of the neighborhood and a bed of colorful flowers about to pop through the ground. There's a [**screened porch that's ideal for lazy-day relaxation or entertaining, double garage, full basement, and central air for those sultry days ahead**]. It's available now at a price any groundhog will love, [**$147,900**].

UR
HOME REALTY
555-8200
www.ur-home.net

ALTERNATIVE HEADING

Check Your Shadow

LINCOLN'S BIRTHDAY

228

Log Cabin Special

Actually, it's not made of logs and it's a great deal more than a cabin, but a future ABE LINCOLN might call it home. This [**traditional American ranch**] in [**Orchard Heights**] has [**3BRS, 2 baths, 2½-car garage, a huge family room, fireplace, fenced yard, and it's move-in perfect**]. Built to fulfill the American dream, it's fit for a President at [**$239,500**].

UR
HOME REALTY
555-8200
www.ur-home.net

229

Abraham Lincoln

would feel at home in this [**3BR, 2-bath, white clapboard American Traditional**] in [**Weston Heights**]. He would love the [**wooded site, antique brick fireplace, fine woodwork, rocking-chair front porch, and sun-filled rooms**] but would be amazed at the [**kitchen with every convenience imaginable and the whirlpool in the master suite**]. A home for tomorrow with the charm of yesterday—yours for [**$179,500**].

UR
HOME REALTY
555-8200
www.ur-home.net

ALTERNATIVE HEADING

George Washington

230

Honest Abe!

Trust us when we say this sparkling [**2BR, 1½ bath end unit**] in [**Clinton Woods**] is your ideal escape from shoveling walks and mowing lawns! [**Soaring ceilings, white marble fireplace, private balcony, sun-drenched interior, underground parking, and resort amenities.**] Affordably priced at [**$197,500**].

UR
HOME REALTY
555-8200
www.ur-home.net

→ The ad above is for a condo or co-op.

VALENTINE'S DAY

231

World's Best Valentine

Don't settle for a box of chocolates! This [3BR, 1½-bath,] postcard-perfect [Cape Cod] with [fireplace, hardwood floors, garage, and fenced yard] can be yours for a low-down payment and a sweet price of only [$187,500].

UR
HOME REALTY
555-8200
www.ur-home.net

232

A Forever Valentine

Here's a chance to live your love in this [1-year old, 3BR, 2-bath, 2-plus car, Florentine Villa in Westwood] with [double garage, huge family areas, dining patio,] and much more. You can make every day Valentine's day for a low-down payment and a price of only [$154,500].

UR
HOME REALTY
555-8200
www.ur-home.net

ALTERNATIVE HEADING

Keep Your Valentine
in this . . .

233

Don't Buy Flowers!

Get your Valentine a lasting gift. This [3BR, 2-bath, 2-car garage Cape Cod] in [Northwoods Estates] is [only 3 years old] and move-in ready. This home comes with a lifetime of colorful flowers, trees, and a sea of green lawn. Call now and ask about the low-down financing alternatives. We'll put a ribbon around it for you at [$219,500].

UR
HOME REALTY
555-8200
www.ur-home.net

PRESIDENT'S DAY

234

Presidential

This [3BR, 2½-bath New England Colonial] has [high ceilings, expansive areas for formal affairs, a colorful garden setting perfect for news conferences and pinning on medals, a private home office for signing documents, a 2-limousine-sized garage, and a full basement that could be finished to keep your secret service agents]. Best of all, it's Calvin Coolidge-priced at [$289,500].

UR
HOME REALTY
555-8200
www.ur-home.net

→ You can use Lincoln and Washington birthday ads for Presidents' Day.

235

George Washington

couldn't tell a lie, and when we say this [almost-new 3BR, 2-bath Santa Fe Contemporary in Highland Springs] is superb by anyone's standards, it's the absolute truth. It offers [an open, sun-filled design with flowing tile floors, beamed family room with bee-hive fireplace, whitewashed cabinets, 2½-car garage, fenced yard] and so much more. Honest George would recognize it as an opportunity not to be ignored at [$179,500].

UR
HOME REALTY
555-8200
www.ur-home.net

ALTERNATIVE HEADING

Cherry Tree Special!

In honor of George Washington we axed the price on this . . .

236

George Washington

nearly froze his tush at Valley Forge, but you can enjoy year-round comfort in this totally climate-controlled [3BR, 2-bath, double garage New England Colonial]. The Colonial charm would be familiar to George, but he would have marveled at the skillfully integrated systems and state-of-the-art conveniences of this fine residence. We "cannot tell a lie." One look and you'll want it at [$219,500].

UR
HOME REALTY
555-8200
www.ur-home.net

237

George Washington Would Have Slept Here

and felt right at home, had this [newer 3BR, 2½-bath Virginia-inspired Colonial] in [Williamstown] been around in 1776. He would have loved [the rich detailing, high ceilings, sunlit rooms, garden veranda, flowering shrubs, and colorful plantings, as well as the private home office/music room]. In terms of 1776 dollars, George would think it a fantastic bargain at [$194,500].

UR
HOME REALTY
555-8200
www.ur-home.net

238

Washington Cries "Ouch"

Even he never dreamed a dollar could stretch this far.

[$219,900]

for a [calendar-perfect 3BR Cape Cod] on an idyllic [Walnut Grove] site, and there's practically no down payment. Sorry, only one home like this, so it's first-come, first-served.

UR
HOME REALTY
555-8200
www.ur-home.net

239

You Don't Have To Be Irish

to become the lucky owner of this [3BR, 2½-bath, brick Irish Ranch home in Middleton], with a [2½-car garage, family room, full basement, lawn of Irish green, and ancient oak] tree said to have its own Leprechaun. [Mrs. Kelly] of our office says, "If you say you're Irish, I'll help you become the owner for [$234,500]."

UR
HOME REALTY
555-8200
www.ur-home.net

240

Little Green Men

[Mr. Kelly] of our office swears [he] spotted a lucky Leprechaun in an [old oak tree in the back yard] of this [nearly new, 3BR, 2-bath Colonial] in [Westlake]. Of course, [Mr. Kelly] may have started celebrating St. Pat's Day early, but you will love the bright, spacious rooms, [hardwood floors, dream kitchen, formal dining room, breakfast patio, 3-car garage,] and lucky Shamrock price of [$177,777].

UR
HOME REALTY
555-8200
www.ur-home.net

ALTERNATIVE HEADING

I Never Touched A Drop
said [Mr. Kelly] of our office who swears [he] . . .

241

Shamrock Green

will be the color of your friends' faces when you invite them to your [3BR, 2½-bath, 3-car garage Tuscany Mediterranean] in [Woodside Estates]. With [pool, spa, soaring ceilings, huge covered veranda, and landscaping to make a leprechaun jealous], they'll think you robbed the little people. They needn't know it just took a phone call, a wee bit of a down payment, and a price of just [$179,500].

UR
HOME REALTY
555-8200
www.ur-home.net

242

Shamrock Special!

When putting up the For Sale sign on this [3BR, 2-bath West Side Colorado-inspired Ranch], we found a 4-leaf clover. That practically guarantees good luck to the next owner. Oh! The house has a [large, bright family room, cut-stone fireplace, formal dining plus kitchen dining nook, patio surrounded by colorful plantings, 2½-car garage,] and emerald-green lawn. Lucky-priced at [$197,500].

UR
HOME REALTY
555-8200
www.ur-home.net

➤ This "lucky" house ad is not limited to the Irish in its appeal.

243

Savin' o' the Green

No son or daughter of Erin would think of spending thousands more when this [3BR, 2-bath, 3-year old Dublin Style Ranch] in quiet [Sandpoint Village] with [2-car garage, formal and family dining areas, finished basement—perfect for grand parties, and leprechaun-perfect landscaping] can be purchased for a paltry [$187,500].

UR
HOME REALTY
555-8200
www.ur-home.net

APRIL FOOLS' DAY

244

No April Fool [Westhaven] [$219,500]

and that's for a [3BR, 1½-bath, postcard-perfect Cape Cod with attached double garage and screened breezeway] in a haven of [pristine air], gentle breezes, and respectful neighbors. With low-down financing, call now or it will be opportunity-lost.

UR
HOME REALTY
555-8200
www.ur-home.net

EASTER

245

Easter-Egg Special

Nooks and crannies in this [3BR, 2-car garage West Side Traditional] plus flowering shrubs and colorful plantings are Easter eggs-hiding perfect. There's also [a high-poured basement that awaits your imagination, summer patio, friendly neighbors, and a family of squirrels]. It can be purchased for very little if any down payment, and it's priced to hop away at [$98,900].

UR
HOME REALTY
555-8200
www.ur-home.net

ALTERNATIVE HEADINGS

Easter Bunny Special

For the Easter Bunny

For the Easter Parade

246

Bunny-Slipper Special

A snuggle-up fireplace [in the master suite, warm hardwoods, soaring ceilings, and natural vistas that can't be captured on canvas] are yours with this [3BR, 2-bath, 2-car garage, Tennessee Colonial] on [⅓-acre of magnificent landscaping] in [Clinton Woods]. There's also [a family room with built-in bookcases and entertainment center, BBQ deck, basement fitness center, photographer's darkroom,] and a great deal more. It's hop-away priced at [$264,500].

UR
HOME REALTY
555-8200
www.ur-home.net

MOTHER'S DAY

247

Liberate Mother

From housework drudgery. This **[Westlake 3BR, 2-bath traditional]** with every conceivable labor-saving built-in is priced at only **[$178,500]**. Tour #21 *www.ur-home.net*

UR
HOME REALTY
555-8200
www.ur-home.net

CINCO DE MAYO

248

Cinco De Mayo

Celebrate liberation in a **[3BR, 2-bath Westside]** home of your own for just **[$127,900]**. See your future #68B *www.ur-home.net*

UR
HOME REALTY
555-8200
www.ur-home.net

MEMORIAL DAY

249

Memorial Day

It's a time to reflect, and this **[Norman Rockwell Traditional]** brings back the days when life centered on family and friends. Offering **[3BR, spacious family areas, polished oak woodwork and hardwood floors, formal dining area that will hold everybody, old-fashioned front porch, delightful garden,]** and more, it reflects memories of joy and can be your future for only **[$139,500]**.

UR
HOME REALTY
555-8200
www.ur-home.net

FATHER'S DAY

250

For Dad Alone

There's a **[lion-size]** den in this **[3BR, 2-bath Lakeland Colonial]** that Dad will love. It's Dad-friendly priced at **[$169,000]**. See #48 now at *www.ur-home.net*

UR
HOME REALTY
555-8200
www.ur-home.net

ALTERNATIVE HEADINGS

Father's Day Special!

Dad's Place

4TH OF JULY

251

If Betsy Ross

had chosen **[peach]** and **[cream]** for the flag, we could advertise this **[3BR, 2-bath Cape Cod]** as our July 4th Special. Set **[behind a white picket fence]** in a friendly family neighborhood with **[hardwood floors, fireplace, bright sunlit rooms, a garden to be envied, and a 2-car garage]**, this is as good as it gets. Family priced at **[$219,500]**.

UR
HOME REALTY
555-8200
www.ur-home.net

252

1776 Well Almost

This [Pennsylvania Colonial] in [Ojibwa Heights] has the classic lines of the fine estates that originally witnessed that first 4th of July. It's painstakingly authentic with its modern systems integrated so as not to detract from its charm. Featuring [3BR, formal dining, library/home office, country kitchen, 2½ baths, wide-planked maple floors, 10-foot ceilings,] and so very much more. It's a home built for now and the future, and it's firecracker-priced at [$205,000].

UR
HOME REALTY
555-8200
www.ur-home.net

ALTERNATIVE HEADINGS

Independence Day
Say goodbye to your landlord when you see this . . .

Red, White, and Blue!
As American . . .

253

Watch the Fireworks

from the [view-deck] of this [3BR, 2½-bath, double garage Colorado-style ranch in Pinehaven]. This [better-than-new residence] features [landscaping that puts the ordinary to shame, 2 fireplaces, private den/office, and it is decorated in soft, neutral colors]. It's a new listing and not going to last long at [$219,500].

UR
HOME REALTY
555-8200
www.ur-home.net

254

It's Like Fireworks

since we started advertising this [3BR, 2-bath Colonial with its 2½-car garage, and park-like landscaping] in [Weston Hills]. Neighbors have been calling saying we're depressing values by asking only [$189,500].

UR
HOME REALTY
555-8200
www.ur-home.net

LABOR DAY

255

Labor Day Not

Every conceivable labor-saving device has been skillfully integrated into this [like-new 2,400-square-foot, 3BR, 2½-bath Vermont Contemporary] on [a tree-shaded, estate-size lot in Orchard Hill]. It doesn't need a thing, and it only takes a phone call to see your future. Offered at [$239,500].

UR
HOME REALTY
555-8200
www.ur-home.net

COLUMBUS DAY

256

In 1492

Columbus made his discovery. In **[2004]** you'll discover a **[2,200-square-foot Mediterranean Ranch]** in **[Orchard Ridge]** with **[3 royal-sized bedrooms, 2½ baths sheathed in Italian Marble, private home office, magnificent landscaping, 3-car garage,]** and so much more. You'll have discovered your future at **[$269,500]**.

UR

—— **HOME REALTY** ——

555-8200
www.ur-home.net

257

Be Like Columbus

Discover this **[3BR, 2-bath Salt box Colonial]** in **[Morningside Heights]**. You'll be delighted with **[sun-filled rooms, fine woodwork, rose-brick fireplace, formal dining area, colorful plantings,]** and even the **[large garage with workshop area]**. It's a whole new world at **[$217,500]**.

UR

—— **HOME REALTY** ——

555-8200
www.ur-home.net

HALLOWEEN

258

Boo!

Actually, there's nothing about this **[authentic Massachusetts Cape Cod]** that'll scare you, and there's no "Trick," either. With **[3BR, 2 baths, 2½-car garage, enclosed breezeway, fireplace, family room, fenced yard, magnificent trees,]** and a choice **[Mapleton]** setting, it's a delightful TREAT at **[$169,500]**.

UR

—— **HOME REALTY** ——

555-8200
www.ur-home.net

259

Halloween Special

Contrary to popular opinion, **[Mr. Fredericks]** of our office doesn't wear a mask, but he has informed us you needn't be scared of this **[3BR, 2½-bath Pennsylvania Dutch Colonial]** in **[Almond Acres]** that **[he]** has just listed. Priced at a mere **[$176,500]**.

UR

—— **HOME REALTY** ——

555-8200
www.ur-home.net

ALTERNATIVE HEADING

Pumpkin Patch Special

260

A Haunted House?

Yes! This home in [East Westchester] is haunted with memories of a gentler time when life centered on home and family. This [3BR Traditional] has brought joy to generations of Americans and now is ready for your family. It's been carefully preserved and skillfully updated to meet your most demanding needs without detracting from its charm. The home offers [large, bright rooms with high ceilings, 2 baths, huge screened and glassed sunporch, 2 fireplaces, woodwork to be envied, and 2-car garage], all in a setting that'll delight and at a price that won't scare you off: [$97,500].

UR
HOME REALTY
555-8200
www.ur-home.net

VETERAN'S DAY

261

Veterans— Can We Help?

A phone call will explain your eligibility for a no-down-payment VA loan. We can also qualify you, so you'll know how much you can borrow, compute your monthly payments, and even show you homes that you can own. There's no obligation, just call.

UR
HOME REALTY
555-8200
www.ur-home.net

➤ While not an ad for a specific home, it nevertheless is an effective ad that will bring in buyers.

THANKSGIVING

262

Ain't No Turkey [$149,500]

You wouldn't expect to get a [3BR Cape Cod with attached garage] in great condition [with a homebuyer's warranty] in [Westchester Township] for such a price. Right now, such a home is available, but we don't think it'll be available very long.

UR
HOME REALTY
555-8200
www.ur-home.net

ALTERNATIVE HEADINGS

Pilgrim's Pride

Gobble It Up

263

Let's Talk Turkey

The owner wants to sell this impressive [3BR, 2-bath Dutch Colonial on a wooded acre in Westchester]. It's just stuffed with features that would delight any pilgrim. Call now and find out why we think it's worth a great deal more than just [$179,500].

UR
HOME REALTY
555-8200
www.ur-home.net

ALTERNATIVE HEADING

The Right Stuff-ing!

264

Easy as Pumpkin Pie

to buy this [3BR, 2-bath Colonial] on [desirable Washington Blvd]. With [owner financing] you can move in for about [5 percent down], and your monthly payments will likely work out at no more than you've been paying for rent. With a full price of only [$189,500], this is bound to be gobbled up fast.

UR
HOME REALTY
555-8200
www.ur-home.net

CHRISTMAS

265

Santa! Stop the Sleigh!

Why freeze at the North Pole when you can have a year-round climate-controlled environment in this [3BR, 2-bath American Colonial] on the nicest [wooded lot in Westport]? There's [a great fireplace in the family room, a garage big enough to hold 2 sleighs and 8 reindeer, a full basement that makes a great elf workshop, and Mrs. Claus will love the huge country kitchen with every modern convenience imaginable]. A home any jolly, portly man in a red suit would love at [$197,500].

UR
HOME REALTY
555-8200
www.ur-home.net

ALTERNATIVE HEADING

Santa Baby

266

Jingle Our Bell

and we'll show you this [3BR, Northside, white Colonial] with [shutters, fireplace, hardwood floors, fenced yard, garage, and built-ins]. Available with low-down financing, it's Santa priced at [$192,500].

UR
HOME REALTY
555-8200
www.ur-home.net

267

Silent Nights

and joy-filled days can be yours in this [3BR, 2-bath, almost new Hillside Estates Colonial]. There's [a 2½-car garage, full basement, screened rear porch, magnificent wooded site,] and so much more. Delightful, tranquil, and yours for only [$192,500].

UR
HOME REALTY
555-8200
www.ur-home.net

268

Yes! Virginia

There's a [white-shuttered, 3BR, 2-bath Colonial] on a tree-lined street in a friendly [West Side] neighborhood where children's laughter fills the air. On an [oversized corner lot with family garden, spacious sun-filled rooms, formal dining room, hardwood floors, and a brick fireplace for Santa], this home is priced for you at [$179,500].

UR
HOME REALTY
555-8200
www.ur-home.net

269

All You Want for Christmas

in one large package. A [newer, 3BR, 2-bath Cape Cod] on a quiet friendly street in [Newton Heights] that comes complete with [fireplace for Santa, huge family room for the tree, formal dining for Christmas dinner, 2½-sleigh garage, and dog door to the large fenced yard]. A gift for a lifetime, available now with low and possibly no-down financing at [$187,500].

UR
HOME REALTY

555-8200
www.ur-home.net

ALTERNATIVE HEADING

Be A Scrooge!
You won't have to buy any other presents if you give this . . .

270

Dreamin' of a White

[picket fence,] a quiet tree-lined street, friendly neighbors, and a [3BR American Traditional with light, bright rooms, screened summer porch, fenced yard, and double garage] in the nicest neighborhood imaginable. Call and you can own your dream at [$127,500].

UR
HOME REALTY

555-8200
www.ur-home.net

ALTERNATIVE HEADING

Home For The Holidays
A quiet tree-lined street . . .

271

The Chimney

isn't big enough for Santa, but there's plenty of room for your family in this [3BR, 1¾-bath Cape Cod with family room] in friendly [Deerskin Heights]. There's [a family room with fireplace, formal dining room, screened porch, double garage,] and a Santa-sized list of extras. Almost a gift at [$97,500].

UR
HOME REALTY

555-8200
www.ur-home.net

ALTERNATIVE HEADINGS

He Won't Fit!
The chimney isn't big enough . . .

No Room In The Stocking
but there's plenty of room for your family in . . .

272

After Xmas Sale

A [3BR, 2-bath, Westhills Contemporary] marked all the way down to

[$189,500]

Not a stripped-down model, it includes spacious sunlit rooms, [stone fireplace, 10-foot ceilings, 2½-car garage, park-like grounds, and financing too good to be true]. Call now as this SALE is unlikely to be repeated.

UR
HOME REALTY

555-8200
www.ur-home.net

CHAPTER **FOURTEEN**

Homes, Acreage

Homes with acreage are generally located beyond the suburbs. This type of property has strong appeal to many buyers for a wide variety of reasons including the following:

- Privacy—Neighbors are not typically located in close proximity to each other.

- Self Sufficiency—Owners can raise their own food.

- Safety—There's a general feeling that rural life is far safer than living in the city.

- Children—Some families prefer raising children in rural and semirural areas.

- Economics—In some cases, living in a rural area can be less costly than living in many urban areas.

- Taxes—Rural areas offer lower tax rates than urban areas.

- Animals—This type of property provides ample space for a variety of pets, such as horses.

If your newspaper does not include a special section for homes with acreage, consider featuring the size of the property in your ad's heading.

Please see Chapters 24 (Horse Property) and 36 (Vacation Homes) for additional ad themes that can be used for Homes, Acreage.

273

Twice The House Half The Taxes

[2,200 sq. ft.] home on [4] acres with taxes under [$3,000] and a full price of just [$189,500]. Tour your future in [Bayfield County], #63 www.ur-home.net

UR
HOME REALTY

555-8200
www.ur-home.net

274

Arrivederci City!

Go where children actually study and neighbors forget to lock their doors. This [young, 3BR, 2½-bath Colorado Contemporary on a wooded acre] is a world away from but minutes-close to [the city]. Now all the amenities you could want with the ambiance of small-town life can be yours and your family's for [$189,500].

UR
HOME REALTY

555-8200
www.ur-home.net

275

Grow Your Own

vegetables and children. [An updated 3BR, white clapboard American traditional] on [over an acre], and it's only [20 minutes from the city with school bus service at your driveway]. The home offers [large bright rooms, extensive hardwood trim, a brand new kitchen, 2-car garage plus a small barn]. It's your chance to live life the way it is intended to be lived for an affordable [$87,500].

UR
HOME REALTY
555-8200
www.ur-home.net

276

A Rustic Lane

leads to this very private place with [peaceful woods] and a [cedar, stone, and glass] home set in [a sun-streaked glen]. This [commuting close, 3-acre] site is home to a host of friendly [forest] creatures. The [1,800 square foot, 3BR] home has [2 baths sheathed in tile, a bright open concept plan with high ceilings and walls of glass that make nature your decorator, large double garage, and the most modern amenities and conveniences]. If ever there was a "MUST SEE" this is it at [$237,900].

UR
HOME REALTY
555-8200
www.ur-home.net

277

We Lost Charlie

He went to show this [older 8-room Colonial] on [2] lovely [wooded] acres last week, and we haven't seen him since. While the rooms are large, we should have found him by now. The office took up a collection, and we're offering a reward of $39. Oh, unless Charlie sold it, the house is still available at [$89,500], but please return Charlie if you find him.

UR
HOME REALTY
555-8200
www.ur-home.net

278

Sanctuary

The creatures of the forest and your family will feel free and secure in this serene [7-acre] private world that's just [30 minutes from the city]. You will fall in love with this [3BR, 2½ bath, cedar and stone home that seems even better than new and features high ceilings, paneled den, delightful deck, warm, orchard-stone fireplace, sun-drenched country kitchen, spectacular master suite, and woodland views from every window]. There's too much to list, so call now to see your future at a family price of [$287,500].

UR
HOME REALTY
555-8200
www.ur-home.net

ALTERNATIVE HEADING

Pinecones and Chipmunks

279

Where Hawks Soar High

and the air is free and clear, you'll find this [3-bedroom, 2-bath Arizona Contemporary] set on [5] of the most beautiful acres this side of heaven. It is a home that will make all of your toil seem worthwhile. Located in a very private world that's only [a short commute from town], this happy residence offers unparalleled vistas, [a sense of spaciousness with its high ceilings and walls of glass, a private den or office, and indoor-outdoor entertaining areas that merge together in perfect harmony]. More than a new home for you, at [$279,500] this is a whole new outlook on life.

UR
HOME REALTY
555-8200
www.ur-home.net

280

Telecommuters

will love the bright home office/computer center in this [5-year-old, 3BR, 2½-bath, 3-car garage Irish Manor House] set on [2] very private [wooded] acres near [Parsons' Ferry]. With [formal and intimate dining and entertainment areas, plus every modern amenity including a state-of-the-art security system], there's no reason to ever leave home. It can be your private haven for far less than a plain city home just [$289,500].

UR
HOME REALTY
555-8200
www.ur-home.net

281

The Great Escape

Off a quiet country lane near [Abbotsford] on [3 magnificent acres] sits a [white clapboard farmhouse] with [3BR, totally updated systems, and state-of-the-art kitchen], guarded by magnificent [beeches and maples]. There's [an old barn perfect for a studio as well as a 2-car garage]. It can be your family's haven for just [$164,900].

UR
HOME REALTY
555-8200
www.ur-home.net

ALTERNATIVE HEADINGS

Buy The Farm

Barn-House [3] Acres

Holsteins and Guernseys

will be your neighbors . . .

282

Recharge Your Batteries

living in this [2BR and den Victorian farmhouse] just [45 minutes from the city]. The [3-acre] site includes [century-old trees, a wide expanse of lawn, gardens, and a barn perfect for any artist's studio or hobby]. See it and be charmed. [$249,500].

UR
HOME REALTY
555-8200
www.ur-home.net

ALTERNATIVE HEADINGS

Town Close—Country Fresh

A Touch of Country

283

Out of the Tension Zone

On [½ acre] off a quiet lane set [amidst meadows and woods] is a [3BR, 2-bath Quaker Village Colonial] with green lawns and colorful plantings. You will love the [intricate detailing, formal and family dining areas, gleaming hardwood, quiet music room, and the workshop/garage]. A place to unwind naturally at a relaxing [$139,500].

UR
HOME REALTY
555-8200
www.ur-home.net

ALTERNATIVE HEADINGS

Be Laird of the Manor

[1932] Farmhouse

Artists, Writers, and Lovers

Country Addiction

Don't Need a Country Girl
City girls will love this . . .

Harvest the Benefits
of this . . .

284

Good Ol' Country Livin'

will be yours as the owner of this [3BR, 1½-bath, white clapboard American Traditional] set on [a tree-studded knoll] on [3] of the prettiest acres you will ever see. There's even [a rocking-chair front porch, a separate garage, and an old barn with possibilities limited only by your imagination]. It's just waiting at [$227,900].

UR
HOME REALTY
555-8200
www.ur-home.net

285

The Walton's Place [3 Acres]

A large, [white] house, [10] rooms with [3BR, 1½ baths, "welcome-home" front porch, 2-car garage, and a small red barn that awaits your imagination]. It's only [30] miles from the [city], but it seems a century away. Waiting for you at [$237,900].

UR
HOME REALTY
555-8200
www.ur-home.net

ALTERNATIVE HEADING

Farm In The Dell!

286

Country at Its Best

[2 tree-studded acres] a fast [45 minutes] away, a [2,400-sq.-ft.], [3-year-old, Cedar Ranch] with [2 master suites, home office or third bedroom, screened summer porch, 2 river-rock fire places, 3-car garage,] and natural beauty that can't be duplicated. It's your future at [$375,000].

UR
HOME REALTY
555-8200
www.ur-home.net

ALTERNATIVE HEADING

An Old Red Barn
is just part of the package . . .

287

Unlocked Doors

There's a place where a crime wave would be [children snitching apples from the 6 trees that surround this 3BR, white clapboard traditional on a full half-acre]. It's a world where graffiti is practically unheard of, children learn in school and neighbors and merchants know your name. Call and we'll show you this fascinating place, available for only [$87,500].

UR
HOME REALTY
555-8200
www.ur-home.net

288

Green Acres [6] The Place To Be!

Trees, grass, and a [3BR white house that's been meticulously maintained] plus [a red barn that offers a multitude of opportunities] in the most delightful [Washburn County] setting. Priced less than a city lot at [$137,500].

UR
HOME REALTY
555-8200
www.ur-home.net

ALTERNATIVE HEADINGS

Armchair Farmer

Grandma's Farm

Currier and Ives Farm

Lemonade Spring— Cigarette Trees

It is not as idyllic as the Big Rock Candy Mountain but it's close.

289

Your Green Acres

Picturesque [3BR farm home in immaculate condition, barn, apple trees,] and [30] acres only [45 minutes] from the [Civic Center] make this a very rare opportunity to better your life. Priced to make one family happy at [$179,500].

UR
HOME REALTY
555-8200
www.ur-home.net

ALTERNATIVE HEADING

Lost River Farm

→ If a property has a local name, it can be used as in the example above.

290

Giving Away the Farm?

Well practically, because all the owner wants is

[$289,500] for [20] Acres

and that includes [a great 3BR, 2-bath home that's just 6 years old, 4-stall barn, machine shed, family orchard; it's commuting close, too]. If you want to put down roots, call now.

UR
HOME REALTY
555-8200
www.ur-home.net

291

Abandoned [Apple Orchard]

Only [60 minutes] from [the city], there's [a 3BR home that's almost livable, a barn in need of paint, and a few assorted sheds] that come with [40] acres of natural beauty. What it needs is lots of hard work, but it's priced accordingly at [$229,500].

UR
HOME REALTY
555-8200
www.ur-home.net

→ The heading could be modified for a dairy farm, family farm, blueberry farm, etc.

ALTERNATIVE HEADINGS

Down A Winding Road

Refuge From the City

Pastoral Perfection

Commuter's Dream

292

As the Crow Flies

This [3BR American Traditional, with its little red barn] and [5] acres, isn't very far from the city, but one look and you'll realize it's at least [50] years away. On a quiet, [tree-canopied lane], the home features [a huge, old-fashioned pantry; a claw-footed tub; high ceilings; and a rocking-chair front porch]. It appears to have been carefully preserved in a time warp from a far gentler period. It's worth the extra drive to live a dream. Yours at [$219,500].

UR
HOME REALTY
555-8200
www.ur-home.net

293

Never-Never Land

[1½ acres of forests and glens] just [40 minutes] from [the city] is the site for this [3BR, 2-bath, brick, cedar and glass Contemporary] that seems at one with its natural surroundings. You'll delight in [the open, bright floor plan, huge family room with raised hearth fireplace, walk-in closets, delightful BBQ deck,] and so much more. It's your chance to escape at a very reasonable [$239,500].

UR
HOME REALTY
555-8200
www.ur-home.net

ALTERNATIVE AD

Believe in Fairy Tales?

If you don't, forget about this [castle] on [1½] enchanting acres. For just [$239,500], your fantasies can become a reality. Tour your future. #183 at *www.ur-home.net*

UR
HOME REALTY
555-8200
www.ur-home.net

294

Chickens and Ducks

will find a home in [10 acres] of [pastoral] splendor. There's a [solid, 3BR, American Victorian home] with [high ceilings, woodwork to be envied, and totally updated systems] as well as [a sturdy red barn, machine shed, family orchard, great garden spot, and rolling oak-studded hills]. It doesn't get any better than this at [$187,500].

UR
HOME REALTY
555-8200
www.ur-home.net

295

60 Minutes

from [the Civic Center] but this [7-year-old, 3BR, 2½-bath New England Colonial] set amidst [7 acres of wooded splendor] seems a lifetime away, with the friendly warmth of an earlier era. It offers [hardwood floors, orchard-stone fireplace, paneled home office/music room, garden kitchen, and BBQ deck]; your neighbors will be [raccoons, squirrels, and a curious fox]. A better life can be yours for no more than the cost of an ordinary city home [$197,500].

UR

HOME REALTY

555-8200
www.ur-home.net

ALTERNATIVE HEADING

Is It Worth The Drive?

[60] Minutes from . . .

296

Doesn't Taste Like Medicine!

Will be your reaction when you sample the cold, pure water from the well that comes with this [3BR, 1½-bath American Traditional] set on [a full acre] in [Wilson Township]. You'll love the [huge trees, home to dozens of chattering squirrels], as well as the [family-sized garden, double garage] and beauty of this exceptional residence. Call, look, and own at [$189,500].

UR

HOME REALTY

555-8200
www.ur-home.net

➡ This heading can be effective in an area where city water has a strong chlorine taste.

297

Shack Up

with a raccoon and a porcupine. If you want to get back to nature, this is your chance:

[10] Acres

and a [2BR cottage] that's a bit more than a shack. In fact, it's very livable. The good news is that you can find this magnificent setting just [45 minutes] from [the city] with its [woods and sun-filled glens]. The bad news is that the raccoon snores and the porcupine will want to sleep in your bed. A few inconveniences must be expected for just [$94,900].

UR

HOME REALTY

555-8200
www.ur-home.net

Homes, Bargains

A bargain is a purchase that can be made for less than what is considered to be the value of a particular property. Some ads claim to be describing bargains, while others hint or imply that a bargain is possible. For example, an ad that states that a "seller is highly motivated" implies that the owner will accept less than what he or she would ordinarily accept. Other ads give the impression that there is a bargain where one may not exist (e.g., an ad that indicates that a price has been drastically reduced).

Because everyone loves a bargain, ads describing bargains bring in calls even from people whose needs are significantly different from the features advertised for the bargain property.

Before you advertise a property as a bargain, obtain the owner's permission, because this ad type implies that the owner is not asking enough for the property. Never reveal an owner's motivation to sell without his or her permission, as this really invites offers lower than the asking price and reduces the owner's power in negotiations. In the same vein, never indicate that a price quoted is not firm without the owner's express consent.

For additional ad ideas, please see Chapter 19 (Homes, Low Price).

298

Bank Has Grandma's House!

At least it sure looks like it. A [3BR American Bungalow], set amidst [flowering shrubs and colorful plantings] on a quiet tree-lined street in [Washburn Corners]. There's a [country-size sunlit kitchen, polished hardwoods, full basement, and even a double garage]. A lot to love at just [$97,900].

UR

H O M E   R E A L T Y

555-8200
www.ur-home.net

299

Bank-Ordered Sale [$127,500]

A foreclosed bargain [3 BR, 2-bath, double-garage, brick home on the desirable West Side] with low-down financing available. Call quickly or send regrets.

UR

H O M E   R E A L T Y

555-8200
www.ur-home.net

300

Beat the Sheriff

Your last chance to buy this [almost new, 2,000-plus square foot home in sought-after Westwood Estates] before

FORECLOSURE

This light, bright home features [soaring ceilings, window-wrapped living area, huge walk-in closets, spa, and a quiet music room suitable for use as a home office]. It can be purchased NOW at a price unlikely to ever be duplicated [$187,500].

UR
HOME REALTY
555-8200
www.ur-home.net

ALTERNATIVE HEADING

Beat The Bank

301

The "F" Word

We didn't want to say it but it's almost here.

Foreclosure

Here's an opportunity for one buyer to obtain a [3BR, 2½-bath, 2,400-square-foot California-inspired Ranch] with [a "success" address in Washburn Heights]. This picture-book residence offers [a quiet home office, expansive family areas, sun-filled rooms, 2 fireplaces, 3-car garage, professional landscaping,] and lots more. Don't be deceived by the low price. It's a top-of-the-line residence and your window of opportunity at [$229,500].

UR
HOME REALTY
555-8200
www.ur-home.net

302

Ordered Sale

You can own a [3BR, 2½-bath, California-style Ranch with a 3-car garage] on [a choice wooded site] on the most desirable street in [Westlake]. It features [a huge family room, baths sheathed in marble, cathedral ceilings, central air,] and every built-in imaginable. Auction-priced at only [$179,500].

UR
HOME REALTY
555-8200
www.ur-home.net

➡ The ad does not state that this is a court-ordered sale but gives that impression. It could have simply been ordered sold by the owners, in which case it would be an ordinary listing. "Auction-priced" gives the very strong impression of a bargain.

303

Coming Soon

In just a few days we'll be able to show you this lender-owned

[Westchester] Foreclosure

It's a [3BR, 2½ baths, double-garage Quaker Colonial that's just 4 years old]. Call now so you can have the first opportunity to be the proud owner at a bargain price of just [$249,900].

UR
HOME REALTY
555-8200
www.ur-home.net

➡ This is an effective ad for a foreclosure that is not yet available for showing.

304

Lender says "Sell It!"

A [3BR, 2-bath center-hall Colonial] in desirable [Westlake] with all the extras thrown in can be yours for less than the price of a much more modest home. Fast action is required as it's priced to move quickly at [$197,500].

UR
HOME REALTY
555-8200
www.ur-home.net

305

By Virtue of Default

on a security agreement, this [3BR, brick, American Traditional with a huge lot and double garage] must be sold by the lender. This is your opportunity for an exceptional purchase at only [$97,500].

UR
HOME REALTY
555-8200
www.ur-home.net

➤ This is simply another way to show foreclosure. If more than 1 bath exists, it should be noted. If location is not mentioned in the newspaper category and the location is desirable, mention it in the ad.

306

HUD HUD HUD

[6] foreclosed homes available at bargain prices and great terms. View them at *www.ur-home.net* then call

UR
HOME REALTY
555-8200
www.ur-home.net

307

R-E-P-O

spells "bargain!" [3BR, 1½-bath,] well-located [West Side Colonial] with [double garage, hardwood floors, and new Berber carpet; it's in really great shape, except the lawn needs mowing]. The price seems too good to be true; but if you check it out, you'll want to own it. [$149,500].

UR
HOME REALTY
555-8200
www.ur-home.net

308

Repo-Man

is on the way. Your last chance to buy this [6-year-old, 3BR, 2-bath 2,200-plus square foot Carolina Colonial] on [a quiet Westlake lane] without paying foreclosure costs and new loan fees. Assume the [low-interest] loan with practically nothing down and it's yours. At just [$147,500] it's probably far less than the neighbors paid.

UR
HOME REALTY
555-8200
www.ur-home.net

ALTERNATIVE HEADING

Buy It or The Bank Will!
Your last chance to . . .

309

Take the Bank!

The bank must sell this [3BR, 2-bath, custom built, brick Ranch] in [West Corona] that has everything: [massive fireplace, 2-car garage, family room, breakfast patio, huge garden,] and more. The bank's problem can be your gain at [$199,500].

UR
HOME REALTY
555-8200
www.ur-home.net

310

Robin Hood Almost

Take from the bank and keep it for yourself: a [3BR, 2-bath, 2-car garage, solid Carolina Colonial] amidst [an estate-size tree-studded setting] in [Williams Woods]. It's been

Foreclosed

so, let the bank's loss be your gain. You can be the owner with very little if anything down at an embarrassingly low [$294,900].

UR
HOME REALTY
555-8200
www.ur-home.net

311

Desperation Time

If we don't sell this [6-year-old, 3BR, 2-bath Westchester Colonial] with [family room, fireplace, 2½-car garage, and professional landscaping] within the next [30] days, it's

Foreclosure Time

and it will be lost to the lender. Your chance for tremendous savings and low-down financing is available. The neighbors won't believe the price [$169,500].

UR
HOME REALTY
555-8200
www.ur-home.net

312

Attention Martians!

An out-of-this world value is possible on a [4-year-old Sunset Heights, 2,000+ square foot, 3BR, 2½-bath, 3-car garage French Mediterranean] because of the dreaded "F" word

Foreclosure!

A bargain any earthling would relish can be yours at [$184,500].

UR
HOME REALTY
555-8200
www.ur-home.net

ALTERNATIVE HEADING

Are You From [Venus]?

313

It Hit the Fan!

Desperate owner must sell this [almost-new 2,600 square foot, 3BR, 2½ bath Monterey Colonial] in [Washburn Heights]. Priced far below appraisal at [$277,777] it offers every amenity you ever wanted plus some you never knew you needed. Opportunity doesn't knock twice, so call.

UR
HOME REALTY
555-8200
www.ur-home.net

ALTERNATIVE HEADINGS

Foreclosure—Almost

Stop Foreclosure!

314

It's Panic Time

Owner can't hold out, so this [3BR, 1½-bath brick ranch home with 2-plus car garage] that's [walking-close to Washington Park] has been reduced to [$99,500]. Call now because it's below rock bottom.

UR
HOME REALTY
555-8200
www.ur-home.net

ALTERNATIVE HEADING

Buy Before the Bank

315

It's Not for Sale

[Ms. Jones] of our office says the [3BR Cape Cod in Westport] with the [double garage, fireplace, hardwood floors, and full basement] isn't really for sale. [She] says It's a Steal at [$139,500].

UR
HOME REALTY
555-8200
www.ur-home.net

316

It Takes a Thief

to take advantage of the desperate owner who must sell this [3BR, 2½-bath English Tudor Estate] in prestigious [Shorewood]. With its [showplace grounds, 3-car garage, fantastic wood-work, paneled library, magnificent public areas,] and so much more, you'll feel guilty only paying [$319,500].

UR
HOME REALTY
555-8200
www.ur-home.net

317

Guilty at [$164,500]

If you can't take the guilt trip, then don't buy this [3BR, 2-bath Rancho Heights Colonial]. It's certainly a great home. That's the problem: It's too nice for the price. See the steal, #41 at *www.ur-home.net*

UR
HOME REALTY
555-8200
www.ur-home.net

➡ Very little is said about the house, but this ad will attract a great many inquiries.

318

For Sale No!

We have a [6-year-old, 3BR, 2-bath Cape Cod with attached screened breezeway and double garage] on a prime [wooded lot in Westchester] but it's not really for sale.

A STEAL YES!

Unusual circumstances have made this home available at a price that will likely never be seen again for a home such as this. If you don't mind being called a thief, an offer of [$179,500] will make it yours.

UR

HOME REALTY

555-8200

www.ur-home.net

319

Steal Home

No one wants to be considered a thief, but someone will benefit by buying this [3BR, 1¾-bath center hall Colonial] on [almost ½ acre of manicured grounds] in [the estate area of Westchester]. The home is in [pristine condition] and has [an antique brick fireplace, formal dining area, well proportioned rooms, soft maple cabinetry and woodwork, new plush carpeting, every conceivable built-in, double garage,] and lots more. You can ignore this ad and let someone else reap the benefits of this unique opportunity, but we think you should call now and STEAL HOME at [$169,500].

UR

HOME REALTY

555-8200

www.ur-home.net

320

Certified Steal
[$139,500]

It's true! A [3BR, 2-bath California-style ranch home] on a [full ¼-acre wooded lot in Northridge] that should sell for far more is available at this almost ridiculous price because of very unusual circumstances. Call now and we will tell you more.

UR

HOME REALTY

555-8200

www.ur-home.net

ALTERNATIVE HEADING

PSSST! Wanna Steal?

321

The Scene of the Crime

You'll return to this [3BR, 2-bath, 3-car garage, French Chateau] in [Woodland Estates] time after time. You'll love the [high ceilings and happy feeling from the sun-filled rooms] and everything you would expect in a luxury residence.

The Crime?

You stole it at [$257,500].

UR

HOME REALTY

555-8200

www.ur-home.net

322

A Bloomin' Steal
[$127,500]

A [3BR, 1½-bath, 2-car-garage Cape Cod] in [Weston Hills] surrounded by colorful plantings and flowering shrubs, plus a down payment so low it doesn't deserve mention. It's first-come, first-served on this one so call now.

UR
HOME REALTY
555-8200
www.ur-home.net

323

Receiving Stolen Property!

That's what they'll say if you buy this [3BR, 2-bath Cape Cod] on the nicest street in [Winston]. With its [spacious sunlit rooms, raised fireplace, bay windows, delightful garden, 2-car garage, and special low-down financing], everyone will know it was stolen at [$184,500].

UR
HOME REALTY
555-8200
www.ur-home.net

324

Attention: Jesse James!

You don't need a mask to steal this [3BR, 2-bath Carolina Colonial Ranch] in [Winston] complete with [family room, basement recreation/fitness center, dining patio, 2½-car garage, and landscaping that will knock your spurs off]. It's a real heist at [$179,500].

UR
HOME REALTY
555-8200
www.ur-home.net

325

Owner Wants Out!
[$99,500]

Priced to move fast, this [3BR, 1½-bath Cape Cod with full basement, fireplace, fenced yard, and 2-car garage] in [Westport is in exceptional condition]. It's a one-time opportunity with low or even no down financing, so call:

UR
HOME REALTY
555-8200
www.ur-home.net

ALTERNATIVE HEADINGS

S.O.S.! Must Sell

Hysterical Owner!

→ Again, never indicate an owner is desperate without the owner's express written permission to do so.

326

Owner Wants Out!

It's as simple as that. The owner of this [Dutch Colonial set in a secluded wooded enclave of quality homes] wants a sale NOW! The home features [3BR, 2 baths, study or home office, garden kitchen with a step-out breakfast patio, double garage plus RV parking,] and a whole lot more. Don't be the second caller because it's priced to move fast at [$189,500].

UR
HOME REALTY
555-8200
www.ur-home.net

327

Sacrifice [$179,500]

While no one really wants to profit from the problems of another, that's exactly what is about to happen. Because of unusual circumstances, the owner of this [3BR, 2-bath American Traditional] in [Holiday Hills] has set a price significantly below the appraised value that is bound to be accepted by the first buyer. If you want to be the one to make money the day you make your purchase, hurry or be sorry.

UR
HOME REALTY
555-8200
www.ur-home.net

→ The above bargain ad is not subtle. This type of ad effectively motivates buyers to call and can result in a sale even when a house fails to meet the buyer's needs fully. No one likes someone else to get a bargain when they were there first.

328

A Bargain To End All Bargains

Sure, you've heard it before but not about a home like this. A [3BR, 2-bath, 4-year-old, Tuscany Mediterranean] in [Northland Heights] for [$247,500]. This home features [a huge family room with fireplace, delightful breakfast patio, formal and family dining areas, a master suite you can get lost in, basement fitness center, double garage with workshop,] and a great deal more. Call and check it out for yourself.

UR
HOME REALTY
555-8200
www.ur-home.net

329

A Bargain Antique

Sure, it's getting on in years but it's kept in shape and will continue to be a great house for many more tomorrows. There are [3BR, 1½ baths, a huge old-time kitchen with walk-in pantry, formal dining room, full basement, garage,] and it's in a fine [West Side] neighborhood. It's priced at [little more than the value of the lot], and we think it's one heck of a bargain at [$149,500].

UR
HOME REALTY
555-8200
www.ur-home.net

330

Thank God for Bargains

We all love bargains but real bargains in homes are as scarce as hen's teeth. Even with a low price, you can pay too much because of poor condition, design, or location. Because of unusual circumstances, we have a [3BR, 2-bath, brick rambler in move-in condition with the desirable split bedroom plan for privacy on an oversized lot] on one of the finest streets in [West Astoria]. If you're a shopper and have looked at similar homes, you'll snap it up fast at [$147,500].

UR
HOME REALTY
555-8200
www.ur-home.net

331

Bargain Home No Bargain Price Yes

A [3BR, 2-bath Colonial] with [2-car garage] set on [a wooded corner lot] in [Wilson Village] for just

[$237,500]

Unusual circumstances require a quick sale. Call now or you'll have a lifetime to say "I could have . . ."

UR
HOME REALTY

555-8200
www.ur-home.net

332

Too Low a Price!

The owners of this [3BR, 2-bath, solid English Tudor] in [Northridge] priced their home too high and buyers stayed away. They became disgusted, and we think they overreacted in slashing the price. After all, the home [is in excellent condition with great landscaping and features such as leaded glass entry, bright spacious rooms, like-new decorating and carpeting, fully fenced yard, double garage, and RV parking]. It won't be available very long at [$187,500].

UR
HOME REALTY

555-8200
www.ur-home.net

333

Pinch-Me Price!
[$89,500]

for a [3BR brick] home in friendly [Middleton] it is unbelievable but true. Unusual circumstances force an immediate sale so it's priced to MOVE. But there's more: [super landscaping, fenced yard, almost new carpeting, and double garage] make this a value unlikely to be seen again. First one here will be the winner, call:

UR
HOME REALTY

555-8200
www.ur-home.net

334

Parlez-Vous Bargain?

A [3BR, 2½-bath French Provincial in desirable Westgate] for only:

[$329,500]

This isn't a stripped-down model. Call and you will see it has everything.

UR
HOME REALTY

555-8200
www.ur-home.net

335

The Price Is Wrong

[$299,900] We don't know why the owner set the price so low on this [3BR, 2½-bath Florentine-inspired Villa] on the [best-view site in Claridge Hills]. Check #41 at *www.ur-home.net*, then act quickly.

UR
HOME REALTY

555-8200
www.ur-home.net

336

Priced below REPO
[$189,500]

Unusual circumstances allow us to offer this [3-year old Mediterranean Villa with twin master suites, walk-in closets, and 2-car garage] at this price. Tastefully decorated in [soft, earth tones], it includes [formal and intimate dining areas, flower-bedecked veranda, and a kitchen that will impress a chef]. As an investment or as a fine home, it should demand your immediate attention.

UR
HOME REALTY
555-8200
www.ur-home.net

ALTERNATIVE HEADING

Auction Priced [$189,500]

337

911

A real emergency! Owner must sell this [3BR, 2-bath, 2-car garage, Quaker Village Colonial] in [Winslow Acres] IMMEDIATELY or SOONER! With [a dramatic window-wrapped family room, family and formal dining, breakfast patio, expansive green lawns and colorful plantings, it's move-in ready]. One look and you'll realize what you're getting for less than the price of an ordinary home. [$187,500].

UR
HOME REALTY
555-8200
www.ur-home.net

338

Free Home!

The [Westlake] lot under this [3BR, brick Bungalow] is worth the [$149,500] total price. It's #71, at *www.ur-home.net*

UR
HOME REALTY
555-8200
www.ur-home.net

339

Owner Is Tired

of making payments on a vacant house and has ordered us to get it off his hands. It's a [3BR, 2½-bath, proper English Townhouse] on [desirable Spruce Street]. With [hardwood floors, two fireplaces, high ceilings, generous-sized rooms, and a 2-car garage], it's an imposing residence that exudes success. Your chance to be [lord or lady of the manor] for no more than an ordinary home: [$287,500].

UR
HOME REALTY
555-8200
www.ur-home.net

340

HELP! [$179,500]

Because of unusual circumstances, this [3BR, 2-bath, brick, split ranch with double garage in Orchard Ridge] must be sold within [30] days. We priced it to sell to the first viewer.

UR
HOME REALTY
555-8200
www.ur-home.net

341

Insult Us!

Anything's possible. Take a look at this [2,000 square-foot, 3BR, 2-bath Santa Fe Ranch near Northridge County Club] with [2½-car garage, huge family room, and dream landscaping]. Owner wants [$284,500] but said, "Please! Get me an offer!"

UR
HOME REALTY
555-8200
www.ur-home.net

➤ Never indicate a property can be purchased for less than list price without owner's express permission.

342

No Brainer!

You don't need to be a genius to know you should check it out when a [3-year-old, 3BR, 2-bath Colonial with a 2½-car garage] in [Weston Hills] is available at only [$187,500].

UR
HOME REALTY
555-8200
www.ur-home.net

343

It's Gotta Go!

And fast! That's why this [3BR, 2-bath, 3-year old, Cape Cod with double garage] in [Shorewood Heights] is priced at only [$167,500].

UR
HOME REALTY
555-8200
www.ur-home.net

344

Forget the Appraisal

This [3BR, 2-bath, brick, Arizona Ranch in Clifton Hills] with [a 2½-car garage, family room, and magnificent landscaping] must be sold now so it's being offered at [$50,000] below appraisal at only [$189,500].

UR
HOME REALTY
555-8200
www.ur-home.net

ALTERNATIVE HEADING

[$50,000] Below Appraisal

345

Forget Fixers

when you can buy a [7-year old, 3BR, 2-bath Southwest Ranch] in [Cambellsport Acres] with [a huge family room, fireplace, country-size kitchen, formal dining, breakfast patio, 2-plus car garage, and breathtaking landscaping] in move-in condition that's priced like a fixer at only [$174,500].

UR
HOME REALTY
555-8200
www.ur-home.net

346

Take It Please!

We've offered this [3BR, 1½-bath Middleton Heights Cape Cod] for so long that it's an embarrassment. This light, bright home is in a great family neighborhood and includes [a child-safe fenced yard, lovely landscaping, a full basement, 2-car garage,] and a lot more. The desperate owner has reduced the price [for the second time]. Take advantage of us at [$79,500].

UR
HOME REALTY
555-8200
www.ur-home.net

347

Let's Make a Deal

Owner wants to sell and if you want to buy we have a [nearly new 3BR, 2-bath, double-garage California Contemporary] in a great [West Side] neighborhood with a long list of upgrades and special features. We told the owner it's worth [$199,500]. SO, WHAT'S YOUR OFFER?

UR
HOME REALTY
555-8200
www.ur-home.net

ALTERNATIVE HEADING

Bring an Offer

348

Ripe for an Offer

The owners gave us permission to let you know they are desperate to sell their [immaculate 3BR, 1½-bath brick] home in a very desirable section of [Westhaven]. It has [park-like grounds, large bright rooms, and a double garage, and it's close to schools and shopping]. Flexibly priced at [$197,500].

UR
HOME REALTY
555-8200
www.ur-home.net

349

Notice

We have been ordered to sell a [2-year-old, 3BR, 2-bath, double-garage Nantucket Colonial], having approximately [2,000 sq. ft.], on [a wooded acre] in [Westwood] for the price of [$149,500]. Interested parties should contact the agent.

UR
HOME REALTY
555-8200
www.ur-home.net

350

[$12,000]/Room

But you must take all 9 rooms of this [Westport Traditional]. Take a tour. #18 at *www.ur-home.net*

UR
HOME REALTY
555-8200
www.ur-home.net

351

[72] Hours To Sell

The owner must sell quickly or lose it all. This is a once-in-a-lifetime opportunity to buy a **[2,000 square foot, like-new split ranch with 3BR, den, 2½ baths, and double garage in Hilton Estates]**. Hurry, as the first caller will be the new owner at **[$204,000]**.

UR
HOME REALTY
555-8200
www.ur-home.net

352

A Fixer Not

this **[3BR, 2-bath Tennessee Ranch]** has **[1,800 square feet]** for perfect living. It's **[better than new]** with **[a 2-car garage and fabulous landscaping]** plus it's in a friendly and quiet neighborhood. However, it is fixer-priced at **[$149,500]**.

UR
HOME REALTY
555-8200
www.ur-home.net

353

Wife Walked Out!

and put a deposit on a new home. They need **[$189,500]** for their **[3BR, 2-bath Westside Rambler]**, and we think it's a bargain. See it, #402 *www.ur-home.net*

UR
HOME REALTY
555-8200
www.ur-home.net

ALTERNATIVE HEADING

Two Homes—One Spouse

Must dispose of one, preferably the **[3BR, 2-bath Westside Rambler]** . . .

→ Note: Never give the reason for a sale without the owner's written permission.

CHAPTER SIXTEEN

Homes, Family

Family issues are a motivating factor for many buyers because most parents want to do whatever they can for their children. The selection of a home, in this situation, is largely influenced by the parents' perception of the benefits it offers their children.

Familial bonds can be the focal point of effective advertising. While many ads featured elsewhere in this book also appeal to benefits associated with children, the ads in this chapter are specifically centered on the family.

Please see Chapter 18 (Homes, Large) for additional ads that emphasize features that are attractive to families.

354

No Screeching Brakes!

On this child-friendly cul-de-sac. Check out this [3BR, 2½ bath, split ranch] that's family-priced at [$147,500]. #826
www.ur-home.net

UR
HOME REALTY

555-8200
www.ur-home.net

355

If You're Raising

more than just your standard of living, then you will appreciate the [child-safe tree-shaded fenced yard] that comes with this [2,100-square-foot, 3BR, 1½-bath brick Ranch] in the finest neighborhood of [West Chesterton]. The home, which has an unassuming charm that complements the environment, offers [a sun-drenched garden kitchen with breakfast room that opens to the flower-decked garden veranda, separate formal dining area, a family room that will hold a Cub Scout pack, high ceilings, two fireplaces, and a 3-car garage with room to spare for a dozen bikes, trikes, and a red wagon]. Call today to see where your family's going. Offered at [$329,500].

UR
HOME REALTY

555-8200
www.ur-home.net

356

The Schools You Hoped For

Await your children as the owner of this [brick split level] in highly regarded [Cranston School District]. The [spacious] home has [3BR, 1½ baths, a family room that opens to a relaxing patio, full basement, double garage], and it's family priced at [$214,500].

UR
—————
H O M E   R E A L T Y

555-8200
www.ur-home.net

ALTERNATIVE HEADING

[Avondale] School [$189,500]

➤ If the school or school district is highly regarded, use it in the heading. The school or district could be combined with a price that seems reasonable. Please note: some real estate industry professionals consider ads that emphasize school districts as a form of discrimination. Please use caution and your own judgment when using this type of ad.

357

Private Schools Not Needed

This [4-year-old, 2,450 square foot Colorado Contemporary] in the highly regarded [Newhall School District] offers [3BR, 2½ baths, private home office/computer center, formal and family dining areas, 3-car garage plus RV parking,] and a great deal more. Exceptional in every way except the price; it's affordably yours at [$337,500].

UR
—————
H O M E   R E A L T Y

555-8200
www.ur-home.net

358

Emphasis on Education?

In the highly regarded [Harding School District] [just 1 block] from [Adler Elementary School], there's a [3BR, 2-bath, 2-car-garage, captivating Cape Cod] with [a child-safe fenced yard, basement recreation/fitness center, private home library, orchard stone fireplace, and a family room with French doors that open onto a delightful garden patio]. Call, look and evaluate; you'll find it's a SMART buy at [$247,500].

UR
—————
H O M E   R E A L T Y

555-8200
www.ur-home.net

359

Friendly Dog

is not included with this [3BR] home [in the Hillside School District. With a short walk to schools and parks], this is the ideal home for happiness. It features [a fireplace to gather 'round on cold wintry nights and a tree-shaded, fenced yard children will love. The full, dry basement makes a perfect rainy-day playroom, and the double garage has room for cars, bikes, trikes, and a red wagon]. It's the perfect home for Fido and the rest of the family at [$218,500].

UR
—————
H O M E   R E A L T Y

555-8200
www.ur-home.net

➤ Adding the name of the school district tends to give an area more prestige, even though it might not really be that outstanding. And, again, while the authors do not believe advertising school districts is discriminatory, some people feel this is a gray area.

360

Attention Kids

How would you like a yard big enough for six puppies and a dozen friends, [a perfect place for a tree house, a garage that will hold 2 cars and your own rock band? A family room with its own fireplace that would be great for slumber parties, a high basement that would be a great place for a Ping-Pong table, two kids' bedrooms, and a kids' bath that's separated from parents' so you can have your privacy. And you will be only a short bike ride to the mall, school, and the park]. All a kid could ask for, including lots of friends waiting for you. Tell your parents the house is [only 6 years old], and it's a heck of a value at [$197,500].

UR

HOME REALTY

555-8200
www.ur-home.net

361

Bare Feet Wiggling

in the grass, and [almost a half-acre for your children to roam on this pleasant, wooded site]. Besides the [large family room, the full, dry basement is a great place for a rainy-day playroom]. Incidentally, the house has [3BR, 2 baths, a double garage,] and a lot more for optimum family living. [$187,500].

UR

HOME REALTY

555-8200
www.ur-home.net

362

Even Little Legs

can walk to the [grade school] from this [3BR, 1½-bath, perfect Cape Cod] in [Weston Estates]. Offering [a fenced yard with a swing-perfect tree, sun-drenched rooms, toe-toasting fireplace, a dry basement perfect for a rainy-day playroom, and an oversized 2-car garage with space for a dozen bikes]. With low-down financing, a call will make it your future at [$194,500].

UR

HOME REALTY

555-8200
www.ur-home.net

ALTERNATIVE HEADING

Children's Chauffeur?

Even little legs can . . .

363

Blessed with Children?

Then you'll want to see this [3BR, 2-bath American Traditional] in a friendly neighborhood in the [Finchey School District]. The home offers [a fenced yard for your children and their dogs, full basement, kitchen with lots of built-ins that will hold the biggest family, sun-filled rooms, double garage that will also hold wagons, bikes, and trikes, and it's walking-close to park and grade school]. Priced for the family at [$170,000]. Call and ask about low-down and possible no-down financing.

UR

HOME REALTY

555-8200
www.ur-home.net

364

Family Affair

A tree-canopied street, sidewalks with children playing, and well-kept homes and lawns—that's the setting for a move-in ready **[3BR, 1½-bath, brick and cedar home]** in delightful **[Northridge]**. The sun-filled rooms will delight you. There's **[a fenced backyard that's perfect for small children and puppies, a full, dry, rainy-day-playroom basement, and a garage with plenty of room for bikes and trikes]**. Load up the station wagon and let us show you your new home. Family priced at **[$147,500]**.

UR
HOME REALTY
555-8200
www.ur-home.net

365

Your Family

is all that's needed to fill this **[3BR, 2-bath, double garage Deane-built Cape Cod]** surrounded by colorful plantings **[on a child-safe cul-de-sac in Westhaven]**. There's **[room for toddlers, puppies, and a garden in the fenced yard, kitchen big enough for a troop of Brownies, dining room that will hold everybody including assorted relatives, a corn-poppin' fireplace, huge basement playroom,]** and a lot more. Let us show you how easy it will be to make this your home. Total price only **[$169,500]**.

UR
HOME REALTY
555-8200
www.ur-home.net

366

All for the Family

The **[West Side]** neighborhood you dreamed of, with quiet tree-lined streets, well-kept homes and lawns, friendly people and children laughing. The house has **[3BR, 1½-baths, double garage, full basement, family kitchen with all the built-ins, gated yard with room for an RV, family-size garden, and colorful plantings]**. It's happiness for your family, in move-in condition, priced at **[$124,500]**.

UR
HOME REALTY
555-8200
www.ur-home.net

367

A Boy and His Dog

will love bunking in their own **[paneled, sun-drenched]** bedroom. There are **[2 more bedrooms, an extra bath perfect for kids, a family room with a corn-poppin' fireplace, fenced yard just made for horsin' around, a garage that will hold 2 cars and a dozen bikes, and a whole lot more to this kid-perfect ranch]** on the friendliest street in **[Westport]**. It's smart-parent priced at **[$189,500]** with low-down **[FHA]** financing available.

UR
HOME REALTY
555-8200
www.ur-home.net

368

Brady Bunch [4BR]

[and they're big], plus [formal dining room, country-sized kitchen, double garage, fenced kid-sized yard,] and so much more in this [Montana Traditional] in the friendly neighborhood [of Westhaven]. Best of all, it's priced for your bunch at [$167,500].

UR
HOME REALTY
555-8200
www.ur-home.net

ALTERNATIVE HEADINGS

Room for Grandma

BIG FAMILY?

The [original owner] of this home had [9] children . . .

369

Family Matters?

Then you'll want to see this [immaculate, 3BR, 2-bath Cape Cod] in [Fillmore] known for its parks and fine schools. Offering [a toddler-safe fenced yard, large family room, tribe-sized kitchen, 2-car garage, and flowering shrubs], it's more than just a house, it's home at [$97,500].

UR
HOME REALTY
555-8200
www.ur-home.net

370

Family Values

A quiet, [tree-canopied street,] neighbors who know each other by name, and children skating and playing hopscotch [on the sidewalks]. It's all here plus a [3BR American Traditional] that Norman Rockwell could have painted, complete with [front porch for those lazy summer evenings, family-sized kitchen, formal dining room for Thanksgiving turkey,] and so much more for just [$94,500]. For your family's sake call:

UR
HOME REALTY
555-8200
www.ur-home.net

371

If My Son Ralph

should find a nice girl, this [3BR, 2-bath, 2-car garage Mediterranean] in [Washburn Estates] would be perfect for them. There's [a family room with fireplace, formal dining. For me, the kitchen is good enough. A fenced backyard that would hold a dozen grandchildren, I should be so lucky,] and a lot more. Even Ralph could come up with [this down payment]. And the price? Reasonable at [$187,500].

UR
HOME REALTY
555-8200
www.ur-home.net

→ Of course, this ad is a spoof but it will be read.

372

[16] Hops, Skips, and Jumps from the [High School]

That all-too-familiar trauma of playing "taxi driver" for your growing family can become a distant memory in this [3BR, 2-bath West Side Colonial], and it's only

- a munched, play lunch from the [grade school],
- within ball-bouncing distance from the [playground],
- a short skateboard ride from the [bus stop],
- hand-holding distance from the [middle school], and
- change-jingling distance from the [mall].

This fine home features [a relaxing family room, a kitchen with positively everything, a 2+car garage, and a huge, fenced yard with a giant oak]. At only [$149,500], you better hop, skip, or run to

UR
HOME REALTY
555-8200
www.ur-home.net

373

Walk the Kids

[across the street to school and park]. This [3BR, 1½-bath Cape Cod] is in the friendliest neighborhood and offers [a corn-poppin' fireplace, finished basement fitness center/rainy-day playroom, child-safe fenced yard, 2-plus car garage], and [it's only 4 years old]. A great family opportunity at just [$194,500].

UR
HOME REALTY
555-8200
www.ur-home.net

374

Hopscotch and Rollerblades

on the sidewalks of this quiet, tree-lined street. You will hear the sound of rollerblades and carefree laughter. This [3BR, 1½-bath Cape Cod], set back from the street [behind a white board fence and colorful plantings], offers a [full basement, hardwood floors, formal dining room, country kitchen, and a basketball hoop on the double garage]. Waiting for your tomorrow at an old-fashioned price [$187,500].

UR
HOME REALTY
555-8200
www.ur-home.net

ALTERNATIVE HEADING

Rollerblade Perfect

sidewalks on this quiet . . .

375

A Basketball Hoop

on the oversized, double garage awaits you at this [3BR, 1½-bath Cape Cod] in friendly [Centerville Heights]. There's a [basement recreation/fitness center, fireplace, intimate and formal dining areas, garden patio plus RV parking]. A definite slam-dunk with a low down payment and a price of [$94,500].

UR
HOME REALTY
555-8200
www.ur-home.net

376

There's Room in the Sandbox

for lots more children. [Greenfield Park and Wilson Elementary School] are just [1 short block] from this [3BR, 1½-bath, 2-car garage Cape Cod]. There's [a fenced yard, both family and formal dining areas, full basement that's great as a rainy-day playroom,] and a lot more. It's family-friendly priced at [$99,500].

UR
HOME REALTY
555-8200
www.ur-home.net

377

A Hill for Sledding

[sidewalks for skating], and a great field for playing. What more could a child hope for? This [3BR, 2-bath Spanish Colonial] has [a large fenced yard perfect for small children]. You will love the [distinctive architecture, the lush landscaping,] and the friendly neighborhood where people obviously care about their homes and each other. We consider this to be an exceptional opportunity at [$249,500].

UR
HOME REALTY
555-8200
www.ur-home.net

378

Round up the Kids

pack them in the van and take a look at your new home. [3 oversized bedrooms, 2 full baths, great family room, corn-poppin' fireplace, country-sized kitchen, 2-plus car garage, and a kid-sized yard], all in the friendliest neighborhood you can find and [walking-close to park and schools]. Available with unbelievable financing at [$149,900].

UR
HOME REALTY
555-8200
www.ur-home.net

379

A Very Exclusive Club

it is said meets in the backyard tree house of this [3BR, 2-bath New England Colonial] on [a quiet, shaded street] in [Westlake Estates]. There's [a family room/country kitchen with fireplace, and picnic-perfect patio in a park-like setting]. You get the keys to the club with little or possibly nothing down at [$174,500].

UR
HOME REALTY
555-8200
www.ur-home.net

380

Junior's Rock Band

plus [3] cars will fit in the oversized garage that comes with this [3BR, 2½-bath Southwest Contemporary] in [Summerset]. The [split floor plan] offers the ultimate in privacy with the master suite far removed from Junior's stereo. There's [a sun-filled family room, 10-foot ceilings, state-of-the-art kitchen, beehive fireplace, 40-foot flagstone veranda, and knock-your-socks-off landscaping]. Priced for you to maintain your sanity at [$249,500].

UR
HOME REALTY
555-8200
www.ur-home.net

381

Sleeps [37]

That was the count at a recent slumber party. Besides the [3BR, they used the large family room and music room/home office] supported by the [3½ baths]. There's also a [country-sized kitchen] that fed the entire tribe and [a 40-foot, covered patio, pool, spa, and triple garage]. Your future guests are waiting, and the price is just [$274,500].

UR
HOME REALTY
555-8200
www.ur-home.net

382

A Teen Suite

that will be the envy of the high school comes with this [3BR, 3½-bath, 3-car garage, split-plan Mediterranean] in [Hilton Grove]. There's also [a home office/music room, family room, formal and family dining areas, 2 fireplaces, and dining patio plus room for a pool]. If you don't have a teenager, [Mrs. Hodgkins] in our office says she will throw one in at no charge. It's an unusual offer at [$339,500].

UR
HOME REALTY
555-8200
www.ur-home.net

→ Preteens will love the idea of a "Teen Suite."

383

Married with Children

A split floor plan gives the master suite of this [3BR, 2½-bath California Ranch] absolute privacy. [Only 4 years old,] this home is set on [an oversized, wooded site] in [Weston Hills] and offers [a home office or 4th bedroom, family room, granite fireplace, tons of tile, fountain entry, and more]. Pleasantly priced at [$229,500].

UR
HOME REALTY
555-8200
www.ur-home.net

384

You Got the Family We Got the House

a [3BR, 1½-bath, expanded Cape Cod] in [Northshore] with [a 30-foot dormitory-sized children's bedroom, fireplace, formal and family dining areas, 2-car garage,] and so much more, packaged on [a tree-studded lot amidst colorful plantings]; it's yours with a low down payment at only [$229,500].

UR
HOME REALTY
555-8200
www.ur-home.net

386

All My Children

and the neighbors' too, plus assorted cats and dogs will enjoy the [huge fenced yard] with [3 apple trees] that come with this [3BR, 2-bath, brick split level] in a quiet enclave of well-cared-for homes and lawns. With [a family room, corn-poppin' fireplace, sun-filled kitchen, and 2-plus car garage], it's very special at [$219,500].

UR
HOME REALTY
555-8200
www.ur-home.net

385

Happiness Is

a tree-lined street with children playing, neighbors who greet each other by name, and a [3BR] picture-perfect home with [welcome-home front porch, a large apple tree that has perfect branches to hang a swing,] and a price of [$147,500]. We only have one house like this, so call now if you desire happy tomorrows.

UR
HOME REALTY
555-8200
www.ur-home.net

387

Kids Kids [4BR]

Forget planned parenthood, this [brick Traditional] is for the old-fashioned family. [It's reported that the original owner had 8 children]. In a friendly East Side neighborhood, this solid residence has [two full baths, full basement, unfinished walk-up attic, double garage, two apple trees, and is walking-close to schools, park, and bus line]. Call now, because this is a very special home that is priced within reach at [$165,000].

UR
HOME REALTY
555-8200
www.ur-home.net

ALTERNATIVE HEADING

Lots of Tots [4BR]

CHAPTER SEVENTEEN

Homes, General

You will have no difficulty quickly tailoring a number of the ads in this chapter to fit just about any home you have for sale! If you wish to have an ad structured to a specific feature, or you are searching for creative language that will help you highlight that special feature, be sure to use the Index and Ad Generator to locate the language or ad that best meets your needs.

388

Scarce as Hen's Teeth

to find a [10-room Henry Street Victorian] for [under $300,000]. Check it quick. #47 www.ur-home.net

UR
HOME REALTY
555-8200
www.ur-home.net

390

Spend More for Less

or check out this [3BR, Westside Cape Cod] for just [$157,500], #90C at www.ur-home.net

UR
HOME REALTY
555-8200
www.ur-home.net

389

See Before the Agents

Agents will view [7] new listings in [Westchester] on [Wednesday]. View them NOW at www.ur-home.net

UR
HOME REALTY
555-8200
www.ur-home.net

➤ The ad can be easily modified for one specific property.

391

Search the Web

And you won't find a finer home than this [Edgemont, 3BR Colonial] with all the xtras at just [$219,500]. #82 www.ur-home.net

UR
HOME REALTY
555-8200
www.ur-home.net

392

It's on the Web

For a virtual tour of an exceptional [3BR, Colonial] with everything that's priced right at [$219,000], check #112 www.ur-home.net

UR

HOME REALTY

555-8200
www.ur-home.net

393

Orthodox Druid

wishes to sell her home so she can commune with nature. See her [3BR, 2½-bath Edgewood Heights Mediterranean] [with her magnificent plantings]. #42D www.ur-home.net. Getaway-priced at [$249,500].

UR

HOME REALTY

555-8200
www.ur-home.net

→ Note: It is very important that you have the owner's permission in writing to insert an ad such as the above.

394

House

[Bedroom-Bedroom-Bedroom, Bath-Bath, Garage-Garage, Family Room, Den, Porch, Fruit Trees, Garden View.] [$159,900].

UR

HOME REALTY

555-8200
www.ur-home.net

→ Of course, it is a 3BR, 2-bath house with a double garage. Readers will decipher this ad.

395

Get High on Living

You won't want to leave home owning this [3BR, 2½-bath Tuscany Mediterranean] set amidst [colorful plantings and flowering shrubs] in [Crabapple Acres]. There's [a private home office/computer center, soaring ceilings, bright, open family areas, dramatic fireplace, 40-foot, covered veranda overlooking the pool and hot spa, 3-car garage,] and so much more. An investment in you and yours at [$367,500].

UR

HOME REALTY

555-8200
www.ur-home.net

396

You Said You Wanted

a [3BR, 2-bath, tiled Spanish Colonial] with [a fenced yard and double garage] on [a quiet cul-de-sac] in [the Wilson School District] and you didn't want to pay more than [$10,000] down, with monthly payments under [$1,500] and a full price under [$200,000]. Well, here it is, but it's going to require quick reflexes to own it.

UR

HOME REALTY

555-8200
www.ur-home.net

397

License To Thrill

[Hampton Estates] is the site of this exceptional [3BR, 2½-bath tile-roofed Mediterranean. Only 4 years old], it features [dramatic, soaring ceilings, imported tile fireplace, Corian and white-washed oak kitchen, Berber carpets, home office/computer center, spacious family areas, master suite fit for a movie star with jacuzzi jet tub and fitness center, 40-foot covered veranda, magnificent plantings, and a 3-plus car garage]. Without a doubt, it's the very best at a surprisingly modest [$374,500].

UR
_____
HOME REALTY

555-8200
www.ur-home.net

ALTERNATIVE HEADINGS

House and Block Beautiful

Stop! Circle! Call!

398

Doesn't Get Any Better

than this [3BR, 2-bath Colonial Ranch] on [park-like grounds] in [Weston Hills]. There's [a huge family room with fireplace, formal and intimate dining areas, breakfast patio, 2½-car garage, a kitchen to surpass your dreams,] and great financing at a price of only [$198,500].

UR
_____
HOME REALTY

555-8200
www.ur-home.net

399

California Dreamin'

[Milwaukee] livin'. This is a sprawling California-style, [3BR, 2-bath ranch] home with a [fireplace and a huge family room with sliding glass doors that open to a delightful covered patio]. Hey! It doesn't get any better than this at [$199,500].

UR
_____
HOME REALTY

555-8200
www.ur-home.net

400

Woe Is Me

I waited too long to call about this [3-year-old, 2,100-square-foot Colonial] in [Northport Gardens] with [3BR, 2½-baths, 3-car garage, and private home office]. If I could find anything as nice, it would likely cost [$20,000] more. The owner only wanted [$194,500].

UR
_____
HOME REALTY

555-8200
www.ur-home.net

401

Simply

the best [3BR, 2-bath, 2-plus car garage California Ranch] in [Walnut Terrace]. With [window-wrapped family room, site-picked rock fireplace, breakfast patio surrounded by colorful plantings and flowering shrubs, master suite fit for royalty, extensive use of ceramic, new Berber carpeting, and light, happy decor], the fact is it's the best even though lesser homes are priced higher than [$229,500].

UR
HOME REALTY
555-8200
www.ur-home.net

ALTERNATIVE HEADING

If You Ain't Seen It
you ain't seen the best . . .

402

Definitely Slow Lane

This respectable [brick, 3BR, 2-bath Edwardian] in a dignified [West Side] setting is perfect for the person who is comfortable and secure. [The rich detailing and marvelous built-in cabinetry] exude an unpretentious elegance of one who takes the best for granted. Of course, there's [a paneled home office with built-in bookcases, two fireplaces, hardwood floors, formal and intimate dining, breakfast patio, colorful private garden, and 2-car garage]. It's priced no more than one would pay for a small tract home [$189,500].

UR
HOME REALTY
555-8200
www.ur-home.net

 This is an ad for an older home in a mature area.

403

Crackerjack

and the surprise is the price. This [3BR Colonial ranch] in the nicest [South Side] neighborhood is offered on a first-come, first-served basis at [$89,500].

UR
HOME REALTY
555-8200
www.ur-home.net

 The words first-come, first-served lend a sense of urgency to this ad. The unusual heading invites people to read on.

404

Endangered Species

A [3BR, 2-bath Ranch with attached double garage, family room, and fireplace] in [Kingsley]. We thought they were extinct under [$150,000], but we're holding this one for you at [$139,500].

UR
HOME REALTY
555-8200
www.ur-home.net

405

Couch Potato?

A [3BR, 2-bath, 2-car-garage West Side Ranch] built just for you. Room for [4] sofas in the [large] living room, [family room made for relaxing, screened porch perfect for doing nothing, a couple of trees that could hold a hammock, and landscaping that's close to maintenance free] at a very relaxing [$149,500].

UR
HOME REALTY
555-8200
www.ur-home.net

406

You'll Call in Sick

rather than leave this [3BR, 2-bath, white-clapboard Pennsylvania Colonial] on [a huge tree-studded lot] in [Northaven]. With [gleaming hardwoods, state-of-the-art kitchen, cut stone fireplace, formal and intimate dining areas, relaxing screened porch, breakfast patio, double garage with hobby room, and colorful plantings]. Check your sick days. It's not going to last at [$175,000].

UR

H O M E   R E A L T Y

555-8200
www.ur-home.net

407

Rare Bird

It isn't very often that a [Shorewood Hills] home comes on the market. Even then it's unusual for it to be a [brick, 3BR, 2-bath Georgian Colonial] of this caliber. Set on [an oversized, tree-studded view site] with [gleaming woodwork, paneled home office, formal and intimate dining areas, screened porch, finished basement fitness center, and double garage] plus so much more; it's cheep-cheep-cheep at [$239,500].

UR

H O M E   R E A L T Y

555-8200
www.ur-home.net

408

Never Again

are you going to have the opportunity to own a [newer, 3BR, 2-bath, California-inspired Ranch] on [an estate-sized lot] in [Northridge] with [attached 2-car garage and finished basement recreation area] for a price this low. Act quickly or it will be opportunity lost: [$197,500].

UR

H O M E   R E A L T Y

555-8200
www.ur-home.net

409

Wishing Won't Cut It

but calling us to see this [3BR, 2-bath, almost-new Western Village Colonial] can change your life. There's [a lovely patio garden, 2-car garage, RV parking, family room with fireplace, formal and intimate dining,] and a lot more. With low and even a possible no-down payment, there's no need to wish. It's just [$219,500].

UR

H O M E   R E A L T Y

555-8200
www.ur-home.net

410

It Doesn't Compute

Why would anyone sell a [3BR, 2-bath, 4-year-old Williamsburg Colonial] with [family room, fireplace, garden patio, and 2½-car garage] on [a wooded estate setting] in [desirable Hinsdale Estates] for just [$249,000]?

UR

H O M E   R E A L T Y

555-8200
www.ur-home.net

411

Ooh! Aaaah!

Words can't describe this [3BR, 2½-bath Mediterranean Ranch] in its estate setting in [Northridge]. With [knock-your-socks-off landscaping, soaring ceilings, huge family areas, sinfully sumptuous baths, home office/computer center,] and even [a 3-car garage]. "Magnificent" is an understatement, but you can call it "home" at [$347,500].

UR

HOME REALTY

555-8200
www.ur-home.net

412

A Brake Slammer

A [3BR, 2½-bath House-and-Garden Colonial] that really turns heads. [While only 7 years old, it has the charm of centuries] with its [intricate woodwork, high, bright rooms, window boxes, and crown moldings]. There's [a home office, large flowing family areas, dramatic master suite, walk-in closets, 3-car garage, fantastic landscaping,] and every modern amenity skillfully integrated so as not to detract from its charm. If you don't mind being ogled, it's a great home at only [$214,500].

UR

HOME REALTY

555-8200
www.ur-home.net

ALTERNATIVE HEADING

Valhalla!

413

It Will Do, But!

Don't settle for less than everything when you can have it all for the same price. A [2,500-square-foot, 3BR, 2½-bath, brick French Regency] in [the finest area of Northview Estates] with [high ceilings, handsome detailing, home office/computer center, expansive living areas, 3-car garage, and landscaping that must be experienced], it's priced less than you would imagine at [$234,500].

UR

HOME REALTY

555-8200
www.ur-home.net

414

One Potato, Two Potato

Can't decide between homes that aren't quite what you want? Why compromise when you can own a [3BR, 2½-bath, brick and glass California style Ranch] in [Weston Hills] with [2,400 square feet of luxury, huge family room, home office/music room, delightful dining patio, oversized, 2-car garage, and all set amidst colorful plantings and flowering shrubs]? You can own the exceptional for the price of the ordinary: [$297,500].

UR

HOME REALTY

555-8200
www.ur-home.net

415

On The Street

where you live [a park just a short walk away], fine homes and friendly neighbors, plus your own [3BR, 2½-bath, double garage Colonial, complete with fireplace, family room, family garden, and colorful plantings] for a price that we believe can't be duplicated [$189,500].

UR
HOME REALTY
555-8200
www.ur-home.net

416

Stop Wasting Time

looking at overpriced small homes in undesirable areas. We have a [young and spacious, 3BR, 2½-bath Classic Mediterranean] with [10-foot ceilings, huge family room, breathtaking garden, and 3-car garage], and it's in desirable [Westport]. Priced to make you the owner at [$197,500].

UR
HOME REALTY
555-8200
www.ur-home.net

417

Hard To Get

a [3BR, 2½-bath California Ranch with 3-car garage, fireplace, family room, and a home office] in [Shorewood Hills] under [$300,000]. Well, we have one and it's priced at only [$268,500].

UR
HOME REALTY
555-8200
www.ur-home.net

418

Take the Cure

from the house-hunting blahs. Now we have a home as individual as you are. This [3BR, 2½-bath California Regency] estate on the most desirable site in [Westmont] offers [over 3,000] sq. ft. of luxurious living. You'll delight in the [fantasy master suite with sensuous Roman spa, dream kitchen, and private music room]. Of course, there's [a 3-car garage, family room,] and all the extras you dream about. Priced to end your looking at [$695,000].

UR
HOME REALTY
555-8200
www.ur-home.net

419

Coulda-Woulda-Shoulda

Sad laments of those who failed to grasp opportunity. You can join in their despair or check out this [magnificent 3,800-square-foot French Norman Estate] in [Hawthorne Glen] offering [3BR, 3½ sumptuous baths, private estate office/computer center, baronial-sized fireplace, window-wrapped conservatory, 3-car garage, and grounds ablaze with color]; unusual circumstances make it available [for the first time]. The owners demand a quick sale so it's opportunity-priced [far below appraisal] at [$529,000].

UR
HOME REALTY
555-8200
www.ur-home.net

420

12 Reasons To Buy

First, there's January. Every month will seem like a vacation in this [3-year-old, 2,400+ square foot, 3BR, 21/2-bath, double garage Colonial] in [Westwood] with [a four-season conservatory, dining patio, a garden to make a green thumb start to itch, get-lost-sized closets, therapeutic hot spa plus sauna,] and so much more. A home for all seasons and all reasons at [$347,900].

UR
HOME REALTY
555-8200
www.ur-home.net

422

Batteries Not Included

[Two-year-old], all electric, [3BR, 2½-bath Irish Manor] on a [magnificent ½-acre] site in [Hampton Estates]. With [high ceilings, stone fireplaces, private estate office, expansive family areas, luxury appointments, and a 3-car garage], it sets the standard as to what civilized living should be. Conservatively priced to avoid shock at [$369,500].

UR
HOME REALTY
555-8200
www.ur-home.net

421

Priceless Not

While this [3BR, 2½-bath Tuscany Mediterranean] in [Morningside Heights] is an exceptionally fine residence, with [soaring ceilings, sun-drenched spacious rooms, private home office, family room, fireplace, 3-car garage,] and every extra you would expect and then some, the owner has set a price to sell quickly: [$274,500].

UR
HOME REALTY
555-8200
www.ur-home.net

423

Don't Just Live Have a Life

A [4-year-old, 3BR, 2½-bath, 2,600-square-foot American Contemporary] in [Westlake Estates] that provides for the soul as well as the body. [Soaring ceilings, sun-drenched rooms, soft hues, colorful gardens, and shaded patio] provide a lift to the spirits. Come and see what a happier way of life looks like at an affordable [$329,500].

UR
HOME REALTY
555-8200
www.ur-home.net

424

Step Inside

and be surprised at what this [3BR, 2½-bath American Ranch] in [Cedarburg] offers your family. A [private home office/music room, expansive family areas, whirlpool tubs, walk-in closets, and a kitchen that puts everything you've seen to shame]. Of course, there's also a [3]-car garage [and professional landscaping]. It's a must-see inside and out at [$234,500].

UR
HOME REALTY
555-8200
www.ur-home.net

426

Peek-a-Boo House

Look inside and you'll be surprised by the vitality of this [3BR, 2-bath, 2-car garage Amish-inspired Colonial] on a [wooded setting] in [Mayberry Hills]. With [11-foot ceilings, sun-filled rooms, light cream and white decor, whitewashed oak cabinetry, window-wrapped family room overlooking a flower-bedecked dining patio, formal and intimate dining areas,] and so much more; it's a pleasant experience at [$197,500].

UR
HOME REALTY
555-8200
www.ur-home.net

425

Not What It Appears

from the street. [Behind the gated entry, this newer, 3BR, 2½-bath New England Colonial] offers a new dimension in luxury living. [High ceilings, intricate woodwork, random-planked oak floors, home office, family room, fireplaces, French doors, sumptuous master suite, 3-car garage, and private patio garden], all hidden, await your discovery at [$279,500].

UR
HOME REALTY
555-8200
www.ur-home.net

→ This ad is for a house that is much nicer than it appears from the curb.

427

Hey! Look Me Over

[Dramatic, almost new, 3BR, 2½-bath Mediterranean] set [amidst giant cypress] on [an estate setting] in [Claridge Hills] with [soaring ceilings, sunlit rooms, soft, muted tones, formal and intimate dining areas, freestanding fireplace, master suite that puts Hollywood to shame, and 2½-car garage]. Worth seeing and worth buying at [$237,500].

UR
HOME REALTY
555-8200
www.ur-home.net

428

Let There Be Light

Spacious sun-filled rooms, [vaulted ceilings, and magnificent windowed walls] merge the indoor/outdoor areas of this [Hampton Hills, 3BR, 2½-bath Mediterranean masterpiece] together in perfect harmony. [A private garden patio, tons of tile, whirlpool tubs, home office, and 3-car garage] should make this number 1 on your "must-see" list. Even the price will delight you [$249,500].

UR
HOME REALTY
555-8200
www.ur-home.net

➤ The ad should include location if it is not mentioned in the heading of the ad.

429

You Want It?

We've got it! A [3BR, 2-bath Ranch] with [shake roof, family room, and double garage] in [the Hinsdale School District] under [$100,000], and we'll throw in [a full finished basement, cut stone fireplace, garden patio plus RV parking] for [$99,900].

UR
HOME REALTY
555-8200
www.ur-home.net

430

Take Me! I'm Yours!

Just [a 3BR, 2-bath, 3-car garage, red-headed/tiled Mediterranean] in [Winston Cove]. I'm [2,000-plus square feet] of love with [a home office/music room, family room, master suite with sumptuous oversized spa, high ceilings, fireplace, garden patio, and magnificent plantings]. I'm definitely not cheap, but I'm extremely reasonable at [$168,500].

UR
HOME REALTY
555-8200
www.ur-home.net

431

What's Not To Like

about this [3BR, 2-bath French-inspired hillside villa overlooking the city]? It offers [European charm] with a floor plan designed for entertaining. You'll love the [intimate private patio just off the family room]. Of course, all the usual amenities you expect in one of the grand homes are present, but it's priced to like at [$249,500].

UR
HOME REALTY
555-8200
www.ur-home.net

432

Not Blowing Smoke

when we say this [3BR, 2½-bath, 2-plus car garage California Contemporary] in [Bridgeford Heights] is a tremendous buy [in an almost new home. The stone and glass residence seems to blend with the sweeping lawns, colorful plantings, and century-old trees. With 12-foot ceilings, walls of glass, Ansel Adams view, dramatic fireplace, and expansive decks], it has everything and more. If you want the best, look and buy at [$229,500].

UR
_____
H O M E   R E A L T Y

555-8200
www.ur-home.net

434

Free Guest House

included with this [3BR, 2½-bath, 2-car garage Mediterranean] set amidst [flowering shrubs, colorful plantings, and mulberry trees] in [Washburn Heights]. With [a window-wrapped family room, soaring ceilings, dramatic fireplace, and garden kitchen plus master suite that should be in House and Garden], it's priced without adding for the guest house at [$229,500].

UR
_____
H O M E   R E A L T Y

555-8200
www.ur-home.net

433

Cost Took a Back Seat

to quality when this [8-year-old, 3BR, 2½-bath, 2,200-square-foot, Classic Colonial] was built on [its estate-sized view site] in [Washburn]. With its [hand-pegged matched maple floors, Corian counters, Maytag appliances, whirlpool tub, Pella windows, and river-rock fireplace], the best was demanded. The part you'll love is that, because of unusual circumstances, this house can now be purchased at the price of an ordinary home: [$319,500].

UR
_____
H O M E   R E A L T Y

555-8200
www.ur-home.net

435

Don't Waste Time

You can keep on looking, but this [2,400-square-foot, stone and glass Colorado Contemporary] with [3BR, 2½ baths, 3-car garage, soaring ceilings, sweeping decks, and views to dream about] on [a ½-acre site on Skyline Drive] is more impressive than any home you'll see, regardless of price. Warning! It won't last long at [$279,500].

UR
_____
H O M E   R E A L T Y

555-8200
www.ur-home.net

ALTERNATIVE HEADINGS

Be First in Line
or be sorry. You can . . .

Better Take A Look
or be sorry . . .

436

Like To Fool Around?

We have a [huge] workshop that's a tinkerer's delight, and it comes with a [6-year-old, 3BR, 2-bath Cape Cod] in [Newport Heights]. With its [oversized double garage, screened breezeway, family and formal dining areas, family room with fireplace,] and so much more, it's beyond expectations at a price well within your reach: [$154,900].

UR

HOME REALTY

555-8200
www.ur-home.net

437

The Morning After

you move into this [almost-new, 3BR, 2½-bath tiled Mediterranean] in [Newberry Hills] you'll awake to the sounds of dozens of songbirds in the stately [maple and hickory] trees. You'll bathe in the [sumptuous therapy hot spa] in your master suite and choose your wardrobe in the [get-lost-sized walk-in closet]. You'll go [through the French doors from the sun-drenched country kitchen] to have breakfast on the [flower-bedecked] patio. If you don't decide to call in sick, you'll take your car from the [3]-car garage and drive through your neighborhood of well-kept homes and lawns. But first you have to call, see and buy at a very reasonable [$219,500].

UR

HOME REALTY

555-8200
www.ur-home.net

438

Wake Up Smiling

with morning light in the huge master suite of this [3BR, 2½-bath Tennessee Stone Ranch] in [Bermuda Dunes]. You'll love the [invigorating whirlpool tub and get-lost-sized closets] as well as the [family room with wet bar and fireplace, flower-bedecked flag stone patio, and decorating that will knock your socks off]. Best of all, you'll show your white pearlies when you find out it can be yours for [$247,500].

UR

HOME REALTY

555-8200
www.ur-home.net

439

Call for Directions

While this [3BR, 2½-bath Colorado Contemporary] may be hard to find, your search will be amply rewarded. With [over 2,400 square feet of flowing space, walls of glass, incomparable views, sweeping decks,] and all the expected extras as well as many that will astound you. Your search is over. Proudly offered at [$247,500].

UR

HOME REALTY

555-8200
www.ur-home.net

440

Have an Affair

The expansive open floor plan of this [3BR, 2½-bath Mediterranean master-piece] in desirable [Northridge Estates] is suited for small intimate gatherings as well as entertaining on a grand scale. There's also [a private music room/home office, huge flower-bedecked patio for entertaining under the stars, 2-plus car garage,] and best of all, no one will believe you only paid [$349,500].

UR
HOME REALTY
555-8200
www.ur-home.net

441

Forget about the Price

If you don't like it or it doesn't fit your needs, you're paying too much no matter what the price. See this [4-year-old, 3BR, 2½-bath, 3-car-garage Colonial Ranch] on [its estate setting] in [East Hills] with [over 2,400] square feet, [a family room with orchard stone fireplace and built-in bookcases, private home office or 4th bedroom, master suite with twin walk-in closets and Jacuzzi tub, break-fast patio, and gorgeous landscaping]. The price will seem like a bargain after one glance [$267,500].

UR
HOME REALTY
555-8200
www.ur-home.net

442

Lucky [3s]

[3BR, 3 baths, 3-car garage, almost 3,000 square feet], this [3-year-old, New England Colonial] on [a triple-sized lot] in [Westin Estates] is only 3 minutes from [the freeway]. [Three] is your lucky number at [$245,000.03].

UR
HOME REALTY
555-8200
www.ur-home.net

443

The [Workbench] Stays

with this [3BR, 1½-bath Clifton Hills ranch]. The [basement] workroom would delight any craftsman, tinkerer, or hobbyist. The home offers [hardwood floors, brick fireplace, garden kitchen, formal dining area, fenced yard, 2-car garage plus RV parking]. We're sorry that it doesn't need any fixing but it's priced like a fixer-upper at [$94,500].

UR
HOME REALTY
555-8200
www.ur-home.net

444

It's Your Move

and we have just the home. A [3BR, 1½-bath Cape Cod] in the nicest area of [Winston] that comes complete with [2-car garage, white picket fence, flowering shrubs, and colorful plantings]. Available with low or even no down payment, it's yours at [$137,500].

UR
HOME REALTY
555-8200
www.ur-home.net

445

The Leave-Behinds

The owners indicated that they will leave behind [the patio furniture, fireplace equipment, lawn mower, workbench,] and possibly [a mother-in-law] for the buyer of this [3BR, 1½-bath, 2-car-garage Cape Cod] in [Weston Estates]. It's [in perfect move-in condition with family and formal dining areas, a finished basement/fitness/recreation center, hardwood floors and trim] plus a lot more. It's yours with a very low down payment at a full price of just [$149,500].

UR
HOME REALTY
555-8200
www.ur-home.net

446

It Ain't Bad

In fact, this [3BR, 1½-bath, white Cape Cod in Thurston Heights] is quite nice. It's been meticulously maintained and has [a white picket fence, great landscaping, fireplace, new neutral carpeting, new roof, and 2-car garage]. The price is really good: [$119,500].

UR
HOME REALTY
555-8200
www.ur-home.net

ALTERNATIVE HEADING

It's BAD! BAD! BAD!

When we say bad, it's good. This . . .

447

We Guarantee It!

A home warranty protection package comes with this [3BR, 1½-bath Cape Cod] in [Shorewood]. With [both formal and family dining areas, fireplace, hardwood floors, delightful garden, 2-car garage,] and low or even no down financing; it's your opportunity for the future at [$77,500].

UR
HOME REALTY
555-8200
www.ur-home.net

448

Priced Too Low
[$189,500]

That's all the owners want for this [3BR, 1½-bath, 9-year-old Rambler] in [Thompson Heights]. We'll show you recent sales data that indicate the price is $1,000s below other sales in the area, and this house includes [ceramic tile kitchen, hardwood floors, marble fireplace, finished basement recreation/fitness center, 2-car garage,] and more. Call quickly or you may be too late.

UR
HOME REALTY
555-8200
www.ur-home.net

449

A Kodak Moment

Picture your family in this spotless [3BR, 1½-bath, sparkling white Cape Cod] set [amidst flowering shrubs and colorful plantings] on a quiet tree-lined street in [Westhaven]. With [hardwood floors, marshmallow-roasting fireplace, garden patio, 2-car garage,] and a lot more, it doesn't get any better than this. Priced to put you in the picture at [$169,500].

UR
HOME REALTY
555-8200
www.ur-home.net

450

Say "Cheese!"

You'll want a picture of yourself in front of this [pampered, 3BR, 2-bath, 2-car garage New England Colonial] in order to show off your new home to your friends. You'll love the [intricate detailing, matched hardwood floors, rose-brick fireplace, sun-drenched garden kitchen, screened summer porch, and mature landscaping]. With low-down financing, it's your chance to capture it on more than film at [$187,900].

UR
HOME REALTY
555-8200
www.ur-home.net

451

100 Paintings

could be displayed on the walls of this [9-room, 3BR, 1½-bath, brick Traditional] on a quiet street [just a short walk from the Financial Center]. Offering [high ceilings, rooms awash in natural light, updated systems, walled garden with delightful patio, colorful plantings, garage,] and so much more, it's available at a surprisingly affordable [$79,500].

UR
HOME REALTY
555-8200
www.ur-home.net

➡ The heading above will appeal to persons who consider themselves artistic. It can be effectively used for older homes in central city areas as well as for loft condominiums.

452

Once You Come In

You won't want to leave this picture-postcard [3BR, 1½-bath, white Cape Cod] in [Thurston Woods]. It's perfect in every way with [intimate and formal dining areas, brick fireplace, built-in bookshelves, finished basement fitness center, and 2-car garage]. Not to be confused with an ordinary house despite its price: [$169,500].

UR
HOME REALTY
555-8200
www.ur-home.net

453

Not a Clone

This distinctive [2,400-square-foot, 4-year-old, 3BR, 2½-bath Tennessee Contemporary] situated on [a commanding Riverview wooded acre site] won't last long, because it's priced like a plain tract home [$219,500].

UR
_____
HOME REALTY

555-8200
www.ur-home.net

454

It's Hard To Be Humble

when we have the finest [6-year-old, 3BR, 2-bath Westlake Ranch] home with [2-car garage, formal and family dining areas, home office, full basement, and almost one-third of an acre of landscaped grounds] at a price that blows the rest away: [$174,500].

UR
_____
HOME REALTY

555-8200
www.ur-home.net

455

Cutting Edge Not

It's just a solid [brick American Traditional] in a nice friendly neighborhood. It has [3BR, 1½ baths, large bright rooms, full basement, garage, and fenced yard]. While not high-tech, it's low-key comfortable living at a price that's even lower than you would expect [$124,500].

UR
_____
HOME REALTY

555-8200
www.ur-home.net

456

Like an Old Shoe

You will relish the sheer comfort of living in this [3BR, 1½-bath, red brick Traditional] with its [hardwood floors, built-in cabinetry, mantled fireplace, and light, bright rooms]. Conveniently located on a quiet street [close to everything], there's also [a 2-car garage, fenced yard, and 2 apple trees]. Comfortably priced at only [$134,500].

UR
_____
HOME REALTY

555-8200
www.ur-home.net

457

Gotta Pay Your Dues

Sitting on the couch won't crack it. Check out the housing market carefully. Then make an informed decision to buy this [3BR, 1½-bath West Side Traditional] with [maintenance-free aluminum siding, double garage, fenced yard, garden patio and light, bright rooms]. With super low-down or even no-down payment, you will find it's a best buy at [$94,500].

UR
_____
HOME REALTY

555-8200
www.ur-home.net

458

[45] Tons

That's the approximate weight of this seldom available [3BR, 1½-bath Cape Cod] in [Williamsburg]. It's move-in ready with [hardwood floors, full basement, fenced yard, and double garage]. Pound-for-pound, it's a best value at [$139,500].

UR
HOME REALTY
555-8200
www.ur-home.net

459

No Gimmicks

Just a nice solid [3BR, 1½-bath Split Ranch with 2-car garage on a wooded lot in Northridge]. It's light and bright, but there are no mirrored walls or whirlpool tubs. It's the house for you if you want a good home at a good value [$97,500].

UR
HOME REALTY
555-8200
www.ur-home.net

460

The Other Side of the Fence

offers greener grass, [taller trees,] and a friendly [3BR, white clapboard American Traditional with a 2-car garage, high bright rooms, woodwork to be envied,] and a lot more. With no or low down, it's "come on over" priced at [$94,500].

UR
HOME REALTY
555-8200
www.ur-home.net

461

25 Cents to Happiness

A phone call can mean your own [3BR] home [on a friendly West Side Street] with [a fenced yard perfect for puppies, a garage, light bright rooms] plus a lot more. With possible no-down payment and a price of just [$64,500], call:

UR
HOME REALTY
555-8200
www.ur-home.net

→ Please note: Headline above may vary depending upon local pay phone charges in your geographical area.

462

Believe in Miracles

They can happen. With just a phone call and hardly any cash, you can become the owner of this [3BR-plus American Traditional] in a friendly neighborhood of people who respect their homes and neighbors. There's [a fenced yard, garage, unfinished area that awaits your imagination, vegetable garden plus flowering shrubs and colorful plantings]. Call and see what happens. It's priced at just [$94,500].

UR
HOME REALTY
555-8200
www.ur-home.net

463

A Push-Over Not

This [3BR, 1½-bath ranch home] in [Sunset Estates] is solidly built of [brick with oak and ceramic floors, stone fireplace, generously sized rooms, poured basement, fenced yard, and 2-car garage]. It's a well-cared-for, substantial home. However, because of unusual circumstances, the owner is willing at [$74,500].

UR
HOME REALTY
555-8200
www.ur-home.net

464

Need a Lift?

Then take a look at this [3BR, 1½-bath Cape Cod] in [Westover] that's just a little better than perfect. It shines with its [brick fireplace, new soft beige carpeting, hardwood floors, sun-drenched kitchen, lazy-day porch, 2-car garage with work room, and magnificent trees and plantings]. Your spirits will soar, because it's easily affordable at [$164,500].

UR
HOME REALTY
555-8200
www.ur-home.net

465

The Numbers Game

Check them out. A [6]-room, [3]BR home on [4th] Street with a [2-]car garage. With practically [0] down, call now as it's a winner at [$74,900].

UR
HOME REALTY
555-8200
www.ur-home.net

466

A Most Wanted Poster

prepared by homebuyers would perfectly describe this [3BR, 1½-bath Cape Cod] on [a wooded setting] in [the Lakeland School District]. It has all the identifying features: [2 plus-car attached garage, hardwood floors, both family and formal dining areas, brick fireplace, full basement with finished recreation/fitness center, and all the built-in appliances]. The reward is happy living at just [$157,900].

UR
HOME REALTY
555-8200
www.ur-home.net

467

Attention! Elephants!

At last, the [3BR, West Side] home you wanted with [low-maintenance, vinyl siding, fenced yard, full basement and 2-car garage] that can be purchased for PEANUTS!

[$87,500]

With low-down and possibly no-down payment, it's going to move like a Cheetah! So call and bring the herd to:

UR
HOME REALTY
555-8200
www.ur-home.net

468

Workaholic!

You'll hate this maintenance-free **[brick and vinyl-sided, 3BR, 1½-bath Cape Cod]** with **[finished basement recreation area, RV parking,]** and more in a highly desirable West Side neighborhood. It doesn't need a thing so the **[workbench in the 2-plus car garage]** will gather dust. With low down financing, it's NO SWEAT priced at **[$137,900]**.

UR

HOME REALTY

555-8200
www.ur-home.net

470

200 Years from Now

This **[4-year-old Wilson Grove Colorado Contemporary]** with **[2,400 square feet, 3BR, 2½ baths, and home office]** will be regarded as a classic left behind from a time when life centered on home, family, and gracious living. Future generations will marvel at the spaciousness, clean lines, and sheer beauty. They won't believe it was once available at just **[$429,500]**.

UR

HOME REALTY

555-8200
www.ur-home.net

469

Don't Wait till Spring

to buy, when you can have the perfect home right now at an off-season price. A **[3BR, 1½-bath, 2-car-garage Cape Cod]** that's **[even better than new]** with **[river-stone fireplace, large sun-filled rooms, formal and family dining areas, magnificent cabinetry, 3-season porch, and delightful garden patio]**. With great financing available now, it's winter-priced at **[$184,900]**.

UR

HOME REALTY

555-8200
www.ur-home.net

471

Dreams Don't Last

but this **[5-year-old, brick and stone New England-Style Ranch]** in **[Clinton Hills]** was built to last for generations. Set **[behind a screen of greenery]** with **[3BR, 1½ magnificent baths, 2-car garage, woodwork to be envied, finished basement recreation/fitness center, formal and intimate dining areas, flower-bedecked patio]**, and exceptional financing, it's yours for a long future at **[$164,500]**.

UR

HOME REALTY

555-8200
www.ur-home.net

472

Rare and Well Done

It isn't often that a superb [Mediterranean Masterpiece] such as this [3BR, 2½-bath, 3-car garage] residence becomes available in [Emoryville]. With [2,500] square feet of luxury appointments and landscaping that exceeds your highest expectations, it's call now or be sorry at [$249,500].

UR

HOME REALTY

555-8200
www.ur-home.net

473

Why Gamble

when you can have a tried-and-true sure thing? A [3BR, 1½-bath Cape Cod] in a friendly [West Side] neighborhood of well-cared-for homes and lawns, and it's as desirable now as it was when it was new, [32] years ago. With [fine hardwoods, formal and family dining areas, full basement, sun-filled rooms, patio, fenced yard plus garage,] and low-down financing, it's a winner at [$129,900].

UR

HOME REALTY

555-8200
www.ur-home.net

ALTERNATIVE HEADING

Want a Sure Thing?

Don't gamble . . .

474

[$1.19] / Lb.

With an approximate weight of [80 tons], this [3BR, 2½-bath Mediterranean Colonial] in [Whitewater Estates] is a great value. Offering [a private home office, family room, stone fireplace, a master suite that will knock your socks off, expansive family area, and 3-car garage], it's a weighty value at [$190,000].

UR

HOME REALTY

555-8200
www.ur-home.net

475

Can't Hold a Candle

Whatever you've seen doesn't compare with this [3BR, 1½-bath, 2-car-garage English Traditional] on [Western Blvd.] with its [classic brick exterior, magnificent trees and flowering shrubs, sun-filled rooms, marble fireplace, built-in china cabinetry and bookcases, and glass-wrapped conservatory]. Incomparable at [$219,500].

UR

HOME REALTY

555-8200
www.ur-home.net

476

The White House

on a quiet [West Side] tree-lined street, [expansive lawns, flowering shrubs, 3BR, double garage, large sun-filled rooms, fireplace, garden area, patio,] and so much more; it's a better way of life at just [$114,500].

UR

HOME REALTY

555-8200

www.ur-home.net

477

Free and Easy

Looking's free and buying's easy. A [3BR plus bonus room, 1½-bath Cape Cod] in desirable [Wilson Estates] with [full basement, fenced yard, 2-car garage plus RV space] that is yours with low-down or even no-down payment and monthly payments less than you would have thought possible. Call for details, the price only [$94,500].

UR

HOME REALTY

555-8200

www.ur-home.net

478

Extinction Imminent

This is the only [2BR expandable Cape Cod built by Levitt] with [2-car garage] in [Middlebury], that we know of, priced under [$100,000]. This one also has [a fenced yard, delightful patio, and finished basement recreational/fitness center]. The price just [$89,500].

UR

HOME REALTY

555-8200

www.ur-home.net

479

When Elephants Fly

you might find as good a deal as this [meticulously maintained 4-year-old New Hampshire Colonial] on [a wooded estate-sized site] in [Western Hills]. With its [hardwood floors, brick fireplace, formal and family dining areas, window-wrapped studio, and 2½-car garage, it's worthy of a Currier and Ives print]. Available now with exceptional financing and a full price of only [$179,500].

UR

HOME REALTY

555-8200

www.ur-home.net

ALTERNATIVE HEADING

Pigs Will Fly

when you find . . .

480

It Feels So Good

to lie in the [whirlpool bath in the huge master suite] of this [3BR, 2½-bath, red tile Mediterranean-inspired Villa] in the most sought after area of [West Covington]. Over [2,400] square feet of luxury include a [quiet home office/music room, 10-foot ceilings, incomparable views], every conceivable amenity for the good life, and [a 3-car garage]. Priced no more than an ordinary home at [$249,500].

UR

HOME REALTY

555-8200

www.ur-home.net

481

Drive-By

Call then buy this [3BR, 2-bath Colonial in immaculate condition] located on [an estate-sized lot] in friendly [Westlake]. At [$189,500], see it now [2238 Longhorn Blvd].

UR
HOME REALTY
555-8200
www.ur-home.net

ALTERNATIVE HEADINGS

Look—Call!

Drive-By—Buy!

→ With the exception of an open house, a property's address is not usually included in an ad. However, this approach can be effective when the house has great curb appeal for its price.

482

Bring Your Camera

Your friends will want to see photos of your new home [in Westhaven]. It has [3BR, 1¾ baths, country stone fireplace, family room, finished basement, two-car garage, fenced yard, and a great deal more]. Pictures don't lie; your friends will know you paid a great deal more than the [$117,500] price tag.

UR
HOME REALTY
555-8200
www.ur-home.net

483

Plain Wrapper
[$247,500]

Don't judge a book by its cover and don't judge this [3BR, 2-bath Ranch home in Torrance] by its rather plain exterior. From the street you would never guess that there are [almost 2,000 square feet] of quality, sun-filled living space with amenities normally found only in higher priced homes. You also wouldn't know about the [very private yard with country club landscaping]. If you're more interested in the quality of life for your family than impressing those passing by, call!

UR
HOME REALTY
555-8200
www.ur-home.net

484

Ain't What It Seems

from the street. This [3BR, 2½-bath, 3-car garage center-hall Colonial] looks like just another fine home on a quiet, tree-lined street in [Morningside Heights]. Once inside, WOW! The [11-foot ceilings, floating staircase, sink-to-the-knees carpeting, kitchen to fry for, sinfully sumptuous master suite with whirlpool tub and get-lost-sized closets, private home office/music room] plus a long list more. Best of all, it's priced no more than an ordinary home at [$267,500].

UR
HOME REALTY
555-8200
www.ur-home.net

485

Easy To Love

Falling in love is not only wonderful, it will be instantaneous when you see this [young-in-years but timeless-in-design red brick Georgian Colonial set on a large wooded site in Claridge Heights]. This fine residence offers [3BR, 2½ baths, two dining areas, den or home office, screened summer porch, double garage,] and a price you will love [$117,500].

UR
HOME REALTY
555-8200
www.ur-home.net

486

THIMK!

and you will have to tour the [3BR Westside Colonial] offered at [less than $200,000]. #48C at *www.ur-home.net*

UR
HOME REALTY
555-8200
www.ur-home.net

487

You Must See

and we must sell this [3BR, 1½-bath, double garage, brick split level in Worchester]. With everything you expect and more, it's priced to sell fast at [$119,500] so it's first-come, first-served.

UR
HOME REALTY
555-8200
www.ur-home.net

488

Wish No More

for all your wishes come true in this [3BR, 2½-bath Westchester Colonial that's right out of Currier and Ives]. We're not going to list its features because this [2,800]-square-foot home has them all and more. Call, look, and see that we're right. Proudly offered at [$312,000].

UR
HOME REALTY
555-8200
www.ur-home.net

489

Something's Definitely Wrong

When we listed this [3BR, 2-bath, brick English Tudor] in [Brentwood], we assumed it would sell in just a few days. It's in the best area, in great condition, and it has [superb landscaping, double garage, den or home office, magnificent fireplace, all the built-ins,] and a lot more. [Mrs. Jones] of our office says, "There's a credibility gap. At only [$179,000], people feel that there must be something wrong with it. If it doesn't sell quickly, we'll just have to raise the price!"

UR
HOME REALTY
555-8200
www.ur-home.net

490

Don't Need a Wishbone

Your wish is here. A [3BR, 2-bath, double-garage, dramatic Colonial on a choice corner in Northridge] that you can afford and financing that makes sense. The spacious home has everything from [all the built-ins, great views, delightful garden, tree-shaded patio, and it's walking-close to Finch School]. With a price of [$238,900] call now as others may share your wish.

UR
HOME REALTY
555-8200
www.ur-home.net

491

Care Free

living will be yours in this [cedar shake, 2BR cottage by the sea]. An [unbelievable location, old-fashioned stone fireplace, plank-wood flooring, and large screened sleeping porch] make it our most desirable offering.

Call Free

Use our 800 number now. To delay will mean a lifetime of saying, "I could have" when it's priced at only [$119,500].

UR
HOME REALTY
1-800-555-8200
www.ur-home.net

➤ If you advertise outside of your calling area, use of an "800" number will significantly increase responses.

492

Have You Seen a Unicorn?

They're almost as scarce as [3-BR custom-built homes in Apple Ridge priced under $200,000]. Well we found one at

[$189,500]

It has everything you'd expect and more, including [a private home office, 2-car garage plus RV parking, 2½ sumptuous baths, and a garden that will make your green thumb itch]. We don't expect it to last more than a few days so call before it becomes extinct.

UR
HOME REALTY
555-8200
www.ur-home.net

493

Buy Your Spouse

the house of his or her dreams— [a sparkling white house on a tree-lined lane set back behind a picket fence amidst flowering shrubs and guarded by century-old oak trees]. This warm and inviting [3BR American Traditional] is what dreams are made of. There's a [drawing room big enough for a family reunion, front parlor with a bay window, and a sun-drenched kitchen that will hold a harvest crew]. Once you cross the threshold you'll want to call it "home." The dream-fulfilling price is only [$97,500].

UR
HOME REALTY
555-8200
www.ur-home.net

494

Trust Me!

When I say this [3BR, 2½-bath, exciting Mediterranean in Westhaven] is as close to perfect as it can get with its [high ceilings, French doors, euro-kitchen, sumptuous master suite, home office/music room, and landscaping to be envied]. But why trust me when you can

Trust Yourself!

Take a look and you will know that it's not only the perfect house, it's perfect priced at [$249,500].

UR
HOME REALTY
555-8200
www.ur-home.net

495

Take Me! I'm Yours!

I was designed with flair and built with care on the most gorgeous [wooded half-acre] in [Brentwood Estates]. I have [3 bedrooms, including a breathtaking master suite, 2½ luxurious baths, sheathed in tile including a hot spa, a sun-filled study or home office, 3-car garage,] and so much more. I'm the one at [$249,500].

UR
HOME REALTY
555-8200
www.ur-home.net

496

Bring Your Sunglasses

You'll be dazzled by the sunlit rooms of this [West Side Mediterranean Masterpiece] that features [2 master suites, a garage big enough for 2 cars and a golf cart, vaulted ceiling, a formal dining room plus a breakfast room off the garden kitchen, tons of tile, landscaping to be envied,] and every amenity you could imagine and more; it looks far more expensive than just [$217,000].

UR
HOME REALTY
555-8200
www.ur-home.net

497

Carpe Domus

That's Latin for "Grab This House." This [American Traditional] situated in [the gate-guarded community of Westbrook] has it all; [soaring ceilings, garage space for 3 cars, room for an RV, fully fenced and professionally landscaped, and the view alone is well worth the] price of [$229,500].

UR
HOME REALTY
555-8200
www.ur-home.net

498

Don't Buy a House

yet. This [3BR, 2½-bath Tennessee Colonial] with [home office, 3-car garage, drop-dead landscaping,] and a choice [Wilson Heights] setting won't be available for showing until [October 10th]. With a price of just [$269,500] you'll want to call immediately to be first in line.

UR
HOME REALTY
555-8200
www.ur-home.net

499

Been Fooled By Ads?

Well, we have a [3BR, 2½-bath, brick front Colonial] that is everything we say it is and a lot more. Set on an [over-sized lot] in one of the nicest streets in [Roseburg], this [7-year-old residence has been meticulously maintained] and features a wish list of amenities such as [an orchard rock fireplace, huge 2-car garage, dream kitchen with every conceivable built-in, and landscaping that would turn any gardener green with envy]. The only surprises this house has for you will be pleasant ones such as the price, only [$199,500].

UR
HOME REALTY
555-8200
www.ur-home.net

500

Wait Not Want Not

Don't miss the opportunity to buy an [almost-new 3BR, 2½-bath 3-car garage Santa Fe Contemporary] in [Wilson Heights] for

[$174,500]

and that includes [a home office, Corian countertops, whitewashed oak cabinetry, beehive fireplace, and captivating landscaping]. Call now, because to delay will likely be disastrous.

UR
HOME REALTY
555-8200
www.ur-home.net

501

Bring Your Checkbook

as you will want to own this [3BR, 2-bath, double-garage, white clapboard Cape Cod] that was designed for those whose life centers around family values. Set on [a tree-lined street] in the friendliest neighborhood in [Westhaven], the home features [a fenced yard with a sunny garden spot, mature landscaping, and a full basement that would make a great rainy-day play or hobby room]. With a friendly price of only [$169,500], it deserves your immediate attention.

UR
HOME REALTY
555-8200
www.ur-home.net

502

Love Potion

Just one look and you'll want to possess this **[3BR, 2½-bath Dutch Village Colonial]** in a romantic **[wooded]** setting in **[Northridge]**. Offering **[intimate and formal dining areas, cuddle-up stone fireplace, expansive family areas, and sumptuous master suite with double-sized shower and hot tub]**, it's priced to love at **[$279,500]**.

UR
HOME REALTY

555-8200
www.ur-home.net

ALTERNATIVE HEADING

Magic Potion

503

Beyond Perfect

Whatever you imagine, this **[3BR, 2-bath Cape Cod]** on the nicest street in **[Newton Heights]** will exceed your expectations. A home where your family won't feel cramped, **[a kitchen that has everything, landscaping your neighbors will envy, a garage with space for a workshop plus 2 cars,]** and a perfect price **[$194,500]**.

UR
HOME REALTY

555-8200
www.ur-home.net

504

Goose Bumps All Over

will be your reaction to this **[3BR, 2½-bath, triple-garage Quaker Colonial]** on a delightful **[tree-canopied lane]** in the nicest area of **[Westhaven]**. Everything on your wish list has been meticulously combined to make this not only a "must see" but a "must buy." At **[$239,500]** it won't last long.

UR
HOME REALTY

555-8200
www.ur-home.net

505

Nothing's Perfect

but this **[near-new, 3BR, 2½-bath, 3-car garage Mediterranean in Weston Estates]** has to be as close as it gets. It features **[11-foot ceilings, a spacious flowing floor plan, quiet den or home office, sumptuous master suite, separate family room, and a delightful veranda accented by colorful plantings]**. We know it's perfectly priced at **[$379,500]**.

UR
HOME REALTY

555-8200
www.ur-home.net

506

Now Hear This!

If you act fast, you can own a **[3BR Cape Cod with all the extras]** in desirable **[Dorchester with a down payment too low to print]** and a price of only **[$169,500]**.

UR
HOME REALTY

555-8200
www.ur-home.net

507

Bad Hair Day?

If everything is going wrong, turn your day and life around with the welcome warmth of this [Sunset Hills 3BR 1½-bath, expandable Cape Cod with sun-drenched rooms, screened porch, and double garage.] With special financing it's easy to own at just [$194,500].

UR

HOME REALTY

555-8200
www.ur-home.net

508

Country Boy Special [$149,500]

A [3BR, 1½-bath American Traditional] in [Westhaven] with [a huge down-home kitchen, garage for two pickups, fenced yard perfect for hound dogs, front porch for watching, perfect trees for a hammock,] and best of all, it don't need nothin'. For real livin', call:

UR

HOME REALTY

555-8200
www.ur-home.net

509

In Your Price Range

At last a [3BR, 1½-bath Center-Hall Colonial] with [all the built-ins, fireplace and two-car garage] on the nicest lot on the nicest street in [Westport]. Call now, because at this price others will be interested: [$229,500].

UR

HOME REALTY

555-8200
www.ur-home.net

510

BANG! BANG!

Now that I have your attention, I would like to tell you about a [3BR, 2½-bath English Tudor] in [Highland Estates]. Magnificent [landscaping, three-car garage, library/home office, garden kitchen, and three-season porch] make this a MUST SEE NOW at only [$319,500].

UR

HOME REALTY

555-8200
www.ur-home.net

511

You May Never Have Known

that you could have had a [3BR, 2-bath Colorado Contemporary with a million-dollar view, wraparound decks, soaring ceilings, fireplace,] and every conceivable convenience at the price of an ordinary home for only [$264,900].

UR

HOME REALTY

555-8200
www.ur-home.net

512

Settle for More

Don't compromise. You can have a great [3BR, 2-bath Contemporary in Clifton Hills] with [a postcard view, fantastic landscaping, 2½-car garage, central air, fireplace, breakfast patio, walk-in closets] plus a lot more. Have it all for only [$237,500].

UR

HOME REALTY

555-8200
www.ur-home.net

513

All Things Bright and Beautiful

[and practically new] in this [3BR, 2½-bath brick and cedar Ranch] on a [huge wooded] lot in [Westridge]. It comes with all the extras, [2½-car garage, huge sunlit master suite with whirlpool, family room, and garden patio]. The best part is, it's priced no more than an ordinary home at [$319,500].

UR
HOME REALTY
555-8200
www.ur-home.net

514

Be the New Kid on the Block

in this [3BR, 1½-bath, white Salt box Colonial in Westhaven]. Your neighbors will envy [your park-like lawn with its giant elm trees, the gleaming hardwood floors, formal dining room with built-in buffet, and the finished basement with its authentic English Pub]. They will really be upset when they find you only paid [$189,500].

UR
HOME REALTY
555-8200
www.ur-home.net

515

Telephone Junkie

Phone jacks in every room including the [3 baths] of this [3BR New Hampshire Colonial] in [Eston Heights]. You can talk all day with friends about the [sumptuous master suite, private home office/computer center, Corian and bleached oak kitchen, river-rock fireplace in the family room, dining patio, 3-car garage, and you'll even find words to describe the fabulous landscaping]. You won't tell them the price; let them think you paid more than just [$344,900].

UR
HOME REALTY
555-8200
www.ur-home.net

516

Gone to Heaven?

No, but this [3BR, 1½-bath, 2-car garage, captivating Cape Cod] in [Murray Heights] comes close. With [sun-drenched rooms, neutral colors plus colorful accents, mantled fireplace, basement fitness center, dining patio, and magnificent trees and flowering shrubs], it's as close as it gets to the real thing. Heavenly priced at [$197,500].

UR
HOME REALTY
555-8200
www.ur-home.net

517

Warning! Contagious!

If you see it, you'll be infected, it's as simple as that. This postcard-perfect [3BR, 1½-bath, 2-car garage, white Cape Cod behind a picket fence] in [Glen Cove] will give you the "I Want It!" bug. You will dream about the [gleaming hardwood floors, mantled fireplace, fenced yard, century-old trees, colorful plantings, and flowering shrubs]. If you succumb, it will be yours for [$194,500].

UR
HOME REALTY
555-8200
www.ur-home.net

518

Prepare To Arm Wrestle

other buyers who read this ad. A seldom available [3BR, 2-bath, 2-car-garage Classic Colonial] in [Westley Hills] with [sun-filled rooms, formal and intimate dining areas, family room, magnificent master suite, fireplace, dining patio,] and more. It's priced for immediate sale at [$287,500].

UR
HOME REALTY
555-8200
www.ur-home.net

519

Show and Tell Time

We'll show you this [3BR, 2-bath, West Side Florentine Villa] with its [huge family room, delightful dining patio, 3-car garage, and magnificent landscaping]. We'll tell you about the great financing. Then it's your turn at [$324,500].

UR
HOME REALTY
555-8200
www.ur-home.net

520

What?

An [almost-new 3BR, 2-bath, Virginia-inspired Colonial] with [family room, fireplace, Corian counters, and 2½-car garage] in absolutely the best neighborhood in [Clintonville] for only [$347,500].

UR
HOME REALTY
555-8200
www.ur-home.net

521

A Poet

would appreciate the simple beauty of this [Shaker Colonial] in [Westhaven] set amidst [magnificent oaks and green lawns]. With [wood shutters that work, 3BR, 2½-bath, 2-plus car garage, magnificent craftsmanship evident in the woodwork and cabinetry, hand-picked stone fireplace, joyful sun-filled rooms,] and much more, we think it's life's fulfillment at [$367,500].

UR
HOME REALTY
555-8200
www.ur-home.net

522

Adopt a [6]-Year-Old

Abandoned and vacant, this delightful [3BR, 2-bath Mediterranean in [Shorewood Heights] just needs a little washing plus love. There's [a bright family room opening onto a veranda, a garden that needs some care, a magnificent master suite, step-down living room with dramatic fireplace, a better-than-perfect kitchen plus a 2-car garage]. It's yours to love at [$229,500].

UR
HOME REALTY
555-8200
www.ur-home.net

524

Do It!

SEE: This [3BR, 2-bath, 3-year-old, Cape Cod] in [Westchester] with its [2-car garage, screened summer porch, family room, fireplace, and magnificent landscaping].

COMPARE: The quality, size, condition, and location.

BUY: It's an outstanding opportunity at [$164,500].

UR
HOME REALTY
555-8200
www.ur-home.net

523

The Condo Alternative

A [3BR, 2-bath, low-maintenance, private, single-family home] with [10-foot ceilings, light-bright rooms, fireplace, family room with wet bar, dining patio, and double garage] in the [master planned, gated community] of [Summerset]. A low homeowner fee includes [all of the recreational facilities]. It's the best of 2 worlds at [$247,500].

UR
HOME REALTY
555-8200
www.ur-home.net

525

[Brown] Is Beautiful

trim on this [white brick, 3BR, 2-bath California Ranch home] in [Scarsdale]. There's [a window-wrapped family room, ceramic kitchen and baths, rich plush carpeting, fireplace, screened summer porch, 2-car garage, and landscaping that would make a gardener jealous]. With [owner financing and a low-down payment] it's very definitely a best buy at [$254,500].

UR
HOME REALTY
555-8200
www.ur-home.net

526

[$247,000] Buys

a [3BR, 2-bath, newer Mediterranean] on [a large, professionally landscaped estate-sized lot] in [Norwood Heights], and it includes [a huge family room opening to the garden patio, family-sized kitchen with washed oak cabinetry, top-of-the-line fixtures and appliances, 3-car garage,] and a great deal more. Call now or this opportunity will have passed you by.

UR
HOME REALTY
555-8200
www.ur-home.net

➤ If the strongest feature is the price, use it in the heading.

527

Unfulfilled Needs?

Then see this [spacious, 2-year-old, 2,000-plus square foot, 3BR, 2-bath, 2-car garage, Pennsylvania Colonial near Websters' Corners]. It has what you want, [a private home/office, family room with fireplace, formal and intimate dining areas, breakfast patio, heavenly landscaping,] and so much more. Priced to satisfy at [$274,500].

UR
HOME REALTY
555-8200
www.ur-home.net

528

Grown-Ups Can Play

While we don't have a sandbox or a jungle gym, this [3BR, 2-bath, newer, Mediterranean Ranch] has [a pool plus spa and room for adult as well as kid toys in the 3-car garage]. It's also within [5 minutes of public courts and Westlake Golf Course]. You could play [Ping-Pong in the family room because the ceilings are 11 feet high, and the manicured lawn could be used for croquet or putting around] plus other sport opportunities abound. It's playfully priced at [$279,500].

UR
HOME REALTY
555-8200
www.ur-home.net

529

The Same to You!

We have a [3BR, 2-bath, newer Cape Cod] with [whitewashed oak cabinetry, bay windows, garden patio, oversized double garage, full basement,] and all the extras on a magnificent landscaped setting in desirable [West Point Estates]. If you want one too, call us now; it's priced at only [$227,500].

UR
HOME REALTY
555-8200
www.ur-home.net

530

A Penny Saved

is nice, but here's your chance to save [over $30,000 from the original selling price] of this [2-year-old, 3BR, 2-bath, 2½-car-garage California Ranch] on [a wooded site] in [Wilson Estates]. There's [a window-wrapped family room overlooking the breakfast patio and garden, cut stone fireplace, formal and family dining areas, master suite with get-lost-sized closets,] and so much more for a savings price of just [$247,500].

UR
―――――――――
HOME REALTY

555-8200
www.ur-home.net

➡ While not necessarily a bargain, the house is offered for less than what it originally sold for.

531

A Month of Sundays

and you still wouldn't find a [3BR, 2-bath, Center-Hall Colonial] as nice as this one in [Westchester] without paying many thousands more. On [a huge tree-studded lot] there's [a window-wrapped family room, stunning master suite, screened summer porch, and double garage]. Oh! The price is just [$247,500].

UR
―――――――――
HOME REALTY

555-8200
www.ur-home.net

532

An Offer You Can't Refuse

A [7-year-old, 3BR, 2-bath, postcard-perfect Colonial] with [2½-car garage] on [an estate setting in Manley Hills]. There's [a great family room with cut stone fireplace, dining patio,] and all the extras you expect in a quality residence. The offer—a price less than the competition. [$247,500].

UR
―――――――――
HOME REALTY

555-8200
www.ur-home.net

533

Trophy Husband?

Then buy him something special. This [4-year-old, 3BR, 2-bath, 2-car-garage Colonial] in [Washburn Estates] offers [a quiet trophy room/home office where you can display his photos, delightful breakfast patio, colorful plantings and flowering shrubs for his green thumb, workroom for tinkering, master suite to get lost in, and expansive sun-drenched living areas]. A special place to keep your trophy at [$369,000].

UR
―――――――――
HOME REALTY

555-8200
www.ur-home.net

534

Like in the Movies

you expect to see your favorite star in this, too-good-to-be-true, [3BR, 2-bath French Mediterranean] in [Wilson Acres]. There's [a practically sinful master suite, soaring ceilings, fantastic vistas, Hollywood landscaping, and even a 3-car garage]. Put yourself in the picture with a buy-now price of [$347,500].

UR
HOME REALTY

555-8200
www.ur-home.net

535

[Maxine] and [Marvin] Slept Here

for [10] years, but [Marvin] was transferred to [Phoenix], so they must regretfully take their bed and leave this [3BR, 2-bath, red-brick Georgian Colonial] in the nicest area in all of [Woodland Glen]. The home features [a tantalizing Jacuzzi tub in the master bath, which is why the shower is practically new; walk-in closets; music room for little Ralph, who is learning to play the drums; and a kitchen any chef would fry for]. Priced to get [Maxine] and [Marvin] on their way at [$337,500].

UR
HOME REALTY

555-8200
www.ur-home.net

→ This is a spoof of "George Washington Slept Here."

536

Hard To Get

It isn't often that a [pristine 3BR, 2-bath Southern Ranch] in [Hilton Cove] becomes available and even then you wouldn't expect a price of just [$244,500].

UR
HOME REALTY

555-8200
www.ur-home.net

537

The Good Life

begins at home in this [3BR, 2-bath Massachusetts Cape Cod] on [a wooded half-acre] in [Newport]. Offering [large, sunlit rooms, formal and family dining areas, French doors, breakfast patio, 2-car garage with workshop,] and much more; all it needs is you at a very affordable [$167,500].

UR
HOME REALTY

555-8200
www.ur-home.net

538

There's No Competition

When you see this [Westhaven] [3BR, 2-bath Georgian Colonial] on its [huge wooded lot] with [3-season porch and sun-drenched kitchen], you'll realize that nothing else compares at [$287,500].

UR
HOME REALTY

555-8200
www.ur-home.net

539

Search the World

and you will not find a nicer [3BR, 2-bath Williamsburg Colonial] than this picture-postcard home [on a wooded half-acre in West Town]. With its [formal dining room, antique brick fireplace, delightful garden patio, and 2-car garage], it's better than perfect and priced like an ordinary home at [$247,500].

UR
HOME REALTY
555-8200
www.ur-home.net

540

Call Me!

And I will tell you why this [2,200 square foot, 3BR, 2-bath Colonial Ranch] with [huge family room and 3-car garage on ½ acre] in [Clifton Hills] is the best buy on the market at [$297,500].

UR
HOME REALTY
555-8200
www.ur-home.net

541

Your Grand Piano

will have room to spare in the expansive [living room] of this [2-year-old, 3BR, 2-bath Mediterranean Colonial] in desirable [Wilson Estates]. There's also [a home office/computer center, country-sized kitchen, master suite with sitting room, BBQ-patio, 3-car garage, and landscaping to be envied]. Priced on-key at [$419,500].

UR
HOME REALTY
555-8200
www.ur-home.net

542

Dungeon!

Wine cellar, rainy-day playroom, darkroom, or hobby room. This [3BR, 2½-bath California Ranch] has a sprawling basement that can meet any or all of these needs. Set on a [wooded, corner site in Northridge] this [three-year-new] residence features [a huge family room, home office or guest room, breathtaking landscaping, 2½-car garage,] and every conceivable amenity and built-in. Your castle awaits you at [$289,500].

UR
HOME REALTY
555-8200
www.ur-home.net

543

Nostalgia Strikes

This [almost-new Southern Victorian] captures the spirit of a gentler time. With [3BR, 2½ baths, family room, hardwood floors, and intricate detailing], it embodies the warmth of the past combined with every modern amenity to make a spectacular residence. Proudly offered at [$437,500].

UR
HOME REALTY
555-8200
www.ur-home.net

544

Fat Cat?

You won't be, this [3BR, 2-bath Spanish Colonial] in [Westchester] has its own fitness center. With [bright spacious rooms, window-wrapped conservatory, magnificent fireplace, tons of tile, hewn beams plus room for all the toys in the oversized 3-car garage]; it's priced lean at [$337,500].

UR
HOME REALTY
555-8200
www.ur-home.net

➤ An open, finished basement can be referred to as a fitness center, home gym, game room, billiard room, recreation room, pub room, party room, ballroom, and so on.

545

A Step Back

in the right direction. A return to architectural splendor and great value. [While almost new], this [3BR, 2½-bath Victorian] in [Wrightwood Estates] offers [high ceilings, sunlit rooms, magnificent woodwork, both formal and family dining areas, home office/computer center, two fireplaces, garden patio, and magnificent vistas]. A gentler way of life can be yours at [$347,500].

UR
HOME REALTY
555-8200
www.ur-home.net

546

Tall People

will love the [11-foot ceilings] of this [3BR, 2-bath California Contemporary] in [sought-after Wilson Ridge]. With [expansive living areas, walls of glass, bleached oak cabinetry, master suite with giant-sized Jacuzzi tub, garden patio, colorful plantings, 2-plus car garage,] and more, it's a tall deal for just [$176,800].

UR
HOME REALTY
555-8200
www.ur-home.net

ALTERNATIVE HEADINGS

Basketball Players

In The NBA?
You will love . . .

TOPLESS!
Ceilings seem to soar forever in this . . .

The Sky's the Limit!
Soaring ceilings in this . . .

547

Sandman Special

There's a master suite to make bedtime your favorite activity. This [3BR, 2-bath Kentucky Colonial] in [Willow Estates] includes a [family room/country kitchen with fireplace, huge double garage, circle drive,] and everything you would expect in a quality [4-year-old] residence. It's a "snooze-you-lose" bargain at [$184,500].

UR
HOME REALTY
555-8200
www.ur-home.net

548

A Cool House

You will love the [zone-controlled high-efficiency] air-conditioning in this [3BR New Hampshire Traditional] in the sultry days that lie ahead. Set in [a park-like setting in Westlawn], this home offers [light, bright, and spacious rooms, 1½ tiled baths, a full dry basement perfect for a year-round workroom, 2-car garage,] and a price that won't turn you cold: [$124,500].

UR
HOME REALTY
555-8200
www.ur-home.net

549

Frigid They Said

when they entered this [3BR, 2-bath brick English Tudor] with central air. A home with everything including [an intimate den, full basement awaiting your imagination, double garage, and a garden to make your green thumb itch]. A hot value in a cool house at [$149,500].

UR
HOME REALTY
555-8200
www.ur-home.net

550

Poker Night

will be great in the [finished basement game room with wet bar] in this [3BR, 1½-bath, brick split level near Clifton Corners]. With [large sun-filled rooms, cut stone fireplace, 2-car garage, and terrific landscaping], it's in a neighborhood of beautiful homes and poor poker players. Your chance to win the pot at only [$197,500].

UR
HOME REALTY
555-8200
www.ur-home.net

551

Need a Workshop?

We have the [mother] of all workshops, [a separate 20′ × 30′ heated and air-conditioned shop with 10-foot ceilings and overhead door] set amidst colorful plantings [behind this newer 3BR, 2½-bath Cape Cod] on [almost ½ acre] in [Newberry Estates]. Offering [bright, spacious rooms, charming fireplace, formal and family dining areas, screened summer porch,] and a great deal more; [there is even additional workshop space in the full, dry basement, and oversized double garage]. Call now as it's offered at a price that doesn't need fixing [$269,500].

UR
HOME REALTY
555-8200
www.ur-home.net

552

5,000 Books

will fit in the quiet library that comes with this [3BR, 2-bath Arizona Contemporary behind the gates] in [Newberry Heights]. This home has [10-foot ceilings, walls of glass, family room plus a free-flowing floor plan for intimate entertaining or a grand affair, exceptional landscaping, and a 3-car garage]. It's an exceptional offering at [$247,500].

UR
HOME REALTY
555-8200
www.ur-home.net

553

Bring the Hot Dogs

A BBQ patio surrounded by colorful plantings comes with this [3BR, 2-bath American Traditional, and it's only 3 years old]. There's also [a bright family room with walls of glass, fireplace, formal and family dining areas, a master suite that will knock your socks off, and a 2-car garage]. The only thing not impressive is the price [$267,500].

UR
HOME REALTY
555-8200
www.ur-home.net

554

Morning Coffee

on the [patio] overlooking the [garden] of this [3BR, 1½-bath Cape Cod] on the nicest lot in [Washburn Heights]. You'll love the [bright sunlit rooms, matched hardwood floors, orchard-stone fireplace, and there's plenty of room for cars and more in the over-sized 2-car garage]. Best of all, the price won't keep you awake: [$249,500].

UR
HOME REALTY
555-8200
www.ur-home.net

555

Bingo!

You'll be a winner with this [3BR Townhouse] in [New Berlin]. With [spacious rooms, brick fireplace, hard-wood floors, full basement, fenced yard, and garage], it's a "lotto" house for very little: [$84,500].

UR
HOME REALTY
555-8200
www.ur-home.net

ALTERNATIVE HEADING

Jackpot!

556

Lazy!

Then you will love this practically maintenance free [3BR, 1½-bath Cape Cod] in [North Haven] with its [white aluminum siding and shutters]. Offering light, bright rooms, [full basement, garage plus RV parking] on a quiet street in a friendly neighborhood, you'll relax and watch your neighbors work. The price no chore at [$159,500].

UR
HOME REALTY

555-8200
www.ur-home.net

ALTERNATIVE HEADING

Couch Potato!

557

The [3rd] Day

on the market and we haven't sold this [young, 3BR, 2-bath Colonial] in [Westchester]. It's in the most desirable neighborhood, [in immaculate condition,] and all the extras are here, from [sumptuous whirlpool tub and sitting room in the master suite, to private home office, 3-car garage, landscaping that surpasses your imagination,] and much more. We were sure it would sell the first day, priced at only [$519,500].

UR
HOME REALTY

555-8200
www.ur-home.net

➤ This type of ad could be inserted for three days with a different day each time (3rd, 4th, 5th, etc).

558

Get Here First

or be sorry. We only have one [brick and stone split level] with [3BR, 1¾ baths, 2½-car heated garage in showroom fresh condition] on the loveliest site in [Clifton Hills]. The first to see it will call it "home" at [$139,500].

UR
HOME REALTY

555-8200
www.ur-home.net

559

Don't Dilly Dally!

This [3BR, brick ranch] in a friendly area of [Westport] won't last long. It's in great shape with [mature landscaping, fenced yard, garage plus RV parking]. Priced to move at [$167,500].

UR
HOME REALTY

555-8200
www.ur-home.net

560

Be Nimble Be Quick

or be too late. Just listed a [3BR, 1½-bath, perfect Cape Cod] in [the Thomas School District] with [fireplace, 2-car garage, RV parking, and more]. Because of unusual circumstances, it's priced at only [$187,500].

UR
HOME REALTY

555-8200
www.ur-home.net

561

Fire Sale!

A sizzling price of [$197,500] for a hot [3BR, 2-bath brick Northridge Traditional]. Tour #23 www.ur-home.net, then rush over in your red wagon.

UR
HOME REALTY
555-8200
www.ur-home.net

562

Warning!

If you don't act now, this [3BR, 1½-bath Cape Cod] with [double garage, hardwood floors, and fireplace] on [a wooded ½-acre site] in [Westchester] will be sold to a faster buyer. REASON? It's priced at only [$184,500].

UR
HOME REALTY
555-8200
www.ur-home.net

563

"I Should Have Called"

will be your lament when you find out that you could have purchased this [4-year-old, 3BR, 2½-bath Arizona Traditional] in [Hillside Estates] with a [3-car garage, 2 fireplaces, sweeping decks,] and all the extras for only [$337,500].

UR
HOME REALTY
555-8200
www.ur-home.net

564

No Time To Wait

New on market, a seldom-available [3BR, 2½-bath Carolina Ranch] in [Jackson Heights], with [family room, home office, fireplace, whirlpool tub, 10-foot ceilings, and 3-car garage]. It won't last at [$367,500].

UR
HOME REALTY
555-8200
www.ur-home.net

565

No Place for a Turtle

because the winner will be the first family to see this [Charlotte Woods, 6-year-old, 3BR, 2-bath Saltbox Colonial available for the first time]. With [light, bright rooms, gleaming hardwood floors, kitchen with everything, family room with fireplace, 2½-car garage plus landscaping any gardener would envy]; it may be sold by the time you read this ad because it's priced at [$325,500].

UR
HOME REALTY
555-8200
www.ur-home.net

566

Don't Blink!

Because it won't last. The only [3BR, 2-bath, 2-car garage, newer Ranch] available in [Weston Estates] that's priced under [$250,000], and this one is far under at a call-now price of [$214,500].

UR
HOME REALTY
555-8200
www.ur-home.net

567

It's Been Sold!

will be our response if you delay in calling about this [3BR, 2-bath, 2½-car garage, 4-year-old Cape Cod] on a [wooded site] in [Blueberry Estates]. With its [window-wrapped family room, flower-bedecked dining patio, old-brick fireplace, both family and formal dining areas,] and so much more; it's likely to be sold to the first viewer priced at just [$199,500].

UR
_____
H O M E   R E A L T Y
555-8200
www.ur-home.net

568

Don't Confuse It

with an ordinary house. Check out the [3BR, 2½-bath Spanish in Moorpark] priced under [$400,000]. #47 at _www.ur-home.net_

UR
_____
H O M E   R E A L T Y
555-8200
www.ur-home.net

569

We Have the Key

to your future. A [3BR, 2-bath brick Ranch on a wooded site] in desirable [Weston Hills School District]. This home offers [bright and spacious rooms, country-style fireplace, two-car garage, huge fenced yard, park-like grounds,] and more. Call and you will see everything tomorrow offers at [$229,500].

UR
_____
H O M E   R E A L T Y
555-8200
www.ur-home.net

ALTERNATIVE HEADING

Here's the Key!

570

Turn the Key

and come home to this outstanding [American Colonial] on prestigious [Westlake Blvd.]. This [3BR, 2-bath, double-garage residence] has [white clapboard siding, shutters, a private den with fireplace,] and a long list of delightful features. You will love the feeling of spaciousness and warmth in this fine residence. Call, look, and you will own at [$289,500].

UR
_____
H O M E   R E A L T Y
555-8200
www.ur-home.net

571

Honey! Stop the Car!

This is it! A [3BR, 2-bath Cape Cod with fireplace, hardwood floors, huge kitchen, 1½-car garage] in [Shorewood] priced at [$189,500].

UR
HOME REALTY
555-8200
www.ur-home.net

572

Hug a Tree

Smell the flowers and enjoy this [4-year-old, 3BR, 2-bath Vermont Colonial] in desirable [Westhaven Estates]. With its [10-foot ceilings, sun-drenched rooms, finished basement workout center, garden deck, and 2½-car garage], it's a lot of love at just [$184,500].

UR
HOME REALTY
555-8200
www.ur-home.net

573

Lovely To Look At

but better to live in. This [3BR, 2½-bath, center-hall Virginia-inspired Colonial] offers the ultimate in gracious living. With [spindled banisters, glorious woodwork, mantled fireplaces, paneled library/home office, expansive family areas, terrace, delightful garden, and oversized garage], it's an impressive estate at a surprisingly affordable [$269,500].

UR
HOME REALTY
555-8200
www.ur-home.net

574

Lights! Camera! Action!

This [3BR, 2½-bath Vermont Cape Cod] was originally a model home for [Westwood Estates and was featured in advertisements]. This explains its [large corner lot, magnificent landscaping, and every conceivable appliance and upgrade]. Due to unusual circumstances, it's available now for no more than a lesser home [$249,500].

UR
HOME REALTY
555-8200
www.ur-home.net

→ This approach can be used for a home that, while not new, was formerly a model home for a development.

575

If Looks Could Kill

this [3BR, 2½-bath Mediterranean Colonial] in [Windsong Estates] would wipe out the neighborhood. Both inside and out, it's better than perfect with [tons of tile, 11-foot ceilings, spacious family areas, private home office, wide dining veranda, lush landscaping, 3-car garage,] and every luxury amenity imaginable. It's a "killer" at [$347,500].

UR
HOME REALTY
555-8200
www.ur-home.net

576

Posed for Pin-ups

This [3BR, 2-bath Mediterranean Ranch with 2-plus car garage] was a model home at [Eastdale Estates] and was used in its advertising. This explains the fantastic landscaping and upgrades. Bring your camera so you can show your friends photos of your new home. Yours at an ordinary home price [$229,500].

UR

HOME REALTY

555-8200
www.ur-home.net

577

Your First Impression

will be "Wow!" when you see this [3BR, 2½-bath, red brick Georgian Colonial set back on a tree studded acre] in [Woodhaven]. You'll be impressed [by the long curved drive, bright open floor plan, two magnificent fireplaces, private den/home office, and state-of-the-art kitchen]. Another "Wow!" when you find that it can be yours for [$387,500].

UR

HOME REALTY

555-8200
www.ur-home.net

578

Beauty in the Best

"Pretty" doesn't begin to describe this [3BR, 2-bath, double garage, white clapboard Colonial] on a perfect lot in [Northport] with its [dining patio and sun-filled rooms]. But, with just one look, you'll want to call it "home." Your future at [$247,500].

UR

HOME REALTY

555-8200
www.ur-home.net

579

Come in from the Cold

A warm, [mantled] fireplace awaits you in this [3BR, 2-bath, 2-car garage, brick and stone French Normandy] in fashionable [William's Acres]. With [leaded glass, massive oak doors, high-timbered ceilings, private home office, expansive family areas, flower-bedecked dining patio, and park-like grounds], it's a hot opportunity at [$294,500].

UR

HOME REALTY

555-8200
www.ur-home.net

580

Marshmallow-Roasting Fireplace

comes with this bright and cheerful [3BR, 1½-bath, 2-car garage, cream brick ranch] on a [quiet cul-de-sac] in friendly [Westport] known for parks and fine schools. There's [a full, dry basement, 2-car garage plus RV parking, toddler-safe fenced yard, and delightful plantings]; with low-down or even possible no-down make sure it's your #1 must-see at [$149,500].

UR

HOME REALTY

555-8200
www.ur-home.net

581

Wait for Spring

by [the orchard-stone] fireplace in this [3-year-old, climate-controlled Colonial] in sought-after [Wilson Acres] or [enjoy the steaming whirlpool in the sumptuous master suite, work out in the basement/fitness/recreation room, listen to music in the private office/music room, or watch TV in the window-wrapped family room]. It won't be long till the colorful plantings push through the soil so you can enjoy the [very private garden and breakfast patio]. Meanwhile, it's midwinter priced at just [$298,500].

UR
HOME REALTY
555-8200
www.ur-home.net

582

Live and Work Here

A large bright home office or studio [with a private entrance] is a special feature of this [3BR, 2-bath, brick and stone French Regency home behind the gates in Westchester]. The [2,400] square foot residence offers every amenity and convenience you could possibly desire and is set amidst [giant chestnut trees on almost one half-acre of resplendent grounds]. Come and see your future; it's available today at [$379,500].

UR
HOME REALTY
555-8200
www.ur-home.net

ALTERNATIVE HEADINGS

Work at Home

[6] Steps to Work

583

The Great American Novel

is waiting to be written in the [large, sun-drenched studio] of this [3BR, 2-bath Tennessee stone ranch] set on a [secluded], tree-lined street in [Westhaven]. [Beneath a towering oak], it's truly the place for quiet contemplation. Your escape from the world at [$239,500].

UR
HOME REALTY
555-8200
www.ur-home.net

584

Humongous Closets!

[2½ sumptuous baths, 2BR plus home office or 3BR and a huge family area] are just a few of the features that will delight you about this [Western Hills, better-than-new Mediterranean Villa]. Of course there are [both formal and intimate dining areas, breathtaking landscaping, breakfast patio, and a 3-car garage]. Unexpected, it's priced to sell IMMEDIATELY at [$349,500].

UR
HOME REALTY
555-8200
www.ur-home.net

585

You May Be Dead!

If this [9-room, Hillside Villa] doesn't excite you, check your pulse. Available for tours. #62 at *www.ur-home.net*

UR
HOME REALTY
555-8200
www.ur-home.net

586

Get-Lost Closets

likely bigger than the bedroom you had as a child, come with this [tiled, 3BR, 2½-bath Tuscany Mediterranean] in [positively the finest area of Westwood]. Included are [10-foot ceilings, music room, huge flowing entertaining areas, garden kitchen, French doors opening to the 40-foot terrace, triple garage, and landscaping to be envied]. Offered to those who refuse to compromise on quality at [$539,500].

UR
HOME REALTY
555-8200
www.ur-home.net

587

The Third Little Pig

built this home of brick to endure. It has [3BR, hardwood floors, spacious rooms, finished basement fitness room to trim that excess weight, fenced yard, and garage]. Built to keep the wolf from your door at a price you can afford [$149,500].

UR
HOME REALTY
555-8200
www.ur-home.net

588

Ah-Choo! No More

This [3BR, 1½-bath Cape Cod] in [Northberry] is equipped with a state-of-the-art electronic air cleaner that removes [99%] of the pollen from the air. This home also has [allergy-free hardwood floors, light, bright rooms, a farm-sized kitchen with all the built-ins, finished basement fitness center, and attached 2-car garage]. The price won't make your eyes water [$237,500].

UR
HOME REALTY
555-8200
www.ur-home.net

589

White-Glove [Colonial]

Bound to please even the most fastidious buyer, this [3BR, 2-bath Westhaven] residence reflects the owner's pride in its blue-ribbon condition. The home offers [a country kitchen right out of House and Garden, window-wrapped living area, generously proportioned bright rooms, two-car garage, and a garden ablaze in color that's the envy of the neighborhood]. Best of all, it's priced no more than an ordinary house at [$229,500].

UR
HOME REALTY
555-8200
www.ur-home.net

590

Built Like a Brick

[Georgian Colonial] on a wooded estate lot in [Ridgeway Heights]. There are [3BR, 2½-bath, private home office, both formal and intimate dining areas, delightful dining patio, and a 3-car garage]. Unusual circumstances make this [better-than-new] residence available at only [$419,500].

UR
HOME REALTY
555-8200
www.ur-home.net

591

If Condition Counts

You will want to see this better-than-new [6-year-old, 3BR, 2-bath Cape Cod] sited [behind a white picket fence on a tree-studded lawn] in [Westley Acres]. There's [a sun-drenched family room opening to the flower garden and breakfast patio, rose-brick fireplace, whitewashed cabinets with Corian counters in the family kitchen, a 2½-car garage,] and much more. It's priced no more than an ordinary home at [$267,500].

UR
HOME REALTY
555-8200
www.ur-home.net

592

Feed an Army

A [huge country-style kitchen plus formal and family dining areas] come with this [3BR, 1½-bath Cape Cod] in a desirable [West Side] neighborhood. There's [a dining patio, marshmallow-toasting fireplace, fenced yard, 2-car garage,] and lots more. At this price you can feed them steak: [$179,500].

UR
HOME REALTY
555-8200
www.ur-home.net

593

Dinner for [12]

A tribe-sized country kitchen plus banquet-sized formal dining in this [3BR, 2½-bath Oakridge Mediterranean]. Plus [a family room with fireplace, BBQ patio with room for 100 or more, lovely garden, 2-car garage,] and a low-down payment that won't eat up your savings. Price [$239,500].

UR
HOME REALTY
555-8200
www.ur-home.net

594

Car Collectors

A [4]-car garage comes with this [3BR, 2-bath American Traditional] in [Westport Estates]. There's also [a huge family room with river-rock fireplace, home office, whirlpool in master suite, dining patio,] and a lot more at just [$289,500].

UR
HOME REALTY
555-8200
www.ur-home.net

595

Garage Sale

[an oversized, 3-car] garage goes with this [4-year-old, 3BR, 2-bath Santa Fe Colonial] in [Longview Heights]. With [10-foot ceilings, spacious family room, beehive fireplace, covered veranda, colorful plantings, and views to dream about], it's available [from the first owner] at a secondhand price [$264,500].

UR
H O M E   R E A L T Y

555-8200
www.ur-home.net

596

[4]-Car Garage

comes with this [3BR, 1½-bath American Traditional] on a [double-sized wooded lot] on the nicest street in [Maywood]. The home has [large, bright rooms, hardwood floors, updated systems, and all kitchen built-ins], and it's available with no or low down payment financing at an affordable [$99,500].

UR
H O M E   R E A L T Y

555-8200
www.ur-home.net

ALTERNATIVE HEADING

[4] Car Garage [$99,500]

➡ If a home has a 3-or-more car garage and is in a price range where that size garage ordinarily would not be expected, the garage size can be a strong ad heading, because it is a very desirable feature to some readers. It can be combined with the price.

597

Free [2-Car] Garage

comes with this [3BR, West Side ranch on desirable McKinley Blvd.] With [large, spacious rooms and terrific landscaping], it's an exceptional offering at [$139,500].

UR
H O M E   R E A L T Y

555-8200
www.ur-home.net

598

Garage! Garage!

Two [double garages] go with this [newer, 3BR, 1½-bath Federal Colonial] in friendly [Westhaven]. There's [a large family room with fireplace, greenhouse kitchen, formal dining area, and a feeling of quality in the fine craftsmanship and intricate woodwork]. Available for all your cars and toys at [$149,900].

UR
H O M E   R E A L T Y

555-8200
www.ur-home.net

ALTERNATIVE HEADING

Garage! Garage! Garage!

A three-car garage comes with this ...

599

Immediate Occupancy

If your credit checks, you can move into this [3BR, 1½-bath] picture-perfect [Cape Cod] in [Wild Rose] today. The home is set [amidst flowering shrubs and magnificent chestnut trees] and features [a warm brick fireplace, screened summer porch, 2-car garage] plus friendly neighbors. Because of special financing, you can be the owner with [a down payment so low you won't believe it's true]. Priced right at [$169,500].

UR
HOME REALTY
555-8200
www.ur-home.net

ALTERNATIVE HEADINGS

Buy Today!

Move in Tomorrow

600

Need It Quick?

Vacant and perfect, a [3BR, 1½-bath Cape Cod on a wooded site] in a friendly [West Side] neighborhood. It comes complete with [fenced yard and 2½-car garage], low down financing, and a price of only [$97,500].

UR
HOME REALTY
555-8200
www.ur-home.net

601

Split Personality

We have the home for both of you. A [2BR, 2-bath, sophisticated Mediterranean] in [Western Estates] with [twin master suites, 2-car garage, intimate and formal dining areas, and spacious rooms to keep you apart]. The best of two worlds at [$237,500].

UR
HOME REALTY
555-8200
www.ur-home.net

602

Insomniac Special

If you're going to be awake all night, this [3BR, 2-bath Cape Cod] in [Westin Estates] will keep you entertained. Included are [a state-of-the-art satellite dish, home office/music room, family room with wet bar and built-in bookcases, finished basement fitness center plus room for a photographer's darkroom, oversized 2-car garage that's great for tinkering, and a garden that is beautiful by moonlight]. We're sorry but the price won't help keep you awake at [$269,500].

UR
HOME REALTY
555-8200
www.ur-home.net

603

Psychic?

Then you already knew about this [3BR, 2-bath, 2-car-garage Wisconsin Traditional] on the nicest street in [Bay View]. We hope you liked [the large wooded site, family-sized garden, two apple trees, new Berber carpeting, generous, sun-drenched rooms, and the latest built-ins]. You probably know that it's going to be your future home at [$187,500].

UR
HOME REALTY
555-8200
www.ur-home.net

604

Harry Potter

with all his wizardry couldn't duplicate this [6-year old, 3BR, 2-bath Colonial] in [Farmington] at just [$264,900]. Check the magic box #44 at *www.ur-home.net*

UR
HOME REALTY
555-8200
www.ur-home.net

605

People's Court

declared this [3BR + den, 2½-bath Mediterranean] in [Walnut] to be the best buy at [$269,500]. Check out the verdict #14 *www.ur-home.net*

UR
HOME REALTY
555-8200
www.ur-home.net

606

Dream On

You want an estate home such as this [tiled Spanish Colonial with huge beams, 3BR, 2½ baths, home office/music room, massive fireplace, expansive family areas, delightful dining patio, landscaping to be envied] plus all the extras in a most desirable neighborhood. But you can only afford a cookie-cutter tract home. Don't give up your dream, it can be fulfilled for [$249,500].

UR
HOME REALTY
555-8200
www.ur-home.net

607

Home Improvement

not needed for this [Westchester, 3BR Cape Cod] that fulfills any wish list. Worth checking at [$187,900]. #18 *www.ur-home.net*

UR
HOME REALTY
555-8200
www.ur-home.net

608

Price Is Right
[$187,900]

for a [Shorewood Hills Georgian Colonial]. All the bells and whistles, and it's better than new. #414 at *www.ur-home.net*

UR
HOME REALTY
555-8200
www.ur-home.net

609

Thirtysomething?

No matter what your age, you will love living in this [3BR, 2-bath, center-hall Colonial]. Offering [a quiet home office or 4th bedroom, matched hardwood floors, limestone fireplace, high ceilings, crown moldings, expansive sun-filled living areas, and a 2-plus car garage] set on [a tree-studded site with an enviable Scarsdale Heights address], it's impressive but not expensive at [$384,500].

UR
_____
HOME REALTY
555-8200
www.ur-home.net

610

Jeopardy?

Not this [3BR, 2½-bath Neapolitan Villa] is [behind the gates on a quiet lane in Palmer Ranch] where you'll relish the friendly small-town atmosphere. Featuring [a home office/music room, sun-drenched family areas, 3-car garage, and landscaping that's the envy of the neighbors], it's one house you'll want to call home at an amazingly affordable [$349,500].

UR
_____
HOME REALTY
555-8200
www.ur-home.net

611

Designing Women

will love this [3BR, 2½-bath Mediterranean Villa] with [tons of tile, bubbling fountain entry, 12-foot ceilings, intimate and formal dining areas, expansive sun-drenched living areas, home office/music room, 3-car garage, and garden setting] in sought-after [Western Estates]. Designed for that special person at [$329,500].

UR
_____
HOME REALTY
555-8200
www.ur-home.net

612

Mad about You

Then tell your spouse to buy you this [3BR, 2½-bath, pampered Mediterranean] in the [quiet community of Bay Ridge]. With its [soaring ceilings, walls of glass,] and over [2,800] square feet of sheer luxury, it has all the extras you can imagine. Lead your spouse to a new life at far less than one would expect: [$349,500].

UR
_____
HOME REALTY
555-8200
www.ur-home.net

613

Spin City—Not

No hype—this [Orchard Ridge, 3BR, 2-bath Ranch] is going to knock your socks off at [$229,500]. See if we're right. #14 *www.ur-home.net*

UR
_____
HOME REALTY
555-8200
www.ur-home.net

614

Judge Judy

would award the verdict to this [3BR, 2-bath Brownstone] in [Newhaven] at [$197,500]. Check the evidence. #403 at *www.ur-home.net*

UR
HOME REALTY
555-8200
www.ur-home.net

615

Get Smart!

Why buy a cookie-cutter tract home on a tiny lot when you can own an [impressive Colonial Ranch] on an [estate site] in [Northpoint]? Offering [3BR, 2 luxurious baths, expansive family areas, orchard-stone fireplace, 2-plus car garage, magnificent landscaping,] and great financing, it can be yours for [$189,500].

UR
HOME REALTY
555-8200
www.ur-home.net

616

Keeping Up Appearances [$239,500]

Others will think you're real society living in this [Eastside, 10-room Edwardian town house]. Tour the good life. #90 at *www.ur-home.net*

UR
HOME REALTY
555-8200
www.ur-home.net

617

Wheel of Fortune

You'll be the lucky winner with this [3BR, 2-bath, red brick Georgian Colonial] on [a wooded estate setting] in [Northridge]. With its [private music room/home office, twin fireplaces, fabulous cabinetry, finished recreation room/home gym, 2-car garage,] and many luxury appointments, you'll be the envy of your friends. Don't tell them you lucked out and paid only [$197,500].

UR
HOME REALTY
555-8200
www.ur-home.net

618

Touched By an Angel

Tour this [$239,000] miracle-priced [3BR Eastside Colonial]. #62 at *www.ur-home.net*

UR
HOME REALTY
555-8200
www.ur-home.net

619

Days of Our Lives

and pleasant evenings can be yours in this [young, 2,400-square-foot, 3BR, 2-bath Colonial Ranch] in [Westhaven]. Decorated [in soft earthen hues]. There's [an orchard-stone fireplace, delightful gourmet kitchen, whirlpool tub, walk-in closets, 3-car garage, and a flower-bedecked dining patio]. The best for now and forever at [$197,500].

UR
HOME REALTY
555-8200
www.ur-home.net

620

America's Most Wanted!

A [Newport, 3BR, Colonial] under [$300,000]. See it at #106, *www.ur-home.net*

UR

HOME REALTY

555-8200
www.ur-home.net

621

One Life To Live

so start enjoying it now. A [3BR, 2½-bath Colorado Contemporary] in [Weston Hills] just 15 minutes from [tennis, golf, bridle trails,] and the [town mall]. This home has [a sparkling pool and hot spa, delightful dining patio, fenced yard, flower and vegetable garden, double garage, and large, bright rooms]. Definitely a happy home at a price to make you smile. [$179,500].

UR

HOME REALTY

555-8200
www.ur-home.net

622

Guiding Light

If you look to the [Eastern] sky you will see a bright star. Follow it to your future home in [Midvale]. With [3BR, 2½ luxurious baths, 3-car garage, family room, and home office/den] packaged in [soft hues in a delightful tiled Spanish Colonial] set amidst [landscaping to be envied]; even the price shines [$347,500].

UR

HOME REALTY

555-8200
www.ur-home.net

623

Another World

This quiet [West Side] neighborhood of well-kept homes, manicured lawns, and friendly neighbors can provide you with a way of life you might have thought had disappeared. This solid [3BR, 1½-bath Cape Cod with double garage, full basement, fenced yard, garden, and two apple trees] is as pleasant inside as it appears from the street. Look and you'll want to stay at [$279,500].

UR

HOME REALTY

555-8200
www.ur-home.net

624

The Tabloids Hate It!

A picture-postcard, [3BR, 2-bath Federal Colonial] on a quiet tree-lined street in friendly [Northport Estates]. Nothing that would interest the media ever happened here, just happy, family living. The home offers [gleaming hardwood, a magnificent spindled staircase, river stone fireplace, home office/den, garden patio, colorful plantings and flowering shrubs as well as a 2-car garage with workshop]. With no hidden secrets, it's priced at just [$247,500].

UR

HOME REALTY

555-8200
www.ur-home.net

625

Say the Secret Word

and we'll take you to this [3BR, 2-bath, 2-car-garage Colonial] on [a quiet tree-lined lane] in [Morgan Woods]. You'll be PLEASED by the [intricate detailing, hardwood floors, ancient brick fireplace, private home office, formal and family dining areas, delightful garden patio,] and a great deal more. PLEASE call. It's priced at only [$174,500].

UR
HOME REALTY
555-8200
www.ur-home.net

626

Flintstone Special

Built of [natural stone and glass], this [3BR, 2-bath, 2-car-garage, Arizona-inspired Contemporary] is [nestled among giant oaks and boulders] in [a hillside setting near Glen Cove] with [high ceilings, dining patio big enough to roast a dinosaur, fireplace, and family room], it's Yabba-Dabba-Doo priced at [$184,500].

UR
HOME REALTY
555-8200
www.ur-home.net

627

Scotty
Beam Me Home

to this [3BR, 2-bath, 2-car-garage, American Traditional] on [a quiet, tree-lined West Side street]. With [large, spacious rooms, quiet home study, fireplace, intimate and formal dining areas, polished hardwoods, and starlight patio], it's a safe haven for the traveler at a down-to-earth price: [$189,500].

UR
HOME REALTY
555-8200
www.ur-home.net

628

007

Would love the [sumptuous master suite with double-sized hot spa] in this [3BR, 2½-bath Mediterranean Villa] in [Westchester] with [the wet bar and snuggle-up fireplace in the family room, and a garage for 2 Aston-Martins]. He might even appreciate [the colorful plantings and specimen trees]. He would probably put it on his expense account at [$329,500].

UR
HOME REALTY
555-8200
www.ur-home.net

629

Arnold Schwarzenegger

would love the large home fitness center in [the finished lower level] of this [3BR, 1½-bath, brick ranch home] in friendly [Tilsdale Downs] with quiet streets perfect for jogging, biking, or just strolling. There's [a great fireplace for warming tired muscles, both formal and family dining areas, 2-car garage plus RV parking], and best of all, it's available with low down and really light monthly payments, and full price of only [$197,500].

UR
HOME REALTY
555-8200
www.ur-home.net

631

John Wayne

would have loved the rugged natural look of this [newer, 3BR, 2-bath, stone and Cedar Ranch home], on its [huge wooded setting] in [Northridge]. There's [a paneled den/home office, orchard-stone fireplace, family room, 40-foot covered veranda for relaxing after the day's chores are done, as well as a 2-plus car garage big enough to hold a herd of horses]. It's pilgrim priced at [$198,700].

UR
HOME REALTY
555-8200
www.ur-home.net

630

Nominated for an Oscar

Well, it should be. This [3BR, 2½-bath, brick California Ranch with its 2-car garage] in [Cedarburg] is the best we've seen considering space, [2,000-plus square feet, landscaping, and pristine condition]. It's a definite award-winner at [$219,900].

UR
HOME REALTY
555-8200
www.ur-home.net

632

Designed by Cecil B. DeMille?

A scene right out of Hollywood: a [3BR, 2½-bath, sparkling Mediterranean] that's [nestled on a hillside in Century Estates]. With [high ceilings, walls of glass, spacious master suite, marble fireplace, expansive living areas, 40-foot flower-bedecked veranda, rockscaped waterfall pool, sensuous hot spa, sculptured hedges, 3-car garage,] and more, your fantasies can come true at [a fraction of the reproduction cost]: [$389,500].

UR
HOME REALTY
555-8200
www.ur-home.net

633

What Frost Is to Poetry

this [3BR, 2½-bath Tennessee Colonial] is to gracious living. With [intimate and formal dining areas, wet bar and fireplace in the family room, covered BBQ patio, delightful plantings plus a 2½-car garage], it's move-in perfect and priced for your future at [$325,500].

UR
HOME REALTY
555-8200
www.ur-home.net

➤ This ad is likely to be most effective with readers who are attuned to the arts.

635

If Thomas Edison

hadn't figured out the light bulb, it would take about 1,200 candles to light this [2,400-square-foot, 6-year-old, 3BR, 2½-bath Colonial] in [Orchard Ridge]. With [a private home office, family room with fireplace, formal and intimate dining areas, breakfast patio, and 2-plus car garage] set [amidst flowering shrubs, colorful plantings and stately oaks], it's low-voltage priced at just [$284,500].

UR
HOME REALTY
555-8200
www.ur-home.net

634

If Ben Franklin

had never flown his kite, this all-electric [3BR, 2-bath Arizona Contemporary] would be "all gas." [Halfway up a gentle hill] in [Meadow Wood Estates,] this [4-year-old home] features [walls of glass, mountain vistas, sweeping decks, dramatic river stone fireplace, expansive family areas, a master suite that will electrify you, and a 2-plus car garage]; but the price won't shock you [$294,500].

UR
HOME REALTY
555-8200
www.ur-home.net

636

A Rich Relative

must have left you a fortune. That's what your friends will say when they see this [3BR, 2½-bath, 3-car garage Seville Mediterranean] on [an estate setting] in [Winslow Heights]. They'll be impressed by the [11-foot ceilings, walls of glass, delightful breakfast patio, magnificent marble fireplace, state-of-the-art kitchen, private home office, sumptuous master suite,] and luxury amenities that whisper "quality." Don't tell them you paid [less than 10% down] with a price of just [$289,500].

UR
HOME REALTY
555-8200
www.ur-home.net

637

Be The Joneses

Friends and relatives will try to keep up with you as the owner of this [3BR, 2½-bath Mediterranean Villa] in [Coswell Grove]. They will envy the [breathtaking landscaping, soaring ceilings, twin fireplaces, paneled music room, huge family areas, Hollywood-style master suite, and even the 3-car garage]. Don't tell them you paid only [$249,500].

UR
HOME REALTY

555-8200
www.ur-home.net

638

Green with Envy

will describe your friends when you show them this [2-year-old Seville Mediterranean] on [its estate site] in [Wilson Acres]. With [2,000-plus square feet, 3BR, 2½-bath, 3-car garage, spacious family areas, 2 fireplaces, home office, dining patio] plus luxury appointments, they will be certain that a rich uncle must have remembered you in his will. They would never guess you only paid [$249,500].

UR
HOME REALTY

555-8200
www.ur-home.net

➡ How other people feel about a home is a strong motivator for many buyers.

639

Beyond Your Means

will be what your friends will say when they see this [3BR, 2-bath, 3-car-garage Colonial] in [prestigious Wilson Acres]. With its [10-foot ceilings, huge family room, formal and family dining areas, stone fireplace, dining patio, and magnificent landscaping], they'll be sure you robbed the kid's college fund or sold your soul. Don't tell them you paid [nearly nothing down and] just [$239,500].

UR
HOME REALTY

555-8200
www.ur-home.net

ALTERNATIVE HEADING

Doing Something Illegal

will be what your friends . . .

640

Want to Impress Friends?

Imagine a [3-year-old, tiled Spanish Mediterranean] with [3BR, 2 baths, family room and 3-car garage] in [a Glenwood Acres estate setting]. Imagine [soaring ceilings, marble fireplace, whitewashed oak cabinetry, formal and family dining areas, and a master suite to get lost in]. Combine this with [intricate detailing, a breakfast patio, and landscaping to be envied] and you've done it. Don't tell them you only paid [$289,500].

UR
HOME REALTY

555-8200
www.ur-home.net

641

Make Them Jealous

When you have your friends over for dinner at this [3BR, 2½-bath, 3-car garage, Carolina Colonial] in enviable [Cleveland Heights], they'll marvel at [the huge living and family room, cut stone fireplace, garden patio, movie-star master suite, intimate and formal dining areas, Berber carpeting, and luxurious appointments]. They'll be curious to know how you could afford it, but don't tell them you paid only [$267,500].

UR
HOME REALTY
555-8200
www.ur-home.net

642

A Fool and His Money

Your friends will be certain that you used the kids' college money plus your retirement savings when they see this [3BR, 2-bath, 2½-car-garage New England Colonial] set [amidst flowering shrubs and colorful plantings] on [its estate setting] in [Williams Bay]. They will be green with envy when they see the [11-foot ceilings, intricate detailing, huge family areas, twin fireplaces, formal and intimate dining areas plus a master suite suitable for royalty]. Let them think what they want, but it will be yours with a low and possibly no down payment at only [$237,500].

UR
HOME REALTY
555-8200
www.ur-home.net

643

Lie to Your Friends

No one will believe you only paid [$189,500] for this [3BR, 2-bath American Traditional in the most desirable area of Westchester]. One look at the [bright spacious rooms, magnificent landscaping, screened-in summer porch, and 2½-car garage] and your friends will think you won the lottery. Call and see, we're telling the truth!

UR
HOME REALTY
555-8200
www.ur-home.net

644

Filthy Rich?

You don't have to be in order to have the very best with this [3BR, 2½-bath Mediterranean Villa] that is unsurpassed in charm and ambiance of the good life. On [a secluded site in Westport], this home offers everything you would expect in a world-class residence. Your friends will think you paid far more than just [$289,500].

UR
HOME REALTY
555-8200
www.ur-home.net

645

Status Seeker?

Want to live among the rich and famous? We have a [spacious 3BR, 2½-bath American Traditional] with the most sought-after address imaginable that comes with [magnificent detailing, high ceilings, music room, 2-car garage, and landscaping that will be the envy of any garden club]. It's hard to believe but it's priced like an ordinary home at [$269,500].

UR
_____
HOME REALTY

555-8200
www.ur-home.net

➤ This ad is for an older home in an area that still retains an aura of quality.

646

Putting on the Ritz

You'll impress your [mother-in-law] with this [3BR, 2-bath, 2-car-garage Carolina Colonial] in [Newport Estates]. With [private home office, family room with hand-picked stone fireplace, master suite with sitting room and therapeutic spa, trellised breakfast patio, colorful plantings, and flowering shrubs], it's a "How did they do it?" home at a price that answers the question: [$269,000].

UR
_____
HOME REALTY

555-8200
www.ur-home.net

647

Dear John

I know this comes as a shock, but I've finally found a [9-room, 3BR, 2-bath, brick Victorian] in [Wilson Cove] that I can afford. There are [high ceilings, 2 magnificent fireplaces, updated systems, a kitchen that leaves me breathless, and a garden that is positively sinful. There's also a 2-car garage]. Oh! Don't forget to forward my mail.

Love, Victoria.

P.S. Would you believe all they wanted was [$269,500]?

UR
_____
HOME REALTY

555-8200
www.ur-home.net

648

Lucky House
[$249,500]

Luck and good fortune came to the previous owner of this [3BR, 2-bath Mediterranean] in [Leesburg]. Check the positive energy at #49 *www.ur-home.net*

UR
_____
HOME REALTY

555-8200
www.ur-home.net

ALTERNATIVE HEADING

Lottery Winner's House
[$249,500]

➤ Many people believe strongly in luck. A lucky occurrence related to a house will be a positive factor.

CHAPTER EIGHTEEN

Homes, Large

A home featuring more than three bedrooms is an attractive bonus for many buyers. When scanning a sea of ads, many readers on their quest to find a four-bedroom home (or more) will only look at ad headings that highlight the number of bedrooms—or at best—the ads that indicate that a home is larger than normal.

Ads in other sections can readily be modified for larger homes. Please see Chapters 4 (Architecture) and 20 (Homes, Luxury).

649

Too Big? [12] Rooms

There's room for everything you've ever collected plus kids and assorted cousins in this fine **[Ballard Avenue]** residence. You will be delighted by the **[high ceilings and bright rooms flooded with natural light]** as well as the many amenities for gracious living. Gather your clan and view this offering; you'll find that the only thing modest is the price at **[$239,500]**.

UR
HOME REALTY
555-8200
www.ur-home.net

650

Dozens of Cousins

and in-laws too will fit in this **[5BR, 3½-bath]** **[Westlake Traditional]** at **[$329,000]**. A tour is a must. #51 at *www.ur-home.net*

UR
HOME REALTY
555-8200
www.ur-home.net

651

Mother Goose [5BR]

View this "really big shoe" in a prime **[Westhaven]** location that's fairy-tale priced at **[$169,900]**. #480 at *www.ur-home.net*

UR
HOME REALTY
555-8200
www.ur-home.net

652

Claustrophobic?
[11] Rooms

Never feel shut in again with this [4BR, 2-bath American Traditional] on its [hillside site] in [Meadowood]. Offering [high ceilings, sun-drenched rooms, 2-car garage,] and friendly neighbors, it's expansive but not expensive at [$179,500].

UR
HOME REALTY
555-8200
www.ur-home.net

653

Tired of Compacts?
[10] Rooms

and [4,800] square feet of incredible space make this [Tuscany Villa] one of the most impressive residences we have seen. A home with everything you expect, including [the most beautiful setting in sought-after Brentwood], the only negative feature is that you'll need to shop for furniture to fill these estate-size rooms. A spectacular residence that demands your immediate attention at [$895,000].

UR
HOME REALTY
555-8200
www.ur-home.net

ALTERNATIVE HEADINGS

Don't Cramp Your Style

Ease the Squeeze

Go to the Big House

In-law Solution

Get Lost [10] Rooms

654

Twice the Room
[4BR]

Half the Price
[$159,500]

A [9-room] family-sized home in a great [West Side] neighborhood with [2-car garage, RV parking, magnificent woodwork, hardwood floors, and lazy-day porch] for less than the price of an ordinary home. Call now; you won't be disappointed.

UR
HOME REALTY
555-8200
www.ur-home.net

655

Call It [5-] Bedroom

or [4] plus [home office/music room]. This [sprawling California-style Ranch] in [Western Hills] also has [2 baths, 2-car garage, family and formal dining areas, family room with built-in entertainment center, dining patio, and low-maintenance natural landscaping]. With a low down payment, it's a lot of home for [$187,500].

UR
HOME REALTY
555-8200
www.ur-home.net

656

Big [4BR]
Big Lot [½ Acre]
Small Price [$169,500]

UR
HOME REALTY
555-8200
www.ur-home.net

657

[4] Big Bedrooms
[$169,500]

[A country-like setting] in a friendly neighborhood, [2 full baths, light, bright rooms, loads of gleaming hardwood, stone fireplace, country kitchen, 2-car garage, RV parking, fenced yard,] and perfect financing await your call.

UR
HOME REALTY
555-8200
www.ur-home.net

658

Amazing Space [4BR]

[Huge family room] and so much more, this [7-year-old West Side Colonial] is the best buy foot-for-foot that we know of at [$314,500].

UR
HOME REALTY
555-8200
www.ur-home.net

659

Think Big [5BRS]

Plus [family room, formal dining, country-sized kitchen, huge yard,] and [3]-car garage to hold all the toys, all packaged in a(n) [7-year-old Federal Colonial] in [Boyenton Heights]. Everything big but the price [$274,500].

UR
HOME REALTY
555-8200
www.ur-home.net

660

Need [4] Bedrooms?

Plus [a family room, fenced yard, garden patio, extra deep double garage in the Fillmore School District]; well, we have it, and it's priced far less than you would imagine at [$195,500].

UR
HOME REALTY
555-8200
www.ur-home.net

661

Big Deal [5] BRS

[2 baths, formal and family dining areas, finished basement recreation area, huge fenced yard, 2-car garage plus workshop, great landscaping,] and it's in a desirable [West Side] neighborhood of well-maintained homes and lawns. Priced no more than a small house at [$167,500].

UR
HOME REALTY
555-8200
www.ur-home.net

662

Sleeper [4] Bedrooms

[2 baths, 2-car garage], and it's in [the desirable Newcastle School District]. On a [large, professionally landscaped] site, it's ready for your family right now at only [$219,500].

UR

HOME REALTY

555-8200
www.ur-home.net

ALTERNATIVE HEADINGS

Needs Children [4]BR

Kids—Kids—Kids [5]BR

663

Full House [4] BRS

plus [home office/5th bedroom, huge family areas, basement recreation area/gym, stone fireplace, and 2½-car garage] packaged in a delightful [New England Colonial] on [an oversized wooded lot] in [the nicest area of Northport]. Stretch out, not spaced out at [$279,500].

UR

HOME REALTY

555-8200
www.ur-home.net

664

Don't Squeeze [5] BRS

Why be cramped when for the price of an ordinary home you can own this [11]-room [Dutch Colonial] on a [tree-canopied street in the most sought after neighborhood of Kingston Heights]? You'll love the classic lines and [the magnificent garden], but you'll have to see the interior, as words won't do it justice. Call now if you want a solution to the space problem at an affordable [$214,500].

UR

HOME REALTY

555-8200
www.ur-home.net

665

Extended Family?

Do relatives and not-quite relatives have you squeezed? Here's your chance to space out in this

[9]-Room, [4]BR

[Brick American Traditional] in [Westwood]. With [high ceilings, sunlit rooms, magnificent woodwork, 2 baths, fenced yard, double garage plus RV parking, and great financing], it's breathing room at a very affordable [$92,500].

UR

HOME REALTY

555-8200
www.ur-home.net

666

Need Space?

for a large family, the in-laws, a home business, or just room to stretch, we have it:

[12] Rooms [$139,000]

A [brick solid] residence in a friendly [West Side] neighborhood that will hold everybody and everything. There's even [a 2-car garage, fenced yard,] and a lot more than you would think is possible at this price. [With low-down payment terms available], it's move it or lose it.

UR
HOME REALTY
555-8200
www.ur-home.net

667

Space Odyssey [3,000] Sq. Ft.

of sheer luxury in [Weston Hills]. With [3BRS, 3½ baths, home office, flowing family areas, marble fireplace, get-lost-sized closets, and 3-car garage], it will make everything else you have seen seem small. Impressive, except for price [$479,500].

UR
HOME REALTY
555-8200
www.ur-home.net

668

H-U-G-E [5] Bedroom

Gather the clan and hurry to see this [11-room residence in move-in condition] that can handle all of you with room to spare. You will love the [huge living area, bright kitchen, 3 fireplaces, and even the unfinished walk-up attic]. In a great [Elmwood] location, it's ready for you at [$214,500].

UR
HOME REALTY
555-8200
www.ur-home.net

669

The Biggie [5]BR

A whopping [3,800] square feet of living in this Texas-size [brick, stone, and glass Contemporary in Westlawn]. This home has it all from [soaring ceilings to views that would make *National Geographic* envious]. It's [just a little better than new] and probably the most beautiful home you will ever see. No need to be cramped at [$439,500].

UR
HOME REALTY
555-8200
www.ur-home.net

670

Price and Size

are not necessarily related. In fact we have

[5]BR—[$139,500]

a solid house in a solid neighborhood perfect for an extended family. The home offers [gleaming hardwood floors, fenced yard, landscaping you will love, double garage,] and a lot more. While it's big, it will move fast, so call now.

UR
HOME REALTY
555-8200
www.ur-home.net

672

[4] BRS
Room for Granny

assorted cousins or lots of kids in this [sparkling Dutch Colonial] in a quiet and friendly [South Side] neighborhood. It has it all: [farm-sized kitchen, separate dining room, 1¾ baths, double garage, and delightful plantings]. Everything about it is well proportioned except the price [$169,500].

UR
HOME REALTY
555-8200
www.ur-home.net

671

Hordes of Kids and a Mean Mother-In-Law

will all fit in this [11-room, 4BR, 2-bath American Traditional in delightful West Salem]. The [brick and cedar home] has what you want and a lot more. Call now, as it's a great house for a small price [$209,500].

UR
HOME REALTY
555-8200
www.ur-home.net

673

In Your Face—Not

Room for privacy in this [7-year-old, 2,400-square-foot, 3BR, 2½-bath Southern Colonial] on [an estate-sized, wooded lot] in [Weston Estates]. With [a private study/home office, spacious family room, massive master suite, relaxing garden patio, and 2-plus car garage], it's your space at [$294,500].

UR
HOME REALTY
555-8200
www.ur-home.net

674

[4] B-I-G Bedrooms

in this [2½-bath New England Colonial] in desirable [Sylvan Estates]. The [light and bright 2,400-square-foot home is decorator-perfect and offers a large family room that opens to a delightful garden patio, private den or home office, and an oversized double garage] in a setting of [oak trees and flowering shrubs that's only a short walk to schools and park]. You're not going to find a comparable home at [$249,500].

UR
HOME REALTY
555-8200
www.ur-home.net

675

BIG Is Beautiful
[11 Rooms]

This [American Traditional] on [an oversized lot in Westbury] is impressive in size and design [and flanked by magnificent oaks]. It solves the space problem for only

[$197,500]

Special features include [a full bath plus powder room, sun-filled rooms of generous proportion, gleaming hardwood, magnificent detailing, a huge walk-up storage attic that could be converted to a studio,] and a list of amenities that could fill a book. If it's time to expand, call.

UR
HOME REALTY
555-8200
www.ur-home.net

676

Big—Vacant—Beautiful

[3BR, 2½-bath New England Colonial on an estate-sized wooded lot] in [Northridge] featuring [magnificent hardwood floors, two mantled fireplaces, tribe-sized kitchen, formal dining, finished basement fitness center, and extra-deep 2-car garage]. It's [move-in ready] with exceptional financing at a price of only [$249,500].

UR
HOME REALTY
555-8200
www.ur-home.net

677

Lost in Space
[11] Rooms [5] BRS

Immense, rambling [American Traditional] in a quiet neighborhood of fine homes and manicured lawns offering [2½ baths, window-wrapped studio, library/home office, high ceilings, exquisite woodwork,] and so much more. The only thing that is not of Herculean proportion is the price. Act fast and it's yours at [$149,500].

UR
HOME REALTY
555-8200
www.ur-home.net

678

Do You Save Things

such as tinfoil, balls of string, old mayon-naise jars, and more? Afraid to throw out anything in case you'll need it later? This [3BR American Traditional] in [a friendly West Side neighborhood] has [a full basement, walk-up storage attic, lots of nooks, crannies, and closets, and a 2½-car garage] to hold all your stuff. You can also save money because it's available with a low-down payment at only [$149,500].

UR
HOME REALTY
555-8200
www.ur-home.net

679

Collector?

Room for your collectibles and a lot more in this [7-room, 3BR, 2-bath American Traditional] in [Westlake]. With [nooks and crannies, full, dry basement, walk-up storage attic, 2½-car garage with storage loft/studio, spacious family room, and large fenced yard], there's room to hold everything. You can collect this fine home with a low down payment and a price of only [$197,500].

UR
HOME REALTY
555-8200
www.ur-home.net

680

Hard To Fill

a [4-year-old, 2,000-square-foot Ranch] in [West Avian] with [3BR, 2 baths, family room, full basement, 2-car garage] on [a ¼-acre] estate site. There's room for everything you own and a few more children or assorted cousins at only [$169,500].

UR
HOME REALTY
555-8200
www.ur-home.net

681

A "Lotto" House

for the money. One look at this [7-room, 3BR, English Traditional] on a [quiet tree-lined] street in [Shorewood] and you will agree this is a "sure thing," not a gamble. With [large sun-filled rooms, brick fireplace, gleaming hard-woods, welcome-home front porch, fenced yard, and double garage], it's the big payoff at [$99,900].

UR
HOME REALTY
555-8200
www.ur-home.net

682

Too Much House

for the present owners of this [3BR, 2½-bath, 2,400-square foot sprawling Mediterranean] with [3-car garage, family room, and magnificent landscaping] in a choice [Westport] setting. Take advantage of an unusual opportunity at [$329,500].

UR
HOME REALTY
555-8200
www.ur-home.net

683

Go Buy Furniture

With [2,400-plus square feet], this [3BR, 2½-bath, 8-year-old Quaker Colonial] in [Clinton Estates] is going to need a lot of furniture. There's even [a home office, family room, formal and family dining areas, 40-foot veranda, and workroom in the 2-plus car garage]. With a low-low-low down payment, you'll have cash to spend, and it's priced at only [$249,500].

UR

HOME REALTY

555-8200
www.ur-home.net

685

Astronauts!

You'll be spaced out by [3,000-plus square feet] of luxury living. This [3BR, 3½-bath Mediterranean Contemporary] in [Cathedral Hills] has [walls of glass, sky-reaching ceilings, vast areas for family living, private home office, a kitchen that's out of this world, two sumptuous master suites, garden patio plus a 3-car garage,] and a price that won't send you into orbit: [$349,500].

UR

HOME REALTY

555-8200
www.ur-home.net

684

Two Grand Pianos

plus a country-western band will fit in the [huge family room] of this [3BR, 2½-bath New Hampshire Colonial] in [Shorewood Gardens]. This [3-year-old] residence [decorated in soft hues] features [a Corian and tile kitchen, walk-in closets, finished basement fitness center, 2½-car garage, and knock-your-socks-off landscaping]. Oversized in everything but price at [$289,500].

UR

HOME REALTY

555-8200
www.ur-home.net

CHAPTER NINETEEN

Homes, Low Price

While price is relative, these ads are written for the lower end of the market—many aimed at first-time buyers. These ads stress affordability.

Many of the ads in other chapters can also be used for lower-priced homes. Please see Chapters 9 (Financing), 15 (Homes, Bargains), and 22 (Homes, Old).

686

[$89,500]
Not a Misprint

That's all the owner is asking for this [3BR, 1½-bath brick rambler in a quiet West Side neighborhood]. The home has [a huge country-style kitchen, garage, full dry basement,] and a great deal more. With [low-down FHA financing], it will likely sell to the first caller.

UR
HOME REALTY

555-8200
www.ur-home.net

ALTERNATIVE HEADINGS

[$89,500] Buys What?

**Love at Purse Sight
[$89,500]**

687

Are You a Slave
to Rent?

Continue to rent and all you will have is receipts. With a down payment so low we can't mention it and monthly payments likely less than you're giving your landlord, you can own a [3BR Cape Cod] on a delightful street in [Chesterton]. The special home has [a fenced yard, garage, RV parking], and it's move-in ready. Call and it can be your freedom. Full price [$98,500].

UR
HOME REALTY

555-8200
www.ur-home.net

ALTERNATIVE HEADINGS

Want to Rent Forever?

Renter's Revenge [$98,000]

688

Ernie the Fish

Plunks down more each month in rent than it would take to own this [3BR, Cape Cod] in [Westhaven] at [$129,500], see what Ernie's missing. #41 at *www.ur-home.net*

UR
HOME REALTY
555-8200
www.ur-home.net

689

Tightwad

You'll squeeze your dollars until George Washington hollers "Uncle." At [$118,500] you won't do better than this [Westwood 3BR]. See what's possible #49 at *www.ur-home.net*

UR
HOME REALTY
555-8200
www.ur-home.net

ALTERNATIVE HEADINGS

Miser!

Cheapskate!

690

Tired of the Apartment?

Want privacy, a [West Side] neighborhood, [your own fenced yard for puppies and children, a garden, 3 bedrooms, 1½ baths, fireplace,] and more, but you don't have much of a down payment and can't pay more than [$800] per month? Don't despair; your relief is just a phone call away.

UR
HOME REALTY
555-8200
www.ur-home.net

➤ This ad sells terms.

691

Stick the Landlord!

Why make his mortgage payments when you could be buying a [3BR Cape Cod] in the friendliest neighborhood in [Kingston] with [a possible no-down payment and] monthly payments less than you are probably paying in rent. Call now and see what your rent money will buy.

UR
HOME REALTY
555-8200
www.ur-home.net

ALTERNATIVE HEADINGS

Fire the Landlord!

Kiss Your Landlord Goodbye!

➤ Price is not really essential. The ad sells terms.

692

Help Your Landlord

make his mortgage payments, put cash in his pocket, and give him the tax breaks. But if you don't want to be this nice, you can own a great [3BR, 1½-bath Cape Cod with your own fenced yard, basement, and double garage] in [Westhaven] for possibly

No or Low Down

and monthly payments likely less than you pay for rent. Don't call and you will keep your landlord happy.

UR
HOME REALTY

555-8200
www.ur-home.net

694

So Much—So Little

A [3BR, 2-bath Modern Victorian] on a choice lot in [Glendale] with all the extras including [two-car garage, fireplace, built-ins, 10-foot ceilings] and more. Act now or it will be sold at only [$174,900].

UR
HOME REALTY

555-8200
www.ur-home.net

ALTERNATIVE HEADING

On A Budget?

693

Kick the Habit

of paying rent. For [almost a no-down payment] you can own a [3BR home] in a choice [South Side] neighborhood priced for you at

[$89,500]

and it includes your own [garage plus RV parking, fenced yard, 2 apple trees, full basement,] and payments likely to be less than rent. Interested? Then call:

UR
HOME REALTY

555-8200
www.ur-home.net

695

How Low Can We Get?

This [3BR, 2-bath, brick Traditional] in [Sandpoint Village] has been reduced below the bargain point to just

[$159,500]

and that's for a home [in great condition] on [the nicest street] with [fireplace, garage, formal and family dining areas.] It's now a matter of call or be sorry.

UR
HOME REALTY

555-8200
www.ur-home.net

696

Sweet and Low

A sweet [3BR, 1½-bath, 2-car garage, brick Split-Level in great condition] with [fabulous landscaping and large sunny rooms] in the [Midvale School District], and because of unusual circumstances, it's priced at a low [$98,500].

UR
HOME REALTY
555-8200
www.ur-home.net

697

You Can Pay More But Why?

when this [3BR, 1½-bath brick Split-Level] with [2-car garage, hardwood floors, finished recreation/fitness area,] and a lot more is available in a choice [West Side] neighborhood for only [$114,500].

UR
HOME REALTY
555-8200
www.ur-home.net

698

Off the Deep End? No!

You don't have to drown in debt to own this [3BR, 2-bath New Mexico-inspired Ranch in Clydesdale Estates] with [fireplace, family room, 2-car garage and all the extras]. We have one and only one at [$169,500].

UR
HOME REALTY
555-8200
www.ur-home.net

699

Closet Cheapskate?

You can own a [3BR, 2-bath, Arizona-inspired Ranch] in [Clifton Heights] with [2½-car garage, fireplace, family room, dining patio,] and all the extras. No one will ever guess you only paid [$149,500].

UR
HOME REALTY
555-8200
www.ur-home.net

700

Pie in the Sky?

No! You can actually own a terrific [3BR, 2-bath, brick ranch] in a friendly [West Side neighborhood with good schools] for close to

Nothing Down

and payments likely less than you are paying for rent. Hurry as we only have this one.

UR
HOME REALTY
555-8200
www.ur-home.net

701

Forget the Appraisal

View this [3BR, 1½-bath white clapboard Cape Cod] on a quiet tree lined street in [New Lisbon] #62, *www.ur-home.net*. The appraiser says its worth [$108,000]. We only want [$89,500].

UR
HOME REALTY
555-8200
www.ur-home.net

702

If Mother Goose

knew she could have purchased this [Westlake Village], Cape Cod with [3BR, huge bonus room, and 2 baths] with almost nothing down, she would have given the shoe to the Salvation Army. There's also [a fenced yard, garden patio, garage plus RV parking]. It's priced so as not to ruffle your feathers at [$87,500].

UR
HOME REALTY
555-8200
www.ur-home.net

703

Rent a Truck

and start moving! This [3BR] solid [West Side] home is available right now with low-down and possibly no-down payment and monthly payments likely less than rent. With [private fenced yard, full basement, garage, and garden], it certainly beats renting. You better call now because it's priced at only [$89,500].

UR
HOME REALTY
555-8200
www.ur-home.net

704

Be a Wise Guy

or gal. Why pay rent when you can own this [2BR, 1½-bath, expandable Cape Cod with fireplace and garage] in a great [West Side] neighborhood for almost nothing down and low monthly payments? At [$84,500], it's smart to call.

UR
HOME REALTY
555-8200
www.ur-home.net

705

Spend Less Get More

[3BR, 1½ baths, 2-car garage, over-sized lot] in [the desirable Claymore School District] with low-down or no-down payment and a price of only [$67,500]. The second one to call will likely be too late.

UR
HOME REALTY
555-8200
www.ur-home.net

ALTERNATIVE HEADING

Pauper Priced [$69,500]

but you'll live like a prince in this . . .

706

Same as Rent

After a low or even possibly no down payment, your monthly payments will likely be no more than you are presently paying for rent, but you will be buying a [3BR, 1½-bath Cape Cod with a fenced yard, private patio, basement recreation room, oversized garage] in [a garden setting] on [a quiet street] in friendly [Northport]. Better call now because we only have one home like this. Oh! The price is just [$99,500].

UR
HOME REALTY
555-8200
www.ur-home.net

ALTERNATIVE HEADING

Why Mortgage the Kids?

707

Not a Condo
[$89,500]

A free-standing [3BR] home with its own [fenced] yard and garage plus more-more-more, in [convenient Westport]. You'll be glad you called:

UR
HOME REALTY
555-8200
www.ur-home.net

ALTERNATIVE HEADINGS

[$89,500] Buys What?

[$89,500] Not A Fixer

[$89,500] Budget Saver

708

Yes! You Can!
[$79,500]

and a low-low down payment will make you owner of this [3BR, brick American Traditional] in a quiet and friendly [West Hills neighborhood]. This house has [full basement, garage, fenced yard, and is bright and cheery]. Call! See! And it will be "HOME."

UR
HOME REALTY
555-8200
www.ur-home.net

709

Go for It!

With low-down or even no-down payment and monthly payments that are likely less than your monthly rent, it's no gamble to buy this [2BR, expandable Cape Cod] with [fenced yard, full basement, and attached garage] in [Wilson Heights]. Act fast because others are reading this ad. Oh! The price? [$84,500].

UR
HOME REALTY
555-8200
www.ur-home.net

ALTERNATIVE HEADING

Don't Rent Your Dream

710

Start Packing
[$69,500]

at this price and with a low-low down payment, your monthly payments will likely be less than your rent plus you'll be building equity in a solid [3BR, brick home in West Templeton] with [hardwood floors, full basement, garage, and a backyard you won't have to share with anyone]. Some lucky renter is going to be an owner, so call and get lucky.

UR
HOME REALTY
555-8200
www.ur-home.net

711

Starving Artist?
[$87,500]

Even you can afford this **[6-room, brick traditional]** with sun-filled rooms. See your new home at *www.ur-home.net*

UR
HOME REALTY

555-8200
www.ur-home.net

712

Dirt Cheap [$89,500]

This **[2BR Rambler on a choice corner lot]** in **[Westchester]** is available for lot value.

The House Is Free

It's a no-lose situation so act fast and call.

UR
HOME REALTY

555-8200
www.ur-home.net

→ This is an effective approach where lot value is equal to or exceeds price of an older home.

713

Free House

We mean it! A **[great 3BR, 1½-bath Cape Cod]** in a desirable **[estate area of Northampton]** is available right now for the value of the land alone. Check it out, and compare with lot values; it's only **[$94,500]**.

UR
HOME REALTY

555-8200
www.ur-home.net

Homes, Luxury

Luxury and expensive are relative terms. A home that you consider middle-range might be considered luxury by a person at a lower economic level. Therefore, it is important to remember that the language in luxury ads can be used effectively for homes over a wide spectrum of quality and value.

In luxury home ads, point out features that aren't often found in homes of lesser quality. Because many people buy expensive homes for the prestige they feel it gives them, this factor can be effectively used in your ads.

Ads from other Chapters such as (4) Architecture and (26) Location may also be applicable to luxury homes.

714

A Price on Priceless [$899,500]

Unmatched quality, [unparalleled views,] and a [Woodland Hills] address that's second to none. You must experience this striking [3,800-square-foot Mediterranean masterpiece] with its [tile, 12-foot ceilings, walls of glass, get-lost size closets, Phoenician baths, private home office, marble fireplaces, fountain pool and spa, dining veranda, landscaping that puts everything you've seen to shame,] and so very much more. This is what success is all about.

UR
H O M E   R E A L T Y

555-8200
www.ur-home.net

ALTERNATIVE HEADINGS

OOOH! AAAH! [$899,500]

A Definite 10 [$899,500]

715

Drop-Dead Gorgeous

That's the way [my daughter] described this [almost-new Modern Mediterranean masterpiece] in [Weston Heights]. There are [three stunningly conceived bedrooms, 2½ opulent baths, sky-high ceilings, window-walls that invite the beautiful setting into the home, a terrace overflowing with flowers,] and a great deal more. Expect the best and your expectations will be exceeded. Everything about this fine residence is impressive except the price: [$449,500].

UR
H O M E   R E A L T Y

555-8200
www.ur-home.net

716

[$3,000,000]

If you are one of the fortunate few who can get beyond the price, you will want to see this magnificent [14-room Brentwood Estate]. #47 at www.ur-home.net

UR
HOME REALTY
555-8200
www.ur-home.net

717

Reflect Your Success

Don't you deserve a home that mirrors your achievements? This [brick and stone English Regency] on an estate setting in [Woodridge Heights] combines architecture and craftsmanship in a home that whispers "success." With its [high ceilings, massive beams, and gleaming hardwoods], this spacious [3BR and den, 2½-bath home] provides [over 3,000] sq. ft. for gracious living. You'll love the [rock-scaped pool, your own championship tennis court, and the impeccably maintained grounds] that provide an ambiance of quality living. For a very special few at [$890,000].

UR
HOME REALTY
555-8200
www.ur-home.net

ALTERNATIVE HEADINGS

Rich and Famous!

Life Is Full of Compromises
compromise no more . . .

718

Absolutely Fabulous

Need we say more about this [near-new 3BR, 3½-bath Mediterranean Villa] on an estate setting in [Northridge]. Of course, there's [a private music room, expansive family areas, walk-in closets, 3-car garage,] and all the rest. What makes it special is the feeling of elegance tempered with simplicity created by the architect for this one-of-a-kind masterpiece. The lifestyle you deserve. [$595,000].

UR
HOME REALTY
555-8200
www.ur-home.net

719

It's Expensive but Worth It

[3,000] square feet of luxury packaged in [a like-new Mediterranean Contemporary] on an estate site in [Weatherby Hills]. With [3BR, 3½ baths, 3-car garage, dual master suites with spas, home office, 12-foot ceilings, walls of glass, garden patio overlooking pool, spa, and gazebo, and set amidst award-quality landscaping], it offers the ultimate in living for the family unwilling to compromise: [$535,000].

UR
HOME REALTY
555-8200
www.ur-home.net

ALTERNATIVE HEADINGS

If You Didn't Care
what it costs, consider this . . .

Tomorrow May Never Come
if you don't see this . . .

720

World-Class Residence

Once in a rare while will a truly magnificent home such as this be available. Built without compromise, the home reflects only the very best. This [17-room American classic] has [baths sheathed in Grecian marble, woodwork of American walnut, leaded-glass windows, a slate roof,] and all the amenities present on your wish list including a [lighted championship tennis court, heated Olympic pool, and home theatre with surround sound]. Set on [12 rolling acres], it is what success is all about. If you promised yourself the best in life, you can keep that promise at [$2,600,000].

UR
HOME REALTY
555-8200
www.ur-home.net

ALTERNATIVE HEADINGS

The Art of Living!

**Reached the Top?
Live There!**

721

Old-World Opulence

is combined with every modern convenience in this [4-year-old Mediterranean in Tuscany Estates]. With [3BR, 2½ baths, 3-car garage, 12-foot ceilings, walls of glass, private home office, expansive family areas, landscaping to be envied, and a master suite that will surpass your dreams], luxury is an understatement. Offered at [$398,500].

UR
HOME REALTY
555-8200
www.ur-home.net

722

Former
[Du Pont] Estate

The [Du Pont] family called this [11-room English Traditional] their home. Set [behind stately maples], this impressive [brick and stone residence] features [a slate roof, 3-car garage, 3½ baths, music room, library, 4BR, 50-foot flagstone veranda, magnificent plantings,] and so much more. This [impeccably maintained residence] reflects the epitome of quality for gracious living. Superlatives apply to everything but the price: [$697,500].

UR
HOME REALTY
555-8200
www.ur-home.net

ALTERNATIVE HEADINGS

Five Oaks

A Robber Baron

is reputed to have called this [...] home ...

→ A well-known owner or former owner can add a great deal of desirability to a home. People like to point out to their friends that a famous person or family once owned their home. If an estate has a name the use of the name could give an ad prestige.

723

No Earthly Reason

to accept second best when you can own this [3BR, 3½-bath Italian Renaissance masterpiece] in an estate setting [behind gates in Westport]. This exceptional residence includes [rooms of baronial proportions masterfully decorated in soft tones, a private home office, tons of marble and tile,] and every modern amenity imaginable plus [a pool, tennis court, and formal gardens]. Truly a residence to reflect your success at [$975,000].

UR

H O M E   R E A L T Y

555-8200
www.ur-home.net

724

The ? Home

The [celebrity] owner of this delightful [3BR, 2½-bath California Regency] in the estate section of [Southport] must, because of unusual circumstances, sell [his/her] dream home. Built to exacting specifications with almost no regard to cost, the home features a [huge game room for informal gatherings; a walnut, paneled den; a breakfast patio overlooking the pool and gardens]; and all the other amenities one can wish for. The impeccable taste of this owner is yours for [$895,000].

UR

H O M E   R E A L T Y

555-8200
www.ur-home.net

➤ Without revealing his or her name, the ad indicates that the home has a famous owner. This adds prestige to the house. You could also refer to the owner as world-renowned or well-known.

725

A Power House

Magnificent [English Tudor] in a [Westridge] estate setting that gently whispers "success." This [3BR, 2½-bath] masterpiece boasts [a paneled home office/music room, public areas of immense proportion, intricate detailing, 3 fireplaces, French doors to the 50-foot veranda, formal rose garden, and 3-car garage]. Truly a home to be envied at [$379,500].

UR

H O M E   R E A L T Y

555-8200
www.ur-home.net

ALTERNATIVE HEADINGS

Presidents

of corporations will be your neighbors when you own this . . .

Caesar's Palace

offers fewer delights than this . . .

A Home to Hate

if you want to hide your success from the world . . .

726

A Trophy House

Forget understated elegance. This [12-room, 5BR, 5½-plus bath English Manor] on [4 acres] with a [Winslow Hills address] exudes quality in every inch of its [6,000-plus] square feet. It has everything including [pool and courts]. Offered to the very few who have achieved such success at [$2,000,000].

UR

H O M E   R E A L T Y

555-8200
www.ur-home.net

727

Accept No Substitutes

This [almost-new New Hampshire Colonial] was designed by [Royal Berry Wills] and built by [Barton Brothers] in [a garden setting behind gates] in [Windsong]. With [2,600 square feet, 3BR, home office, 3½ baths, 3-car garage,] and every civilized amenity, don't even think of duplicating it. We are proud to offer the original at [$389,500].

UR

HOME REALTY

555-8200
www.ur-home.net

➤ Use of architect and/or builder name(s) tends to add prestige.

728

Doctors' Row

A block party in this [Pinewood Cove] community will seem like a medical convention. This [3BR, 2½-bath English Tudor estate] is the perfect home for a hypochondriac. When not providing the neighbors with your symptoms, there's [a heated pool and spa for therapy and a fantastic garden guaranteed to lower your blood pressure]. This home has all you expect and more with its [fine French doors; leaded crystal, cut windows; exquisite woodwork; a kitchen that will make you want to eat at home; and a richly paneled library]. Hurry, or a doctor will beat you to it at [$469,500].

UR

HOME REALTY

555-8200
www.ur-home.net

➤ This ad treats the home's neighbors in a very light manner.

729

Clone Proof

To reproduce this [2,800-square-foot, 3BR, 3½-bath, 3-car garage French Chateau] in [West Wind Estates] would cost far more than the owner's price. While [only 8 years old], it's evident that cost took a back seat to the quality in the [luxurious landscaping, quality amenities, paneled home office, Corian-copper-tile kitchen, twin master suites with sitting rooms, walk-in closets, whirlpool tubs,] and so much more. It's certain to remain a "one of a kind" at [$689,000].

UR

HOME REALTY

555-8200
www.ur-home.net

730

Are You Pretentious?

If so, you'll love the lifestyle normally reserved for the "Rich and Famous" offered by this [8-year-old, 3BR, 2½-bath Southwestern Colonial]. The [expansive family areas overlook colorful plantings, pool, spa, and BBQ patio]. There are [high ceilings, white marble fireplace, tons of tile, 3-car garage, walls of glass,] and a seldom experienced feeling of "success," yet it's comfortably priced at [$389,500].

UR

HOME REALTY

555-8200
www.ur-home.net

ALTERNATIVE HEADING

Social Wannabe?

731

Who Used the Tub?

We suspect [Mr. Buckley] of our office has been bathing in the Italian [marble] tub in the sumptuous master bath of this [3BR, 2½-bath Italian Renaissance] estate in [Westhaven]. Every afternoon [he] visits the house and takes along a towel. When [he] returns, [he's] singing Italian arias. When you see the tantalizing Roman baths, you'll understand why. The estate has an aura of elegance that makes you want to pamper yourself. With [more than 3,500] sq. ft. of sheer luxury and [almost a half-acre] of grounds, this is your chance to be good to yourself for [$549,500]. After all, who deserves it more?

UR
HOME REALTY
555-8200
www.ur-home.net

➡️ This ad's heading is a real attention-getter. The ad can be used with any Mediterranean architectural style.

732

Who Deserves It More?

You've worked for what you have, and it's time to pamper yourself with a home that reflects your success. A [Mediterranean Villa] that's better than you ever dreamed with [12 rooms, 3½ marble baths, soaring ceilings, intricate detailing,] and it's on a superb estate site in [Prentice Hills]. A definite must-see for the fortunate few, offered at [$690,000].

UR
HOME REALTY
555-8200
www.ur-home.net

733

So You've Made It!

It's time to live your success in this [Brick English Tudor] in desirable [Hillside Estates]. It has everything and more, including [a private library or 4th bedroom, baths everywhere, magnificent formal dining room, English rose garden, and a flagstone dining patio]. Best of all, you don't have to spend it all with a price of [$449,500].

UR
HOME REALTY
555-8200
www.ur-home.net

734

Soap Opera Home

It's exotic, daring, and dramatic. This [3BR, 2½-bath, 2,800-square-foot, West Hills masterpiece] melds design and decor to excite the senses. Built of [stone and glass], this home features [soaring ceilings, an enormous fireplace, flowing open floor plan, loads of tile, lush carpeting, a mix of soft hues and vibrant accents as well as a 3-car garage and a garden that's an extravaganza of color]. You can be the star of your own production for [$649,500].

UR
HOME REALTY
555-8200
www.ur-home.net

735

Flaunt It!

Don't be ashamed to let others know of your success. After all, what good is success if you can't live it? This **[9-room, 3,400-square-foot, 3BR, 3½-bath Mediterranean Villa behind gates at Ironwood]** offers the ultimate in fine living. You'll love the **[spacious rooms, 10-foot ceilings, fairway view, 3-car garage,]** and so much more. A home to be experienced is offered as an investment in yourself at **[$749,500]**.

UR
HOME REALTY
555-8200
www.ur-home.net

ALTERNATIVE HEADINGS

Are You There Yet?

Rich?

736

Butler Not Included

With this **[3BR, 2½-bath, brick and stone Edwardian Estate]** in **[Westmorland, set back from the quiet street and guarded by stately trees and manicured hedges]**; it projects an aura of permanence and quality. You will love **[the gleaming woodwork, leaded cut glass, private home office and spacious, sun-drenched family areas]**. A proper residence for gracious living at a surprisingly modest **[$347,500]**.

UR
HOME REALTY
555-8200
www.ur-home.net

ALTERNATIVE HEADING

Room For the Bentley

and **[3 other cars]** with this . . .

737

Success Is The Best Revenge

What better way to get even than to turn them green with envy? A **[3BR, 2½-bath, brick Edwardian behind wrought iron gates with a Hilton Head address and dramatic courtyard entry]**, featuring **[leaded glass, slate, high ceilings, intricate woodwork,]** and countless luxury amenities. There's **[an office/music room, royal-sized dining room, great room with massive fireplace, wine cellar, 3-car garage,]** and everything you would want if fine living was placed before cost. Reproduction cost probably **[$2 million]**, but don't tell them you only paid **[$475,000]**.

UR
HOME REALTY
555-8200
www.ur-home.net

➤ This ad would be appropriate for an impressive older estate.

738

Alarmed

and protected in **[the gate-guarded]** community of **[Glen Oaks]**, this **[3BR, 2½-bath Tuscany Villa]** features **[high ceilings, bright, spacious rooms, home office, magnificent fireplace, delightful dining patio, 3-car garage, and even a hidden home safe]**, and it's conservatively priced at **[$479,500]**.

UR
HOME REALTY
555-8200
www.ur-home.net

739

Regrets

Unfortunately, only one buyer will be able to experience the joy of owning this [9-room, 3BR and den French Regency Masterpiece]. With [10-foot ceilings, baths sheathed in marble, and a kitchen that would be the envy of a "Michelin" chef], this premier residence commands [a coveted location] in [an enclave of fine estates]. Of course, all the amenities one associates with a home of this caliber are included as well as [sparkling pool, spa, and garden resplendent in a rainbow of colors]. Everything will impress you except the price, an amazingly reasonable [$595,000].

UR
_____
HOME REALTY

555-8200
www.ur-home.net

740

The Guests Live Well

This [5,000-square foot 4BR, 4½-plus bath English country estate] on [4 acres] in [River Hills] includes [an additional spacious suite over the 4-car garage for live-ins, in-laws, or guests]. With every amenity one would expect in a world-class residence, imagine the very finest and you will still be delighted. Proudly offered to just a few at [$2,800,000].

UR
_____
HOME REALTY

555-8200
www.ur-home.net

741

Wanna Be a Snob?

People will know you have class living in this [3BR, 2½-bath, older Georgian Colonial]. This very fine residence is in an area where the same families have lived for generations, intermarrying, and producing clone offspring with names like Buffy and Carleton. There's an [old carriage house with a large, bright studio that's beyond perfect if you're an artist, even if only in your own mind]. When you move in, make certain the neighbors see your polo mallets. Positive snob appeal at a surprisingly reasonable [$485,000].

UR
_____
HOME REALTY

555-8200
www.ur-home.net

→ While this ad also makes fun of old money, it will attract people who have social aspirations.

CHAPTER TWENTY-ONE

Homes, New

While display ads are often used to advertise new homes, classifieds are still a very effective method of generating interest in a particular piece of property, especially considering that some readers may bypass display advertising altogether in their search for a "bargain" or "affordable housing!" (The smaller classified ads also have a significant price advantage over display ads.)

Ads for particular features or types of homes found in other sections in this book can also be readily tailored for new homes, as can open house ads.

742

The Last of the Best

When we sell this new [model] home in [Clairborne Estates] there won't be any more. This [3BR, 2½-bath, 2,100-square-foot Regency plan features soaring ceilings, glass-wrapped living area, very private home office, garden kitchen, an unbelievable master suite, and just about every conceivable upgrade]. Call now because it's your last chance at [$289,500].

UR
HOME REALTY
555-8200
www.ur-home.net

743

Builder Liquidation [2] Left

Builder is closing out [Chadwick Hills] development and has asked us to unload the last of these [3BR, 2-bath, 1,800-square-foot Mediterranean Ranch homes]. They have "everything" including [den or home office, quality carpets and tile, built-ins galore,] and more. While you could buy similar homes for much more, it's your last chance at [$189,500].

UR
HOME REALTY
555-8200
www.ur-home.net

ALTERNATIVE HEADING

Get In Line!

744

Feng Shui Approved [$279,500]

Brand-new, [Westhaven 3BR, 2-bath Contemporary] that embraces harmony and balance. Check #88 at www.ur-home.net

UR
HOME REALTY
555-8200
www.ur-home.net

➤ Feng Shui is an important Chinese philosophical design system that creates a balance of flow and containment. A house design approved by a Feng Shui consultant is believed to offer health and luck.

745

Ralph Washington Slept Here

It's reputed that Ralph, no relation to George, spent at least 1 night in this new [3BR, 2-bath Colonial] while it was under construction. Despite Ralph's brief occupancy, the home turned out extremely well. The [wood floors and trim, used-brick fireplace with a mantle made from an ancient beam, and brick, copper, and tile family kitchen] all add a feeling of warmth. You'll love the [bay windows and the family room that opens onto your own wooded grove]. All the amenities are present, [air conditioning, a 2½-car garage, and a full basement awaiting your finishing touches]. After Ralph, you can be the second person to sleep here for [$197,500]. This moment in history is brought to you by

UR
HOME REALTY
555-8200
www.ur-home.net

➤ This ad is a takeoff on ads used by some brokers to sell historic homes.

746

Why Buy Used?

when for the same money, you can buy new with everything under builder's warranty. A very special [3BR, 2-bath brick Ranch on an estate-size lot in Clifton Hills] is just a phone call away from being yours. Honest, it's priced at only [$157,500].

UR
HOME REALTY
555-8200
www.ur-home.net

747

A New Reproduction

Too many extra amenities were built into this new [3BR, 2-bath Mediterranean Executive Ranch] on [a prime site in Wedgefield Estates]. Of course, there's [a 3-car garage, family room, fireplace, home office/music room, and professional landscaping], but the upgrades must be seen to be appreciated. If you act quickly, you can own it at no more than the cost of an ordinary home.

UR
HOME REALTY
555-8200
www.ur-home.net

ALTERNATIVE HEADINGS

New But No Squeak
this . . .

A Brand New Classic
this . . .

748

Not Quite Finished

but if you wait 'til then, there'll be someone else's name on the mailbox. A [3BR, 2-bath, 2,000-square-foot luxury Colonial with a 2-car garage] on [an estate lot] in [Lockridge]. Featuring [a Corian and tile kitchen, mantled fireplace, Jacuzzi tub, get-lost closets,] and much more; you will have to act fast, as the builder is only asking [$227,500].

UR
_____
H O M E   R E A L T Y
555-8200
www.ur-home.net

ALTERNATIVE HEADING

The Paint Isn't Dry!

749

New Deal Raw Deal

It won't take much to finish this [3BR, 2-bath Colonial in Chesterfield Heights]. It needs [varnish, paint, tile, landscaping,] and just a bit more, but when the work is done, you should have a home worth far more than you invested. The home has [a 3-car garage, whirlpool tub in the master suite,] and many more luxury amenities. Because of unusual circumstances it is available as is, and it's only [$189,500].

UR
_____
H O M E   R E A L T Y
555-8200
www.ur-home.net

ALTERNATIVE HEADING

Unfinished Opportunity

750

Some Assembly Required

[The lawn isn't in and the garage could use some cabinets] but otherwise this [Northport 3BR, 2½-bath, Mediterranean Villa] is darn near perfect. At just [$287,900], check it out. #815 at *www.ur-home.net*.

UR
_____
H O M E   R E A L T Y
555-8200
www.ur-home.net

751

Wanna Peek?

Not quite completed [2,000-square-foot Pennsylvania Ranch in Ripon Heights] with [3BR, 2½ baths, family room, two fireplaces, whitewashed oak kitchen, Berber carpet, whirlpool tubs, and professional landscaping]. If you wait until the decorators are finished it will be too late because it's priced at [$259,500].

UR
_____
H O M E   R E A L T Y
555-8200
www.ur-home.net

ALTERNATIVE HEADINGS

Just Finished Hammering

Wear Your Boots

The lawn isn't ready on this . . .

752

Naked and New

You get to pick the [cabinets, tile, carpeting, appliances, light fixtures, and paint] of this almost-finished, [3BR, 2½-bath, 3-car garage, almost 2,200-square-foot Tuscany Mediterranean] in [Washington Heights] that will reflect your individual taste at a "must see now" precompletion price of just [$169,500].

UR

HOME REALTY

555-8200
www.ur-home.net

ALTERNATIVE HEADINGS

Bare Naked

No Body Slept Here!

753

Buy the Model

[Clifford Estates has sold out], so this upgraded [3BR, 2½-bath, 2,000-square-foot, red-tiled Mediterranean] with [3-car garage and professional landscaping] plus everything is builder-liquidation priced at only [$239,500].

UR

HOME REALTY

555-8200
www.ur-home.net

754

Undressed

This brand-new, [3BR, 2-bath, double-garage Colonial] is awaiting your individual touch. There's still time to choose the colors. You'll love the [high ceilings, authentic moldings] and the feeling of bright spaciousness. Set on an estate-sized lot on the most desirable street, this is an opportunity that won't last long at [$179,500].

UR

HOME REALTY

555-8200
www.ur-home.net

→ The above heading will ensure that the ad is read. A racier heading would be the following.

ALTERNATIVE HEADING

Undressed and Waiting

755

Brand New Almost

Hardly lived in [3BR, 2½-bath Dutch Colonial] in a magnificently landscaped setting in [Westwood has been tastefully decorated with soft hues and colorful accents]. With over [2,400] square feet of luxury plus a [3-car garage and flower-bedecked dining patio]. It can be yours at only [$229,500].

UR

HOME REALTY

555-8200
www.ur-home.net

Homes, Old

Architectural detailing, size, workmanship, and construction material: These and other unique features of "older homes" continue to attract buyers' attention. Instead of following the familiar "newer is better" philosophy, many individuals purposely seek out the historical appeal offered by this category of housing.

Ads for older homes emphasize traits such as quality, size, beauty, and value—enviable features that may appeal to the buyer's desire for a genteel way of life. Some ads suitable for older homes are also found in other sections in this book such as in Chapter 4 (Architecture).

756

A Sordid Past! [$149,500]

Rumor has it this **[9-room Woodhaven Victorian]** was once used for nefarious purposes. Forget the past and see a splendid future. #601 at *www.ur-home.net*

UR
H O M E   R E A L T Y

555-8200
www.ur-home.net

ALTERNATIVE HEADINGS

A Lady with A Past

A Fallen Woman

757

Do I Have the Girl for You!

She's a bit old-fashioned, actually **[Victorian]**, and she will never see 100 again, but she has her feet on the ground in **[Westhaven]** and her head in the sky. She is anything but cheap, however, she's affordable at **[$239,500]**. Check her out for the good life. #103 at *www.ur-home.net*

UR
H O M E   R E A L T Y

555-8200
www.ur-home.net

→ This ad is for an older Victorian home.

Social Wannabee?

A [3BR, 1½-bath] [Edwardian brick] in [Westhaven] that looks like old money but is available at [$149,900]. Check it out at *www.ur-home.net* #403

UR

HOME REALTY

555-8200
www.ur-home.net

759

$1,000,000 Home [$189,500] Price

See why you can afford a [9-room Victorian masterpiece] that only a millionaire could build today. #402 at *www.ur-home.net*

UR

HOME REALTY

555-8200
www.ur-home.net

760

Country Modern?

If modern means indoor plumbing, this [9-room Westlake clapboard traditional] qualifies. See what comfortable living is all about for just [$175,000]. #61 at *www.ur-home.net*

UR

HOME REALTY

555-8200
www.ur-home.net

761

Once Upon a Time

a man carefully crafted a [9-room, white clapboard Riverdale] home for his family that has endured for generations. See what it can offer you at just [$187,900]. #401 at *www.ur-home.net*

UR

HOME REALTY

555-8200
www.ur-home.net

762

Historic [Breckinridge] House

Built by [a Civil War hero] in [1871], this exceptional residence comes with a history as colorful as its beautiful setting. This [9] room, [3]BR, [2-]bath monument to American artisans has been meticulously maintained and updated with integrity so as not to detract from the elegance of its design. There's a **[parlor wrapped in glass, high ceilings, gleaming oak, generously proportioned rooms, exquisite detailing, and the carriage house loft would be perfect for an artist's studio]**. This elegance of a time when life centered on home and family can be yours for the future at a conservative [$379,500].

UR

HOME REALTY

555-8200
www.ur-home.net

→ The original owner of an older home can be effectively used even when that person is not well known.

763

The Prolific [Swits] Lived Here

[Jonathan Swit] built this [9-room, 3BR American Victorian] in [1847] for [his bride]. They reportedly had [11] children. Since then, dozens more children have been born here. With its [11-foot ceilings, sun-drenched rooms, covered front porch, magnificent garden setting, large garage, and updated systems], it will continue to nurture families. You must see this special home priced at an ordinary [$176,500].

UR
HOME REALTY

555-8200
www.ur-home.net

➤ Families of the Victorian era tended to be large. A local historian might provide information for a very appealing marketing presentation.

764

Romantic Wanted

to appreciate the [200] years of living that has given this [3BR, 2-bath Virginia Colonial] its unique charm and warmth. Set back from a quiet street [amidst ancient hardwoods], this home seems to echo centuries of laughter and happiness. You'll love the [floating staircase and museum-quality woodwork]. Proudly offered for your future at [$279,500].

UR
HOME REALTY

555-8200
www.ur-home.net

➤ If a house has been extensively renovated, you should say so in your ads.

765

Time Forgot

about this [3-bedroom] remnant of a gentler past [embraced by its wraparound, covered porch]. You'll fall in love with the [polished oak paneling, dramatic staircase, high ceilings, light, bright rooms, double garage, and country garden] in its quiet community of fine homes, [towering trees,] and friendly neighbors. This is a home your family deserves at the old-fashioned price of [$149,500].

UR
HOME REALTY

555-8200
www.ur-home.net

ALTERNATIVE HEADINGS

Ante Bellum
Time forgot about this . . .

100 Years Behind the Times
Time forgot about this . . .

Remember Grandma's House?
Time forgot about this . . .

Yearning for Yesterday?
Time forgot about this . . .

A Call From the Past!
Time forgot about this . . .

Love With Yesteryear?

return to a quieter and gentler
e where pride in family and home is
dent by happy children playing,
well-cared-for homes, and neighbors
who pause to talk to one another. We
have the key to this solid [3BR American
Traditional] with everything you could
want for your family in friendly
[Southport]. The price of your return,
only [$112,500].

UR
HOME REALTY
555-8200
www.ur-home.net

ALTERNATIVE HEADINGS

Why Buy New?

Back to Your Future

Steeped in History

Norman Rockwell Traditional

American Gothic

Yearning for Yesterday!

767

[1878] Charm [2004] Value

A [3BR American Classic] with [white-
columned veranda, gleaming hardwood
floors, family and formal dining areas,
large, bright rooms, mature landscaping,
and a delightful garden] make this an
impressive residence. Priced less than
any newer home at only [$79,900].

UR
HOME REALTY
555-8200
www.ur-home.net

768

New in [1914]

when they built homes with care. This
[3BR, American Traditional] in a friendly
[West Side] neighborhood offers
[gleaming hardwood floors, large,
bright rooms, formal and family dining
areas, full dry basement, fenced yard,
garage, mature landscaping, and a
delightful covered front porch]. It's available now with excellent financing and
a price far less than new cookie-cutter
homes [$87,500].

UR
HOME REALTY
555-8200
www.ur-home.net

769

From Out of the Past

The dignity, mystery, and excitement of
this [American Colonial] needs to be
restored, but it'll be well worth the effort.
There are [3BR, 1½ baths, formal dining,
sun-filled kitchen, exquisite detailing, and
even a screened summer porch]. On a
desirable [wooded] site in [Dorchester],
it can be your future at [$229,500].

UR
HOME REALTY
555-8200
www.ur-home.net

770

[1896]

Civil War veterans led the July 4th parade, horsepower still referred to horses, and a family's home was truly its castle when this [turreted, 10-room Victorian, with its lavish wood trim and high ceilings], was built for gracious living. If you desire to recapture the joy of a gentler time, call today for a private showing. Offered at [$214,500].

UR
_____
HOME REALTY

555-8200
www.ur-home.net

ALTERNATIVE HEADING

Step Back [100] Years

when Civil War veterans . . .

→ The year an older home was built can make an effective heading. The ad body creates a pleasant, nostalgic image.

771

Like Them Mature?

A stately [white Traditional showing Queen Anne influence] in a [magnificently landscaped site] on [homeowner-proud Wilson Avenue]. With [9 perfect rooms, 3BR, 1½ baths, high ceilings, intricate detailing, polished hardwoods, beveled glass, wide-covered side porch, and modern systems that have been carefully integrated so as not to detract from the charm of yesterday], it's a home any millionaire would be proud of for just [$227,500].

UR
_____
HOME REALTY

555-8200
www.ur-home.net

772

A Cocked Hat

was worn by the first owner of this [3-bedroom Carolina Colonial] built with timber likely hewn from giant trees in this prestigious [Oakmont] setting. Craftsmanship can be seen in every detail. The [high ceilings, bright rooms, and polished woodwork] echo years of gracious living. There's an exquisite [carriage house, currently used as a workshop, and a garage that will make a charming studio for an artist or writer]. Carefully preserved and updated with every modern convenience, this glorious home can be yours at far less than you would imagine [$379,500].

UR
_____
HOME REALTY

555-8200
www.ur-home.net

773

As the World Turns

things are supposed to change, but time has stood still for this [3BR, American Traditional] on a quiet, tree-lined street in [Northaven] known for its well-kept homes and lawns. There's [a covered front porch perfect for quiet summer nights, several giant trees, light, bright rooms, woodwork to envy, and totally updated systems combining the best of today with the charm of a gentler time]. Even the price seems out of the past, [$189,500].

UR
_____
HOME REALTY

555-8200
www.ur-home.net

774

Old? Yes!
Decrepit? No!

A [3BR, white clapboard, American traditional] on a quiet tree-lined street in [Westhaven]. No restoration needed. It's been lovingly maintained and is ready for your family. Offering [a friendly front porch, gleaming woodwork, high ceilings, spacious, light rooms as well as a 2-car garage with loft/studio], it's better living at a budget price: [$179,500].

UR
—————————
HOME REALTY

555-8200
www.ur-home.net

ALTERNATIVE HEADINGS

Forget about Restoration

You'll Respect Her in the Morning

775

Money Was No Object

when this [3BR, 2-bath Edwardian residence] was built on [Highland Blvd.]. The [slate entry, marble baths, exceptional woodwork, leaded glass, and magnificent fireplace] reflect success. There is also a [solarium, formal and family dining areas, 2-car garage, and 4 huge oak trees]. Available at a small fraction of reproduction cost: [$214,500].

UR
—————————
HOME REALTY

555-8200
www.ur-home.net

776

The Butler's Gone

but this [Auburn Road, 11-room Brownstone Town House] retains all of the charm of long ago with its [polished woodwork, dramatic staircase, high ceilings, sun-drenched rooms, walled garden, and carriage house]. It's been skillfully updated with all the modern conveniences and systems so as not to compromise the ambiance of a time of gracious living. Truly an impressive residence at a less than impressive [$349,500].

UR
—————————
HOME REALTY

555-8200
www.ur-home.net

777

Crystal and Old Lace

At last, the perfect place for your collectibles. A [9-room, 3BR, Edwardian Manor House with 2 baths, double garage, fenced yard, walk-up storage attic, nooks and crannies galore, polished oak, leaded glass,] and a premier [Washington Heights] address. A proper residence for those who truly understand what quality is all about. Everything far exceeds the ordinary except the price [$327,500].

UR
—————————
HOME REALTY

555-8200
www.ur-home.net

778

Age of Innocence

Nostalgic **[3BR, American classic]** with **[high ceilings, intricate molding, sitting-room, parlor, gleaming hardwoods, and 2-car carriage house]**. This light, bright home set amidst colorful plantings offers a gentler way of life at a very affordable **[$169,500]**.

UR

—————
HOME REALTY

555-8200
www.ur-home.net

779

Herbert Hoover

was President and prosperity was just around the corner when this **[3BR, 1½-bath Washington Blvd., brick and stone New England Traditional]** was new, and it has only improved with time. **[All systems have been updated including the kitchen with every conceivable built-in]**. There's **[a lovely fenced yard, 2-car garage,]** and so much more. Priced conservatively at **[$209,500]**.

UR

—————
HOME REALTY

555-8200
www.ur-home.net

780

Fiddler on the Roof

This house has tradition. Built in **[1870]**, this **[8-room, 3BR Edwardian]** masterpiece has seen America grow from the days of horse-drawn carriages to modern times. It has been home to suffragettes and Civil War veterans. The **[long, covered porch]** has heard tales of the days when the country was new, and the **[front parlor]** held many nervous young beaus who came courting. This happy home of the past has much happiness to give for your family's future. A rare bit of Americana can be yours for only **[$245,500]**.

UR

—————
HOME REALTY

555-8200
www.ur-home.net

ALTERNATIVE HEADING

History Revisited

➡ This ad sells a mood to make the home desirable.

781

Bogart and Cagney

would seem at home in this prohibition-era **[red brick Traditional]** in **[its wooded estate setting]** in **[Northridge]**. With **[3BR, 1½ baths, wide front porch, high ceilings, exquisite woodwork, and large sun-drenched rooms]**, it conveys a solid image of the past at a price to please you now: **[$169,500]**.

UR

—————
HOME REALTY

555-8200
www.ur-home.net

782

The Roaring Twenties

Rumor has it that the [2] bathtubs of this [Gatsby-era, 3-bedroom brick home] were once used to manufacture gin. If true, it's the last exciting thing that happened here. Of course, it has all the goodies of its era: [rich, solid walnut paneling, leaded glass, high ceilings,] and magnificently proportioned rooms. Definitely more the home of a successful banker than a bootlegger, it is respectfully priced at [$219,500].

UR
HOME REALTY

555-8200
www.ur-home.net

→ This ad conveys the image of a proper, solid, quality home that doesn't have a great deal of flash. This is the kind of home many buyers desire.

783

William Howard Taft Would Love the Bath

Of course, back then, he would have taken a [huge, claw-footed, cast-iron tub with sparkling brass] for granted. But what would he think about the [copper, brick, and oak kitchen with its microwave and built-in conveniences?] It would be a wonder of wonders. This [3BR] period piece has been preserved and thoughtfully updated for the family who is tired of plastic. A far better way at [$213,500].

UR
HOME REALTY

555-8200
www.ur-home.net

784

Born Again [Victorian]

Completely and lovingly restored to [1880] standards of elegance and skillfully combined with systems and conveniences of tomorrow, this [10-room, 3BR, 2½-bath] masterpiece is now ready for your adoration. Set amidst [flowering shrubs, colorful plantings, and century-old trees] on [an estate-sized lot on fashionable Newhall Street], this home offers [woodwork detailing and leaded glass that is unmatched with bay windows, wrap-around porch, high ceilings, sun-drenched rooms, and even a 2-car carriage house]; it's better than new [at half the price: $447,500].

UR
HOME REALTY

555-8200
www.ur-home.net

ALTERNATIVE HEADING

Great Dame!

785

Antiques Roadshow

would likely appraise this [9-room Eastside Victorian] for more than the [$284,000] sale price. See why. #44 at *www.ur-home.net*

UR
HOME REALTY

555-8200
www.ur-home.net

786

Restorable [Colonial]

While the [West Side] neighborhood is considered fashionable, this [3BR, 9-room Federal Colonial] with its classic lines has seen better days, probably [150] years ago. [Original detailing intact, this house appears structurally sound; however, the "modern" systems are now about 70 years old]. While still elegantly livable, you'll find much that you would want updated. It's priced far less than you would expect to pay for so prestigious a residence: [$169,500].

UR
HOME REALTY

555-8200
www.ur-home.net

ALTERNATIVE HEADINGS

Faded Glory

Faded Beauty

787

[125] Years of Potential

have been accumulating on this [Highland Blvd.] circa [1879 Victorian] masterpiece. While a little worse for wear, it's still impressive with its [7 rooms, 2 baths, high, sun-filled rooms and separate 2-car garage] set amidst [landscaping to be envied]. There is an air of gentility so necessary for sympathetic renovation. A fine home now, a grand home with your effort; proudly offered at [$139,500].

UR
HOME REALTY

555-8200
www.ur-home.net

ALTERNATIVE HEADING

[115] Years of Grime

→ This ad would attract fixer-upper buyers.

Homes, Small

Homes that have less than three rooms suitable for bedrooms are usually regarded as small homes, and they often sell at significantly lower prices than larger homes located in the same neighborhood.

Singles, couples, and single parents are typically attracted to smaller homes, but be careful not to write ads that may exclude other potential buyers. Of course, careful and creative ad building may still target specific buyers without alienating other potential buyers.

Many of the ads in Chapter 7 (Condominiums and Cooperatives) can also be tailored for smaller homes.

788

Writers and Artists

A [2BR, 1½-bath English Cottage] set amidst [giant boulders and soaring pines] just [5 minutes] from [Santa Fe] on a quiet [½-acre] site. There's a [loft studio, sun-drenched rooms, and river-rock fireplace plus every modern amenity]. Truly tonic for the creative mind at just [$179,500].

UR

HOME REALTY

555-8200
www.ur-home.net

ALTERNATIVE HEADINGS

Attention Hedonists!

Enchanted Cottage

Hansel and Gretel Cottage

789

No Room for In-Laws

There's [a master suite, nursery, huge living room, fireplace, garden patio, 2½-car garage, and lovely landscaping], but this picture-perfect [white Cape Cod in Oakhill Heights] has no guest room. Guess they'll have to stay at a motel. It's yours, with this one fault, at [$179,500].

UR

HOME REALTY

555-8200
www.ur-home.net

 This ad makes a virtue out of a 2-bedroom home. An opposite approach would be the following.

ALTERNATIVE HEADING

Put Mother In a Home
There's [a master suite, sewing room . . .

790

Writer's Studio

This is the perfect spot for a writer or artist. There is a [massive living room/ dining area with room for bookcases, easels, or even a grand piano]. The bedroom is [large enough for a king-sized bed as well as a desk. You'll love the orchard-stone fireplace, delightful dining patio, and colorful garden. The garage can be converted to a separate studio or guest suite]. This is a home created for your very special needs at an amazingly affordable [$99,500].

UR
HOME REALTY

555-8200
www.ur-home.net

→ This ad gives a one-bedroom home desirability. It is aimed at single people who regard themselves as artistic.

ALTERNATIVE HEADINGS

The Great American Novel
could well be written in this perfect writer's hideaway . . .

Love Size?
One large bedroom on this . . .

Home Alone?
Then you will want to see this 1BR . . .

Think Small

Studio/Home

Honeymoon Cottage

Beginner's Luck
This is the perfect spot for newlyweds . . .

791

Goose Bumps All Over

said [Mrs. Callahan] of our office after viewing this [2BR, ivy-covered cottage secluded in its woodland setting. Snuggle up to watch the flames and hear the crackle of burning wood in the stone fireplace. With its rich wood paneling, leaded-glass entry,] and ambiance of comfort and quality, this home will seem a fulfillment of all your fantasies at a price bound to excite [$137,500].

UR
HOME REALTY

555-8200
www.ur-home.net

792

Think Small

This [stone and cedar] residence offers you [an opulent master suite with whirlpool bath sheathed in tile, an open concept living area with soaring ceilings, a wall of glass overlooking the walled garden,] and a whole lot more. Good things do come in small packages and the price matches at [$137,500].

UR
HOME REALTY

555-8200
www.ur-home.net

793

Why Pay for Big

when you can own the ultimate in luxury at a size that suits your lifestyle? A [Tuscany Mediterranean] in [Walnut Grove] with [a huge master suite plus home office/guest suite, 2 marble baths, 10-foot ceiling, magnificent fireplace, open concept for entertaining, and glass walls opening to the sumptuous hot spa, dining patio, and colorful garden]. Complete with [2-car garage], it proves that the best can be found in smaller packages at a realistic [$249,500].

UR
HOME REALTY
555-8200
www.ur-home.net

ALTERNATIVE HEADINGS

Mini-Château

Mini-Mansion
Why pay for BIG when you can own . . .

794

Why Pay For 3

when 2 bedrooms will do. See this [Northside sophisticated] residence that can be your future at just [$187,900]. #11A at *www.ur-home.net*

UR
HOME REALTY
555-8200
www.ur-home.net

CHAPTER TWENTY-FOUR

Horse Property

To horse owners, or buyers with a desire to own horses, a place to stable their animals is every bit as important—and in some cases more important—than the homes they live in.

Ads for horse property can be written whenever a property has the appropriate room and meets the specific zoning requirements for horses, even if the property does not currently have the facilities to house these animals. The following ads were written to appeal to "horse people." Please note that the headings specifically indicate that the ads are for horse property, but certainly another feature can be emphasized in a heading when a newspaper has a separate section for horse property.

795

A Horse of Course

should go in the [2-stall stable with tack room] that comes with this [2½]-acre ranch. The [California-style, 3BR, 2-bath ranch] home set [beneath a giant oak] seems to blend into the landscape. You'll love the [bright family room with its native stone fireplace and rich wood paneling as well as the brick and tile kitchen with room for an entire roundup crew]. [Sparkling white board fences and an irrigated pasture] make this the place where you'll want to hang your spurs. Better hurry at [$398,500].

UR
HOME REALTY
555-8200
www.ur-home.net

796

Where's the Pony?

your children will cry when they see the [4-stall red barn] that comes with this ranch-perfect [brick and cedar, 3BR, 1½-bath home] packaged on [5] beautiful acres. The home has [central air, stone fireplace, ranch-sized kitchen and country vistas]. Blue-jean priced at [$189,500].

UR
HOME REALTY
555-8200
www.ur-home.net

ALTERNATIVE HEADING

Buy Me A Pony!

797

Awaits Your Horse

[A red 4-stall barn, pipe corral and watered pasture] on a [2-acre] spread [just west of Carriage Falls] is more than any horse could hope for. There's also a [3-year-old, 3BR brick and redwood Ranch] with [2 baths, family room, ranch office, and 2-car garage plus workshop]. A great place for 2-legged and 4-legged critters at a realistic [$284,500].

UR
_____
H O M E   R E A L T Y

555-8200
www.ur-home.net

ALTERNATIVE AD

Awaits Your Horse

Barn, corral, pasture, and almost-new [3BR] home on [12 acres] for [$284,500]. #12 at www.ur-home.net

UR
_____
H O M E   R E A L T Y

555-8200
www.ur-home.net

ALTERNATIVE HEADINGS

Happy Horse

Make Your Horse Happy

Whoa! Nellie!

Get a Horse!

Animal House

Animal Planet

798

Buy the Horse [$284,500] Get the Home FREE!

That's right, a [like-new, 3BR, 2½-bath brick Carolina Ranch] on [2 fenced acres] including [a 3-double-stall horse barn] comes with [a well-mannered, 6-year-old quarter-horse]. This home offers a [huge tiled family room, movie-perfect master suite, home office/study, and a 3-car garage with workshop]. Don't hold your horses, act now at [$229,500].

UR
_____
H O M E   R E A L T Y

555-8200
www.ur-home.net

➡ The owner must be willing to include a horse with the sale for you to use this ad approach. A reverse approach would be the following:

ALTERNATIVE HEADING

A Free Horse

goes with this . . .

799

Hold Your Horses

in the [3 corrals and quaint western-style barn with 6 stalls]. This [20]-acre ranch [adjoins miles of riding trails] and comes complete with a [3BR, 2½-bath ranch] home that will delight any cowboy or cowgirl. It has every modern convenience set in a down-home decor of [rich wood paneling and antique rose brick]. It's the life you deserve at [$368,500].

UR
_____
H O M E   R E A L T Y

555-8200
www.ur-home.net

800

Keep a Cow

or horses in the [3-stall red barn] that comes with this [sprawling 3BR, 2-bath Colorado Ranch on 2 acres just minutes from Weston Center]. It's a mighty purty spread with its [white board fencing]. This [tastefully decorated home offers spacious sun-filled rooms and a front porch made for relaxation after your day on the range]. Call quickly, as some city slicker will likely try to beat you to it because it's priced at only [$279,500].

UR
HOME REALTY
555-8200
www.ur-home.net

801

Cowboy—Cowgirl

If you love the smell of horses, you'll be ecstatic about this [3BR, 2-bath] ranch home on [5] acres. [Zoned for 10 horses, there's even a Dutch barn with 4 double stalls, a large tack room and 2 corrals]. The whole package is tied together with [white-board ranch fencing]. A "mighty purty spread." Offered at less than the price of a city home, [$297,500].

UR
HOME REALTY
555-8200
www.ur-home.net

ALTERNATIVE HEADING

[Appaloosas] Lived Here

802

Camels, Llamas, Buffalo,

horses, or just lots of kids on this [fenced and cross-fenced, 4-acre ranch] in [the Midland School District]. There's a [newer Montana-style] home with [3BR, 2 baths, ranch office or guest room, family room with Western stone fireplace, covered patio, 2½-car garage, 4-stall barn with tack room and shower, and a pipe corral]. A mighty purty spread at [$279,500].

UR
HOME REALTY
555-8200
www.ur-home.net

803

Horse Manure

not included with the [3-stall] horse barn that comes with this [Colorado-style, 3BR, 2½-bath ranch] home set on [5] acres only [40 minutes] from [the city]. The house has [every conceivable built-in, a screened porch, a 2-car garage, and central air]. [Fenced and cross-fenced], you'll want to put your brand on this spread at [$219,500].

UR
HOME REALTY
555-8200
www.ur-home.net

804

A Horse and Pony Show

can be yours as the owner of your own **[3-acre]** ranch complete with **[a three-stall barn, tack room, corral, white board fencing, watered pasture, and New Mexican-style ranch house that looks to be right out of House and Garden]**. There's a bright feeling with its **[3BR, 2½ baths, high ceilings, spacious, sun-filled rooms, and open floor plan. The country kitchen has a storage pantry plus every convenience you would want. There's even a den/ranch office and an oversized double garage]**. This is not the time to hold your horses because it's priced to gallop off at **[$189,500]**.

UR
HOME REALTY

555-8200
www.ur-home.net

Investment/
Income Property

Buyers of residential rental property are motivated by a number of financial opportunities: locating a new source of income, the potential for the property to appreciate in value, and the tax advantages that come with ownership.

The most common residential income property is the duplex home, although a single property can contain hundreds of units. Most of the ads in this section have been written for residential income property. Ads for other types of income property can be prepared by using language from the Ad Generator at the back of this book.

It is important to note that buyers who express an interest in residing in one of the property's units will also have the same concerns and desires as any other homeowner.

805

The Color of Money

If [net spendable income] is important, you'll want to see and buy this [brick 8-unit building that seldom has a vacancy]. The bottom line is profit and the price: [$429,000].

UR
HOME REALTY
555-8200
www.ur-home.net

ALTERNATIVE HEADING

Money in Your Pocket

806

Forget Potential [10] Units

These [6-year-old, low-maintenance, brick 2BR, 2-bath units] show [10%] cash-on-cash return RIGHT NOW with a minimum down payment and, because of tax shelter, it's almost tax-free. It doesn't get any better than this at [$620,000].

UR
HOME REALTY
555-8200
www.ur-home.net

ALTERNATIVE HEADING

Positive Cash Flow

807

Smells Like Money
[12] Units [$840,000]

Fully rented [with mostly long-term tenants at rents that have not been increased in 4 years. 12 garages and no deferred maintenance] make this a MUST SEE.

UR
HOME REALTY
555-8200
www.ur-home.net

808

Nothing But Money
[16 Units [6] × Gross]

[Low vacancy, professionally managed. All 2BR units in elevator building with parking that's walking-close to Civic Center]. Starker Exchange welcome. A definite best buy at [$920,000].

UR
HOME REALTY
555-8200
www.ur-home.net

➤ Starker Exchange benefits the buyer by deferring taxes on income from the sale of other income or investment property.

809

Wanted!
Future Millionaire

[Low-vacancy, low-maintenance 2BR brick units at below-market rents and close to hospital and university].

[16 Units 6.4 × Gross]

With [less than 15%] down, it will buy itself plus give you a tax-sheltered cash flow. A wealth builder will buy it fast at [$248,000].

UR
HOME REALTY
555-8200
www.ur-home.net

ALTERNATIVE HEADING

Raisable Rents

810

[$100,000] =
[$1,000,000]

That's right, [$100,000] down payment on [38 brick, 2BR units] will give you an investment that will not only buy itself but give you a tax shelter and a hedge against inflation. In the low-vacancy [Mercy Hospital area], it's an opportunity that deserves your immediate investigation.

UR
HOME REALTY
555-8200
www.ur-home.net

➤ This ad very simply emphasizes the value of leverage.

811

Wall-to-Wall Income
[18] Units [6] × [Gross]

[All 2BR in a low-maintenance elevator building, south of Highway 17]. The books are open to you. Full price [$595,000]. Try [15%] down.

UR
HOME REALTY
555-8200
www.ur-home.net

812

Easy Money

Just collect the rents. [Low-maintenance brick building in a great rental area].

[24] Units, [$630,000]

Will show positive cash flow. Try [10%] down.

UR
HOME REALTY
555-8200
www.ur-home.net

813

Rake It In
[12] Units [$490,000]

With low vacancy, great rental area [near hospitals and university], [raisable rents and no deferred maintenance], it's definitely see-worthy.

UR
HOME REALTY
555-8200
www.ur-home.net

814

[14%] Cash-on-Cash

Plus tax-sheltered income. If the bottom line is important to you, check out these [24 2BR West Side brick units]. Try [$100,000] down with a price of [$480,000].

UR
HOME REALTY
555-8200
www.ur-home.net

815

Sccess!

We can't spell it without "U." You must analyze an investment and act if you are to ensure your future. We have a [12-unit building] in a desirable rental area [with raisable rents] that offers an exceptional opportunity with [less than 10% down] and a total price of [$480,000]. Call now, analyze, and act.

UR
HOME REALTY
555-8200
www.ur-home.net

816

Convertible [16] Units

All [2BR] with [parking] in [the low-vacancy Mercy Hospital area]. Collect the rents or convert to [condominiums]. The choice of two worlds at a make-sense price of [$520,000].

UR
HOME REALTY
555-8200
www.ur-home.net

→ The approach above can be used where condominium conversions are possible.

817

Keep Your Bankers Happy

Keep your money in low-interest or no-interest accounts so they can lend it out at high interest. Don't even think about the [10% tax-sheltered cash-on-cash return with about 20% down] that you can get by buying [16 2BR, low-vacancy units just 2 blocks from Mercy Hospital]. Forget about an inflation hedge or letting the investment pay for itself. If your bankers read this ad, they might be the ones who buy it at [$590,000].

UR
HOME REALTY
555-8200
www.ur-home.net

➡ For a different approach to the same property, see the following ad.

818

Ask Your Accountant

If a [10% tax-sheltered cash-on-cash return] makes sense. Ask about the benefits of leverage in paying just [20%] down and having the property pay for itself. Ask about real estate as an inflation hedge. Then ask if these

[16 2BR] Units

with [a low vacancy record just 2 blocks from Mercy Hospital] make sense at [$590,000].

UR
HOME REALTY
555-8200
www.ur-home.net

819

Tenants Pay Mortgage

while you collect the rents on this [brick 4-plex] in a prime rental area close to [downtown]. It's available with excellent financing at a price that demands your immediate action: [$244,500].

UR
HOME REALTY
555-8200
www.ur-home.net

820

Be the Landlord [8 Units]

[Low-maintenance brick] apartment in a great [West Side] area with [low rents and long-term tenants]. Priced [6] × gross at [$435,000] [to settle estate]. Delay and be sorry.

UR
HOME REALTY
555-8200
www.ur-home.net

821

Opport-you-nity [4] Units [$289,500] [Low-vacancy 2BR] units [6½] × Gross

[Walking-close to university]. Unusual circumstances allow this offering, so call now or send regrets.

UR
HOME REALTY
555-8200
www.ur-home.net

822

Live Free Almost

Let your tenant make most of the mortgage payment while you enjoy the good life in this [3BR brick duplex] in a desirable [North Side] neighborhood. [Quality landscaping, garage, formal dining room, built-ins, and separate utilities] make this a best buy. Call now and ask about the great low-down financing. Full price only [$179,500].

UR
HOME REALTY
555-8200
www.ur-home.net

823

Two-Family Portrait

A truly luxury [stone] duplex with [3BR, 1½-bath owner's unit and 2BR rental unit, double garage, fenced yard, built-ins, and separate utilities] in a desirable [West Side] neighborhood. We can put you in the picture for a remarkably low down payment and a price of [$189,500].

UR
HOME REALTY
555-8200
www.ur-home.net

824

Upstairs/Downstairs Duplex

These [brick 3BR, 1½-bath units] near [Wilson Park] have [formal and family dining areas, window-wrapped living areas, gleaming oak woodwork, split basement with separate utilities, 2-car garage, and fenced yard]. Enjoy the feeling of single-family living while your tenant makes [most of your payments]. With low-down financing, it makes dollars and sense at [$169,400].

UR
HOME REALTY
555-8200
www.ur-home.net

ALTERNATIVE HEADINGS

Dynamic Duo!

Doubles

2 for 1

Duplex [Wilson Park]

Exacta Two

winning units . . . (for 3 units, your heading could be, "Trifecta.")

825

Not Much Class

but the income is great. A [5-store strip center] with [long-term] tenants in a [high traffic] area. With [a low] down payment and a full price of [$750,000] you can ensure your retirement. Call now for complete information.

UR
HOME REALTY
555-8200
www.ur-home.net

826

Partner-Perfect

Two joined [3BR, 1½-bath West End] luxury units ideal for owner/occupants. With [high ceilings, light, bright, and spacious rooms, new kitchens/baths, 2-car garage plus 2 parking spots,] and low-down financing, the price makes sense at [$220,000].

UR
HOME REALTY
555-8200
www.ur-home.net

827

Pride of Ownership?

You won't show off this [warehouse] to your friends. The only thing your friends will envy is the positive cash flow it generates. If you are able to invest [$100,000] and a [$700,000] purchase price doesn't scare you, call now for details on an exceptional investment.

UR
HOME REALTY
555-8200
www.ur-home.net

CHAPTER TWENTY-SIX

Location

It has often been said that the three most important factors in purchasing a home are "location, location, and location." Location is a primary determinant of value and appreciation. If a property is in a highly desirable area, this should be emphasized in an ad, preferably in its heading. If a newspaper categorizes property by location, don't repeat the location in your ad heading, as this serves no purpose.

You can also emphasize the proximity of a home to schools, hospitals, large employers, and recreational facilities, such as golf courses. "Location" can be combined with other features such as size, price, financing, and so on, when creating an effective ad headline.

828

Almost [Beverly Hills] Half the Price [$879,500]

From the neighborhood, you would swear it's [Beverly Hills] without the high prices [and taxes]. A [3BR, 2½-bath, 3-car-garage Mediterranean Villa] on [an estate-sized lot with pool, spa and magnificent landscaping]. For a home to be proud of, call:

UR
HOME REALTY
555-8200
www.ur-home.net

ALTERNATIVE HEADING

Beverly Hills Almost

829

When [Beverly Hills] Won't Do

A quiet enclave of estate homes [nestled in the foothills] and secluded from the world. [A long driveway lined with colorful plantings and massive oaks] leads to a [monumental Colonial masterpiece with soaring columns and covered portico]. Offering [14 rooms, 4BR, 4½ baths,] and every amenity imaginable, it will be envied by all but its owner. Proudly offered at [$2.4 million].

UR
HOME REALTY
555-8200
www.ur-home.net

→ By using an extremely desirable area in the heading, the location is made to seem a step above it. The actual location need not be specifically stated unless it will excite the reader.

830

Ontogeny Recapitulates Phylogeny

If you understand this, you'll love living [walking-close] to [State University] in this [3BR, brick Traditional] at [$219,500]. Check it #27 at *www.ur-home.net*

UR
_____
HOME REALTY
555-8200
www.ur-home.net

831

Gotta Sell [Beverly Drive]

Take advantage and buy this [3BR, 2-bath, 3-year-old Executive Colonial] with [sun-drenched rooms, marble fireplace, family room with wet bar, formal and family dining areas, master suite that will make you want to stay in bed, breakfast patio, 3-car garage, and exquisite landscaping]. A rare opportunity at [$289,900].

UR
_____
HOME REALTY
555-8200
www.ur-home.net

832

[Westwood] Wannabe

Well, your dream can come true. A [3BR, 2-bath Colonial] not just in [Westwood] but the finest area of [Westwood], priced to be sold tomorrow at [$287,500].

UR
_____
HOME REALTY
555-8200
www.ur-home.net

833

[Westwood] [$237,500]

It's true. You can own a [3BR, 2-bath Pennsylvania Dutch Colonial] with [hardwood floors, brick mantled fireplace, formal and family dining areas, screened summer porch, delightful dining patio, 2-car garage,] and much more in a location you only dreamed of. At this price, you'll have to act fast.

UR
_____
HOME REALTY
555-8200
www.ur-home.net

ALTERNATIVE HEADINGS

[Westwood] Schools [$237,500]

[Westwood] Address [$237,500]

[Westwood] Under [$250,000]

➤ If the location is highly desirable and it is not used in the newspaper ad classification, it should be in the heading. If the price seems low for the area, add it to the heading as we have done in the ad above.

834

Work at [Norton]?

Then you can live only [8 minutes] away. A [3BR, 1½-bath Cape Cod with a 2-car garage] on [a quiet, tree-lined street], and it's [in great condition with hardwood floors, fireplace, formal and family dining areas, full basement, fenced yard,] and more. With a variety of low-down or no-down payment plans, it's available right now at [$149,500].

UR
HOME REALTY
555-8200
www.ur-home.net

836

The Only Modest Home

in [Westwood], an area of luxury residences that cost far more than this [3BR, 2-bath, 2-car-garage Cape Cod]. It offers [finished basement fitness center plus photographer's darkroom, home office/music room, French doors, fireplace, garden patio, and landscaping that rivals any of the neighbors'] at a fraction of the cost: [$274,500].

UR
HOME REALTY
555-8200
www.ur-home.net

835

Ask the Neighbors

what they think about the neighborhood. You'll find friendly people who think they live in the nicest block on the nicest street in [Ridgeway Heights]. You'll also find a [3BR, 2-bath, 2½-car garage, 4-year-old New Brunswick Colonial] with [washed oak cabinetry, family room with orchard-stone fireplace, private home office, sumptuous master suite,] and everything you expect plus more. Don't tell the neighbors the price because they likely paid more than just [$329,500].

UR
HOME REALTY
555-8200
www.ur-home.net

837

Car-Free Living [$139,500]

Walking close to shopping [and schools], this [charming 2-BR American Bungalow has public transportation practically at the door]. You could rent the [2-car] garage or convert it to a studio. The home features [hardwood floors, exquisite detailing, a bright country kitchen, formal dining room with built-in buffet, a lazy-day front porch plus room for your own garden]. If you are looking for a comfortable and uncomplicated lifestyle call!

UR
HOME REALTY
555-8200
www.ur-home.net

ALTERNATIVE HEADINGS

Are We There Yet?
Live just minutes from . . .

Born To Shop

838

Street Smart?

Then you know that [Lewis Lane] is the most desirable street in [Westchester], with its manicured lawns and fine homes. This [young 3BR, 2½-bath Tudor] compares with the finest, offering [circle drive, home office/music room, 40-foot flagstone veranda, rose garden,] and all the embellishments you would expect in a premier residence. Unusual circumstances allow this offering at [$398,500].

UR
HOME REALTY

555-8200
www.ur-home.net

840

Forget the Burbs!

You can have it all just minutes from [the Civic Center] in [an enclave of quality residences]. A [3BR, 2-bath Brownstone] with [extra space to spare, private walled garden, 2-car garage, electronic security,] and more quality features than you can imagine. A proper residence for those who wants the convenience and amenities of city life. Proudly offered at [$197,500].

UR
HOME REALTY

555-8200
www.ur-home.net

839

Don't Ride—Walk

everywhere from this centrally located [3BR, 1½-bath Victorian] with [intricate detailing, bay window, walk-around covered porch, gleaming hardwood, high ceilings, sun-drenched rooms, nooks and crannies for collectibles, full basement, 2-car garage, and private garden]. A home for a city person at [$147,500].

UR
HOME REALTY

555-8200
www.ur-home.net

841

Stop Commuting—
Enjoy

this [Brownstone, 3-story town house] that's [walking-close to the Civic Center]. You will love the [rich paneling and detail work, high ceilings, 3 fireplaces, and high-walled garden with its delightful dining patio]. A sanctuary from the city in the city, available at a reasonable [$219,500].

UR
HOME REALTY

555-8200
www.ur-home.net

842

Nothing to Expose

The National Enquirer would never do a story about **[Colton Glen]**. There are no hidden secrets about this genuinely friendly neighborhood where the Little League is more important than the tabloids. If you can live without scandalous happenings, we have a **[6-year-old brick Traditional Ranch]** on **[a large corner lot]** that has **[10-foot ceilings, sun-drenched family room with fireplace, family and formal dining areas, home office/computer center, breakfast patio, 2½-car garage, and landscaping to be envied]**. The price, a very affordable **[$267,500]**.

UR
HOME REALTY

555-8200
www.ur-home.net

844

Graffiti-Free [Middleton]

When children play tag here, they're not using spray paint. The schools still insist on homework, and life revolves around family and friends. We may be dull, but to us dull is a virtue. If old-fashioned values are of interest to you, we have a **[3BR, 1½-bath, white clapboard Traditional on almost ½ acre with hardwood floors, garage, family-sized garden, apple and plum trees, and it's walking-close to schools and shopping]**. Small-town priced at **[$187,500]**.

UR
HOME REALTY

555-8200
www.ur-home.net

→ The ad above is effective in a big city paper selling a small town property.

843

Escape City Taxes

Great schools, quiet streets, and tranquil parks in the commuting-close **[Village of Blue Mound]**. A **[2,200-square-foot, 3-year-old, 3BR, 2½-bath Carolina Ranch with 10-foot ceilings, family room, fireplace, home office, whitewashed oak cabinetry, rock-scaped patio, and a 3-car garage]**. It's small-town priced at **[$235,000]**.

UR
HOME REALTY

555-8200
www.ur-home.net

ALTERNATIVE HEADING

Be Among the First

to discover the great schools . . .

845

Walk to the Country

from this **[3BR, 1½-bath, brick American Traditional]** on its large garden lot in **[Winston]**. You'll love **[the "Welcome Home" front porch, hardwood floors, gleaming woodwork, formal and family dining areas, sun-filled rooms, and garage/workshop]**. It's a friendly home at a very friendly price: **[$168,500]**.

UR
HOME REALTY

555-8200
www.ur-home.net

846

The House on the Hill

can be yours. With [3BR, 2 baths, 2-car garage, family room, fireplace, full basement, and landscaping to be envied], it's a very special place for just [$192,500].

UR
_____
HOME REALTY
555-8200
www.ur-home.net

847

On a Grassy Knoll

set back on [5 magnificent acres] is a [young 3BR, 2½-bath Colonial] that seems as one with its natural surroundings. Featuring [gleaming hardwood floors, sun-drenched country kitchen, home office/music room, two magnificent fireplaces, 2½-car garage, and paved drive], this is a special opportunity for your family at [$349,500].

UR
_____
HOME REALTY
555-8200
www.ur-home.net

848

Standin' on the Corner

in [Cloverland Estates], a [3BR white clapboard Traditional]. Set amidst [flowering shrubs, manicured hedges, and magnificent maples] with [double garage, full basement, and chef's-delight kitchen], it's not going to be vacant long at [$98,500].

UR
_____
HOME REALTY
555-8200
www.ur-home.net

849

The Young and the Restless

will appreciate the [Westhill] setting for this [3BR, 2½-bath Riviera Mediterranean] that's just minutes from [the Orchard Mall, fine dining, courts, and golf courses]. Offering [a spacious, sun-drenched open floor plan, family room, 2½-car garage, and landscaping second to none], it makes a bold statement as to what life is all about at a surprisingly modest [$279,500].

UR
_____
HOME REALTY
555-8200
www.ur-home.net

850

[10] Reasons To Move

to [Morton Grove] and location is just one of them. The other 9 are the rooms in this [3BR, 2-bath, brick Edwardian] residence with [a huge bay window, gleaming hardwood, sun-drenched rooms, landscaping of your dreams, 2-car garage,] and so much more. An [11th] reason is the price [$238,700].

UR
_____
HOME REALTY
555-8200
www.ur-home.net

CHAPTER **TWENTY-SEVEN**

Lots

In writing an ad for a lot, try to put yourself in the shoes of the buyer: What features would be of interest to that person, besides price? One or more of the following attributes are key features that could be emphasized in a lot advertisement:

- Access (Note the presence of a paved road if many other lots are not on paved roads.)

- Utilities (but only if nearby lots do not offer the same utilities—sewer, water, electricity, gas, phone, or cable TV)

- Water frontage (if applicable)

- Highway frontage (commercial)

- View

- Trees (Wooded lots are desirable.)

- Slope (While lots with steep slopes are normally less expensive because of their greater construction costs, many buyers like lots where split-level or open-basement plans are possible.)

- Zoning (if other than single-family residential)

- Permits (If engineering, approval, or building permits for a particular use have been obtained, say so in the ad.)

- Size (This is very important for other than single-family residential lots. If a residential lot is larger than average, emphasize its size.)

- Terms (If a lot can be purchased with terms or if the owner will subordinate to a construction loan, point this out.)

When a lot ad is under the newspaper category "lots," remember: Do not repeat the fact that you are advertising a lot in the ad. For lots other than single-family residential, see the Ad Generator.

851

Your Piece of the Block

and a fine piece it is. Over [¼ acre] on a quiet street amidst luxury homes in the prestigious community of [Hearthridge] known for its parks and fine schools. Because of unusual circumstances, this site for future happiness is available for only [$89,500].

UR
HOME REALTY

555-8200
www.ur-home.net

ALTERNATIVE HEADING

$89,500—[Hearthridge]

852

Dirt for Sale

[¼-acre] of it [just off Clancy Lane] in a neighborhood of [impressive new homes], and we're throwing in [some magnificent pine trees, a huge boulder, postcard view] plus some ideas for your dream home. They don't make 'em like this anymore, so it's first-come, first-served at [$67,500].

UR
HOME REALTY

555-8200
www.ur-home.net

ALTERNATIVE HEADING

Dirt Cheap!

853

A Lot To Love

The perfect site for your future. This [½-acre in the estate section of Weston Hills] has a view that must be experienced. Landscaping is courtesy of Mother Nature [with giant beech and chestnut trees]. [Utilities are in and] it's ready for you at [$79,500].

UR
HOME REALTY

555-8200
www.ur-home.net

ALTERNATIVE HEADINGS

[Wild Raspberries]

are growing on the site for your . . .

Home For Your Home

If more than one lot were available, you could use headings such as the following.

Lots of Lots

Neighborhood Ready

Tomorrow's Neighborhood

854

The National Enquirer

doesn't know about this spectacular piece of dirt we latched onto [in the quiet, suburban community of Walthaven] among [well-kept homes and manicured lawns]. It's really big, [almost ¼-acre], and it's ready for you to dig into for your dream home. Scoop the rest at [$87,500].

UR
HOME REALTY

555-8200
www.ur-home.net

855

A Lot Less

Because of unusual circumstances, a ['/4-acre, builder-ready site] with [several large maple trees] that's [adjacent to Woodley Heights] can be purchased [with a very low down payment] at just [$64,500].

UR
_____
H O M E   R E A L T Y

555-8200
www.ur-home.net

ALTERNATIVE HEADINGS

Zoned [R-3]

All Approvals

[9] Units Possible

856

Mountain Goat Sanctuary?

What do we do with an [oversized, practically perpendicular lot on McLeon Blvd.]? [Mrs. Smith] of our office, who's afraid of heights, refuses to show it. Of course [she] doesn't like showing 2-story homes either. The view is spectacular, but it's definitely not for the buyer who walks in his or her sleep. The price, however, is not steep at [$49,500].

UR
_____
H O M E   R E A L T Y

555-8200
www.ur-home.net

→ The humorous ad above for a steep lot will stimulate the interest of readers.

Mobile Homes

Mobile homes differ from other housing in that a mobile home is typically located on an area of leased land within a park. The desirability of a particular park, including its amenities and its rental fees, are highly important considerations for the purchaser. Parks are rated by a Woodall's rating system based on the amenities offered. While 5-star parks are rated the highest, both 4-star and 5-star parks are considered superior parks, and their ratings would be important to many buyers.

If a mobile home is to be sold with land, this is a very attractive feature that should be highlighted in your ad, as is the size of the mobile home, especially if it is a double-wide or triple-wide unit.

Certain brands of mobile homes have a quality image and are important to purchasers familiar with mobile homes. However, the brand of mobile home is probably less of a priority for first-time buyers.

Mobile home ads are generally located under a designated category in newspapers. If such a category does not exist, be sure to clearly state that you are advertising a mobile home. While the mobile home industry prefers the designation "manufactured housing," readers are far more familiar with "mobile home."

857

Less Than a Car [$18,900]

buys you a [3BR home] in a delightful [West Side] park [with low-low space rent]. It's move-in ready [with appliances], and it's yours with almost no down payment but call now!

UR
H O M E   R E A L T Y

555-8200
www.ur-home.net

858

Heaven on Wheels

Well, not exactly. The wheels have been removed on this [4-year-old, 1,820-foot triple-wide] in a [4-star, rent-controlled park]. There are [2BR plus music room/guest room, both formal and intimate dining areas, screened lanai, and huge carport]. With every upgrade imaginable, it really must be seen to conceive of what you will receive for [$79,500].

UR
H O M E   R E A L T Y

555-8200
www.ur-home.net

859

Big as a House

[28 × 48, 3BR, 2-bath, screened porch, carport, all appliances and it's 6 years new] in desirable [Clinton Estates].

[$67,500]

Ask us about our unbelievable financing.

UR
HOME REALTY
555-8200
www.ur-home.net

ALTERNATIVE HEADING

You Won't Believe

it really is a mobile home . . .

860

W-I-D-E

[Triple]-wide [1,850]-square-foot, [3]BR, [2-]bath with [screened lanai, double carport, and storage] in [Westward Village]. Save BIG at: [$59,500].

UR
HOME REALTY
555-8200
www.ur-home.net

ALTERNATIVE HEADINGS

[36 × 42] Triple

[5] Star Park—[Triple Wide]

861

[$189] Space Rent

In a [tree-shaded] park in [Newberry Heights]. You'll have [2BR plus studio/ guest room, 1½ baths, all appliances including washer/dryer plus a covered carport, and a storage shed] for only [$24,900].

UR
HOME REALTY
555-8200
www.ur-home.net

ALTERNATIVE HEADING

Low Space Rent—[$24,900]

This is a good approach for a single-wide in an older, low-rent park.

Lucky 55!

You're eligible to become the owner of this [3BR, 2-bath double-wide] in a [4-star, rent-controlled, adult park] in desirable [Westmoreland] with resort-like facilities. It won't last long at [$59,500].

862

UR
HOME REALTY
555-8200
www.ur-home.net

863

Why Pay

high space rents when you can own the land with a [3BR, 2-bath double-wide with double carport, patio, and shed] in desirable [Walden Woods]. It's going to sell fast at [$64,500].

UR
HOME REALTY

555-8200
www.ur-home.net

ALTERNATIVE HEADINGS

You Own the Land

with this [3BR] . . .

No Park Rent

You own the land with . . .

[24 × 50] Rent Stopper

You own the land with . . .

864

Rent Controlled

Space rent in this [4-star park] in [Weston Hills] is just one advantage of this [3BR, 2-bath, 1,820-square-foot, 5-year-old Rolla home] has to offer. There's [a huge screened Florida room, double carport with storage wall, plus it's only steps from pool and recreation areas]. Check the others out first and you'll realize it's a bargain, if it's still available, at [$69,500].

UR
HOME REALTY

555-8200
www.ur-home.net

CHAPTER TWENTY-NINE

Negative Ads

This chapter deals with negative ads that advise readers not to do something. These ads tell the reader what is wrong with a property, why they won't like it, or why it won't suit their needs. Like fixer-upper ads, covered in Chapter 10, negative ads tend to ellicit a large number of inquiries and responses. Informing potential buyers why they don't want, or can't use, something is a challenge many individuals find hard to resist.

At one time, real estate brokers took the position that if you couldn't say anything nice about a feature or property, don't say anything. While taking a positive approach is effective, it took a British real estate agent to show us that very negative ads could also provide extremely positive results.

Roy Brooks, a London, England, real estate agent in the 1950s and 1960s, developed a cult following because his ads showed the world that real estate could be fun and that agents need not abandon their sense of humor. A master of the negative or adverse ad, he thoroughly trashed properties in a manner that at the time was completely unique. His extreme negativism resulted in queues of customers awaiting the opportunity to both view and buy his listed properties. He has been credited as having single-handedly caused the renovation of its crumbling Pimlico and Chelsea neighborhoods by luring well-to-do buyers to these areas. "Brothel in Pimlico," the classified ad which opens this chapter, is an example of one of Roy Brooks's ads.

Brothel in Pimlico

WANTED: Someone with taste, means, and a stomach strong enough to buy this erstwhile house of ill-repute in Pimlico. It is untouched by the 20th Century as far as convenience for even the basic human decencies is concerned. Although it reeks of damp or worse, the plaster is coming off the walls, and daylight peeps through a hole in the roof, it is still habitable judging by the bed of rags, fag ends, and empty bottles in one corner. Plenty of scope for the socially aspiring to express their decorative taste and get their abode in 'The Glossy' and nothing to stop them putting Westminster on their notepaper. 10 rather unpleasant rooms with slimy backyard. £15,000.—Roy Brooks

865

Small and Dreary

Without a view but at [$69,900], this [2BR Westside unit] is a must see. #44 at *www.ur-home.net*

UR

HOME REALTY

555-8200
www.ur-home.net

866

Low Self-Esteem?

This [3BR, 2-bath Quaker Colonial in Ridgefield Heights] is too good for you. You don't deserve to have [your own home office, family room, river rock fireplace, garden patio, landscaping that's picture-perfect, or a 3-car garage]. Don't think you should have it just because it's priced at only [$264,500].

UR

HOME REALTY

555-8200
www.ur-home.net

867

Do You Hate People?

If so, you'll detest living in this [3BR, 2-bath Colonial Ranch] in the friendly community of [Windsor Pines]. Neighbors will greet you by name, and you'll be invited to block parties and Little League games. Anyway, you don't need a house with a [large family room, formal and intimate dining areas, garden patio, and 3-car garage]. Don't even ask about the price [$197,500].

UR

HOME REALTY

555-8200
www.ur-home.net

868

You'll Hate It!

A [3BR, 2-bath, 2-car-garage Contemporary] on [a tree-lined street in Wilson Heights]. The [floor plan is inconvenient, decorating is awful, and little concrete animals clutter the landscaping]. On the plus side is [location, it appears well-built, it's only 6 years old, there's central air,] and it's priced at just [$149,500].

UR

HOME REALTY

555-8200
www.ur-home.net

ALTERNATIVE HEADING

Forget Common Sense

you don't really need a . . .

869

It's Too Good for You

You won't feel right living in this luxury [3BR, 2-bath, Quaker Colonial] in a neighborhood that exudes success. You don't need the [private home office/music room, expansive family areas, intimate and formal dining areas, walk-in closets, whirlpool hot tub, 3-car garage,] or any of the other luxury amenities. Anyway, there must be something wrong with it if the price is only [$297,500].

UR

HOME REALTY

555-8200
www.ur-home.net

→ Telling people what they don't want when you make the property sound attractive can be a very effective advertising technique.

870

Dirty Old House

on a nondescript street. While it has **[3BR, fireplace, fenced yard, garage, and new furnace]**, and would likely rent for far more than the monthly payments with a low-down payment loan, it really isn't much, and we would like to get rid of it. Priced to disappear at **[$92,500]**.

UR
HOME REALTY
555-8200
www.ur-home.net

➤ This is a negative ad that sells a house as a rental property.

871

Shabby But Comfortable

A **[3BR, 1½-bath American Traditional]** in a quiet family neighborhood has just about everything you want including **[full basement, double garage, room for an RV, fireplace,]** and more. The **[garden needs weeding, it could use a new coat of paint, and the carpeting should definitely be replaced]**. However, it's priced to overcome its shortcomings at **[$169,500]**.

UR
HOME REALTY
555-8200
www.ur-home.net

872

Like Action? Then Forget

about this **[3BR, 1½-bath, 2-car-garage, brick Traditional]** in **[the Hoover School District]**. No pool, tennis courts, or wet bar; just a solid **[7-year-old]** home in a desirable neighborhood with **[fenced yard for small children and puppies, several nice trees, full basement, and bright sunny rooms]**. If this is too plain for you, don't circle this ad. The price? Just **[$127,500]**.

UR
HOME REALTY
555-8200
www.ur-home.net

873

We Cannot Tell a Lie

This **[3BR, 2-bath, split-level with a 2-car garage and large maple tree in the front yard]** is just like every other house on the block. The only difference is some homes have garages on the left and some on the right, and **[the brick trim]** varies. They all have **[family rooms and ceramic tile in the baths and kitchens]**. The difference with this house is it's for sale. These homes are seldom on the market. Your chance to live in a friendly, village-type environment for only **[$159,500]**.

UR
HOME REALTY
555-8200
www.ur-home.net

➤ This is an unusual treatment for a tract home where the other homes in the area are almost the same.

874

Boring!

What more can we say? A [3BR, 1½-bath Brick Ranch] with [attached 2-car garage, fenced yard, garden patio, hardwood floors, brick fireplace, formal and family dining areas, and finished basement]. Actually, it describes most of the homes in this quiet [West Side] neighborhood. The only thing different about this home is the exceptional low-down financing and a price of just [$147,500].

UR

HOME REALTY

555-8200
www.ur-home.net

ALTERNATIVE HEADINGS

Monotonous!

Unimpressive!

875

Beavis and Butt-Head

would hate this straitlaced [3BR, 2-bath, 2-car garage, Brick Ranch] on [a quiet, friendly street] in [Middleview Heights]. It's just [2,000] square feet of comfortable living with [flowering trees and shrubs, dining patio, family room with fireplace,] and a lot of convenient but unspectacular features. Comfortably priced at [$184,500].

UR

HOME REALTY

555-8200
www.ur-home.net

876

Color-Blind Decorator

That's our impression of this [3BR, 2½-bath Romanesque Villa] on a quiet street in [Westport]. This spacious, [7-year-old home] does offer [two fireplaces, private study/guest room, walk-in closets, huge family room, garden kitchen, and great landscaping]. While the decorator likely considered the colors vibrant, we think they're ugly and we've priced the house accordingly at [$237,500].

UR

HOME REALTY

555-8200
www.ur-home.net

ALTERNATIVE HEADINGS

Bad Taste Abounds!

Elvis Presley

was the decorator. That's our . . .

Curly, Moe, and Larry

were the decorators . . .

As with any negative ad, obtain the owner's specific permission prior to using this approach. It's effective in that the reader senses a bargain similar to those encountered with fixer-uppers.

877

Looks Like Old Money

is what your friends will say about this dingy monstrosity that skillfully blends the ugly with the vulgar. View the [11 rooms] that [$280,000] will buy, #47C, *www.ur-home.net*

UR

HOME REALTY

555-8200
www.ur-home.net

878

Stripes with Plaids

If you think that's "cool," you'll love this [pink 3BR, 2-bath, 2-car-garage Mediterranean] with [mauve-toned baths, unusual cabinetry, and extensive use of mirrors]. It's a home that truly reflects your taste at far less than reproduction cost: [$239,500].

UR
HOME REALTY
555-8200
www.ur-home.net

ALTERNATIVE HEADINGS

Gaudy!
If you like [leprous yellow tile and pink tubs], you'll love . . .

Is Ugly Your Thing?
If you like [leprous yellow tile and pink tubs], you'll love . . .

A Monument to Bad Taste
If you like . . .

879

Procrastinators!

You won't have to delay long to miss out on this [3BR, 2-bath, 2-car-garage, brick Split Level] in [Kinston Heights] with its [finished recreation/fitness center, sumptuous master suite, window-wrapped family room, formal and intimate dining areas, poolside patio, and neighbor-envied landscaping]. Too bad you didn't call sooner; you could have purchased it with great low-down financing at just [$184,500].

UR
HOME REALTY
555-8200
www.ur-home.net

880

Ignore This Ad

If you don't, you'll want to see this [3BR, 2½-bath Vermont Traditional] on its [½-acre site] in [Northridge]. You'll love the [whitewashed oak cabinetry, huge fireplace, private home office, spacious family room, dining patio, and 3-car garage]. Chances are, you'll end up as the owner so you won't be able to devote any more Sundays to your favorite activity—house hunting. Oh! The price only [$249,500].

UR
HOME REALTY
555-8200
www.ur-home.net

881

Don't Call Tomorrow

as it will likely be too late. This [1-year-old Dickenson-built, 3BR, 2-bath Ranch] on a coveted street in [Westlake] is the perfect family home. It's [better than new with upgrades you wouldn't believe]. The first one who sees will buy. If you don't think we are serious, be prepared to be sorry. You will have missed your chance to own it for only [$159,500].

UR
HOME REALTY
555-8200
www.ur-home.net

882

Don't Do It!

Don't buy a plain-wrapper [$200,000] home until you've seen this exciting [3BR, 2-bath New England Contemporary on an estate setting] in [Northridge]. With [10-foot ceilings, walls of glass, dramatic fireplace, spacious sun-drenched rooms, flower-bedecked patio, and 2-plus car garage], why settle for less when it can be yours at [$198,500]?

UR

HOME REALTY

555-8200
www.ur-home.net

883

Truth in Advertising

This [3-bedroom] home isn't much. It's plain, fairly clean, and fair-sized, but not what you'd call huge. There's no wet bar, soaring ceilings, or breathtaking view. It didn't appear on the cover of *House Beautiful*, and it never will. It is, however, [the lowest-priced] home in [the Edgewood School District], and you won't need to sell your kids to raise the down payment. Call today on this plain-wrapper home priced at a plain [$114,500].

UR

HOME REALTY

555-8200
www.ur-home.net

ALTERNATIVE HEADING

Conformist?

Then you'll love this [3BR] home that looks like every other home on the block. It's plain . . .

884

It's Too Far Away

Why would I buy a [2,200-square-foot, 4-year-old Newport Colonial with 3-car garage and private home office] in [Bayridge]? I could probably find something almost as nice closer in for only [$100,000] more. After all, it's at least [35] minutes from the [Civic Center] and [10] minutes from [Orchard Mall]. Anyway, a home closer in would have higher taxes, which adds to the prestige. I don't think it's a bargain at [$269,500].

UR

HOME REALTY

555-8200
www.ur-home.net

➤ This is an effective negative ad that can be used when the property really isn't that remote.

Open House

While open houses sell many homes, they also generate prospective buyers who can often be switched to a property that is more suitable to their needs. New prospects are often better listing prospects than sale prospects because they must sell an existing home before they can buy a new one.

An open house is popular with buyers because they're allowed to view the home in a nonthreatening environment. Buyers do not feel controlled by a real estate agent. For this reason, an open house ad cannot be subtle. It must clearly indicate the days and/or hours the home is open for viewing. The address should be stated, and if not well known or difficult to find, directions to the location of the open house should also be included in the ad.

Like other ads, the price should be included as well as just enough information to prompt readers to want to discover even more about the property.

The authors feel that open house ads are more effective in geographical area ad categories than in a special open house section in the classified ads as most serious home seekers search the classifieds by area desired. An exception would be papers that categorize open houses by location.

Besides the ads presented here, ads in other chapters of this book can be readily modified for open houses.

885

See Sunday Open House Now!

Check *www.ur-home.net* and click Open Houses to be the first to view our best offerings.

UR
HOME REALTY
555-8200
www.ur-home.net

➤ An ad such as this can be used to encourage Internet viewing prior to the weekend Open House ads.

886

Open House Every Day

Want to see new properties before they're advertised? Want free e-mails and pictures of new listings? Log on to [*www.ur-home.net* and click New Listings e-mails]. You select your area, size, and price range. It's the ultimate shop at home.

UR
HOME REALTY
555-8200
www.ur-home.net

➤ This ad attracts readers with the offer of e-mails of new listings before they come in.

887

BINGO
OPEN HOUSE TOUR
1–4 Today
Win Valuable Prizes

B [3BR, 2-bath Colonial site amidst towering maples. 1820 Woodside Lane] [$218,500].

I [4BR American bungalow with huge fenced yard. 4237 Morningside] [$218,500].

N [3BR, 2-bath, brick split Ranch with finished lower level. 1643 Jacob's Trail] [$227,900].

G [3BR, 2-bath, Contemporary with walls of glass and soaring ceilings. 1521 Woodside Terrace] [$249,000].

O [2BR+ den, 2-bath Cape Cod in a storybook garden. 1207 Tiffany Circle] [$209,000].

You will receive a sealed letter at each home:

5 letters spelling Bingo = 27" color TV

4 of the letters of Bingo = 4-Head VCR/DVD

3 of the letters of Bingo = 5" TV

2 of the letters of Bingo = [Dodgers] baseball cap

UR
HOME REALTY
555-8200
www.ur-home.net

➡ You can get visitors to one open house to visit other open houses with an ad such as the one above. For Bingo or Lotto tours, you want the 5 homes to be in the same general area, preferably about a 5 minute drive apart and be homes in the same general price bracket and size so they will appeal to the same group of buyers. It would be wise if two of the locations were loaded with applicable letters so there could be many cap winners. Instead of [Dodgers] caps, your office logo could be on them. Photos should be taken of large-item winners for press releases.

888

It's Worth Waiting
In Line
to buy a new [3BR, 2½-bath, Ridgefield] home starting at just [$169,500].

Sat–Sun Open Models
1–4 P.M.
[42nd St. at Madison]

UR
HOME REALTY
555-8200
www.ur-home.net

ALTERNATIVE HEADING

Muddy Shoes Opening
It's worth the mud to buy . . .

889

Whotcha Doin' Today?
Forget [football] and see your new home, a [3BR, 2-bath American Traditional] in [Ridgehaven] at an affordable [$179,500].

Open House 1–4 P.M.
[2419 Monarch Ave.]

UR
HOME REALTY
555-8200
www.ur-home.net

890

WIN [$50] MILLION

Every adult visitor to this [3BR, 2½-bath Colonial] will receive a free lottery ticket.

Open [1–4] [2837 Mulberry Lane]

At only [$239,500], you don't have to win the lottery to be the winner.

UR

HOME REALTY

555-8200
www.ur-home.net

891

Open House [Sat 1–4 P.M.] [3128 Tyler Lane]

[Follow the arrows from 1st Ave and Clinton]

GET HERE FIRST?

or you will likely be sorry since the first one to see this [like-new 3BR-and-den New England Traditional] will likely be the buyer. It's definitely not a "drive-by" at [$199,500].

UR

HOME REALTY

555-8200
www.ur-home.net

ALTERNATIVE HEADINGS

Open To Sell

Open—Come Buy

Don't Drive By

Come inside and be surprised . . .

892

Open House [Today] [1–4 P.M.] First Offering Ever

[412 Kingsley Lane] [North off Prairie 1 block East of Elm]. Like-new [3BR and den, 2½-bath, double garage Country Colonial with all the charm of yesterday combined with the amenities of tomorrow]. One glance and you won't believe we are only asking [$239,500].

UR

HOME REALTY

555-8200
www.ur-home.net

893

Never on Sunday

Will you find an [almost-new 3BR, 2½-bath New England Colonial with home office, family room, and 3-car garage] in [enviable Clifford Estates] like the one being offered at our

Open House [1–4 P.M.] [223 W. Orange Blvd.]

Low-down financing, [$214,500].

UR

HOME REALTY

555-8200
www.ur-home.net

894

Lookie Lu's and Buyers Too

[3BR, 2½-bath Greek Revival] that has everything and is priced at just [$294,500].

Open House Sat & Sun [1–4 P.M.] [223 W. Orange Blvd.]

UR
HOME REALTY

555-8200
www.ur-home.net

CHAPTER **THIRTY-ONE**

Owner—(Present, Former)

The identity of a home's former owner does not add intrinsic value to a property. Nevertheless, the fact that a home was built, or was once owned or occupied by a noteworthy person, may foster a certain kind of pride for a new buyer.

Typically, a buyer will talk to others about the former owner and vicariously bask in his or her "fame." If a former owner were a lottery winner, this implies that the home could possibly be "lucky" in the minds of some potential buyers. Former owners of a particular home who had amassed great wealth or owners who had established a notable reputation due to their profession (physician, attorney, political office) may be of interest to some buyers as well.

Even an owner with an unusual hobby could be used as an attention-getting heading as can other unique, personal information about a particular home's owner.

Before you include any information about an owner in an ad, obtain his or her permission, in writing, especially if it is a "spoof."

For other related ads, please see Chapters 20 (Homes, Luxury) and 22 (Homes, Old).

895

Unhappy Owners

must sell their pride and joy, a [3BR, 2-bath, like-new Federal Colonial] in enviable [Northridge Estates] with [a huge family room, brick and copper country kitchen, two fireplaces, Jacuzzi in master suite, a garden that's hard to believe, and 2½-car garage]. It's your opportunity to have the best at a price that falls far short of reflecting the quality: [$219,500].

UR
HOME REALTY
555-8200
www.ur-home.net

896

Seller Has a Job

far away, so must reluctantly sacrifice this [3BR, 1½-bath, white Cape Cod] in [a rustic wooded setting] in [Northport]. You will love [the mantled fireplace, intimate and formal dining areas, breakfast patio, finished recreation/hobby room, and 2+ car garage with workshop]. It won't last long at only [$209,000].

UR
HOME REALTY
555-8200
www.ur-home.net

897

Multimillionaires

formerly owned this [3BR, 2-bath, 2½-car garage Quaker Colonial] on [a quiet tree-lined street in Newport.] [They] enjoyed [the formal and intimate dining areas, delightful garden patio, quiet home office/study, brick fireplace, and magnificent woodwork] of this fine residence. It's available for your family at [$269,500].

UR
HOME REALTY
555-8200
www.ur-home.net

ALTERNATIVE HEADINGS

A Robber Baron

A Notorious Bootlegger

Physician's Home

A doctor formerly owned this . . .

➤ Because a prominent person or person of great wealth once lived in the home, its desirability is increased.

898

Cried All Night!

The owner is heartbroken that [a job transfer] means leaving this [2-year-old 3BR, 2-bath, 3-car-garage French Mediterranean] on a [½-acre site] in [Washburn Hills]. With [high ceilings, oversized family room, warm river stone fireplace, master suite with office alcove, therapeutic hot spa, delightful garden patio, riding-mower lawn,] and exceptional financing, it's available at a price to make you smile: [$287,500].

UR
HOME REALTY
555-8200
www.ur-home.net

899

Owner Going Bye Bye

Must sell this [3BR, 2½-bath, 3-year-old, spacious, sunlit Mediterranean Villa] in desirable [Hyde Park]. Offering [10-foot ceilings, family room, home office/music room, garden patio, 3-car garage, and landscaping to be envied], it's a rare opportunity at [$279,500].

UR
HOME REALTY
555-8200
www.ur-home.net

➤ The heading would be appropriate any time an owner wants to move elsewhere. Use the following if the owner has already left.

ALTERNATIVE HEADING

Owner Went Bye Bye

900

Future Historical Site

[Sally], age [9], who, with her parents, [is leaving] for [Baltimore,] told us that [she] is going to be [the first woman] President when [she] grows up. Thousands of visitors will then admire this [newer, 3BR, 2½-bath Southern Colonial] in [Charleston Heights] with [its fluted columns, circle drive, expansive living areas, twin fireplaces, large family room, home office, 40-foot flagstone veranda, and 3-car garage] set amidst [an acre of magnificent trees, lawn, and flowering shrubs]. Future visitors won't believe it was once available for only [$247,500].

UR
HOME REALTY
555-8200
www.ur-home.net

901

Left in the Lurch

Owner's gone, leaving this [3BR, 2-bath Southwest Ranch] in [River Heights]. Everything is empty, from [the huge master suite to the family room with fireplace and wet bar. The flagstone patio has no chairs, and even the hammock is gone from the two large trees in the fenced yard. The empty 3-car garage looks cavernous.] A lot of empty space at [$269,500].

UR
HOME REALTY
555-8200
www.ur-home.net

ALTERNATIVE HEADINGS

It's An Orphan

Owner Ran Out

and left this . . .

➡ This approach can be used for any vacant home.

902

Tuba Player

is out of breath and must sell this [3BR, 2-bath, New England-inspired town house] located in an area of [prestigious] homes. There's a [separate, not quite soundproof music room, a private sunbathing porch, and a perfect garden spot]. The price won't hit a sour note at [$224,500].

UR
HOME REALTY
555-8200
www.ur-home.net

➡ The hobby of a home's owner can be used to create a catchy heading.

903

Good Luck Home

Ask us why this [newer, 3BR, 2-bath, Westside Colonial] is a lucky house. It isn't because of its [spacious floor plan, home office, 2½-car garage, wooded site,] or even its price, which seems too low at [$167,500].

UR
HOME REALTY
555-8200
www.ur-home.net

ALTERNATIVE HEADING

Lottery Winner

going upscale and selling this lucky . . .

➡ This ad would be appropriate if a former owner has had good fortune such as business success, a promotion, or even winning a lottery.

904

Historic Home

It was just 1 year ago that Homer Clapmeyer invented the electric paper clip while staying as a guest in this [3BR, 2-bath modern American classic] in [Westwood Heights]. He used the [workroom in the 2½-car attached garage] to build his prototype, which was tested before dozens of relatives in the [huge family room]. Today his name is a household word. This is your chance to own a bit of American history for only [$197,500].

UR
HOME REALTY
555-8200
www.ur-home.net

➡ This ad spoofs listings often found in southern and eastern papers for historic homes. It will definitely generate much discussion.

Privacy

Buyers who rate privacy as a priority may be looking to escape the chaos of shared living arrangements. For our purposes, privacy refers to "seclusion" and to properties that provide a comfortable amount of space between neighbors and/or tenants. Certain individuals may consider themselves "very private" and try to avoid as many outside distractions (sights and sounds) as possible, especially if they work out of their homes. You must be careful in creating this type of classified ad in order to avoid giving the impression that privacy means "exclusion" or "discrimination." The ads in this chapter focus on seclusion.

905

HERMIT

People-hater or just on the lam, check out the total seclusion of this [3BR cottage] for [$139,500]. #402 *www.ur-home.net*

UR
H O M E   R E A L T Y

555-8200
www.ur-home.net

906

Hushed Privacy, [$229,500]

[Nestled among trees off a quiet lane] is this [classic 3BR Colonial]. Its [gleaming hardwood floors, mullioned windows and shutters] echo charm of long ago and welcome you to a life where city noise and stress are just a vague memory. It can be your future, begin with a phone call.

UR
H O M E   R E A L T Y

555-8200
www.ur-home.net

ALTERNATIVE HEADING

Run Naked

in total wooded seclusion, but live in this . . .

907

Edge of the World

Remote does not adequately describe this [end-of-the-road European-style cottage] with [a massive beamed family area, 2 oversized bedrooms, and a separate large shop and garage]. Set on [over 2 wooded acres] in [Dodge County], it's hard to find, but it will be even harder to leave. A very private place at [$229,500].

UR
HOME REALTY
555-8200
www.ur-home.net

908

The Fugitive

would love this secluded [2BR-and-den American Traditional] in [Westport] that's hidden from the street and the neighbors by [a wall of greenery]. Offering [large, bright rooms, brick fireplace, full basement that's perfect for storing loot, 2-car garage, sun-streaked garden,] and a great deal more, it's the perfect hideout at [$114,500].

UR
HOME REALTY
555-8200
www.ur-home.net

909

Privacy Is

A [2,600-square-foot, 3BR, 2½-bath Classic Colonial behind the gates] in [Newport Acres sheltered by giant oaks, flowering shrubs, and sculptured hedges]. With [intimate and formal dining areas, quiet library, master suite with sitting room, and garden patio that's surrounded by sunbursts of color], it's a place to refresh yourself. Call and see the joys life has to offer at a very affordable [$267,500].

UR
HOME REALTY
555-8200
www.ur-home.net

910

Through the Gates

at [Parson's Ranch and up a quiet lane] to this [6-year-old, 3BR, 2½-bath Southwest Hacienda] with [red tile roof, massive timbers, Spanish tile floors, bubbling courtyard fountain, home office/music room, spacious sun-filled family areas, tiled fireplace, patio, 3-car garage, and hot spa all surrounded by colorful flowers and ornamental trees]. A delight to the senses at [$297,500].

UR
HOME REALTY
555-8200
www.ur-home.net

911

Lock the Guests Away

in the separate [guest house] that comes with this [3BR, 2½-bath, 2-car-garage Mediterranean] set amidst [flowering shrubs, colorful plantings, and mulberry trees] in [Washburn Heights]. With [a window-wrapped family room, soaring ceilings, dramatic fireplace, garden kitchen plus master suite that should be in *House and Garden*], you get the guest house thrown in for free at [$329,500].

UR
HOME REALTY

555-8200
www.ur-home.net

912

Even the Bloodhounds Got Lost

looking for this secluded [3BR, 2-bath Colonial] buried in the woods. At [$214,900], it's worth looking for. #161, *www.ur-home.net*

UR
HOME REALTY

555-8200
www.ur-home.net

Sports

The proximity of recreational facilities such as golf and tennis is of paramount concern to many buyers.

Sports can be used in attention-getting teaser headlines and copy, such as "Bottom of the 9th—your last chance to buy this . . . ," or "4th Down . . ." These are primarily attention-getting headings rather than headings directly related to features. Baseball headings would be most appropriate prior to the World Series, football prior to the Super Bowl, and basketball prior to the NBA championship.

913

Double Play

We have two [3BR, 1½-bath brick ranch] homes in [Clydesdale Estates]. Each has [a full basement, 2-car garage plus built-ins]. It's a fielder's choice with each at [$184,500].

UR
H O M E   R E A L T Y

555-8200
www.ur-home.net

914

Bases Loaded!

You're at bat! Bring them home to this [3BR, 1½-bath, 2-car-garage Cape Cod] that's [close to school and park]. With [fenced yard, great landscaping, fireplace, basement recreation/fitness center, light, bright rooms, friendly neighbors, and great financing], it's a home run at [$98,500].

UR
H O M E   R E A L T Y

555-8200
www.ur-home.net

915

Grand Slam!

They'll shout with joy when you bring them home to this [3BR, 1½-bath, 2-car-garage, 7-year-old West Side brick Ranch] on a tree-lined, [low-traffic street] of well-kept homes and lawns. With [fireplace, family room, formal and family dining areas, sun-drenched rooms, picnic-perfect patio]. It's a home run at [$188,500].

UR

HOME REALTY

555-8200
www.ur-home.net

916

A Heavy Hitter

is needed for this leadoff spot [3BR, 2½-bath, 3-car-garage, proper Mediterranean] in [Shorewood Hills]. With [12-foot ceilings, home office/ computer center, window-wrapped family room, formal and intimate dining areas, master suite to get lost in, dining patio, and home-run landscaping], it's a steal home at [$489,500].

UR

HOME REALTY

555-8200
www.ur-home.net

917

Bottom of the 9th

Your last chance to buy this [3BR, 1½-bath Cape Cod] on the friendliest street in [Santa Fe Heights]. With [large sunlit rooms, hardwood floors, fireplace, fenced yard, and 2-car garage], it must be sold within [7 days]. We've priced it accordingly at [$139,500].

UR

HOME REALTY

555-8200
www.ur-home.net

918

Foul Ball!

Not this [3BR, 2-bath, 2-car-garage Colonial] in [Ridgeway Heights]. It is a definite hit. With [high ceilings, stone fireplace, family room, formal and intimate dining areas, oversized master suite, killer views, garden patio,] and more, you can be safely on base at [$279,500].

UR

HOME REALTY

555-8200
www.ur-home.net

919

4th Down—
Last Chance

If it doesn't sell [this weekend, absentee owner will move in]. A [3BR, 1½-bath Cape Cod] with [full basement, 2½-car garage, RV parking, just 3 blocks to Finchy School, and it's in terrific shape]. We've priced it to keep the owner away at [$139,500].

UR

HOME REALTY

555-8200
www.ur-home.net

920

Extra Point

We forgot to tell you that this [3-year-old, 3BR, 2-bath Colonial with 3-car garage] in [Woodland Estates] can be purchased for only [$247,500].

UR
HOME REALTY

555-8200
www.ur-home.net

921

The Longest Yard
[80 × 320]

Room for pool, garden, orchard, and archery in the backyard of this [3BR, 1½-bath Federal Colonial] in friendly [Middleton]. This [newer home has washed oak cabinetry, Berber carpets, fireplace, family room, and a flower-covered patio]. It can be yours for the price of an ordinary home [$198,900].

UR
HOME REALTY

555-8200
www.ur-home.net

922

Play Touch Football

on the expansive level lawns of this [3BR, 1½-bath Colonial in Westchester]. It's [walking-close to bus, train, and schools] and has [a basement recreation/fitness area, 2-car garage plus RV space]. It's move-in ready and will definitely score with your family at [$179,500].

UR
HOME REALTY

555-8200
www.ur-home.net

923

[6] Points

You'll score a touchdown with this [3BR, 2-bath, California-inspired ranch] with an enviable [Wilson's Grove] address. There's [a state-of-the-art kitchen, 10-foot ceilings, orchard stone fireplace, formal and family dining areas, stretching-room living areas, sumptuous master suite, dining patio, 2-plus car garage, and a lush floral setting]. The extra point is the price [$289,500].

UR
HOME REALTY

555-8200
www.ur-home.net

924

Want To Score

with your family? Then buy this [3BR, 2½-bath Mediterranean Contemporary] in friendly [Northridge Estates]. It's [4 years new] and offers [soaring ceilings, incomparable views through walls of glass, family room with fire-place, expansive family areas, a master suite that looks like it came from Hollywood, 3-car garage, and landscaping to be envied]. If you don't hurry, someone else will be a hero to their family at [$269,500].

UR
HOME REALTY

555-8200
www.ur-home.net

925

Tell Your [Wife]

that this [3BR Mediterranean] is in the [Midville School District] and it's going to make [her] the envy of [her] friends.

Don't Tell [Her]

It's within [15] minutes of [9] championship golf courses. You will want a tour at [$237,900]. #46, www.ur-home.net

UR
HOME REALTY
555-8200
www.ur-home.net

926

A Birdie

[on the 7th Fairway at Brookside] and it's CHEAP—CHEAP—CHEAP!

[$197,500]

buys this [2BR, 1½-bath, English Town House with fantastic views, breakfast patio, garage,] and so much more. Don't drop the ball, call.

UR
HOME REALTY
555-8200
www.ur-home.net

ALTERNATIVE HEADING

Birdie Lovers!

927

For Golfers Only

A [looks like-new, 2BR and den free-standing home] at the [Lakes Country Club]. This light and bright home has [cathedral ceilings, a wall of glass, 3-sided white marble fireplace, lots of tile, a patio great for entertaining after 18 holes, and a garage that will hold 2 cars and a golf cart]. If you think golf is the most important thing in the world, call now and we will put you among friends at a price that won't put you into the rough: [$247,500].

UR
HOME REALTY
555-8200
www.ur-home.net

ALTERNATIVE HEADINGS

Putt Around!

Fore You

[4] Minutes to Tee Time

Trees and Tees

Wanna Play A-Round?

Score Low—Live High!

Below Par

Your scores will drop as the owner of a [...]

928

Scratch Your Itch
[$189,500]

Itching to have a [2BR condo] on the golf course. Tour your new home. #49, *www.ur-home.net*

UR
HOME REALTY
555-8200
www.ur-home.net

929

Tee Off at Home

Well, practically. This [2BR plus home office/music center Spanish Revival residence with 2 baths, high ceilings, sun-drenched rooms, marble fireplace, garden patio, and 2-plus cart garage] is [just a chip shot from South Hills Golf course], and it's available at a price you wouldn't expect, just [$146,500].

UR
HOME REALTY
555-8200
www.ur-home.net

930

Top Flite

[3BR, 2-bath, 2-plus cart garage, tiled Mediterranean with CONDOR-high ceilings, private breakfast patio, magnificent landscaping, and it's behind gates in the golf community of Ironwood]. The PINNACLE of living at an affordable [$269,500].

UR
HOME REALTY
555-8200
www.ur-home.net

931

Free Golf

The course [plus pool, spas, and courts are] all yours as the owner of this [2BR, 1½-bath garden unit] at [Sun Vista]. With [10-foot ceilings, state-of-the-art kitchen, white marble fireplace, delightful dining patio, and room for car and golf cart in the oversized garage], life doesn't get any better at [$179,500].

UR
HOME REALTY
555-8200
www.ur-home.net

➡ This ad can be used where the owners' association owns the golf course and homeowner dues include golf privileges.

932

Listen to Your Elders

No 90-year-old has ever said he wished he had played less and worked more. See this [2BR, 2½-bath, 2-car plus cart garage, 4-year-old Colonial Ranch] that's [behind the gates at Ironwood Country Club]. With [high ceilings, twin master suites, private office/music room, marble fireplace, and a delightful patio surrounded by flowering shrubs and colorful plantings], this is an exceptional opportunity for fun at [$287,500].

UR
HOME REALTY
555-8200
www.ur-home.net

933

Spouse a Golfer?

Then burn this ad. If you buy this [3BR, 2-bath Tuscany Villa] in [Edgewood Estates], you'll only see your spouse on rainy days because it's only [5 minutes to the first tee at Glenwood]. Don't play golf? Then you'll love the [10-foot ceilings, sun-drenched rooms, lavish use of tile, walk-in closets, whirlpool tub, fountain patio, and breathtaking garden. You can probably rent out the golf cart space in the 2½-car garage]. Because of unusual circumstances, it's priced at [$197,500].

UR

HOME REALTY

555-8200
www.ur-home.net

934

Hookers!

You'll quickly correct your swing living [behind the gates] in the golf-course community of [Ironwood]. A [tiled Mediterranean with 2BR, 2½ baths, 2-plus car garage, soaring ceilings, spacious, sun-filled rooms, magnificent landscaping,] and only [4 years old,] it's yours for a straight-shot price of [$249,500].

UR

HOME REALTY

555-8200
www.ur-home.net

935

A Putting Green

Well, almost. It's a picture-postcard lawn that surrounds this [5-year-old, 3BR, 2-bath Quaker Colonial] with [almost 2,000 square feet] and too many luxury features to list. Within [8 minutes] of the 1st tee, it's a definite must-see at [$249,500].

UR

HOME REALTY

555-8200
www.ur-home.net

936

Duffer's Widow?

Keep your golfer close to home with this [12th] fairway, [2BR villa] at [Claremont] available for just [$198,500]. Take a tour. #34, *www.ur-home.net*

UR

HOME REALTY

555-8200
www.ur-home.net

937

[Husband] Underfoot?

Send [him] out to play [golf, tennis, billiards, pool, and enjoy the spa] that comes with this [2BR town house] at [Lexington Village]. Tour your future. #601 at *www.ur-home.net*.

UR

HOME REALTY

555-8200
www.ur-home.net

938

Bring the Woods

and irons. A [3BR, 2½-bath Spanish Colonial] just [a chip-shot away from the fairway] at [Shorewood Hills]. Spacious and gracious, this home features [tons of tile, massive beams, old-world fireplace, breathtaking landscaping, and garage for 2 cars plus cart]. The home "fore" you at [$247,500].

UR
HOME REALTY
555-8200
www.ur-home.net

939

Free Tennis

The courts [plus pool, spa, and fitness center] are yours as the owner of this [2BR, 1½-bath garden unit] at [Clearwater Villas]. With [10-foot ceilings, state-of-the-art kitchen, fireplace, delightful dining patio, and room for car and cart in the oversize garage], life doesn't get any better at [$169,500].

UR
HOME REALTY
555-8200
www.ur-home.net

ALTERNATIVE HEADINGS

Into the Racquets?

Tennis Anyone?

Come Play With Us!

940

Love in the Afternoon

or any time you please with your very own professional tennis court that comes with this [3BR, 3½-bath, 3-car-garage, tiled Mediterranean] in [Western Estates]. The [3,000-plus]-square-foot residence includes [a private home office, expansive family areas, two fireplaces, teen suite/guest suite plus sumptuous master suite, covered veranda overlooking court/pool/spa, plus landscaping to be envied]. It's LOVE at [$489,500].

UR
HOME REALTY
555-8200
www.ur-home.net

941

A Slam Dunk!

It will take only a moment to decide that this [3BR, 1½-bath Cape Cod] in [Gordon Estates] is a definite 2 points. It's postcard perfect with [2-plus car garage and RV parking, expansive family areas, orchard-stone fireplace, central air, fenced yard,] and a lot more. You'll really score at [$174,500].

UR
HOME REALTY
555-8200
www.ur-home.net

942

[Shaquille O'Neal] Ceilings

They're [11'] high in this [3BR, 2½ bath, 2+car garage Massachusetts Traditional] in [Westport Acres]. With [a flowing floor plan, soft beige dribble-proof carpets, and hall-of-fame landscaping], it's a slam dunk at [$349,500].

UR
HOME REALTY
555-8200
www.ur-home.net

➡ You can use a respected star of a favored professional team for the heading such as Chun-Li or even a retired star like Larry Bird.

943

Rollerblades

on the sidewalk and basketball in the driveway. If you're still interested, we have the perfect home: a [3BR plus bonus room, 1½-bath Cape Cod] in friendly [Hindsdale Estates]. With [intimate and formal dining areas, hardwood floors, fireplace, basement recreation/fitness center, 2½-car garage, RV parking, and landscaping to make your green thumb itch], it's priced to roll away at [$176,500].

UR
HOME REALTY
555-8200
www.ur-home.net

944

Morning Jogger?

Join dozens of others on the quiet streets and paths of friendly [Shorewood Estates], home to a [3BR, 2-bath Quaker Colonial] with [hardwood floors, brick fireplace, formal and family dining areas, flagstone dining patio, 2-car garage,] and lots more. Hurry, or it will sprint away at [$214,500].

UR
HOME REALTY
555-8200
www.ur-home.net

945

Ping-Pong Anyone?

The [9-foot-high] basement has room for a half-dozen or more ping-pong tables. Upstairs, there are [3BR, 2 baths, family room, walk-in closets, breakfast patio, and 2½-car garage] packaged in a [3-year-old tile-roofed Tuscany Mediterranean] on [an estate site] in [Summerset Meadows]. It's your serve at [$269,500].

UR
HOME REALTY
555-8200
www.ur-home.net

946

Bowl

your friends over with this [3BR, 2-bath, 2-car-garage Vermont Colonial] just [5 minutes] from [Johnson Lanes]. [Only 5 years old], this [1,900-square-foot] residence has everything on your wish list and more. It's a solid "300" at [$227,500].

UR
HOME REALTY
555-8200
www.ur-home.net

947

Pool Hustler?

A billiard room comes with this [3BR, 2-bath Federal Colonial] in [Westport], but you have to bring your own table. There's also a [family room with fireplace, formal and family dining areas, 2-car garage,] and every modern amenity you can imagine. At [$164,500], call don't scratch.

UR
HOME REALTY
555-8200
www.ur-home.net

CHAPTER THIRTY-FOUR

Swimming Pools

Swimming pools and hot spas should only be the focus of an ad when the presence of a pool or spa would not be expected features for a particular price range or location. Of course, these ads are more effective in the spring or summer months than they would be in the winter. The following ads were written specifically to sell the virtues of swimming pools.

948

Splish! Splash! and Not Much Cash!

A [3BR, 2-bath Mediterranean] in [Washington Heights] with your own in-ground sparkling pool, available with close to nothing down and a call-now price of just [$154,500].

UR
HOME REALTY

555-8200
www.ur-home.net

ALTERNATIVE HEADINGS

Take the Plunge!

Maui in Your Backyard

String Bikini Special

Wet All Over

949

The Summer of ['04]

will be a fun-time with the sparkling pool [and sumptuous hot spa] that comes with this [3BR, 2-bath Mediterranean Villa] set amidst [flowering shrubs and colorful plantings] in [enviable Northridge]. With its [high ceilings, quiet home office/music room, flowing family areas, sunset views, and over-sized garage to hold all the toys], you will vacation every day for the price of an ordinary home: [$287,500].

UR
HOME REALTY

555-8200
www.ur-home.net

ALTERNATIVE HEADING

Vacation Every Day

Every day will be a vacation with the sparkling pool . . .

950

Family with Swimsuits

will love the [California-style] pool [and spa] with this [3BR, 2-bath Spanish Hacienda], with [tons of tile, huge hewn beams, bubbling fountain, formal and intimate dining areas, two magnificent fireplaces, expansive family areas, colorful plantings,] and much more. It's a home a grateful family will welcome at [$327,500].

UR

HOME REALTY

555-8200
www.ur-home.net

ALTERNATIVE HEADING

Get Wet Together

Your family will . . .

951

Life's Too Short

not to have a pool and spa; and while you're at it, a relaxing flower bedecked patio and a [3BR, 2½-bath, spacious Mediterranean Villa] to go along with it. There should be [a quiet music room, large family areas, fireplace, and a 3-car garage] to hold your toys. Don't dream about it when it can be yours at [$269,500].

UR

HOME REALTY

555-8200
www.ur-home.net

952

The Pool Comes Free

Compare and you'll discover that this [3BR, 2-bath Tuscany-inspired Villa] in [Claridge Heights] with magnificent pool, [spa, and gazebo] is priced no more than an ordinary home. Also included are [soaring ceilings, huge family areas, fireplace, a Corian kitchen with everything, 2½-car garage,] and more for only [$237,500].

UR

HOME REALTY

555-8200
www.ur-home.net

953

Attention Skinny-Dippers

The [French doors of the master suite] open onto a [secluded] sparkling pool [and spa] that make keeping fit fun. You'll love the lush plantings and colorful flowers in the picture-book yard. Incidentally, this all comes with a [3BR, 2½-bath California Colonial] in the choicest [Holiday Hills] location you could possibly want. This fine residence is [model-home perfect] and comes with every amenity in the book for only [$279,000], and unbelievable financing is available. Call today for a refreshing tomorrow.

UR

HOME REALTY

555-8200
www.ur-home.net

ALTERNATIVE HEADING

Swimsuits Optional

Time-Shares

Time-shares are interval-ownership vacation properties where buyers customarily purchase a particular week, or weeks, in a designated unit each and every year. Sales appeal is based on the amenities offered by the time-share development. In some cases, a major selling point is the exchange privileges with other time-share units around the world. Because of high promotion and selling costs, time-share developers frequently allowed markups of 300 percent to around 500 percent.

Time-shares are generally resold at significant reductions in price from original sale prices due to a buyers' resale market with far more sellers than buyers. The price savings can be emphasized in ads with language such as: "Seller paid [$26,500] . . . your price [$14,900]," or "Save [45%] . . . from original sale price."

Lower dollar costs of time-share resales will likely create a higher broker commission structure for these units than for other types of properties in order to allow brokers to advertise. Because a time-share is a type of vacation property, a buyer will be particularly interested in the amenities of a development. So be sure to emphasize those features in your classified ad.

If a newspaper has a separate category for time-shares, they should appear under that category, although they can appear under vacation property categories (providing a time-share is clearly presented as such).

Language from Chapter 36 (Vacation Homes) can be readily adapted to time-share ads.

954

[2 Weeks] in Paradise

Your own [2BR, 2½-bath] luxuriously furnished [ocean-view] unit in [Miami Shores] with pools, spas, golf, tennis, and more, awaiting you each and every year. Or, trade your time as part of our worldwide resort exchange plan. Yours [forever] with about [$2,000] down and a full price of just [$21,400].

UR
HOME REALTY
555-8200
www.ur-home.net

ALTERNATIVE HEADINGS

Sample Paradise
for 2 weeks . . .

Buy the Beach
for 2 weeks . . .

Why Pay
for a year when you only use your vacation home for 2 weeks . . .

955

[Tahoe] Holiday

[2 weeks] every year in your own fabulous [2-BR, 2½-bath Lake Tahoe Chalet]. By day, enjoy [water and mountain sports, golf, and tennis]. By night there are the [legendary shows, casinos, and restaurants]. It's your chance to sample a lifestyle reserved for millionaires. Call and for [$16,500] it's yours.

UR
HOME REALTY
555-8200
www.ur-home.net

956

Question?

Is it possible to vacation in exotic places for [2 weeks] every year and enjoy the amenities of world-class resorts without selling your soul to the devil?

Answer!

As the owner of [2 weeks] at [Hudson Shores], you can enjoy [golf, tennis, and water sports] while living in a [2BR, 2½-bath Chalet] that makes those on "Lifestyles of the Rich and Famous" seem second rate, or your can trade your [weeks] with a worldwide exchange plan. [The South of France, Tahiti, Hawaii, Morocco, Bora-Bora,] and dozens of other choices await you. Call and it's all yours [for less than 10% down and] a full price of [$21,500].

UR
HOME REALTY
555-8200
www.ur-home.net

957

What's Interval Ownership?

It's owning your own luxurious [2BR, 2½ bath, ocean-view unit with dining terrace] for [2 weeks every August] at the world-class resort of [Hudson Shores]. You'll live like the rich and famous with [golf, tennis, water sports,] and more, while others pay for the rest of the year. Call and we'll show you how it saves dollars and makes sense at [$23,500].

UR
HOME REALTY
555-8200
www.ur-home.net

958

[Tennis Club] Resale

[Two] desirable [Hilton Springs] weeks every [April] in a luxurious [2BR, 2½-bath] vacation villa [with worldwide exchange privileges]. Enjoy the [pools, spas, courts, and clubhouse] or just soak in the sun. Call now and take advantage of [a 50%] discount from the original price. Only [$18,500].

UR
HOME REALTY
555-8200
www.ur-home.net

ALTERNATIVE HEADINGS

[50%] Discount

**Owner Paid [$37,000]
Your Price [$18,500]**

Owner's Loss—Your Gain

Vacation Homes

Ads for vacation homes differ from traditional ads because they primarily sell a "lifestyle" rather than brick and mortar. Vacation homes are usually built for a relaxed, casual lifestyle and are frequently sought as retirement homes. In this way, they are similar to ads for retirement homes. In fact, many of the properties advertised as vacation homes are purchased as primary residences by retirees. What were once primarily seasonal communities are now becoming retirement destinations.

Vacation homes are more apt to be fully or partially furnished than are other homes. They often are sold along with boats, vehicles, tools, or furnishings.

For additional ads suitable for vacation homes, please see Chapters 14 (Homes, Acreage), 24 (Horse Property), 33 (Sports), 35 (Time-Shares), 37 (View), and 38 (Water-Related Property).

959

Snowbirds!

For the cost of renting your seasonal place in the sun, you can be the year-round owner of this [2BR, 1½-bath Arizona Traditional with 2-car garage, delightful dining patio, open-concept living area with fireplace, 2 orange and 6 palm trees, and low-maintenance landscaping] on a quiet and friendly street [convenient to everything]. With practically nothing down, let us show you how this home makes dollars and sense at only [$84,500].

UR

H O M E   R E A L T Y

555-8200
www.ur-home.net

960

Sol Searching

For vacations or a lifetime, we have your place in the sun. A [2BR-and-den] sun-filled [Hacienda in Palm Desert with a large covered veranda, graceful arches, high ceilings, beehive fireplace, 2 opulent baths, double garage, walled garden with sumptuous hot spa, colorful plantings, and magnificent palms] all in a delightful quiet neighborhood. It's awaiting your pleasure at [$149,500].

UR

H O M E   R E A L T Y

555-8200
www.ur-home.net

961

Sunrise Sunset

Glorious day will follow glorious day in this **[newer, 2-bedroom mountain chalet]** set amidst **[towering pines]**. You'll relish walking the paths of nature as the seasons change, watching **[eagles]** soar, or reading at night **[by the fireplace]** with your dog at your side. The joy and tranquility of living where every neighbor knows your name but respects your privacy can be yours forever at **[$149,500]**.

UR
_____
H O M E   R E A L T Y

555-8200
www.ur-home.net

➤ This ad is targeted toward retirees. It can be used for most rural or resort areas. If a home has other positive features, expand on them with descriptions such as "the walls of glass make nature your decorator" or "you'll relish the feeling of substance that solid wood paneling brings to one's home."

962

Call Free

and we will tell you about this **[2BR]** vacation or retirement home **[overlooking Lake Sullivan]**. You will love the **[orchard-stone fireplace, large screened sleeping porch, sunset vistas over the water, and magnificent natural landscaping]**. It's priced to sell fast at **[$93,500]**, so call.

UR
_____
H O M E   R E A L T Y

1-800-555-8200
www.ur-home.net

➤ This heading is effective when the property is advertised outside your area and your office has an "800" number.

963

Can't Retire Yet?

This **[3BR, 2-bath, almost new Spanish Colonial]** in delightful **[La Quinta]** can be your vacation home 'til then. Featuring **[spacious sun-filled rooms, tons of tile, beehive fireplace, covered dining patio, soaring palms, and flowering shrubs]**, it's your chance to put a lock on your future at **[$194,500]**.

UR
_____
H O M E   R E A L T Y

555-8200
www.ur-home.net

964

Your Retirement Plan [Bass Lake]

Buy this **[better-than-new 2BR, lakeshore home with 1½ baths, large sleeping loft, double garage, and fishing dock]** now. Use it for vacations and when you're ready for your retirement home. If you like, it can be rented 'til you want it. Advantage is you lock in retirement costs now. Secure your future today for **[$247,500]** with great financing available.

UR
_____
H O M E   R E A L T Y

555-8200
www.ur-home.net

965

Walk to Privy

Just follow the picturesque path to the privy behind this **[7-room cottage]** virtually untouched by the twentieth century. While apparently solid in construction, its needs begin with the barest of necessities. In its favor, this property offers **[3]** acres of the most spectacular scenery you'll ever find. If you love working with your hands, then this is your opportunity to achieve pure rapture at only **[$74,000]**.

UR

HOME REALTY

555-8200
www.ur-home.net

→ The above ad heading draws attention to the fact that the home isn't modern, but the heading is nevertheless so unusual that it invites readers to peruse the entire ad. The ad will attract escapists as well as buyers of fixer-uppers.

966

Run Away from Home

to a private Shangri-la. This **[2BR plus loft Mountain Retreat]** is your place to restore your soul with clean air, magnificent vistas, and a feeling of secure contentment. Words can't describe it; come and experience this very special place that's yours for just **[$99,500]**.

UR

HOME REALTY

555-8200
www.ur-home.net

CHAPTER THIRTY-SEVEN

View

To many buyers, a beautiful view can be more important than the basic physical aspects of the property itself! Ocean-view property in some areas will sell for double the price of similar nonview property located in the same area. Other desirable views include the following:

- Mountains
- Forests
- Park reserves
- Historical monuments
- City lights
- Sunsets

While ads in other sections may also occasionally focus on a property's view, the following examples use view as the specific focal point of the ad.

967

Like Penthouse View

without the lower floors. This **[Hillside Mediterranean]** offers the sense of space, style, sensuality, and city vistas normally reserved for multimillion dollar penthouses. **[On its own ½ acre]**, there are **[3BR, 2½ magnificent baths, and a breathtaking garden/breakfast room]** in **[over 2,700 square feet]** of unadulterated luxury. Of course there is a **[3-car garage and all the accoutrements associated with a premier residence]**. It's a sight that won't last at **[$649,500]**.

UR

H O M E   R E A L T Y

555-8200

www.ur-home.net

968

King of the Hill

You'll feel like royalty looking down at your domain from this **[3BR, 2½-bath Spanish Contemporary]** with everything. See what you can have for **[$279,500]**. #602, *www.ur-home.net*

UR

H O M E   R E A L T Y

555-8200

www.ur-home.net

ALTERNATIVE HEADING

Look Down On Your Neighbors

969

View: To Take Your Breath Away

Price: To Let You Breathe

A magnificent [3BR, 2-bath Hillside Colonial] with [a glass-wrapped studio, private home office, family room, 2 fireplaces, hardwood floors, 2-car garage] and [it's only 4 years old]. Despite its enviable [Weston Hills address, forever views, and picture-postcard landscaping], we're able to offer this premier residence at a price fitting a far more modest residence: [$242,500].

UR
HOME REALTY
555-8200
www.ur-home.net

ALTERNATIVE HEADINGS

The City at Your Feet

Palace in the Sky

Above the Eagles

High on a Windy Hill

970

[Boats] and Sunsets

Ever-changing vistas are yours from this [7-year-old, 3BR, 2½-bath hillside Hacienda]. With [2,400 square feet of casual living, huge beams, warm tile, luxurious baths, 3-car garage, and incomparable vistas], it's a must-see at [$269,500].

UR
HOME REALTY
555-8200
www.ur-home.net

971

Ansel Adams

loved these majestic mountains now framed through the walls of glass in this [Colorado Contemporary]. The view comes complete with [3 bedrooms, 2½ baths, a 30-foot family room opening onto a deck with a stone barbecue, and just about every known convenience]. The view goes on forever, but at [$349,500] your opportunity is right now.

UR
HOME REALTY
555-8200
www.ur-home.net

➤ This ad is targeted at an artistic buyer likely to recognize the name of Ansel Adams, world-renowned photographer known for his mountain vistas. If you are advertising for other than a mountain view, you can say that Ansel Adams "would have loved..."

ALTERNATIVE HEADING

John Muir

972

Why Buy a Painting

when [walls of glass] bring [mountain] vistas right into this [3BR, 2½-bath Spanish Contemporary] on the prettiest [wooded] site in [Westport]? Offering [sky-high ceilings, flowing floor plan, magnificent decks, home office/music room, 3-car garage,] and more, [it's better than new] at [$379,500].

UR
HOME REALTY
555-8200
www.ur-home.net

973

On a Clear Day, You Can See Forever!

You could travel the world and find little to compare with the peace and tranquility of this lovely spot. A [sturdy 3BR, 1¾-bath New England Colonial] set amidst [an acre of lawn and trees]. With unsurpassed [mountain] vistas and a home anyone would be proud to call their own, it's the perfect blend of privacy and convenience. Best of all it's [move-in ready], priced at only [$239,000].

UR
HOME REALTY
555-8200
www.ur-home.net

ALTERNATIVE HEADINGS

Heaven Has a View

God Was the Decorator

974

Star Trek Groupie?

You can watch the skies for the next sequel from the spacious decks of this [3BR, 2-bath Texas Contemporary Ranch] on an [estate-sized hillside setting] in [West Covington]. Offering [a huge Corian and tile kitchen, flowing family areas, French doors, sumptuous master suite with whirlpool, 3-car garage, all the built-ins plus what is likely the most beautiful yard in town], it's a place Captain Kirk could call his own at [$309,500].

UR
HOME REALTY
555-8200
www.ur-home.net

975

Starship Views

[Skylights and moonlit decks] present a heavenly picture from this [3BR, 2-bath, tiled Mediterranean nestled in the hillside overlooking the city]. With [sky-high ceilings, vast open family areas, a master suite to get lost in, walls of glass, whitewashed cabinetry, 2-plus car garage,] and so much more, even Dr. Spock would agree it's an exceptional home at [$282,500].

UR
HOME REALTY
555-8200
www.ur-home.net

976

Free View Preview

Newly available [2,200+ square foot, 3BR, 2½-bath Tennessee Ranch] in [Hilton Heights], with [3-car garage, soaring ceilings, walls of glass, wraparound deck,] and unobstructed views of [lake and fairway]. It's all yours at [$269,900].

UR
HOME REALTY
555-8200
www.ur-home.net

ALTERNATIVE HEADING

Not Just the View

It's the vision of living . . .

977

World Class Sunsets

will be yours from the [deck] of this [2,500-square-foot Colorado Contemporary on Ridgeline Road]. The home features [soaring ceilings, glass-wrapped living area, 3 baths, 3-car garage, home office, family room with floor-to-ceiling rock fireplace, and unparalleled landscaping by Mother Nature]. A celestial value at a down-to-earth price of [$329,500].

UR
HOME REALTY
555-8200
www.ur-home.net

978

[Carolina] Sunsets

and evening breezes can be yours on the [sweeping deck] of this [3BR Southern Colonial Ranch] set on [the hillside amidst colorful plantings]. With [a window-wrapped family room, native stone fireplace, formal and family dining areas, and exquisite cabinetry], it's special for you at [$239,500].

UR
HOME REALTY
555-8200
www.ur-home.net

979

Want To Watch

sunsets on the distance hills and nature in all its nuances? This [3BR, 1½-bath Tennessee stone splitlevel] in [Williams Acres] on an exceptional view site offers [a large family room with fireplace, formal and intimate dining areas, walls of glass, expansive red wood decking, and landscaping second to none]. With exceptional low-down payment financing, it's the home you've been looking for at [$167,500].

UR
HOME REALTY
555-8200
www.ur-home.net

980

[7] Rooms with a View

[3BR, 2-bath, 2-car garage and a sweeping deck] go with this [window-wrapped Mediterranean] in [Kingston Estates]. There's also [11-foot ceilings, sumptuous master suite, fireplace, family room, and it's decorated in a light, neutral decor with colorful accents]. As the proud owner [the world will appear at your feet]; priced no more than an ordinary home [$237,500].

UR
HOME REALTY
555-8200
www.ur-home.net

981

View from the Terrace

and [every] window of this [2,200-plus square foot, 3-year-old, 3BR, 2½-bath, 3-car-garage Renaissance Mediterranean] with an address to be envied in [Hillside Estates]. With [private home office/computer center, family room, white marble fireplace, 12-foot ceilings, red tile roof, covered dining patio, and landscaping that must be experienced], the horizon is within your reach at [$289,500].

UR
H O M E   R E A L T Y

555-8200
www.ur-home.net

982

Front Row Seats

[Soaring walls of glass and sweeping decks] give you unparalleled vistas of [the city below]. This [3BR, 2½-bath, cedar and stone Santa Fe Contemporary] offers [a magnificent rock fireplace, private home office, flowing family areas, sumptuous hot spa in the master suite, and a 3-car garage] in a quiet enclave of fine homes. It's a beauty that must be experienced, available now at [$374,900].

UR
H O M E   R E A L T Y

555-8200
www.ur-home.net

983

Season Tickets

to Mother Nature's spectacular show. [French doors and a 40-foot covered veranda] look out over a postcard-perfect setting. Located in [Wellington Heights] this [3BR, 2½-bath, brick and stone French Normandy] residence features [leaded glass, private home office/music room, expansive living areas, magnificent fireplaces, 3-car garage,] and a great deal more. If you appreciate beauty, it can be your own at [$319,500].

UR
H O M E   R E A L T Y

555-8200
www.ur-home.net

984

Napoleonic Complex?

You will think you are master of all from this top of the world [3BR, 2½-bath Montana-inspired Contemporary]. Fantastic views of a private domain any emperor would love. With [high ceilings, walls of glass, formal and intimate dining areas, home office to plot strategies, 2-plus car garage, and a shield of tall trees], it's a place to rule from at [$294,500].

UR
H O M E   R E A L T Y

555-8200
www.ur-home.net

ALTERNATIVE HEADINGS

Everything Else Is Downhill

Overlooking the World

985

Baywatch

View the ships and surf from this spectacular [3BR, 2½-bath New Hampshire Colonial] overlooking [Dana Harbor]. Featuring [woodwork to be envied; huge, open rooms; magnificent fireplace; paneled captain's office; three-season porch; 2-car garage; and delightful landscaping], it's a special home for sea-lovers at [$549,500].

UR

HOME REALTY

555-8200
www.ur-home.net

986

Get High

above the city and watch the world below from this [3BR, 2½-bath Executive Mediterranean] on a premier site in [Hillside Estates]. This home offers [soaring ceilings, walls of glass, flowing floor plan, generous-sized rooms, 2½-car garage, rock terraced landscaping, magnificent deck, and it's superbly decorated in soft muted tones]. It's definitely a MUST SEE and a BEST BUY at [$279,500].

UR

HOME REALTY

555-8200
www.ur-home.net

CHAPTER THIRTY-EIGHT

Water-Related Property

The proximity of property to an ocean, lake, or river is a very important feature. Being close to water increases property desirability, having a water view is a benefit, and being on the water significantly enhances the property's value. In several areas of the country, a 100-foot vacant lot on the ocean or on a particularly desirable lake can command a sales price of over $1 million.

In creating a classified ad for lake or river property, remember that if the particular lake or river is highly desirable, then the name of the lake or river should be included in the ad heading. If the name of the lake is unlikely to be familiar to the reader, you can use some of the other headings included in this section or in the Ad Generator.

987

Sand Between
Your Toes

the constant sound of the surf, bikinis, and a laid-back attitude are aspects of the beach you'll have to endure as the owner of this **[2BR, cedar-shake cottage just steps from the sand]**. There's **[a large screened porch perfect for summer sleeping and a woodburning fireplace for those brisk mornings]**. Much more than a home, it's a whole new lifestyle at **[$218,000]**.

UR
HOME REALTY
555-8200
www.ur-home.net

988

Reach Out!
Touch the Surf!!!

There's nothing quite like the smell of sea air at your doorstep or the gentle sound of waves to lull you to sleep. An ambiance of quiet contentment encompasses this absolutely unique **[3BR, ocean-front cottage]**. At night you could swim unnoticed in nature's garment or simply sit and watch the variegated lights of paradise. This is the end of the rainbow and the address of your future. Unexcelled for weekends or weeks on end, a rare offering at **[$750,000]**.

UR
HOME REALTY
555-8200
www.ur-home.net

989

A Big Fat Fish

was swimming by the dock **[last week]** as we put out the For Sale sign on this **[4-season]** home with 100-foot frontage on **[crystal-clear Thunder Lake]**. With **[2BR plus huge bunkhouse over the garage and screened sleeping porch]**, you can host a family reunion. The **[kitchen and systems have been totally updated, making this a carefree home]** for weekends, weeks on end, or an eternity. It's a big catch at a small price **[$179,500]**.

UR
HOME REALTY
555-8200
www.ur-home.net

➡️ If the lake is well known, the name should be in the heading. The amount of water frontage is also a prime feature.

ALTERNATIVE HEADING

100 Feet—Thunder Lake

990

The Sound of the Surf

will lull you to sleep, and the morning call of gulls will invite you to walk barefoot in the sand. The beach lifestyle of this **[2-bedroom beach bungalow]** will relieve your stress far more effectively than medication or a psychiatrist's couch. An investment in yourself at **[$389,000]**.

UR
HOME REALTY
555-8200
www.ur-home.net

➡️ This ad presents a rational health reason for buying into this type of lifestyle.

991

The Loon Calls

and your canoe glides over tranquil **[Lake Owens]** to your private dock just steps from the **[tree-shaded deck]** of your **[3BR]** view-ti-ful home. It can be yours: the lake, **[dock]**, home, and tranquility. Call now to find out more about this investment in yourself. Priced at only **[$189,500]**.

UR
HOME REALTY
555-8200
www.ur-home.net

ALTERNATIVE HEADING

Loon Magic

Thoreau would love the call of the loon as your canoe . . .

992

Surfers and Surf-Watchers

will appreciate this **[2BR stone cottage]** that's **[just a short walk to the sand]**. There's **[a mantled fireplace in the great room, state-of-the-art kitchen, delightful patio plus parking for 4 cars]**. It's your chance for an endless vacation at **[$274,500]**.

UR
HOME REALTY
555-8200
www.ur-home.net

993

Shh! Don't Tell the Relatives!

that you purchased this [3BR waterfront home on Bass Lake]. They'll want to sleep [on the large screened porch], use your boats, fish off your [dock,] or even camp on the emerald-green lawn [flowing to the water's edge]. You'll likely discover cousins you have never heard of. The price at least won't scare you, [$89,500].

UR
_____
H O M E   R E A L T Y

555-8200
www.ur-home.net

➤ Because the heading doesn't mention waterfront property, the newspaper category should indicate that it is water-related property. Otherwise, your heading can read as follows.

ALTERNATIVE HEADING

**Bass Lake Frontage/
Don't Tell the Relatives**

994

Life's a Beach

So why not live there? A [2BR, year-round cottage with fireplace, wood paneling, built-ins, breakfast patio, garage plus additional parking] that's [within the sound of the surf and the smell of the sea]. Starving-surfer priced at [$194,900].

UR
_____
H O M E   R E A L T Y

555-8200
www.ur-home.net

995

Blue Water White Sand

Your own cottage [at] the beach. [2BR, fireplace, large, open living area, completely new bath, sleeping porch, and parking for 3 cars] are yours for weekends or weeks on end. Call it yours for [$198,500].

UR
_____
H O M E   R E A L T Y

555-8200
www.ur-home.net

➤ If the property includes water frontage, the heading should indicate this. Also, if it is very close to water, this should be conveyed.

ALTERNATIVE HEADINGS

Fish or Cut Bait

Where Trees Grow Tall

and the sun meets the sea . . .

996

Footsteps to the Sea

Take morning walks with your dog along hardpacked sand enjoying the sights, sounds, and smell of the sea. An idyllic [clapboard] beach home with [3BR, 1½ baths, wood-burning fireplace, huge sun-filled kitchen, garage plus RV parking] will bring happiness to the lucky buyer at [$279,500].

UR
_____
H O M E   R E A L T Y

555-8200
www.ur-home.net

➤ This home is not directly on the water. If it has a view, then this fact should be emphasized.

997

Buy the Sea

The cry of gulls will be your morning call. You'll breakfast on the **[terrace]** to the sound of waves caressing the shore. You'll walk barefoot along the sand in the solitude of your thoughts. This **[2BR cottage]** is just steps from the sand. Tranquility can be yours at **[$269,500]**.

UR
HOME REALTY
555-8200
www.ur-home.net

➤ The property is not on the waterfront, nor is an ocean view implied. If there's a view, change the words to "...on the terrace entranced by the sight and sound of waves gently caressing the shore." If the property is on the water, change the heading to one of the following.

ALTERNATIVE HEADINGS

Ocean Front

Water Front

River Front

Lake Front

On Lake [Charles]

998

One Legged Alligator Hunter

Has decided to sell this **[delightful 2BR cottage with 150' frontage on Lake La Belle]** at **[$189,000]**. Check out #41 at _www.ur-home.net_

UR
HOME REALTY
555-8200
www.ur-home.net

➤ While the heading is intended as an attention-getting spoof, get the owner's permission to use it.

999

Paddle Your Own Canoe

across tranquil waters, walk your dog along **[forest paths]**, view magnificent sunsets from **[your porch]**. As the owner of this **[2BR, 1½-bath American Cedar home near Lakeport]**, you will rejoice in all nature has to offer. This **[year-round home]** has **[open high ceilings in the living area, a loft that could be a 3rd bedroom, solid wood paneling, and large garage]** on **[its wooded ½ acre]**. It's a very special place at **[$284,500]**.

UR
HOME REALTY
555-8200
www.ur-home.net

➤ If the property has water frontage, it should be covered in the heading.

1000

A River Runs Through It

[Tall trees], gorgeous views, and the gentle sound of a river make this [2-bedroom home] on [10] acres more than a "must see," it's a "MUST OWN" at [$187,500].

UR
HOME REALTY
555-8200
www.ur-home.net

➤ If the name of the river carries a positive image, it should be in the heading.

1001

Landlubber?

Watch the real sailors from the [deck] of this [9-room Nantucket Traditional] set on the best lot in [Bayfield Heights]. [$489,000] lets you sea it all at #63, *www.ur-home.net*

UR
HOME REALTY
555-8200
www.ur-home.net

ALTERNATIVE HEADINGS

Sing Sea Chanteys

Dream of Pirates

Ocean 11
(for an 11-room ocean-view home)

Ad Generator

The headings, feature language, and price closings in this Ad Generator may be used to modify the ads in this book or to create original ads. Boldface type indicates the language is suited for an ad heading. Types, features, and amenities of homes are arranged in alphabetical order.

Acreage   (*See* **Land, Undeveloped.**)

Air-Conditioning   Central air; central air for those sultry days ahead; fully air-conditioned; zone control air-conditioning and heat; climate-controlled environment; climate-controlled living; electronically controlled environment; **A Cool House; Cool House—Cool Price; Beat the Heat; A Hot Deal—A Cool House;** even the price is cool—$. **Frigid They Said;** A hot deal on a cool house—$; **A Cool [*Colonial*].**

Alcove   Music alcove; sleeping alcove; reading room; library; office alcove; sewing room.

Animals and Birds   (*See also* **Pets.**) Roaming [*Deer and Curious Raccoons*] will visit you at this . . . ; **Creatures Cavort** in the backyard of this . . . ; the backyard features [*a magnificent oak tree*] that is home to at least one family of squirrels; [*Deer*] **Have Been Seen** on the property; the woodlot is loaded with game; your nearest neighbors are [*squirrels and a friendly family of raccoons*]; **Wild Critters Abound** on this . . . ; presently home to [*deer, quail, and pheasant*]; you will **Feed the [*Deer*]** in your own backyard; you will look out your windows and see [*quail and doves*] at the well-frequented bird feeders; the breakfast area overlooks the well-frequented [*hummingbird*] feeders; a noisy neighbor will be a [*chattering chipmunk*]; you'll be enthralled by the haunting call of [*loons over the water*]; where [*raccoons and deer*] are the only residents and [*eagles*] soar above; your backyard will be host to everything from [*hummingbirds*] to [*quail*] and a [*red-tail hawk*]; the former owner has recorded [*73*] species of birds on the property; wake up to **The Sound of Birds; A Squirrel Lives** in an [*oak*] tree in the backyard of this . . . ; [*Eagles Soar*] over this . . . ; [*Hawks*] **Soar High** over this . . . ; **Geese and Ducks** fly low over this . . . ; **For the Birds** and bird lovers; **The Birds and Trees; Robins and Roses; A Curious [*Raccoon*]** watched as we put up the For Sale Sign on this . . . ; **A [*Goldfinch*] and a [*Hummingbird*]** are frequent visitors at the feeders; [*Robins*] **Perch** on the balcony of this of this . . . ; **Awaken Each Day** to the sound of birds; **Robins and Roses** share the backyard; **A Squirrel Lives** in the [*oak tree*]; **Birds Nest at the Window** of this . . .

Appliances   Like-new appliances; built-in appliances; all built-ins; built-in everything; every conceivable built-in; the [*Maytag*] appliances reflect the quality appointments of this . . .

Architect   **Designed by** [*Frank Lloyd Wright*]; **Frank Lloyd Wright** designed this . . . ; masterfully designed by . . . ; in the style of [*Frank Lloyd Wright*]; **Frank Lloyd Wright**-inspired; detailing that echoes the spirit of [*Frank Lloyd Wright*]; [*Frank Lloyd Wright*] **Original**.

Architecture   **Architecturally Perfect, Architecturally Fresh;** one of a kind; **Architectural Masterpiece;** architecturally designed; distinctively designed; masterful design; exuberant design; featured in [*Architectural Digest*]; architectural award-winner; design award-winner; award-winning design; awe-inspiring; merging aesthetic form with efficiency of function; capturing nature's essence; architecturally unique; a home that breaks the monotony of the ordinary; excitingly different; elegance tempered with simplicity; thoughtfully planned and executed; open concept; one-of-a-kind artistic statement; **Escape the Ordinary; Not a Cookie Cutter** version of every other house; *Architectural Digest* did not feature this [. . .] but they should have; **Rare** means uncommon or unique which describes this . . . ; daringly designed; designed with flair and style; classical symmetry of design (*See also* Floor Plan).

Architectural Detailing   Exquisite architectural details; handsome detailing; classic detailing; the most authentic . . . we have seen; the aesthetic allure of classic design; blending the traditional with the timeless; built with delightful European flair and style; classical embellishments; detailing that echoes the spirit of a time when life centered on the home; [*light, curved*] and elegant detailing; detailing that will excite the most discriminating.

Architectural Style

Brownstone   **Brownstone; Brownstone Classic; Front-Stoop Brownstone; Brownstone Magic; Sophisticated Brownstone; Brownstone Opulence.**

Cape Cod   **Friendly Cape Cod; Captivating Cape Cod; New England Cape Cod; Salt Box Cape; Down-East Cape Cod;** [*New Hampshire*] **Cape Cod; Classic Cape Cod; Nantucket Cape Cod.**

Colonial   Right out of the pages of **Gone with the Wind; Scarlett and Rhett** would be right at home in this . . . ; **Rhett Butler Colonial; Tara; Southern Manor; Pillared Colonial; Columned Colonial; 4-column Colonial; Southern Colonial; Southern Traditional; New Orleans Colonial; Mississippi Gambler;** double-stairs colonial; colonial with a contemporary flair; **Substantial Colonial; Classic Colonial; Nostalgic Colonial; New England Charmer; Clapboard Colonial; Federal Colonial; Colonial Splendor; Head-Turning Colonial; Colonial Revival;** distinctive colonial; **Impeccable Colonial; Picture-Book Colonial; Proper Colonial; Jacobean Colonial;** Touch of **Williamsburg; Williamsburg-Inspired; Virginia-Inspired; Williamsburg Traditional; Georgian Colonial; Virginia Colonial;**

Quaker Charmer; Pennsylvania Dutch; New England Saltbox; for the colonial purist; **Multigabled Colonial;** colonial grace with modern comfort; **A Touch of New England; Stately Colonial; Timeless Colonial; Monumental Colonial; Nantucket Colonial; Saltbox Colonial; Quaker Village Colonial; Pampered Dutch Colonial;** stone-front colonial; **Proud Colonial; Proper Colonial; Shutters and Clapboard; Plantation Colonial; Shaker Colonial; Amish-Inspired Colonial; Colonial Lovers; An American Classic;** crown molding; dental molding; painstakingly authentic; shutters that actually work; **Soaring Columns.**

Contemporary   Refreshing contemporary; dramatic contemporary; outstanding contemporary; stunning; sophisticated contemporary; distinctive contemporary; custom; [*California*] **Contemporary; Southwest Contemporary;** trilevel; splitlevel; earth shelter; solar home; **Art Deco;** excitingly different; imaginative floor plan; contemporary elegance casually designed in the flavor of the Southwest; exuberant design; open-living design; free-flowing floor plan; open concept; versatile floor plan; exciting and spacious; skylit; warm; treetop; **California-Inspired; Beaux-Art; Post Modern;** stunningly conceived; innovative without being trendy; clean; sleek; uncluttered design; sleek and sophisticated yet warm and cheerful. [*Santa Fe Style*]; **Cutting-Edge Contemporary; Exuberant Contemporary; Hercule Poirot** would have loved this Art Deco . . . ; **They Broke the Mold** when they built this . . . ; **Cookie Cutters** are for cookies; in harmony with nature; **One of a Kind; Not for the Timid; Pleasant Under Glass;** window-wrapped; the beauty of simplicity; **Frank Lloyd Wright** eat your heart out (*See also* **Floor Plan, Windows**).

Craftsman   Prairie Style Craftsman; American Craftsman; Stickley Craftsman; Gustav Stickley would have loved this . . . ; Shaker Inspired; Amish Inspired; American Bungalow; [*California*] Bungalow.

English   British Accent; British Town House; Merry Old English; Anglophile; English Manor; English Manor House; Cotswold Manor; Stone Manor House; Proper English; Smashing; A Touch of Old England; English Brick; Yorkshire Tudor; Tiffany Tudor; Handsome Tudor; Flawless Tudor; Tudor Revival; Country English; English Colonial; Queen Anne; Elizabethan; Edwardian; Edwardian Brick; Edwardian Manor House; English Chateau; English Country; English Cottage; Stately Manor House; Tiffany Tudor; Architecturally Smashing; Smashingly Impressive; reminiscent of an **English Country Estate;** patterned after the noble houses of England where entertaining and hospitality were inseparable from a gracious tradition; every conceivable option an Anglophile could possibly want; your opportunity to be **Lord of the Manor; To the Manor Born;** for an extremely civilized way of life; [*Irish*] **Manor House; A Civilized Residence; Proper English Brick** a civilized home offered at an uncommonly reasonable—$; **The British Are Coming!; Charles Dickens** would feel right at home in this . . . ; **I Say Old Chap** would you like a frightfully civilized . . .

French   Sassy French Provincial; French Colonial; French Country Home; sumptuous French country home; French Regency; French Norman; Norman Farmhouse; French Renaissance; Renaissance Revival; Turreted French Norman; French Manor; French Contemporary; Chateau; Chic Chateau; French Chateau; Flemish Cottage; Flemish Country; French Mediterranean; A Touch Of Paris; A Lifetime In Provence; Back to Provence; Fantastique at—$; Magnifique at—$.

Gothic   Gothic; American Gothic; Gothic Revival; Victorian Gothic.

Greek   Greek Revival; Greek Gothic; Grecian Columns; Athens Revisited.

Italian   Mediterranean; Stately Mediterranean; Old-World Mediterranean; Mediterranean Flair; Florentine Mediterranean; lavish villa; Italianate; brick Italianate; Mediterranean Colonial; Romanesque Beauty; Venetian; Venetian Gothic; Neapolitan Villa; Tuscany Villa; Lavish Villa; Italian Renaissance; reminiscent of the grand Mediterranean villas; inspired by old Rome; Baroque; Roman Glory.

Ranch   [*California*] Ranch; Santa Fe Ranch; raised ranch; exciting rambler; brick rambler; long, low and luscious; sprawling ranch; Colonial Ranch; distinctive ranch; contemporary ranch; a real ranch home.

Spanish   A Touch of Spain; Spanish Hacienda; Adobe Hacienda; A True Hacienda; Presidio Spanish; Old-World Spanish; Tons of Tile; flowing tile floors; mission tile; Saltillo tile; adobe fireplace; beehive fireplace; arches; Massive Arches; covered walkways; capturing the glory of old Spain; Spanish Renaissance; Spanish Revival; Latin Flavor; Salsa the Border; California Mission Style; Spanish Omelet; Spanish Eyes would love this . . . ; Pueblo Style; Pueblo Revival; Havana Wrapper; Mariachi Music.

Traditional   Traditional estate; elegant brick traditional; dignified traditional; American Traditional; American Bungalow; White Clapboard Traditional; Brick Traditional; Norman Rockwell Traditional; blending the traditional with the timeless.

Victorian   Country Victorian; charming Victorian; grand and dignified lady; Turreted Victorian; Victorian Showcase; Stately Victorian; Bow-Front Victorian; Victorian Grandiose; Vintage Victorian; Gingerbread Victorian; Queen Anne; Storybook Victorian; Commanding Victorian; Southern Victorian; American Victorian; A Painted Lady; Pretty Woman; Imposing Victorian; A Lady With A Past; shows Victorian influence; Crowning Victorian; ageless dignity; an old fashioned lady; Born Again Victorian.

Assumable Loan   Assumable [*7%*]; VA-Assumable; FHA-Assumable; Assume [*8½%*]; FHA; [*$8,500*] Takeover; pay down to [*7½%*] loan; Super Assumption; No Qualifying—No Credit Check; large; long-term fixed-rate; Seller Wants [*$5,000*] and you assume . . . ; No Loan Costs; Rejected for a Loan; an assumable mortgage that you'll love; Assume

the Best [*7%*]; Can't Get Financing; It's Easy as Pie to own this . . . (*See also* **Financing**).

Atrium Cathedral atrium; glassed-in atrium; fountain atrium; glass-domed atrium; soaring atrium; lushly landscaped atrium; tropical atrium; garden atrium; sky-lit atrium.

Attic Walk-up attic; room for [*2*] additional bedrooms in walk-up attic; storage attic; storage attic could be converted to studio or guest room; skylighted attic; skylit attic; windowed attic; dormered attic; would make ideal **Artist's Studio; Perfect Loft Studio; Attic Studio;** plenty of dry storage in the . . . ; room to store a lifetime of memories in the . . .

Backyard Tribe-sized yard; softball-size backyard; kid-size yard; pool-size yard; fully fenced backyard; playground backyard; **Room To Romp;** room for swing set and sandbox and a gaggle of children; the backyard is just waiting for your children; orchard-size; perfect spot for your garden; garden-size yard; fenced play area; child-safe fenced yard; family-size yard; the backyard is just waiting for a sandbox and swing; the [*old oak tree*] in the backyard is the perfect place to hang your swing; picturesque and private; room for a gaggle of children and their dogs in the . . . ; **Puppies and Children; A Jungle Gym** stands in the . . . ; a tree-shaded [*fenced*] yard your children will love (*See also* **Landscaping**).

Balcony A delightful balcony for [*starlight dining*]; a very private balcony; flower-bedecked balcony; incomparable view from the . . . ; intimate balcony; room for the barbecue on the delightful balcony; a full-body tan is possible on the very private balcony of this . . . ; wrought iron balcony; sheltered balcony; sunset balcony; sunrise balcony; sunny balcony; secluded privacy; iron balconies reminiscent of New Orleans; Spanish balcony; perfect for cocktails at sunset; iron railings (*See also* **Deck, Patio, Porch.**)

Bargain Property (*See* **Homes, Bargain-Priced.**)

Barns **A Weathered Barn; Horse Barn** comes with this . . . ; **A Red Barn; A Wobbly Barn; Old Dutch Barn;** gambrel-roofed barn; **Ancient Barn; Massive Barn;** would make ideal studio; awaits your imagination; century-old [*red*] barn; [*red*] barn has stood for [*nearly 100*] years; traditional [*red*] barn; hayloft barn; pole barn; [*40*]-stanchion barn; steel barn; perfect for boarding and training horses; the [*huge*] barn would make an ideal artist's studio; ideal for an artist's studio or for restoring furniture; [*40'*]-barn is begging for a couple of box stalls. (*See also* **Farms.**)

Bars Wet bar; refrigerated wet bar; sunken wet bar; pub room; friendly pub room; English pub room; Irish pub.

Baseball **The Last Home Run**—we doubt if we will ever see another . . . ; **Steal Home;** steal home at $; **Bottom Of The 9th;** your last chance to buy this . . . ; **Double Play** we have 2 . . . ; it's a fielder's choice at $; you'll really score at $; **Bases Loaded** you're at bat; bring them home to this . . . ; a home run at $; **Grand Slam**—they will shout with joy when you bring them home to this . . . ; **Foul Ball—Not;** you can be safely on base with this . . . ; **A Definite Hit; Season Tickets** to Mother Nature's spectacular show; **A Heavy Hitter** needed for this lead-off spot . . . ; home-run [*landscaping*].

Basement   Full basement; poured basement; block basement; [*8′*] basement; sump pump in . . . ; partial basement; fruit cellar; exposed basement; exposed lower level; walk-out basement; daylight basement; finished basement; partially finished basement; laundry room in; ready for finishing; roughed-in for bath; perfect for rainy-day playroom; plenty of storage room; room for 2 additional bedrooms in . . . ; expansion room in . . . ; future game room; plenty of room in the basement for a [*hobby shop*]; wine cellar; [*5,000*]-bottle wine cellar; temperature-controlled wine cellar; a perfect spot for a photographer's darkroom; fitness center in the . . . ; would make a perfect fitness center; the basement workroom is a hobbyist's delight; the finished basement is ideal for an office party; room for 100 teenagers in the . . . ; recreation center; game room; the full basement offers limitless possibilities; the full basement is perfect for a playroom or dungeon— depending upon your interests; workout room; a sprawling basement you can turn into separate worlds; **A Dungeon—**wine cellar or rainy-day playroom; perfect for potting and storage of bulbs.

Basement Unit   **English Apartment;** room for English apartment; **Terrace-Level Apartment;** could be finished for rental unit; **In-Law Suite;** would make possible in-law suite; could be converted to an English apartment; possible rental unit.

Basketball   **Slam-Dunk Deal;** it's a slam-dunk at $; there's a basketball hoop on the [*oversized, double garage*] of this . . . ; it's a 3-pointer at $; [***Larry Bird***] **Ceiling.**

Bathhouse   Cabana; dressing room with shower; pool house.

Baths   Master bath; opulent master bath; opulent [*Phoenician*] bath; sumptuous master bath; sinfully sumptuous master bath; sensuous master bath; sinfully sensuous master bath; deliciously sumptuous baths; tiled baths; Roman baths; Phoenician baths; Phoenician tile baths; Grecian baths; garden tub; raised garden tub; luxurious sunken tub; step-down tub; oval spa; antique tub; antique claw-footed tub; skylit bath; enchanting garden bath; bath/fitness center; oval tub; tub with whirlpool; whirlpool tub; hot spa; therapeutic hot spa; double tub; double vanities; double shower; his-and-hers vanities; dual vanities; separate shower; powder room; $1/2$-bath; $3/4$-bath; floor-to-ceiling tile in . . . ; intimate hot spa; double-size whirlpool tub; intimate hot spa for two; sheathed in [*tile*]; marble baths; imported marble baths; **It Feels So Good** to sit in the hot whirlpool bath; the master bath is larger than an ordinary bedroom; guest bath (*See also* **Marble, Tile**).

Bedroom   [*26′*] master bedroom; master suite; breathtaking master suite; Arabian Nights master suite; sensuous master suite; lavish master suite; [*2*] bedrooms in children's wing; separate dressing areas; his-and-hers dressing rooms; nursery; **Teen Suite;** maid's room; maid or guest room; guest suite;

separate guest suite; king-size; queen-size; delightful dormered; room for [*2*];
room for additional bedrooms in . . . ; master suite with morning room;
master suite with sitting room; sumptuous master suite; dual master suites;
master suite plus guest room; master suite features a snuggle-up fireplace;
separate suite for guests or live-ins; lower-level bedroom; [*double doors*]
lead to master suite; stunningly conceived master suite; Texas-size bedrooms;
baronial-size bedrooms; royal-size master suite; fantasy master suite; master
chamber; in-laws and teens will love the privacy of the separate suite;
practically sinful master suite; movie-star master suite; Hollywood-inspired
master suite; privacy master suite; master retreat; sinfully indulgent master
suite; [*4*] **Big Bedrooms; A Storybook Nursery** just waiting for you;
possible [*4th*] bedroom; **Rip Van Winkle Dream Home;** a boy and his dog
would love bunking in their [*rugged, paneled*] bedroom; dormitory-size
children's bedroom; sleeping loft; sleeping porch; sleeping alcove; a master
suite right out of the Arabian Nights (*See also* **Baths, Closets**).

Birds   (*See* **Animals and Birds.**)

Brick   Used brick; Tennessee brick; **Brick Solid;** antique brick; Norman brick;
English brick; warm-rose brick; all brick; Adobe brick; vine-covered brick;
brick and stone; maintenance-free brick exterior; exposed brick work;
The 3rd Little Pig would have loved this brick . . . (*See also* **Stone**).

Builder's Sale   **Builder's Closeout; Builder's Liquidation;** builder's final
sellout; **Desperate Builder; Builder SOS; Below Builder's Cost; Builder
Ordered Sale; Builder Says Sell; Builder Must Sell;** built by the builder
as [*his/her*] own residence; **Builder's Own;** built by the builder for [*his/her*]
own family (*See also* **Homes, New**).

Business Opportunities   **The Buck Starts Here; Unbelievable Money-
Maker; A Money Machine; Count Your Profits; Proven Gold Mine;
Impressive Track Record; Fantastic Profits; Whopportunity;
Opportunity Knocks; National Franchise; Captured Clientele;
Immediate Income; Hire Yourself; Work for Yourself;** be master of your
future; **Family Business; Mother and Daughter Business; Father And
Son Business; Recession-Proof Business;** take advantage of [*17*] years of
goodwill; established [*24 years*]; long-established; in operation more than
[*30*] years; books open to serious buyer; the books are open to you and your
accountant; needs a take-charge owner; untapped potential; can be
expanded; proven growth record; owner will train; experienced staff; loyal
staff will remain; employees know of this ad; below-market rental;
advantageous lease; long-term lease; long-term lease at moderate rental;
favorable lease; price includes all inventory; inventory at cost; comes with
all equipment; furnishings and fixtures for efficient operation; all equipment
included for uninterrupted operation; latest equipment; new equipment;
like-new furnishings and equipment; **100% Location;** strategically located
between . . . and . . . ; prominent location; corner location; high-traffic
location; college town; located in affluent community of . . . ; located in
booming . . . ; loads of parking; ample parking; carrying all major lines;
top-line inventory; exclusive dealer for . . . ; steady neighborhood trade;
established clientele; excellent record of repeat clientele; enjoys a substantial

tourist trade; national accounts; national clients; major clients; retiring owner will sign noncompetition agreement; unusual circumstances force the sale of this profitable; owner retiring; [*79*]-year-old owner retiring; business has grown too fast for elderly owner; needs a take-charge owner; **Owner's Doctor Says Sell;** part-time owner reports [*$*] gross; reports [*$*] net with absentee owner; absentee owner wants out; [*3*] generations of family ownership; this business has been a landmark since [*1920*]; needs owner willing to work; no selling; no mechanical experience necessary; this profitable business can be operated right from your home; exclusive dealer for . . . ; your security is only a phone call away; a good operating business that could be even better.

Carpeting   Top-line carpeting; plush [*Karastan*] carpeting; all wool carpeting; sculptured wool carpeting; [*stain resistant*] carpeting; plush sculptured carpeting; plush neutral carpeting; luxurious; wall-to-wall carpet; [*Berber*] carpet; carpeting Fido can't stain (*See also* **Colors**).

Ceiling   Lighted ceiling; softly lighted ceiling; illuminated ceiling; skylighted ceiling; cathedral ceiling; soaring cathedral ceiling; impressive cathedral ceiling; beamed ceiling; open-beamed ceiling; exposed beam ceiling; [*10'*] ceiling; two-story living room; the [*10'*] ceiling adds a feeling of spaciousness and light; a soft ceiling of light gently illuminates the [*charming kitchen*]; crowned by a [*12'*] ceiling; giant-high ceilings; studio ceilings. coved ceiling; vaulted ceiling; dramatically vaulted ceiling; colossal ceiling; double-high ceilings; tin ceiling; the [*14'*] vaulted ceiling enhances the ambiance of the [*great room*]; coffered ceiling; ceilings climb to over [*20'*].

Ceiling Fan   Ceiling fan; plantation fan; paddle fan; Bermuda fan; [*Hunter*] **Fans.**

Clean   Better than a model; **Shows Like a Model; Immaculate; Impeccable; Flawless;** spotless; **Move-in Ready; Squeaky Clean;** reflects caring owners; **Owner's Pride; Whistle-Clean;** handsomely kept; antiseptic clean; **White-Glove Clean; White-Glove [*Colonial*];** it sparkles; pristine condition; blue-ribbon condition; superbly maintained; reflects owner's pride; **Better Than New; Persnickety; Lazy!** Then you'll love this impeccably maintained . . . ; **Beyond Perfect; Nothing To Do** but move into this immaculate . . . ; **All You Have To Do** is move into this . . . ; showroom fresh; wear your white gloves and check it out; bound to please the most fastidious buyer; **Move-in Perfect.**

Closets   Huge closets; his-and-hers closets; walk-in closets; lighted; outrageous closets; mirrored wardrobes; double sliding wardrobes; mirrored doors on the sliding wardrobes; more closets than you have ever seen; loads of closet and storage space; built-in shoe racks; closets you can get lost in; **Get-Lost Closets;** closets bigger than your wish list; closets Imelda Marcos would envy; **Closet Clout.**

Closings   (*See* **Price Closings.**)

Colors   [*Brown*] **is Beautiful** trim on this . . . ; soft terra-cotta tones; rich terra-cotta tones; warm and rich color scheme; warm medley of colors; muted tones; soft tones; softly decorated; basic earth-tone decor; golden earth tones; warm earth tones; muted earth tones; desert colors; desert decor; **The White House;** cool and fresh; cool tones; bright and light; peaches-and-cream decor; a happy decor of . . . ; tasteful neutral tones; subdued tones of [*ivory and beige*]; decorator-perfect; decorator colors; decorator-fresh; decorator-sharp; [*grey*] and [*salmon*] tones complement this . . . ; soft; neutral tones with colorful accents; tasteful neutral decor; a mix of soft hues and colorful accents; bright; lively hues; bright rooms add a sense of happiness; frosty gray; soft beige; pale [*marigold*]; bathed in pastels (*See also* **Decorating**).

Columns   Doric; Corinthian; Greek; Roman; soaring; fluted; pilaster; stately.

Condominium   **Condomaximum;** Choice corner unit; impressive end unit; at last—a corner unit; freestanding unit; garden unit; villa-style; fantasy villa; upgraded model; sought-after model; a hard-to-find model; upgraded appliances; upgraded beyond belief; with just about every upgrade possible; walk to everything from this . . . ; walk to . . . ; strategic location; rental service available; monthly assessments only [*$*]; association fees lower than you ever imagined; low monthly assessment; low condo fee includes everything; maintenance fee includes [*heat*]; **Never a Rent Increase;** very private balcony; [*18*] windows welcome the sunshine in this immaculate [*corner unit*]; manicured greenbelt; soundproofed walls; you won't have to whisper in this soundproof . . . ; **Whisper No More**—fully soundproof building; elevator building; doorman; concierge; full-service building; a condominium that gives you the privacy of a single-family home with none of the worry; offering the seclusion of a private home; an exciting alternative to apartment living; a resort-style lifestyle with big-city sophistication; sophisticated yet so comfortable; for a uniquely comfortable urban lifestyle, free from the burden of maintenance; all the amenities of a fine resort; more than just a place to live—it's a whole new way of living; resort environment; **For the Wild Life** enjoy the two-legged kind around the pool; a world of fun and leisure; country-club recreational facilities; for comfort and uncomplicated living; the closest thing to carefree living; offering the excitement of city living in an almost country-like setting. **A Full Body Tan** is possible on the very private [*balcony*]; when the grass grows, the leaves fall, and the snow piles up, you will appreciate the lifestyle you've worked for; much more than a place to live—it's your entry into the carefree world of fun and leisure; all the amenities of a fine single-family residence with none of the responsibilities; you can travel the world knowing that maintenance will be taken care of; let others do your bidding while you enjoy the . . . ; with the spaciousness and privacy of a single-family home; a wealth of on-site and neighborhood amenities; it's like living in a country club; offering every requisite for the lifestyle you have earned; you will have time for the joys of living while we [*mow the lawn and shovel the snow*]; combining the best of luxurious living and home ownership; for an active yet relaxed lifestyle; luxury reaches a new height with this [*12th*]-floor . . . ; semiattached luxury homes; **Condo in the Clouds; Condo or Castle; No Board Approval;** luxurious privacy and access to a full community life; a recreational ambiance rivaling the world's most exclusive resorts; **Sell The Lawn Mower;**

Junk the Car everything is walking-close to this . . . ; room for flowers on the [*delightful balcony*]; sun-drenched rooms; a balanced environment where you and your family can enjoy the best that life has to offer; a multitude of recreational opportunities; exudes an aura of style; comfort and sophistication; roof garden; sheltered [*balcony*]; [*14*] **Windows; Let it Snow;** chock-full of upgrades; ground-level unit; [*38*] **Steps to** [*Pool*]; **A Gorgeous Hunk** of a very desirable building; [*Lakeshore Drive*] **Address; Big as a House; It's the Tops; Space/Light/Views; 55? You're Lucky—** you qualify for this . . . ; **Getting A Little Gray?** chances are you qualify for this . . . ; a village-like atmosphere; **Unretire—**life's just beginning at 55 in . . . ; no one above or below; detached unit; **Feels Like a House; Big As A House; Lazy Owner Condo; Condo-Charisma** (*See also* **Privacy, Security, Vacation Homes**).

Cooperative   (*See* **Condominium.**)

Courtyard   Stone courtyard; brick courtyard; paved courtyard; fountain courtyard; flower-bedecked courtyard; charming courtyard; tiled courtyard; **Paving Stones and Flowers** in the delightful courtyard of this . . . (*See also* **Patio.**)

Darkroom   Darkroom with sinks; darkroom with stainless-steel sinks; ideal for photographer's darkroom; would make the perfect darkroom; professional darkroom; room for a photographer's darkroom in the . . .

Deck   Wrap-around deck; inviting sun deck; secluded deck; extensive deck area; extensive decking; redwood deck; cedar deck; treated deck; vinyl deck; redwood balcony; wrapped on [*three*] sides by redwood deck; sunset deck; sunrise deck; barbecue deck; cantilevered deck; garden deck; warm, sunny deck; secluded deck; privacy deck; a very private sun deck; experience the inner peace of a breathtaking [*sunrise*] [*sunset*] from the deck of this . . . ; you will want to light the BBQ when you walk out on this . . . ; spy-glass deck; [*south*]-facing deck; **Bake Sale** there's a great sun deck on this; **Nudists** you will love the privacy of the sundeck on this . . . (*See also* **Balcony, Patio, Porch**).

Decorating   Lavishly decorated; tastefully decorated; professionally decorated; decorated by . . . ; dramatically decorated; decorated in [*peaches and cream*]; meticulously appointed; thoughtfully appointed; stunningly decorated; **Decorator-Perfect;** decorating that will knock your socks off (*See also* **Colors**).

Den   Lion-size den; walnut-paneled den; courtroom-paneled den; study; paneled study; library; English library; music room; English drawing room; drawing room; office; home office; office/den; office/studio; estate office; convertible den; the warm [*paneled*] den features a friendly [*orchard-stone*] fireplace; floor-to-ceiling bookcases line one wall of the richly appointed study; the separate entrance makes the den the perfect home office; your perfect quiet spot; sewing room; studio; [*5,000*] **Books** fit in the quiet library; computer center; home office/computer center; your "sneak-away" place.

Dining Room   Separate dining area; formal dining room; elegant dining room; chandeliered dining room; crystal chandelier adorns the formal dining room; banquet-size dining room; gallery dining room; window-wrapped dining room; room for a family reunion in the . . . ; solarium-style dining room; breakfast room; cheerful breakfast room; greenhouse-windowed breakfast room; intimate and formal dining areas.

Doors   Double doors; pocket doors; double pocket doors; solid [*oak*] entry; massive hand-carved doors; rustic carved doors; vintage carved doors; castle doors; handcrafted doors; sculptured double-door entry; [*9'*] doors; massive [*9'*] doors; [*6*] panel doors; double glass doors; sliding glass patio doors; sliding French doors; French-swinging doors; classic French doors; leaded French doors; stained-glass entry door; leaded-glass entry door; leaded-glass accents; crystal doorknobs.

Driveway   Paved drive; concrete drive; cobblestone driveway; circle drive; tree-canopied drive; big enough for [*6*] cars; flower-bedecked driveway; lined with colorful plantings and flowering shrubs.

Entry Hall   Foyer; elegant foyer; tiled foyer; slate foyer; impressive slate foyer; soaring foyer; expansive foyer; two-story soaring foyer; split foyer; vestibule; the lovely slate foyer beckons you into this magnificent residence; the foyer opens to a dramatic [*great room*].

Entryway   Courtyard entry; arched entryway; shaded entry; dramatic entry; slate entryway; turreted entryway; dramatic turreted entryway; massive entryway; grand entryway; towering entry; gallery entryway; gracious entryway; picturesque columned entry enhances this . . . ; cathedral entryway; portico; gated entryway; enter through a stone portal; fountain entryway; drive-through portico; the estate entrance frames this . . . ; the entry is flanked by [*dramatic fluted columns*]; **Wrought Iron Gates** lead to . . . ; flower-bedecked entry.

Estate Sale   **Estate Clearance; Heirs Say Sell; Heir's Selling; Estate Settlement;** priced to settle estate; **Probate Sale;** probate-ordered sale; heirs want cash now. (*See also* **Homes, Bargain-Priced.**)

Exterior Siding   Low-maintenance [*Masonite*] siding; no-maintenance [*aluminum*] siding and trim; maintenance-free [*vinyl*] siding; western cedar siding; cedar log siding; redwood siding; natural cedar siding; cedar shakes; natural textured wood siding; handsome brick exterior; brick and cedar exterior; brick beauty; brick-and-stone exterior; **Brick-Solid;** native stone exterior; solid stone construction; **Stone and Glass.** (*See also* **Brick.**)

Failed Sale   **Sale Failed; Play It Again Sam; It's Back; Blown Sale; Opportunity Knocks Twice; Buyer Backed Out;** opportunity is knocking again—respond or be sorry; because of unusual circumstances this "sold" . . . is back on the market; **A Second Chance.**

Family Room   Family room; [*30'*] game room; club room; recreation room; daylight recreation room; billiard room; there's room for a billiard table and even ping-pong in . . . ; marine room; playroom; family playroom; drawing room; salon; fitness center; home gym; private gym; family room opens onto . . . ; the family room centers on [*a massive stone fireplace*]; warm; window-wrapped family room; leisure room; pub room; English pub room; cozy pub room with [*stone fireplace*]; adult playroom; magnificent salon; grand salon; lounge; drawing room; English drawing room; multiuse room.

Farms

Farmers'   **A Farmer's Farm; Family Farm; Real Farmer's Farm; Double Cropper; Grade-A Dairy Farm;** irrigated [*alfalfa*] farm; **Poultry Ranch;** [*Apple*] **Orchard;** diversified farm; **Farmin' Bargain;** high-producing [*soybean*] farm; **A Working Farm; A Working Ranch;** [*200*] **Acres under Plow;** [*400*] acres of pasture; [*600*] acres tillable; [*100*] acres in government program; [*90%*] tillable; **800 Deeded Acres; 10-Acre Tobacco Allotment;** balance woodlot; [*120*] acres currently in alfalfa; leased grazing rights on [*3,000*] acres; **BLM Lease** for [*3,000*] additional acres; pasture for cows; will carry [*700*] cow units; capacity for [*800*] feeder pigs; [*120*] bushels of corn per acre reported last year; said to be one of the best-producing farms in the area; a self-sustaining cattle operation; capable of carrying [*600*] cattle units; improved pasture; unimproved pasture; native pasture; [*4"*] drilled well; [*3*] wells; natural flowing spring; year-round flowing river; seasonal stream; [*½*] mile of river frontage; irrigation lines; [*120*] acres irrigated and tiled; irrigation allotment; creek could be used for irrigation; creek presently used for irrigation; drip irrigation; overhead irrigation; includes ample water rights; [*4*] ponds; land is well watered; blessed with ample water; milking parlor; automatic feeders; fenced and cross-fenced; [*80*]-stanchion barn; [*42*]-stall barn; [*6*] silos; [*4*] Harvestor silos; [*three 60,000-bu.*] grain bins; [*30' × 120'*] machine shed; [*40' × 100'*] pole barn; [*40' × 100'*] open-loft barn; [*11*]-room house; modern [*11*]-room house; newer [*11*]-room house (*See also* **Barns**).

Gentlemen   **Family Showplace; Country Squire; Weekend Farm; Picture-Postcard Farm; Currier-and-Ives Farm; Old West Ranch;** [*300*]**-Acre Empire;** for the blue jeans wearer; Agricultural Estate; the best in town and country living; farm in style; **Flying Cowboy/Cowgirl Ranch; Flying Farmer;** possible landing strip; miles of white board fencing; abundance of wildlife; just the place for purebred cattle and thoroughbred horses; mouth-watering orchard; **Historic Farm; Storybook Farm; Be Lord or Lady of the Manor; Start a Dynasty** on this . . . ; **Shades of the Old West;** Old West ranch; **Zane Grey** would have felt at home in this . . . ; be monarch of the range; **The Old West Is Alive** and well on this . . . ; established by a federal land grant issued in [*18__*]; manor house built in [*18__*]; this is the first time this farm has been on the market in . . . years; formerly owned by . . . ; Dutch barn; complete cattle-working facilities were specifically designed for easy management; farm pond stocked with [*bass*]; trout-filled stream; abundance of wildlife; professional management available; **Your Own Ponderosa** (*See also* **Barns**).

Hobby   Mother Earth Farm; Self-Sufficiency Farm; Self-Sufficiency Retreat; Cornucopia Hobby Farm; Farmlet; Organic Farm; Organic Orchard; Grandpa or Grandma's Farm; Beginner's Farm; Forgotten Farm; Abandoned [*Blackberry*] Farm; Back to the Farm; starter farm; Farmette; minifarm; ranchette; Pioneer Farm; Retirement Farm; Old-Time Farm; farmlet; your escape from the city; Back To Basics; [*40*] Acres and Independence; Find Your Roots; harvest the good life; traditional farm home; old-time farm home; solid [*5*]-room home; windmill-powered well; hydropower possibilities; possible water generation site; possible dam site for lake and hydropower; contains marketable timber; full complement of modern well-maintained equipment; easy drive to . . . ; not just a home—it's a way of life; a better place to raise a family; escape from city crime and grime; harvest the good life; for the life you deserve; on a country lane; on a quiet country lane; country living at its tranquil best; offering pastoral tranquility; Chickens and Ducks; Old McDonald [*40*] Acres we have his farm; Stone Silo. (*See also* **Barns.**)

Investment   In the Path of Progress; Farm Now—Develop Later; [*$90,000*] lst-year depreciation; owner will lease back; TENANT AVAILABLE; lessee available; [*$200,000*] of depreciable assets; [*½*] mineral rights; development possibilities; exciting potential; The Ultimate Tax Shelter; impressive investment; Tax Farm (*See also* **Land, Undeveloped**).

Fencing   Cyclone fence; white board fence; cedar rail fence; split-rail fence; white picket fence; Tom Sawyer Picket Fence; charming white picket fence; stockade fencing; privacy walls; block walls; completely fenced; fully fenced; perimeter and cross-fencing; fenced and cross-fenced; old stone wall; high-walled garden; hedged with stone walls; framed by . . . ; embraced by stone walls; estate-rail fencing; ranch-rail fencing; wrought iron fencing; Don't Sit on This Fence; a white picket fence frames this; Walled Estate; privacy walls; walled patio.

Financing   Less than [*5%*] down; try [*$1,000*] down; can you afford [*$500*] per month?; old-fashioned financing; down-to-earth financing; hardly anything down; possible [*6%*] financing; possible no-down VA low-down FHA; seller pays points; seller pays points and closing costs; locked-in interest rate; payments like rent; financing has been arranged; financing available; offering extraordinary financial arrangements; exceptional financing; you might qualify for a very special low-interest loan; below-market-rate owner financing; with almost no down payment—it doesn't get any better than this; financing tailored to your personal needs; with simply great financing; Move in Free or close to it; No Down Payment if you qualify for this . . . ; payments likely less than you're paying in rent; the payments will seem like rent; Almost Nothing Down; No Points; Dreamer—do you dream about owning a home but only have [*$*] for a down payment?; Mean In-Laws? No need to borrow a down payment with this . . . ; Rejected for a Loan? we can make you a homeowner with this . . . ; Name Your Terms; owner is flexible; [*7%*] assumable; an assumable mortgage that you will love; Reduced for Cash; It's Easy as Pie to buy this . . . ; Anything Down;

pint-size payments; **Owner Will Finance; No Loan Fees; No Cash?**
negotiate terms with bank; **Not A Vet?** The VA may sell this . . . to a non-Vet
with "0" down; **Down Payment—Whatever; Lease To Own; Easy To
Own;** perfect financing (*See also* **Assumable Loan**).

Fireplace   [*16'*] floor-to-ceiling fireplace; wood-burning fireplace; fieldstone
fireplace; orchard-stone fireplace; river rock fireplace; cut-stone fireplace;
native stone fireplace; massive [*stone*] fireplace; majestic [*stone*] fireplace;
California driftwood fireplace; Tennessee stone fireplace; limestone fireplace; antique brick fireplace; warm rose brick fireplace; marble fireplace;
fireplace sheathed in [*marble*]; cheerful fireplace; corner fireplace; intimate
fireplace; snuggle-up fireplace; country-style fireplace; romantic fireplace;
corn poppin' fireplace; chestnut roastin' fireplace; marshmallow toastin'
fireplace; freestanding fireplace; Beehive fireplace; Danish fireplace; 2-way
fireplace; fireplace insert; Heatilator fireplace; Franklin stove; marble hearth
and mantle; the massive [*oak*] fireplace mantel reportedly came from
[*an ancient sailing ship*]; solid [*walnut*] mantle; brick hearth; raised hearth;
toe-warming fireplace; heartwarming [*brick*] fireplace; cheerful hearth;
soaring fireplace; castle-size fireplace.

Fixer-Upper   **Fixer-Upper; Fixer-Upper—[*4*]-BR; Fix 'n' Save; Fix it Up**
and save a bundle; **Large and Scruffy [*4BR*]; Filthy Old House;
The Roof Leaks; Sweep and Reap; Weed It and Reap; Prewar Wreck;
Magnificent Wreck; A Shambles; Demolition Derby Special; Bit of a
Mess; Heck of a Wreck; Worst House—Best Street;** the worst-looking
house; **An Eyesore; Peeling-Paint Special; Leaking-Roof Special; Bring
Your Toolbox; Bring Your Paintbrush; Fix Or Tear Down; Bring Your
Hammer; Wrecking-Bar Special; Paintbrush Needed; Needs Love;
Needs a Labor of Love; Needs a Face-Lift; Ugly Duckling; Pygmalion—
Needs Prof. Higgins; In Terrible Condition; It's Miserable; Neglected** is
an understatement for this . . . ; **Neglected Giant; Neglected Ranch;
Neglected—Oh Yes!; Needs Everything; High-Class Disaster; It's a
Disaster;** quality construction in need of cosmetic surgery; but the structure
appears sound; solid construction; presently livable; barely livable; livable
but . . . ; make no mistake—there is work to be done; needs a few bushels of
nails and barrels of paint; loaded with potential but needs a barrel of paint;
bring your imagination and some elbow grease; a neglected beauty awaiting
a Prince Charming; this home boasts [*3 bedrooms and 2 baths*]—what it
doesn't boast about is its horrible condition; wear your old clothes and bring
along aspirin; a jungle of overgrown shrubs and trees; it looks as though it
fought in World War III and was the loser; we scraped the bottom of the
barrel to come up with this . . . ; **Deserted; Abandoned; Semi-Fixer-Upper;
Fire-Damaged; Rambling Wreck; Abandoned [*Artist's Chalet*]; It's a
Lemon; Handyperson's Special; Diamond in the Rough; Toolbox
Special; Needs TLC; Dumpy Duplex; Forgotten Cottage; Fixer-Upper
Possibilities; Dilapidated Disaster; Paint, Patch, and Profit;** fixer-upper
priced at $; the lawn shows more bare ground than grass; you'll have to
start your landscaping with a machete; set amidst waist-high weeds; it looks
like you would expect a foreclosure to look like; it will take more than
paint to make this . . . presentable; while it needs a lot; you'll only be
paying $; awaiting your imagination at $, but it's livable; **Almost Livable;**

Easy Money—a little work can mean a big profit; build sweat equity; the neighbors will appreciate any effort to improve this . . . ; we don't have much that's nice to say about this . . . ; if you love to tinker, here's work for a lifetime; the only redeeming feature is the price; **Generations of Grime** have been lovingly preserved in this; **Shabby but Comfortable;** calling it a fixer is a generous description of this . . . ; paint, plaster, nails, and some strong glue will be needed to mend this . . . ; we would be ashamed to advertise it if it weren't for the price $; it looks as if it's never seen a paint brush or a vacuum cleaner; this one makes any other fixer-upper look like a palace; don't take our word for it—come and see what a mess it really is; **A Turkey;** whatever is breakable is broken; the decorating is early medieval; **Dark and Dreary;** you'll be depressed—not impressed by this . . . ; at least one family of [*pigeons*] calls it home; the shame of an otherwise pleasant neighborhood; it's the worst house in an otherwise fine neighborhood; the lawn is nonexistent; the shrubs haven't been trimmed in ages; the house has forgotten what a paint brush feels like; needs a bit of work; needs cosmetic repair; **Older Than Dirt** and just as pretty; **Gaudy**—poor taste abounds in this . . . ; your chance to turn sweat into equity; **Needs Everything;** needs a facelift plus internal surgery; **Vacant; Want To Make [*$60,000*]?** about [*$10,000*] and a lot of hard work should turn this . . . into a showplace; **El Dumpo—El Cheapo** (*See also* **Homes, Bargain-Priced**).

Warning! Never use a negative approach or indicate a home is a fixer-upper without prior written permission from the owner.

Flooring

Tile/Stone   Terrazzo; quarry tile; Mexican tile; Mexican quarry tile; sun-baked Mexican tile; travertine tile; Portuguese tile; easy-care tile; no-wax Congoleum; vinyl floors; pure vinyl floors; flagstone; Saltillo tile; limestone floors.

Wood   Hardwood floors; gleaming hardwood floors; random-plank [*hardwood*] floors; random-width flooring; hand-pegged floors; matched hardwood floors; pegged hardwood floors; parquet floors; inlaid hardwood floors; solid oak floors; maple floors; soft-tone maple floors; refined maple floors; mellow pine floors; pine plank floors; heart oak floors; varnished oak floors; dazzling oak floors; graced with gleaming hardwood and richly carpeted floors; bleached oak floors; original [*wide-plank*] floors (*See also* **Woodwork**).

Floor Plan   Innovative floor plan; versatile floor plan; free-flowing floor plan; exciting and spacious floor plan; California-inspired floor plan; split floor plan; master bedroom is separated for maximum privacy; open concept; free-flowing floor plan; you'll marvel at the feeling of light and spaciousness of the free-flowing floor plan; a flowing floor plan of space and function; gracious floor plan; intimate floor plan; sensitive floor plan; designed for casual living; designed for gracious entertaining; imaginative floor plan; thoughtful floor plan; split bedrooms; the most livable floor plan you have ever seen.

Football   **Want To Score** points with your family?; **The Longest Yard** in . . . ; touchdown priced at $; **Play Touch Football** on the expansive level lawns of this . . . ; **4th Down—Last Chance; Extra Point**—we forgot to tell you that . . . ; **6 Points**—you'll score a touchdown with this . . . ; the extra point is the price—$; **Season Tickets** to Mother Nature's spectacular show.

Foreclosure   **Foreclosure Sale; Near Foreclosure; Stop Foreclosure; Beat Foreclosure Sale; Foreclosure Pending; Last Chance** before foreclosure; **Lender Forces Sale; Beat-the-Sheriff** sale; lender wants sale now; **Lender Orders Sale; Bank Repo; Out of Foreclosure; Government Foreclosure;** for sale by lender; **Lender Sale; Bank Sale; The F Word** it's foreclosure time; **Bank Has Grandma's House; Court Ordered Sale; REPO . . .** (*See also* **Homes, Bargain-Priced**).

Fountain   Fountain courtyard; fountain entry; flower-bedecked fountain; fountain atrium; shimmering fountain; bubbling fountain; Spanish fountain; Mexican fountain; tiled fountain; garden fountain; fountain pool.

Foyer   (*See* **Entry Hall.**)

Furnished Homes   Completely furnished; completely and exquisitely furnished; **Fully Furnished; Furnished—[3]BR;** magnificently furnished; magnificent furnishings; meticulously furnished; extravagant furnishings; extravagant appointments; handsomely appointed; exciting accessories; custom-furnished without regard to cost; most of the custom furniture stays; decorator-furnished; designer-furnished; fully furnished and accessorized; furnishings available; charmingly furnished; a wealth of luxurious appoint-ments; toothbrush-ready; lavishly appointed; decorator appointments; California decorator; decorated and furnished by . . . ; **Turnkey-Furnished;** richly detailed interior appointments; impeccably decorated and furnished; **If You Have Nothing** we have a fully furnished . . . ; [*exquisite*] furnishings are included at $; all you need is your family; **Decorated by [*Chase*]; Toothbrush not Included** but everything else comes with this . . . ; **Forks and Saltshakers** are about all you'll need.

Garage   Heated; 2-car garage; double garage; attached garage; 2½-car garage; oversized double garage; 2+ car garage; detached garage; coach house; carriage house; **A Whole Bunch of Cars** will fit in this . . . ; RV-size garage; plus room to park a RV; could be converted to [*studio*] [*guest house*]; plenty of room for [2] cars plus all your "stuff"; [*4*]-**Car Garage** comes with this; room for bikes and trikes in the . . . ; makes a perfect rainy day playroom; the . . . has room for everything you own; garage/workshop; extra-deep . . . ; boat-deep . . . ; **Car Collectors**—[5]-car garage comes with this . . . ; room for all your toys in the . . . ; **Garage—Garage** two separate [2]-car garages come with this . . . ; **Garage Sale**—an oversize [3]-car garage comes with this . . . ; the commodious garage has room for [3] motorcars.

Garden   Gardener's Showcase; harvest in your own backyard; **A Bountiful Harvest** from this . . . ; **A Garden Gnome; Gherkins and Gnomes;** family-size garden; super-size vegetable garden; productive garden; private garden; **English Garden;** private **Walled Garden;** terraced garden; organic garden; lush tropical garden; excellent garden spot; a quiet garden spot; great spot for vegetable garden; a special sunny garden spot; perfect garden spot; **An Herb Garden;** old-fashioned grape arbor; courtyard garden; solar greenhouse; **A Greenhouse; Your Own Greenhouse;** the perfect plant and putter place; rose garden; formal rose garden; **Strawberry Shortcake** a strawberry patch comes with this . . . ; **Rhubarb Pie** a rhubarb patch comes with this . . . ; **Green is for Garden;** Hawaiian garden; oriental garden; bonsai garden; perennial garden; resplendent in a rainbow of colors; **Orchids and Daisies** will flourish in the greenhouse that comes with this . . . ; **Cholesterol Free** garden . . . ; **Organic Garden;** bright splashes of color; your green thumb will begin to itch when you see the indescribable garden; a somewhat neglected garden awaits your green thumb; colorful plantings; colorful plantings and flowering shrubs; lovingly cared for flowers; starburst of flowers; ablaze with color; a garden that will turn a farmer green with envy; glorious garden; **Robins and Roses;** [*Azaleas*] **and** [*Daffodils*]; [*Geraniums*] line the garden walk; green-thumb priced at $; **Garden for All Reasons; Stop! Smell the Flowers**—the [*roses*] are in bloom at this . . . ; **A Botanical Wonderland** surrounds this . . . ; it's definitely your place to grow at $; A . . . that will keep you busy and healthy; an opportunity to forget the cares of the world while doing what you love; the garden comes with . . . ; **Gardener's Paradise;** the finest [*rose*] garden in the neighborhood; [*Cabbage*] **People** will love this garden . . . ; the envy of the garden club; trellised garden; [*rose bushes*] that are a neighborhood landmark; **Vegetarian's Delight;** the garden produces enough vegetables to fill a [*half-dozen*] freezers; a **Strawberry Patch** comes with this . . . ; **Ramblin' Rose** bushes and colorful plantings; **Luther Burbank** would have loved this botanical wonderland; a garden your neighbors will envy; planting shed; garden shed; planting frames; prize-winning [*roses*]; **Smell the Flowers;** the colorful flowers are about to pop through the ground; romantic [*water garden*]; extravagance of color; a garden to delight you; sumptuous gardens filled with streaming sunshine; **Promise Her a Rose Garden** fulfill that promise with this . . . ; **Seed Catalog Special.** (*See also* **Landscaping.**)

Gate   Wooden; security; wrought iron; gate-guarded; the gateposts stand like stone sentinels; **Behind the Gates** (*See also* **Security**).

Gazebo   Garden gazebo; delightful gazebo; charming gazebo; screened gazebo; gazebo with wet bar and BBQ for your summer entertaining; **A Summer Place** comes with this . . . ; summer house.

Glass   Double-glazed glass; triple-glazed glass; intricately etched glass; frosted glass; stained glass; leaded glass; vintage leaded glass; oval glass; insulated glass (*See also* **Windows**).

Golf   Just off the [*7th tee*]; minutes to the first tee; **On The Fairway;** walk to the clubhouse; golf-cart distance from the course; just a [*chip-shot*] from the course; just off the emerald green fairways; executive course; [*27*]-hole course; designed by . . . ; a [*Jack Nicklaus*] golf course; championship golf course; PGA course; world-class golf course; in the golf community of . . . ; in the golf-course community of . . . ; in a country-club setting; **Affordable Golf; Is Golf Your Bag?;** a championship golf course is in your backyard;

Tee Off practically from your backyard; the [*family room*] has a perfect wall to hold your trophies; **Birdie Lovers; Fore; Fore You;** [*triple*] fairway view; on the emerald fairway; **Duffers Widow?** Keep your golfer at home with this . . . ; **Putt Around** or tee off; **Bring the Woods** and irons too; **A Birdie** [*on the 7th fairway*] and it's cheap-cheap-cheap; your own country club; **For Golfers Only;** live on the green; this one will move faster than a Top Flite off the tee; puttin'-green lawn; **Up The Fairway; Livin' on the Green; Top Flite**—condor-high ceilings; **Pinnacle of Living; Free Golf—** the course is yours as the owner of this . . . ; **Tee Off at Home; Trapped** between [*2*] golf courses; **Hookers!** you will quickly correct your swing living in . . . ; straight-shot priced at $; [*4*] **Minutes to Tee Time; A Putting Green**—well almost; golf-course lawns; the home "fore" you at $; at a price that won't putt you in the rough, $.

Guest Quarters   Guest room; guest suite; private guest suite; self-contained **Guest House;** separate guest unit could be rented; in-law suite; in-law unit; **Room for the Cousins; Room for Grandma; Teen Suite;** for live-ins or guests; delightful dormered guest room; perfect for live-ins.

Handicapped   **Handicapped Accessible;** extra-wide doorways will accommodate a wheelchair; ground level for easy access; parking within [*20'*] of your door; handicapped shower; wheelchair access; lowered cabinetry; handicapped conveniences.

Heating   Forced-air heat; hot-water heat; hydronic heat; baseboard heat; hydronic baseboard heat; zoned heat control; climate zone control; total climate control; [*4-zone*] hydronic heat; [*5*]-ton heat pump for economy and comfort; dual heat pumps; the economy of natural gas; wood-burning stove; combination wood/gas furnace; wood-burning furnace with auxiliary [*gas*] heat; wood stove heats entire house; economical wood heat; wood stove with catalytic converter; energy-saving wood heat; wood heater fireplace insert; Franklin stove; Vermont wood stove; solar heat; partial solar heat; passive solar heat; maximum energy efficiency; **Low Utility Bills** with this energy efficient . . . ; **Buy a Chainsaw** this . . . comes with an auxiliary wood furnace; **Heat For Free** Cut your own wood for this state of the art wood heating plant.

Hedge   English hedge; sculptured hedge; privacy hedge; rose hedge.

Hills   Nestled in the . . . ; on top of the . . . ; **Hilltop Showplace;** above the smog; **Head for the Hills;** the gently rolling hills create a haven for this . . . ; perched **Atop a High Knoll;** knoll top . . . ; sited high in a one-acre knoll; **Above All;** top of the mountain; be king or queen of the hill; on a sheltered hillside; hilltop vistas; embraced by the scenic hills; **The House on the Hill; A Hill for Sledding; Everything is Downhill** from this. (*See also* **View.**)

Holiday Ads

Martin Luther King's Birthday   **If You Had a Dream** it would be about this . . . ; **He Had a Dream** that we share . . . ; **Don't Dream** about owning your own home, do it.

Lincoln's Birthday   **Log Cabin Special**—it's not made of logs and it's a
lot more than a cabin, but future Abe Lincolns will be proud to call it
home; **A Real Log Cabin; Honest Abe!**—trust us when we say . . . ;
Abraham Lincoln would have felt right at home in this . . . log home.

Valentine's Day   **A Valentine Present; Express Your Love** with this . . . ;
World's Best Valentine; don't settle for a box of chocolates; **A Forever
Valentine;** a chance to live your love in this . . . ; make every day
Valentine's Day for $; **Keep Your Valentine** in this . . . ; **Don't Buy
Flowers** Get your valentine this . . .

President's Day   fit for a president at $; **Presidential Candidates** would
love to say they lived in a real log home such as this . . . (*See also*
Lincoln's Birthday, Washington's Birthday).

George Washington's Birthday   **Cherry-Tree Special;** George
Washington would have loved this . . . that comes with [*3*] cherry trees;
George Washington couldn't tell a lie and neither can we when we say
this . . . ; honest George would recognize it as an opportunity not to be
ignored at $; **George Washington** nearly froze at Valley Forge, but
you can enjoy year-round comfort in this climate controlled . . . ; the
colonial charm would be familiar to George but he would have marveled
at the skillfully integrated systems and state-of-the-art conveniences
of this . . . ; we cannot tell a lie—one look and you'll want it at $;
George Washington Would Have Slept Here and felt right at home
had this . . . been around in 1776; **We Cannot Tell a Lie; Washington
Cries "Ouch"** even he never dreamed a dollar could stretch this far.

St. Patrick's Day   **Little Green Men**—[*Mr. Kelly*] of our office swears he
saw lucky leprechauns in the [oak tree behind] this . . . ; **You Don't
Have To Be Irish** to become the lucky owners of this . . . ; **Leprechaun
Disclosure** state law requires that we tell you little green men have been
seen in the [*oak*] tree in the backyard of this . . . ; even if you're not
Irish, it's priced at; $, **Shamrock Special;** while putting up our For Sale
sign . . . found a 4-leaf clover that practically guarantees good luck to the
next owner; emerald-green lawn; lucky-shamrock price of $; **No
Blarney; Savin' O The Green** no son or daughter of
Erin would think of spending thousands more when this . . .

Easter   **Put On Your Easter Bonnet** and come out to see this . . . ; **Easter
Egg Special;** perfect for hiding Easter eggs; priced to hop away; **For
the Easter Parade; Easter Bunny Special; Bunny Slipper Special;
A Place For The Easter Bunny;** it's hop-away priced at $.

Mother's Day   **Mother's Day Present; Mother's Day Special;
For Mother; Liberate Mother** from household drudgery with every
conceivable laborsaving built-in.

Memorial Day   **Memorial Day** is a time to reflect and this . . . brings
back memories of a time . . . ; we owe a lot to those who lived before us
and it's time to reflect on and honor their memories.

Father's Day   **Father's Day Special; Father's Day Present; For Dad;
Dad's Place; Give Father a Lawn Mower** and this . . .

July 4th   Shades of 1776; **Red, White and Blue; It's Like Fireworks; 1776—Well, Almost;** this . . . captures the ambiance of the days when our country was new; firecracker priced at $; **Watch the Fireworks** from the [*deck*] of this . . . ; **If Betsy Ross** had chosen [*peach and cream*], we would advertise this . . . as a **4th of July Special; Firecracker Special; Independence Day**—say farewell to your landlord; **Red, White, and Blue** an all American . . .

Labor Day   **Labor Day—Not**—everything is automatic in this . . .

Columbus Day   **Columbus Day Special**—make a big discovery with this . . . ; **Discover** [*Westwood*]; **In 1492** we had his discovery—in [*2004*] you'll discover this . . . ; you'll have discovered your future at $; **Be Like Columbus**—discover this . . . ; it's a whole new world at $.

Halloween   **Boo!** the price won't scare you; **A Haunted House**—it brings back memories of a gentler time; **Pumpkin-Patch Special; The Great Pumpkin** might be found in the garden of this . . . ; **Halloween Special; Trick Or Treat?**

Thanksgiving   **Ain't No Turkey; Let's Talk Turkey; The Right Stuffing; It's as Easy as Pumpkin Pie** to buy this . . . ; bound to be gobbled up fast at $; it's just stuffed with features to delight any pilgrim; **Not a Turkey; Pilgrim's Pride; Gobble It Up.**

Christmas   **A Home for the Holidays; Home for Christmas; An Early Christmas;** buy this . . . for your family; **A Cool Yule,** and a warm hearth will be yours with this . . . ; **Wrap It Up** in time for the holidays; **Christmas To Come;** room for a [*12′*] tree in the . . . ; **Happy Holidays** will be yours in this . . . ; **Silent Nights** and pleasant days will be yours in this . . . ; **Dreamin' of a White** [*picket fence*]; **The Chimney** isn't big enough for Santa but this . . . has plenty of room for your family and friends; **Christmas Sale** [*$129,500*]; **In Time for Xmas; A Place To Hang** the stockings; **Santa—Stop the Sleigh!** Why spend the rest of the year at the North Pole when you can live in . . . ; **Santa Baby;** there's even a [*full basement that would make an ideal workshop for your elves*]; priced especially for roly-poly men in red suits at $; **Gift-Wrapped, Red-Suit Special** [*$91,000*]; **Jingle Our Bell** and we'll show you this . . . ; **Happy Holidays—Happy Pocketbook; Tell Santa** you want this . . . ; **Yes! Virginia** there is a . . . ; **Dreamin' of a White** [*colonial*]; **Red-Stocking Special; It Won't Fit** in the stockin'; it's gift-wrapped at $; it's Santa-priced at $; a home any jolly fat man in a red suit would love at $; **All You Want For Christmas** is in one large package, fireplace for Santa, [*2½*]-sleigh garage; **No Room in the Stocking** for this . . . ; **Scrooge Special** [*$87,500*]; **Be A Scrooge** you won't have to buy any other presents if you give this . . .

New Years   **New Year—New Home; New Year's Celebration** in this . . . ; **For a New Year** and many years to come.

Homes

Bargain-Priced   Unbelievable price; super buy; **Wow!;** what a value;
Foreclosure-Priced; Panic-Priced; priced for immediate sale; **Must-
Sell-Priced; "Pinch-Me" Priced;** priced below appraisal; speculator
priced; **Desperate Owner; The Bargain of** [*Westwood*]**;** exciting value;
owner transferred; absentee **Owner Wants Out;** partnership dissolution
forces sale; **Bankruptcy Sale;** near-bankruptcy sale; **Attorney Orders
Sale; Court-Ordered Sale;** corporate owner must sell; **Corporate
Liquidation;** buyer backed out; one house too many; below cost;
Below Builder's Cost; below reproduction cost; below appraisal; price
drastically reduced; **The F Word—Foreclosure;** because of unusual
circumstances this . . . ; is available at a price significantly below
[*appraisal*]; if you want to make money the day you buy, hurry and
call . . . ; **Priced To Move; Auction Priced; Desperation Time; Must
Be Sold; Estate Sale; Absentee Owner Says Sell; Owner Needs Cash;
Stop Foreclosure; In Foreclosure; Repossession; Repo; Bank-Owned;**
[*72*] **Hours to Sell;** once-in-a-lifetime opportunity unlikely to be
repeated; **Price Slashed** thousands less than being asked for similar
property; **Time's Run Out; Here's the Deal** [*$180,000*]**;** [*$139,000*]
Firm; Beat the Bank; foreclosure is imminent on this . . . ; **Panic
Priced; Seller Sez Sell!; Thank God For Bargains; Steal Home;
Bank's Super Sale; Bring Me an Offer—**almost anything's possible;
**Catch a Falling Price; The Price is Right; Owner Bites the Bullet;
Giveaway—Almost; Attention Jesse James; Owner Wants It Gone;
Parlez-Vous—Bargain?; Owner Needs Out; Facing Foreclosure;
Pssst! Wanna Steal?; Beat the Bank; Buy it or the Bank Will;
Desperation time; Pre-Foreclosure Sale; Govt. Repo; ALL OFFERS
Considered; Bonafide Bargain; Distress Means Less** [*$85,000*]**;
One-Day Sale** [*$69,000*]**; Take the Bank; Certified Steal** [*$79,000*]**;
Government Resale; Bank Loss—Your Gain; Buy from the Bank**
[*$79,500*]**; Repo Mania; Price Crashed—**[*$89,500*]**; Judge Says
"Sell!"; Best Offer Takes It; Over a Barrel; Help!** (*See also* **Builder's
Sale; Estate Sale; Foreclosure; Price Closings**).

Country/Suburban   On A Country Lane; Rustic Lane; Down a Winding
Road; Country-Fresh; Town-Close—Country-Fresh; Pastoral
Perfection; Country Magic; Bird-Watcher's Paradise; a new way of
life—country-style; God's [*Half*]-Acre; Heaven's Acre; Country
Squire's Estate; Estate in the Country; Country-Quiet;** hassle-free
country life; a friendly lifestyle; city conveniences with country charm;
**Commuter's Dream; Refuge from the City; Sanctuary from the
City;** discover the joy of country life; charming countrified home;
old-fashioned country home; everything you need for country living;
your nearest neighbors are [*squirrels*] and a family of [*raccoons*]; brings
city conveniences to the country; country living with city flair; combines
country charm with city conveniences; the country is right outside your
door; matchless country beauty; where [*hawks*] soar high and the air is
crisp and clean; endowed with country charm; **Currier and Ives
Estate;** calendar-scene estate; you will discover the joy of country life in
this . . . ; old-fashioned country home; a happy alternative to city living;
the charm is country and so is the quiet; enjoy the simple pleasure of

American rural life combined with big-city conveniences; country ambiance with all the conveniences of the city; your family will breathe the clean air of rural America; blends harmoniously with the peaceful country surroundings; leave the city lights behind; for a simpler life; old-fashioned country living can be yours; country living as it should be; enjoy the security of country living; the school bus stops at the driveway; it's a real showplace if showing is to [*raccoons; deer and squirrels*]; in [*a wooded glen*] just [*45*] minutes away; a home for children and dogs; you will be enthralled by nature's surroundings; your children will love the [*miles of trails, trees*] and friendly neighbors [*both 2-legged and 4-legged*]; **A Raccoon** will be your neighbor as the owner of this . . . ; at less than the price of an ordinary city home; **Keep A Cow** or a horse on this . . . ; **Grow Your Own** vegetables and children on this; your chance to live life the way it was intended to be; **Come Home to the Country;** your escape from city drudgery; trails for jogging or just a quiet stroll; **Good Ole Country Livin';** close enough but not too close; serene setting; **A Hound Dog on the Porch** would seem natural for this . . . ; seclusion without isolation; [*bike*] trail starts from your backyard; your very own nature preserve at $; set amidst the [*semirural*] quietness of [*the sunlit hills*]; **Country Quiet;** small-town quiet; it's like living in a country village; the ultimate country fantasy at $; perfectly positioned on [*2*] acres; in a quiet hamlet; **Village Life; A Country Village;** blue-jean special at $; **Country Cottage; Country Style [*$84,500*];** **Out of the Tension Zone; Small-Town Friendly; Enjoy Country Living?; The Waltons' Place; Unlocked Doors** where a crime wave is children snitching apples; **Commuter's Dream; Twice the House—Half the Taxes; All You Survey,** well [*2*] acres of it, goes with this . . . ; **Country Boy Special;** in harmony with its natural surroundings; **Good-Bye City—Hello Country; Arrivederci City; Your Green Acres** (*See also* **Homes, Family and Location; Horse Property; Land, Undeveloped; Vacation Homes**).

Family   **A Happy Home;** family home; roots for your family; **Children Wanted;** designed for children; **A Kid's Home;** for the growing family; needs boys and girls; you provide the family; room for the family; **Room for a Pony;** get settled before school starts in this . . . ; move before school starts; your kids will love this . . . ; a home for family love; room for the family; across from [*the park*]; [*1*] block to the [*playground*]; fenced play area; on a child-safe cul-de-sac; teenager's suite; playroom; rainy-day playroom; nursery; tribe-sized backyard; child-safe backyard; room for bikes and trikes and a red wagon in the . . . ; a very special family home; this . . . reflects the time when the family home was the center of one's existence; a much-loved home of the past for your family future; trees for climbing; a place where children can still run free; if you are tired of driving your children to school; you will appreciate this . . . ; family-size yard; fully fenced; a place to raise your children in all the old ways; the backyard is just waiting for a sandbox and swing; the [*old oak*] tree in the backyard is the perfect place to hang your swing; ready for your family; a happy home; a spouse-pleaser; a spouse-saver; a very special family home; a home that will secure your family's future; buy today and your family will thank you forever;

Rollerblades on the sidewalk and basketball in the driveway of this . . . ; the perfect home to enjoy the closeness of your family; a [*family room*] big enough for [*a troop of Brownies*]; a fenced yard that will hold a gaggle of children and their dogs; in the [*Midvale*] **School District; The Schools You Hoped For;** tribe-sized bedrooms; dormitory-size bedrooms; separate children's wing; waiting for your family's tomorrow at $; what better place for your family?; **Lots of Tots** can play in the . . . ; **A Hill for Sledding** and sidewalks for skating; **Puppies and Children** will love the . . . ; your children's memories will be a quiet tree-lined street; sidewalks for roller skating and [*a park just minutes away*]; a perfect place for Fido and the rest of the family; a perfect spot for hide-and-seek; **Family Values;** . . . known for its parks and fine schools; **What Are You Raising?** If you're raising more than just your standard of living; you'll appreciate [*the child-safe fenced yard*]; **Your Family** is all that's needed for this; **Bring The Kids; Kindergarten** is within [*skipping*] distance of this . . . ; **Blessed With Children?** Then you will appreciate this . . . ; **You Got the Family—We Got the House; Family Find;** A feeling of spaciousness makes this the perfect home for family living; if you don't like children, you won't like this neighborhood, because the lawns and sidewalks appear to be swarming with children of all ages; the best schools and the best home for your family; **No Screeching Brakes** on this child-friendly cul-de-sac; **Even Little Legs** can walk to . . . ; **Family Affair; A Boy and His Dog** would love bunking in their own . . . ; **Big Family?** The former owner had [*7*] children; **Family Matters; A Basketball Hoop** is in the driveway of this . . . ; **Hopscotch and Rollerblade** on the sidewalks . . . ; **Lots of Tots?; The Gang** will love this . . . (*See also* **Homes—Large**).

General   a house with personality; a rare opportunity; captivatingly beautiful; instantly appealing; eye-appealing; bewitching; seductive; elegant; overwhelming; sophisticated; handsome residence; refreshing; dramatic; outstanding; stunning; excitingly different; charming; a home to cherish; enchanting; picturesque; trend-setter; enticing; friendly; breathtaking; refreshingly different; versatile floor plan; built in the European tradition of fine craftsmanship; superbly crafted; finished to an exacting standard; offering heart-stirring warmth that will win you over; sophisticated design; unassuming charm; offering a charm that complements the environment; captures your vision of tomorrow; romance and flair run rampant in this . . . ; captivatingly different; stunningly conceived; amenities to enhance your living pleasure; featuring all the amenities you have dreamed of; enviable amenities; many wonderful amenities; wall-to-wall comfort; vitality radiates from the fresh, sun-filled rooms; comfort and sophistication with a dazzling array of exquisite features to delight the senses; the solid construction and workmanship of this fine home will delight you; everything on your wish list plus things you never knew you had to have; brimming with exquisite details; features every amenity you can find in [*Better Homes and Gardens*]; amenities normally found in only the most expensive homes; exudes a quiet elegance; bound to please the most fastidious buyer; you'll appreciate the quality of this fine residence; the only thing that's not impressive about this fine home is the price $; a captivating home with everything you could possibly want; this fine home is superior in every aspect except the price: $; priced at no more than you would expect to pay for a tract home $; generously proportioned rooms; a warm feeling of spaciousness and quality; **A Home For All Reasons; The Home You Waited For— The Price You Hoped For; Want Everything?** Then have everything with this . . . ; **Once in a Blue Moon** will a . . . such as this come on the market; **Nothing's Perfect** but if you want the closest thing you'll have to see this . . . ; **Happiness Is; Never Move Again; Circle This Ad; Welcome Home;** one of [*Oak Creek's*] most attractive and livable homes; **Fooled by Ads?** Well, this one tells it like it is; **It's Here; Seeing Will Mean Sold;** the first family to visit this . . . will likely be the last; **You're Home;** pardon me for YELLING but you must act fast; **Elbow Room;** this . . . stands by itself on an [oversized site]; **Carpe Domus**—that's Latin for Grab This House; **Regrets**—only one buyer will enjoy this . . . ; **Everything You Want** even if you want everything; **Read Me; Bring Your Sunglasses**—You'll be dazzled by this . . . ; **On The Street Where You Live; Bring Your Money;** find out today why tomorrow will be too late; a home where memories are born; **How Sweet It Is; Setting Pretty; Northern Exposure; No Gimmicks**—we mean what we say; **See What's Inside; Like an Old Shoe**—You will relish the comfortable living in this . . . ; built for casual living and easy entertaining; **Look What We Found; First Week** on the market for this . . . ; **Perfect Marriage;** this . . . seems as one with its natural setting; **Step Inside** and see . . . ; **New?** No, this . . . is better than new; **The Whole Gang** will love this; **Beyond Perfect;** warm and inviting interior; you will have to search for adjectives to describe this . . . ; **Soul Provider; Have It All; Elegant Is a Word** that describes this . . . ; **What Frost Is to Poetry** this . . . is to gracious living; **Touched By an Angel; America's Most Wanted; Throw Away The Wishbone**—Your wish is here; **This Baby Can Be Yours; Buy Your Spouse** a dream house; **Don't Call Tomorrow**—it will be too late; **Soap Opera Home;** an exotic . . . that's camera-ready and family-ready; **Drop-Dead Gorgeous;** filled with life and comfort; refined casual elegance; a home where dreams begin; it would seem that the only way you could go wrong would be to delay seeing this . . . ; **Plain Wrapper [*$89,500*]**— Don't judge a book by its cover; **If Comfort Counts; Former Model Home;** a beauty and tranquility that must be experienced; **Home at Last; Quit Looking; Bang-Bang**—Now that I have your attention, I would like to tell you about this . . . ; **We Have the Key; Double Your Pleasure** with this 2-story . . . ; highlights include . . . ; **Paradise Found; The Reachable Dream;** call now—if you snooze—you lose; **Terms of Endearment**—don't do justice to this . . . ; **Get Here First** or be sorry; **Honey, Stop The Car; Bring Your Camera** to show your friends pictures of your new home; the only thing missing is you; **More Than a Pretty Face; We Have It; A Better Life** can be yours in this . . . ; **You May Never Know** that for the price of an ordinary home you could have owned this . . . ; **Settle For More; Be the New Kid** on the block in this . . . ; **The Right Stuff; Start Here; Absolutely Gorgeous; Check Others**—Buy This; **In Your Price Range; All Things Bright and Beautiful;** the showcase for your life is your home; **Today's Look—Yesterday's Price; Let's Go Home; U Must C** this . . . ;

Groovy to the Max; Rainbow's End—This . . . is your pot of gold; **A Deal for You; Dare To Compare** [*$119,500*]; **Beyond Elegant; Don't Buy** until you see this . . . ; **Easy To Love;** the first to see will call it home at $; **Who Deserves It More?; Wake Up with a Smile** in this . . . ; **Here's the Key** to a new life; **Everything Is Beautiful;** rooms awash in natural light; **No Time To Dilly-Dally; Live the Dream; It's the Jackpot; Warning!** You will fall in love with this . . . ; **Love's Labor Found; One Life To Live; Good Lookin'; A Reachable Dream; Take It All; Love Potion**—Just look and you will desire this . . . ; **A Definite 10; You Won't Believe It,** but we have a . . . ;[*2nd*] **Day** on the market for this . . . ; **Better Than Vanilla,** a home to relax in; **Rent a Truck** and start moving; **The Good Life** begins at home in this . . . ; **No More Excuses**—You can own . . . ; **License To Thrill; Status Seeker?** You will have it in this . . . ; **Good-Luck Home**—ask us why . . . ; **The First** impression will be WOW; **No Earthly Reason** to compromise; **Better Take a Look; Make a Statement; Knock Em Dead; Indulge Yourself;** every conceivable luxury is included in this . . . ; **Wise Guy?** Then you'll appreciate the value of this . . . ; **See Your Future** in this . . . ; **Not for Everyone; Run, Don't Walk; Ready To Move; Innovative— Elegant—Inviting; Scarce as Hen's Teeth** to find a . . . ; **Spend More for Less** or check out this . . . ; **House and Block Beautiful; A Brake Slammer; Batteries Not Included** An all electric . . . ; **Be First in Line** or be sorry; **The Leave Behinds** Owners will leave . . . ; **THIMK** and you'll have to see this . . . ; **Fire Sale** A sizzling price on this . . . ; **Peoples Court** declared this . . . to be the best buy at . . . ; **Home Improvement** not needed for this . . . ; **Judge Judy** would award the verdict to this . . . ; **Keeping UP Appearances** . . . (*See also* **Architectural Style, Floor Plan, Garden, Homes—Family, Landscaping,** and **Location**).

Large Space Odyssey; Room for everything; **Lost in Space** [*5*] **BR; A Lotto House; Captain Kirk** would love to explore the vast space of this . . . ; **Mother Goose** View this really big shoe; **Won't Cramp Your Style; The Biggie; Room To Roam;** room to spare; **Big Is Beautiful;** elbow room; **L-A-R-G-E; H-U-G-E; The Big House;** space abounds inside and out in this . . . ; a whopping [*3,000*] square feet of living space; plenty of room for collectibles in this . . . ; you won't squeeze the children in this . . . ; embassy-size; you'll have room for the children and grandma too in this . . . ; [*4*] **Bedrooms;** [*11*] **Rooms; Kids—Kids;** [*4*] **BR; Forget Planned Parenthood**—this . . . is for the old-fashioned large family; it's reported that the original owner of this . . . had [*12*] children; you'll see that an expansive home need not be expensive; there's room for a large family and assorted cousins in this . . . ; **Hordes of Kids** and a mother-in-law will all fit in this . . . ; there's room for everything you've ever collected in this . . . ; there's room to stretch in this . . . ; there's room for gathering the clan in this . . . ; you'll have trouble finding all your kids in this . . . ; Gather the clan and hurry to see this . . . ; **Big Time**—a big house at a small price—$; **Bed and Breakfast Possibility; Mega-House;** [*5*]**BR; Humongous** [*Colonial*] [*5*]**BR;** [*3,000*] incredible square feet; the main residence features . . . ; **Move to the Manor; Tired of Compacts?;** [*12*] **Rooms;** your chance to win the space race at $; uniquely spacious; rooms of Herculean proportion; expansive dimensions; **Too Big for Most;** you'll need more furniture for this . . . ; **Be Spaced Out** in the huge rooms of this . . . ; sprawling and elegant; **Upstairs—Downstairs;** [*11 Rooms*]; **A Whopper—[*5BR*]; In-Laws and Outlaws—**There's room for all in this . . . ; **Big House—Big Deal; So Much—So Little; Twice the Room—Half the Price; Big as a House [*4BR*]; Big as a Barn [*5BR*]; House of Plenty—[*11 Rooms*]; And It's Big; Brady Bunch [*4BR*]; Need [*5*] Bedrooms?; The Big Guy—[*5BR*]; Try for Size—[*4*]BR; Lost in Space [*5BR*];** seemingly endless living space; it won't cramp your style at $.

Low-Priced   **Budget-Balancer; Budget-Pleaser; EZ on the Budget; Dollar-Stretcher; Easy To Own; Castle on a Budget; Wallet-Watcher;** elegantly affordable; **Kiss Your Landlord Good-Bye; Landlord off Your Payroll?; [*$49,000*]—Not a Misprint; Can't Afford To Buy?** Then you haven't seen this . . . ; **Why Be a Slave** to high house payments? [*$50,000*] can still buy a . . . ; **Priced Right—[*$49,500*];** it's hard to believe that you can still buy a . . . ; at a price a renter can afford; at last, a home in [*Westport*] that you can afford; just about everyone can afford this . . . ; **An Affordable Dream; Renter's Revenge;** your good taste and wallet will both agree that you should be the owner of this . . . ; why make your landlord's mortgage payment when you could be making your own?; If you're paying [*$600*] in rent; you can afford to own this . . . ; it's your opportunity to build equity, not rent receipts; **Renter's Revolt; Cheaper Than Rent; Slave to Rent?; Want to Rent Forever?; Fire the Landlord;** why make your landlord rich? Call now . . . ; **Penny-Pinchers' Paradise [*$49,900*]; Less Than Rent; Lowest Price In [*Middleton*]; Great Beginnings [*$49,900*];** the only thing small about this home is the price—$; **Beats Renting!; Why Rent?** when you can own this . . . ; **The Price Is Right—[*$59,500*]; On a Budget?; Not a Condo—[*$59,500*]; No Mistake [*$59,500*]; Tightwad** squeeze your dollars with this . . . ; **[*$129,000*] Buys What?; Yes You Can [*$59,500*]; Beginner's Luck [*$47,500*]; Kick the Habit** of paying rent; **Love at Purse Sight [*$94,500*]; A Slave To Rent?; Why Rent?** when you can own this . . . ; **How Low Can You Get?** (*See also* **Homes, Bargain-Priced**).

Luxury   [*$3,000,000*] If you are one of the fortunate few who can get beyond the price, you will want to see this . . . ; **Life is Full of Compromises** but compromise no more; **Self Indulgent—Overachiever** At last the home for you; **If You Didn't Care** what it cost, you would want to see this . . . ; **Reached the Top? Live There!; Emperors and Kings** would feel at home in this . . . ; **Caesar's Palace** offers fewer delights than this . . . ; **Room for the Bentley** in the . . . ; Sheer elegance; overwhelming; **Tres Elegant;** the ultra in sophisticated living; **A Great House;** estate; showplace; lavish estate; palatial estate; **Home Extraordinaire;** a showcase home; sleek and sophisticated; magnificent estate; one of [*Akron's*] great homes; conservatively elegant; understated elegance; subdued elegance; **A World-Class Residence;** the ultimate in prestigious living; unexcelled; epitome of elegance; the Dom Perignon of fine estates; just a little better; suited for royalty; impressive; a handsome estate; far from the ordinary; absolutely awesome; muted elegance; top-of-the-line; the standard of excellence; just a little better than anything you have seen; uncompromised quality; uncommon luxury; graciously elegant; quiet elegance; masterpiece; magnificent in its scale and design; thoughtfully planned to provide the ultimate lifestyle; for those accustomed to the very best; built for a lifestyle to be envied; refined elegance; a home that mirrors your achievements; reflecting the goals and ambitions of today's achievers; providing an unexcelled quality of life; reflecting the classic taste and subtle sophistication of the most discriminating buyer; truly an unparalleled home; a charismatic blending of regal splendor with delicate charm; truly a feast for the senses; for the lifestyle you deserve; a home that echoes achievement; the home for those who appreciate the fine art of living; elegance personified; the unmistakable air of elegance is expressed eloquently in its . . . ; a home that knows no compromise; you need compromise no more; what civilized living is all about; an ambassadorial residence; providing a new definition of elegance; a remarkable blend of authentic character and luxury amenities; dramatically combining the best traditional detailing with high-tech amenities to provide the ultimate lifestyle; all the appointments one would expect in a home of this caliber; resplendent with magnificent detail; while life is filled with compromises, you need compromise no more; just a step above anything you have seen; the look of prestige is captured eloquently in this stately . . . ; once in a rare while a home such as this will appear on the market; a gracious style of luxury that soon may no longer be available; provides a new definition of elegance; offering the utmost in gracious living; enjoy the lifestyle others can only hope to match; a new dimension in gracious living; truly the culmination of all your dreams; the ultimate statement of your success; if you promised yourself the best in life, there is no better time than now to keep that promise; defies reproduction; the showcase of your success is your home; includes the amenities normally found only in magazines; dramatically proportioned rooms; **Everything You Want—Even If You Want Everything;** expect the very best and you'll still be pleasantly surprised; unpretentious luxury at $; **When the Ordinary Won't Do;** while the elegance is timeless—the opportunity is not; **Won't Compromise?** you won't have to with this . . . ; **You've Earned It; Reflect Your Success;** don't you deserve a home that mirrors your achievements?; a home that whispers "success"; for a very special few at $; you have worked hard for your family and this . . . reflects that success; an enviable estate at $; the ultimate in material things that life has to offer; built to exacting specifications and almost no regard to cost; a home that makes a statement as individual as yourself; **If You Didn't Care** what it cost and simply wanted the finest—this is the house you would build; a home that makes all others appear plain by comparison; the usual and most of the unusual luxuries; the understated elegance seems to whisper "quality"; an estate for the civilized family at $; proudly offered to qualified buyers at $; offered to the family accustomed to the very best at $; all the amenities money can buy; offered to the person who doesn't know the meaning of "compromise" at $; it represents what others can only wish for; an aura of elegance; isn't it time you began to pamper yourself?; makes everything else look ordinary; **Expect To Be Envied** as the owner of this . . . ; **The Standard Of Excellence** against which all other homes will be measured; an exceptional opportunity for one fortunate family; it may be copied but it will never be equaled; one of the finest estates we have been privileged to offer; offering a whole new meaning to luxury at $; truly the epitome of elegant living; **The Ultimate Residence**—if you're one of the very few in reach of such a residence, call; if your concern is not affording the best but in finding it, look no more; **If Money Didn't Matter** this is the home you would build for your family; offered to the fortunate few at $; **Unlimited Luxury—Limited Availability; Move to the Manor;** the dramatic interiors express themselves quietly but impressively; in a secluded compound of fine estates; richly detailed and dedicated to gracious living; elegant simplicity; a home that challenges all others; offering the quintessential level of luxury; a dizzying array of exquisite features; a delight to the senses; embraces all the quality one would wish for in a truly spectacular residence; a refuge of refinement; **One of the Greats; If Rolls-Royce Built Homes,** this would be their Corniche; lose yourself in splendor; it casts an impressive shadow for all others to follow; anything else is compromise; former [*Du Pont*] estate; elegance tempered with simplicity; in spite of its grandeur it still functions as a comfortable home; a heritage for your family; a gentle ambiance of luxury (*See also* **Architecture**).

New   Builder-Fresh; Pick of the Litter** [*9*] homes left in . . . ;**The Final [*Four*] homes in . . . ; Brand-New Classic; Young and Beautiful; New Is Better; Never Lived In;** be the first to live in . . . still time to pick the colors; **Muddy-Shoes Opening;** be the first owner of this . . . ; **A Future Classic;** a new home with a dramatic flair; one of the most exciting new homes we have seen; you will smell the newness in this . . . ; a rare opportunity to buy one of the original models at . . . ; a sparkling-new rendition of a . . . ; price guaranteed for . . . ; **Exceptional Not Optional**—all the extras are included with this brand-new . . . ; **All the Extras** at no extra price with this . . . ; reflecting the proudest traditions of homebuilding; meticulously finished; sumptuously appointed with an impressive array of amenities; vitality radiates from the fresh sun-filled rooms; every modern expectancy; **Tomorrow's Legend; The Last One; We're Building Your Dream; Some Assembly Required** The [*lawn isn't in*] on this brand new . . . ; **Wear Your Boots** There is no lawn on this brand new . . . ; **Why Settle** for someone else's dream when you can have your own?; **Looking for the First Owner; Pick Your Colors; Be the First** to enjoy this . . . ; **Take Your Pick**—the last [*13*] . . . ; **Only [*6*]—Whoops, [*5*] Left; Bright and New; If You Like New; When the Fat Lady Sings** it's the last of the [*3*] remaining new homes in . . . ; **Be the First Owner;** the paint is still drying on this . . . ; call today, as the owner will only guarantee this price for [*30 days*]; **New But No Squeaks; The Paint Isn't Dry; Why Settle for Hand-Me-Downs** when for the same money you can be the owner of this . . . ; **Undressed** and waiting for you to pick the colors; **Nobody Slept Here; Why Buy Used?; Precompletion Savings;** everything is guaranteed by the builder for [*1 year*]; **Model Home Clearance; It's the Model Home!; Builder S.O.S.; Builder in Trouble; It Smells New** and it is . . . ; **No Need for Extras,** as every imaginable luxury has been included in the price of $;

preconstruction-priced at $; **Tired of Used Homes?; Why Buy Used?; A Young [*Colonial*]; Now Comes the Best; New Home—New Price;** yes, the price has been reduced on this; **New Home—Old Price—**The builder has not yet raised prices on . . . ; you can have a brand-new . . . for the price of a used home; enjoy the newness of this . . . ; **Little Things Mean a Lot—**every detail is covered in this . . . ; **New and Vacant; Not Quite Finished** but if you wait till then, someone else's name will be on the mailbox; **Brand New—Almost; Raw Deal—**It won't take much to finish this . . . ; **Not Brand-New** but almost; **Brand Spanking New; Bare Naked** You pick the [*colors*]; **Newer Than New; Almost Completed** (*See also* **Builder's Sale**).

Old   **A Bit of History;** the grandeur of yesterday; [*Grandpa*] or [*Grandma's*] **Home Revisited; Step Back Into Yesterday; Timeless Elegance; Heirloom Estate; Nostalgic Showplace; Preserved from Yesteryear; Ageless Beauty; Circa [*1830*];** better-than-new; 19th-century perfection; **Turn-of-the-Century [*Ranch*]; A Centurion; A Century Young; Antique Treasure;** antebellum; **Antebellum Beauty; Timeless Beauty; Like Them Mature?; Bed-and-Breakfast Potential; Bed-and-Breakfast Zoning;** inn potential; has been admired since it was built . . . ; embodies the charm and romance of a bygone era; reflects the pride of [*6*] generations of family ownership; time-mellowed; built to endure; [*3,200*] sq. ft. of traditional charm; enjoy the charm and warmth found only in older homes; gracious turn-of-the-century charm; gracious old-world charm; its beauty has increased for [*100*] years; old-fashioned space and grace; you will be struck by the excitement and romance; many children have grown of age in this . . . ; it truly represents the grandeur of the past with all of the modern conveniences of tomorrow; style and tradition are captured in this . . . ; registered with the National Register of Historic Places; **Landmark-Eligible;** possibly eligible for National Registry; **Steeped In History; A Home with a History; A Lady with a Past; A Sordid Past!** Rumor has it that . . . ; **Better Than New; Historic Treasure; The Best of the Past;** time will stand still in this . . . ; **Yesterday's Dream;** old-world charm abounds in this . . . ; artistically restored to functional and aesthetic perfection; painstakingly restored; tastefully restored and updated to meet the living standards of the most discriminating; in museum condition; **Museum Piece; Restored with Imagination** and elegance; **Museum-Quality Restoration; Restorable [*Colonial*];** refurbished with state-of-the-art conveniences; **New Everything;** with old-world detailing and modern amenities; 19th-century elegance combined with 21st-century convenience; unobtrusive improvements; the meticulous and imaginative renovation offers . . . ; masterfully renovated; a once-in-a-lifetime opportunity to secure a piece of America's heritage; **A Diorama of Yesteryear;** offering an elegance unobtainable in today's homes; generations have meticulously maintained this . . . ; every room is filled with classic appointments; a patina of love and care shines from this gentle reminder of the good full life of a long-ago time; offering the charm of yesteryear with the conveniences of tomorrow; your chance to **Live in a Legend;** reflects [*120*] years of loving care; offering a quality of life that only the past can provide; a unique **Vestige of the Past;** an opportunity to live in the opulence that recalls the grandeur of ages past; horse-drawn carriages and parasols recall the days when this . . . was young; one of the finest specimens of [*19th*]-century architecture carefully preserved so you can enjoy its future; reflects a spectacular era in America's past; reminiscent of the **Gatsby Era;** you will step back in history as the owner of this . . . ; for the special few who desire the ultimate in unabashed charm of the early [*1900s*]; the elegance of yesterday can be yours for tomorrow; **Built in [*1903*]** when quality counted; built in the tradition of a bygone era; the opulence of yesterday refreshingly provides the perfect atmosphere for today's gracious living; this . . . reflects the time when the home was the center of one's existence; a much-loved home of the past for your family's future; eclectic merger of the charm of yesterday and the convenience of tomorrow; restored with integrity; meticulously [*renovated*] [*restored*]; comes with a history as colorful as its beautiful setting; **Historic [*Breckinridge*] House;** its modern systems don't detract from the integrity of this . . . ; offering the charm of a gentler time; **Like An Old Shoe** it offers old-fashioned comfort for a happy tomorrow; it appears to have been perfectly preserved in a time-warp from a gentler time; the [*dining room*] has seen [*over a century*] of [*Thanksgiving dinners*]; **The Christmas Tree** was lit by candles when this . . . was new; **A Cherished Remnant** of a gentler past; embraced by its [*wraparound porch*]; old-fashioned priced at $; **Not Good as New—** it's better; **Craftsmanship Like This** is a thing of the past, but its fruit remains in this . . . ; **House of The Year [*1902*];** a place for your vintage collectibles; reportedly built in [*1824*]; **Why Buy a Tract House** when you can buy a classic for less?; for the special buyer who will not accept style as a substitute for quality—we proudly offer this classic at $; **An American Tradition;** built for comfort and enduring beauty; nooks and crannies abound in this . . . ; the [*walk-up attic*] has room for a lifetime of memories; a home that was crafted for generations; **Remember Grandmother's House—**its spirit has been lovingly preserved in this . . . ; combines the best of the past with conveniences of tomorrow; **Don't Look for Reproductions;** when the real thing is available for only $; available at less than the price of an ordinary home—$; offers an elegance unobtainable in today's homes; every room is filled with classic appointments that reflect memories of workmanship and pride; woodwork that has been lovingly polished for [*7*] generations; this home seems to echo its [*century*] of laughter and happiness; the [*long, covered porch*] heard of when this country was new; a rare bit of Americana can be yours for only $; your piece of America's history for $; the front parlor held many nervous young beaus who came a-courting; this happy home of the past has much more happiness to give for your future; in a neighborhood that relives the best of the past; the [*hardwood*] floors are as true today as the day they were laid; the [*oak*] woodwork was matched as to grain and fitted with meticulous precision; built when workers took pride in their labor; reflects the love of [*8*] generations; it's been updated to satisfy the family of tomorrow; it has a feeling of spaciousness so seldom felt in newer homes; your opportunity to continue this legacy of love—$; like previous generations you'll be smitten by the beauty of [*the gleaming woodwork*] and the grace of design; **No Restoration Needed** because this . . . has never been abused; **Haunted** by [*over 100*] years of happy living; **Norman Rockwell Traditional; American Gothic; Fiddler on the Roof**—this house has **Tradition;** it has seen America grow from the days of horse-drawn carriages and parasols to modern time; **Step Back into Your Future;** your escape from today at $; **Grant Wood** could have used this . . . as the model for American Gothic; perfect just the way it is; **Turn Back the Clock** with this . . . ; it was new when your [*great-grandparents*] were young; this [*100*]-year old classic is barely broken-in and should serve as home to many future generations; reflects a time when American craftsmen did not know the meaning of compromise; for less than the price of a house you can own a real home; **Vintage Charm;** [*100*] **Years Young; A New Century** began when this . . . ; **Yearning for Yesterday; A Glorious Past** will lead to a glorious future for this . . . ; modern systems don't detract from the architectural charm; skillfully modernized without sacrificing charm; a product of an era when homes were built for gracious living; [*1896*] was the year when Civil War Veterans led the July 4th parade and this . . . was new; if you desire to recapture the joy of a gentler time—call today for a private showing; [*1926*] was a classic year when homes were built of lath; plaster and solid wood paneling; all systems have been carefully updated to provide the utmost in amenities; nooks and crannies abound for your precious collectibles; the sitting room has entertained generations of friends and neighbors; guests arriving by carriage must have marveled at this then-new . . . ; **Built by a Hero**—the builder was a [*captain*] in the [*Union Army*]; built with care for a bride in [*1871*]; **Class of** [*1930*]; it would be nearly impossible to reproduce this . . . ; **Remember When; George Washington** could have slept here; **Preserved from the Past;** every modern expectancy has been skillfully integrated so as not to detract from this **Classic Beauty; Restore or Enhance; A Cocked Hat** was worn by the first owner of this . . . ; woodwork lovingly polished for [*150*] years; **Ante Bellum;** carriages and parasols are just part of the history of this . . . ; the gracious ambiance of this classic can be yours for $; [*Benjamin Harrison*] was president when this . . . was built; [*100*] **Years** of loving care is reflected in this . . . ; exudes authenticity; warmth and charm; believed to be over [*150*] years old; **Gracious as the 1800s,** yet spacious for the 2000s; preserved from the golden age of American architecture; offering the luxury of a time gone by at $; **A Funny Old House;** [*100*] **Years Of Love;** original detailing; **Antique Lovers; Antiques Roadshow** would likely appraise this . . . at far more than the . . . price; **Old Farmhouse; Live-In History;** steeped in history; **Age of Innocence;** wonderful [*1920s*] detailing; will continue to improve with age; **Revisit Yesterday, You Can Go Back Again;** the dignity; mystery and excitement of this . . . needs to be restored; a piece of history for you to continue; **In Love With Yesteryear; Golden Oldie;** [*1874*] **Charm—**[*2004*] **Value; Time Machine; The Craftsmen Of** [*1892*] didn't know the meaning of compromise (*See also* **Architecture**).

Small   Cottage; Enchanted Cottage; [*1940s*] Cottage; Honeymoon Cottage; Grandma's Cottage; Secluded Cottage; Intimate Cottage; Writer's Cottage; The Great American Novel** could well be written in this writer's [*4*] room hideaway; **Hansel & Gretel Cottage; Artist's**

Studio; **Your Personal Hideaway; Your Pad;** sophisticated home; **Fairy-Tale Cottage; Gingerbread House;** mini-chateau; la petite maison; maisonette; mini-estate; a home for one who deserves a more luxurious environment; the perfect home for a very sophisticated lifestyle; quaint; A [2]-bedroom American [*bungalow*]; **Put Mother In A Home; Why Pay For 3** bedrooms when [2] will do?; **Hermit?** well here's your home; ideal for the writer or artist; there's no room for guests—even if they want to come; priced for those in love at $; intimate [2]-bedroom home; there's no room for in-laws in this; personally priced at $; only 1 bedroom—that's right, you and any guest had better be really close friends; miniature estate; all the space you really need; [*Writer's*] **Studio;** created for your individual needs; **Think Small; Love Size; Home Alone;** at a little bitty price of $; **Better Than a Doll House; Bigger Than a Bread Box;** it's small—only [*2BR*]; there's no view but it has a great location at a price of only $; intimate floor plan; space-engineered for maximum livability; [*Artist's*] **Retreat;** expandable floor plan; a smaller house need not mean a change in lifestyle; quaint hideaway; **Write—Paint—Think** or just enjoy this . . . ; **Goldilocks** we found your cottage; **Small House—Big** [*Garden*]; **Great Big** [*1*] **Bedroom; Attention Hedonists!** A [*1*] bedroom home just for you; **Beginner's Luck** The perfect spot for newlyweds; **Mini-Mansion; Mini-Chateau.**

Horse Property   **Great Place For Horses; Hold Your Horses!;** a place to hang your spurs; **Horse-Lover's Delight; Equestrian Estate; Equestrian Enchanter; Zoned for Horses;** training ring; riding area; lighted riding area; pipe corral; [2] corrals; perimeter and cross-fencing; fenced and cross-fenced; horse barn with [2] stalls; double stalls; tack room; tack room with shower; [5] acres of pasture; [10] acres of watered pasture; **Make Your Horse Happy; Happy Horse; Get a Horse**—or several to fill this . . . barn; **Hey** [*Cowboy/Cowgirl!*] There's room on this range to keep several horses; **Hold Your Horses** in the [3] corrals that go with this . . . ; **Bring Your Horse;** paddocks with accommodations for brood mares; put your brand on this spread for $; **Brand This Spread; Horses and Hounds; Children and Horses; Horses, Hounds, and Hunting Horns;** [*40'*] barn is begging for a couple of box stalls; **The Ponderosa, The Cartwright Ranch**—well almost; **Whoa! Nellie!;** bring your horses; llamas; ostriches, and whatever; priced to gallop off at . . . ; **Want To Horse Around?; Horses—Dogs—Kids** all will love this . . . ; **Where's the Pony?** Just a whinny away; **Horses Allowed; A Horse of Course** would fit in the . . . ; horse barn with [*tack room*]; a delightful [*patio*] where you can relax and gaze out over your spread; a kitchen that can hold a round-up crew; a place where you will want to hang your spurs; blue jean-priced at $; **A Mighty Purty Spread** at $; you'll want to put your brand on this spread at $; **Horse Manure** not included with . . . ; **Buy Me a Pony; An** [*Appaloosa*] **Lived Here;** a place any cowboy or cowgirl would love to call home at $; trade your suit and tasseled loafers for Levi's and boots at $; **Your Trusty Steed** will love this . . . ; **A Horse and Pony Show; Keep a Cow** or horse in this . . . ; **Horse Ranch—Almost** just needs fencing, corrals and a barn; **Awaits Your Horse.** (*See also* **Homes, Acreage**).

Humidifier/Dehumidifier   Power humidifier; furnace with power humidifier; automatic humidifier; automatic power dehumidifier.

Industrial   [*10,000*] **Sq. Ft.;** single level; [*4*] years old; rail siding; heavy industrial; light manufacturing; warehouse; **The Best Little Warehouse in . . . ; Zoned For . . . ;** zoned [*M1*]; 700-sq.-ft. air-conditioned office; [*10,000*]-sq.-ft. showroom; [*10'*] sidewalls; clear span; previously used for . . . ; excellent public transportation; very heavy power; ample power; 400 amps; 3-phase power; EPA-approved waste water system; [*5*]-acre site; parking for [*300*] cars; fenced parking for [*300*] cars; paved parking for [*300*] cars; free-standing building; crane-served; [*10*]-ton crane; [*3*] crane bays; gas heat; [*800*]-sq.-ft. dock; bed-level dock; truck-level dock; recessed dock; enclosed dock; depressed loading dock with Levelators; drive-in door; 16' × OH door; freight elevator; fully sprinklered; security fence; electronic security system; room to expand; good column spacing; showroom and warehouse space; ideal for . . . ; air-conditioned; gas pumps; adjustable dock boards; [*Butler*] building; reinforced concrete construction; tilt-up concrete [*construction*]; fire suppression system; up to code for . . .

Insulation   Fully insulated; R-[*19*] insulation; super-insulated; double-insulated; extra insulation; [*6"*] sidewalls; [*18"*] of ceiling insulation; state-of-the-art energy-efficient construction.

Investment Income Property   **Opportunity; Opportunity Knocks; Investor's Dream; Unique Opportunity;** rare opportunity; **Sleeping Opportunity; Leverage Your Money; Invest in Your Future; Syndicator's Dream; Attention: Syndicators; Be the Landlord; Possible Student Housing; Possible Artists' Lofts; Possible Condominium Conversion;** prime rentals; **A Roof over Your Head—Money in Your Pocket; Raisable Rents;** should rent for [*$2*]/sq. ft.; low rents; high rental demand; no rent increase since [*1988*]; no rent control here; **NYSE Tenant; AAA Tenant; Blue-Chip Tenant; Tenant Waiting List; Sale-Leaseback;** strong tenants; **Always Leased; The Color of Money; Wall to Wall Income; Easy Money;** low vacancy; close-to-zero vacancy; **Bonded Lease;** lease tied to CPI; **Escalating Leases;** inflation-proof leases; **NNN Leases; Percentage Lease;** percentage lease with guarantee; [*$4,800*] **Coming In; Positive Cash Flow; Bottom Line = Profit; Not Beautiful Just Profitable;** [*16*] **Bread-And-Butter Units; Nets** [*12%*]**;** [*12%*] **Cash-On-Cash;** [*12%*] **Cash Flow; Makes U Money;** [*$530,000*] **Spendable;** impressive cash-on-cash return; nearly break even; **Break Even—Almost;** break even with [*15%*] down; let the rents supplement your income; [*$10,000*] **Tax Shelter;** [*$50,000*] lst-year depreciation; **Tax Loss + Cash Flow; The Ultimate Tax Shelter; A Money-Maker;** an investment with a future; exciting potential; the place to watch your equity grow; the bottom line will be profit; **Sanforize Your Dollar**—keep it from shrinking by investing in this . . . ; **Get Rich Slowly** with the steady income from this . . . ; you will never have to say you're sorry if you buy this . . . ; **Below Appraisal; Control-Free Rents;** provision for rent escalation; long-term CPI leases; guaranteed income; insured leases; **No Pride of Ownership—Just Profit; Rake in the Rents; Bread-and-Butter Units—Meat-And-Potatoes Too;** should rent for $; **7 × Gross; $950 Coming In; Seller Will Lease Back or Vacate; Long-Term Lease;**

professional tenants; strong tenants; national tenants; always leased; major tenants occupy [*80%*] of space; national tenants occupy [*80%*] of space; stable rental area; **Uncle Sam Will Hate You; IRS Revenge; Protect Yourself** and your income with this . . . ; **In the Path of Progress;** expanding area; dynamic growth area; high-traffic location; high-traffic corner; heavy foot traffic; best rental location; high-rental-demand area; in-demand rental area; prime rental area; highway visibility; **Traffic—Signage—Visibility;** next to . . . ; across from . . . ; traffic count of . . . cars daily; strategically located between . . . and . . . ; well-maintained; immaculately maintained; like-new; better than new; completely up to code; no deferred maintenance; freestanding; **Ideal Fast-Food Location;** separate meters; tenants pay utilities; ample parking; paved parking; parking for [*300*] cars; off-street parking for [*300*] cars; room for [*30*] additional units; ideal for loft conversion; **Rent Now—Develop Later;** each unit approximately [*1,200*] sq. ft.; redevelopment loans available; professionally managed; management-free investment; EZ management; rezoning possibilities; maintenance-free; almost maintenance-free; an opportunity waiting to happen; for the buyer with vision; the place to watch your equity grow; **Not Much Class** but the income from this . . . is great; [*Time-Share*] **Development Possibilities;** call now, as opportunity seldom knocks twice; **Whopportunity; SCCESS!** We can't spell it without "U"; **The Color Of Money; If Net Is Important to You** let us tell you about this . . . ; **Opportunity Is Knocking; Be the Landlord; Investor's Alert;** raisable rents; **Home + Rental;** [*Brick*] **Duplex;** [*Brick Fourplex*]; [*Duplex*]**—$189,500;** let your tenant pay the mortgage; tenant pays most of mortgage; [*Two*] **Houses—One Lot; Dynamic Duo; Doubles; Exacta** two winning units; **Trifecta** 3 great units; **100% Occupancy; Below Market Rents;** an operating statement your accountant will love; at $ it makes dollars and sense; [*totally*] sheltered income; shows pride of ownership; [*24*] **Units** [*Westwood*]; [*24*] **Units—Accountant Pleaser;** delivered vacant; **Fabulous** [*6*] **Units** . . . ; **Awesome** [*4*] **Units** . . . ; impressive operating statement; **Check the Books**—it's even better than it looks.

Kitchen   a kitchen that puts those in [*House and Garden*] to shame; state-of-the-art kitchen; a kitchen that's better than great; the kitchen you dreamed about; you'll be delighted with the kitchen of tomorrow; **Room for 2 Cooks** in this . . . ; a kitchen that will turn a chef green with envy; French-country kitchen; cupboard-clad kitchen; country kitchen; old-fashioned country kitchen; farm-sized kitchen; tribe-sized kitchen; [*French*] gourmet kitchen; down-home kitchen; ranch-sized kitchen; there's room for a harvest crew in this . . . ; a real chef's kitchen; greenhouse kitchen; island kitchen; dream island kitchen; island cooking center; super-new kitchen; [*St. Charles*] kitchen; sun-drenched kitchen; country-fresh kitchen; country-fresh, bright and airy; sun-filled kitchen; superb culinary center; European; European-inspired kitchen; Eurostyle kitchen; spouse-saver kitchen; work-saver kitchen; skylit kitchen; traditional kitchen; a kitchen a Michelin chef would envy; pass-through kitchen; chateau-size kitchen; a proper English kitchen; the functional kitchen boasts a . . . ; table space in the . . . ; eat-in kitchen; cheerful country kitchen; open work space; salad sink; tiled kitchen; [*granite*] and [*tile*] kitchen; step-saver kitchen; one-step kitchen; Dreamy gourmet kitchen; garden kitchen; designer kitchen; space-age kitchen; kitchen/family room; sun-drenched; brick and copper; energy efficient;

breakfast bar; dining counter; convenient dining counter; built-in dining nook; superb culinary center; the gourmet kitchen is a cook's delight.

Kitchen Appliances   [*Maytag*] kitchen; all the built-ins; self-cleaning oven; built-in microwave; Jenn-Air range; double-door refrigerator with ice maker; top-of-the-line appliances; there are devices for everything except changing junior; with every conceivable labor-saving device built-in; the kitchen includes everything on your wish list; fully applianced [*gourmet*] kitchen; built-in everything.

Kitchen Cabinetry   cupboard-clad kitchen; custom [*oak*] cabinetry; [*oak*] cabinetry; bleached [*oak*] cabinetry; limed [*oak*] cabinetry; solid [*oak*] cabinetry; whitewashed [*oak*] cabinetry; hardwood cabinetry; an extraordinary amount of [*handsome*] wood cabinetry; [*soft pine*] cabinetry; original [*pine*] cabinets; imported European cabinetry; rich [*cherry*] cabinetry; hand-finished [*oak*] cabinetry; [*24'*] of custom kitchen cabinetry to hold all your pots, pans and collectibles; snack bar; breakfast bar; granite counters; Corian counters; Milanese cabinetry; superb handcrafted cabinetry.

Land, Undeveloped   **Future City—[*40*] Acres;** all utilities available; natural gas available; utilities to property; power and phone available; utilities close to property; engineering work completed; completed feasibility study for . . . ; **Zoned [*R-3*] [*40*] Acres;** master-planned for industry; gently rolling; good drainage; favorable percolation tests; [*beech- and oak-*]covered; **Development-Ready—[*40*] Acres;** all mineral and gas rights included; potential for subdividing; **Subdivision Possibilities;** parcel split possible; **An Impressive Investment—[*40*] Acres;** exciting potential . . . ; agricultural lease available; wilderness trails for riding or hiking; **Unspoiled Splendor—[*20*] Acres;** possible dam site for your own lake; you might find arrowheads along the sparkling creek that crosses this . . . ;located in the center of a hunting and fishing paradise; enjoy camping, fishing, and swimming now and build later; a great swimmin' hole; carve your homestead out of the wilderness; marketable timber; timber has not been cut in over [*50*] years; absolute seclusion; enough lumber to build and heat your home forever; **Timber, Fish, and Game—[*10*] Acres**—everything you need is here; possible hydropower site; several excellent homesites; shaded building site; **Subdivision-Ready—[*40*] Acres;** land with a future; **In Path of Progress—[*10*] Acres; In Path of Development; In Path of Annexation; Annexation-Ready—[*40*] Acres;** center of . . . ; squeezed between rapidly growing . . . and . . . ; **Possible Future RV Park—[*40*] Acres; Future Shopping Center?; Your Own Wilderness—[*10*] Acres; Wilderness Domain—[*10*] Acres; Forest Preserve—[*40*] Acres; Private Preserve—[*40*] Acres;** hunting refuge; game refuge; outdoor-person's paradise; bird-watcher's paradise; duck-hunter's paradise; duck-hunter's happiness; undisturbed; forest primeval; your private campgrounds; less than [*10 minutes*] to . . . ; [*150*] **Lots Possible; Thoreau** would have been enthralled with this; **Your Escape—[*10*] Acres; Your Escape from the City; [*40*] Majestic Acres;** destined to become a major development; priced at less than $ per homesite; the [*sun-drenched glen*] would make a perfect homesite; ready for your imagination; this could be your **Shangri-la;** an idyllic spot for your vacation or year-round home, at less than the price of a city lot, $; **Your**

Own [5] Acres; Ah! Wilderness—[5] **Acres;** seclusion from the world for $; **Happy Camper** will love this . . . ; **Your Own Woods** [*and even a hill*]; a place where fantasies become realities; a great place for hermits, children and dogs; [4] acres of a very special love; unspoiled charm; **A Hidden Valley; Your Private Forest** awaits you; [10] **Quiet Acres**—no buildings and no phones; the loudest neighbor is a chattering [*chipmunk*]; [42] **Coveted Acres;** [40] acres of unfenced wilderness; [7] usable acres; the sun-drenched meadow would be perfect for your house and kids; **Own the** [*Valley*] [*Hill*]; **King of the Hill**—[10] **Acres;** where nature excels with her beauty; [10]**-Acre Sanctuary; Roam for Miles; East of the Sun— West of the Moon** is your [10] acres of happiness; **Land—Lots of Land** [40] **Acres** . . . (*See also* **Animals and Birds, Farms**).

Landscaping   Professionally landscaped; **A Sea of Green; Think Green; Knock Your Socks Off** landscaping; estate-like setting; park-like grounds; unrivaled landscaping; landscaping to make your neighbors jealous; native landscaping; water-saving natural landscaping; extensive use of native plants; desert landscaping; impeccable landscaping; flawlessly maintained landscaping; easy-care landscaping; extensively landscaped; lush landscaping; likely the most beautiful yard in town; you will picnic in the park right in your own backyard; featuring exotic plantings; specimen plantings; dream landscaping; rivals any you have seen; unparalleled landscaping by Mother Nature; landscaping to win you a garden club award . . . ; amidst landscaping that would be the envy of any garden club; landscaping you'll take pride in; sculptured hedges; neighbor-jealous landscaping; the lush landscaping reflects loving care; to describe the landscaping as magnificent would be an understatement; model-home landscaping; a screen of greenery; landscaping that is second only to Hampton Gardens; sets a handsome profile on a well-groomed [*acre*]; landscaping that looks too colorful to be real; estate quality landscaping; a [*lawn mower*] goes with the green velvet lawn; verdant; luxuriously manicured lawn studded with stately trees and flower-ing shrubs; impressive plantings; velvet lawn; emerald lawn; landscaping that surpasses your imagination; expansive lawns; magnificent grounds; sweeping emerald lawns; croquet-size lawns; green velvet setting; breathtak-ing grounds; sweeping lawns and towering trees; impeccably maintained lawns; fastidiously maintained grounds; English hedge (*See also* **Garden, Trees**).

Lease   Assumable lease; below-market lease; short-term lease; long-term lease; long-term with escalations; long-term lease at moderate rental; advantageous lease; AAA tenant; **NNN Lease; Triple-Net Lease;** seller will lease back; sale-leaseback; strong tenants; blue-chip tenants; national tenants; always leased; [*100%*] occupancy; major tenants occupy [*80%*] of space; national tenants occupy [*80%*] of space; low vacancy; close-to-zero vacancy; bonded lease; insured lease; guaranteed lease; lease tied to CPI; long-term CPI leases; inflation-proof lease; escalating lease; provisions for rent escalations; short-term below-market lease; raisable rents; percentage lease (*See also* **Business Opportunities, Investment Income Property**).

Lease/Option   **Rent Now—Buy Later; Lease To Own;** renewal option possible; purchase option possible; [*50%*] of rent applies to purchase option; **Lease Till You Buy.**

Living room   26' living room; great room; dramatic great room; drawing room; step-down living room; sunken living room; elegant living room; grand-piano-size living room; entertaining-size living room; mirrored living room with conversation pit; conversation area; intimate conversation area; 2-story living room; vaulted living room; room for a grand piano in this . . . ; dramatically proportioned, open-concept living area; romantic conversation pit in this . . . ; intimate conversation area; expansive living areas; baronial size living areas; a great room that is magnificent in proportion and concept; manor-size living room; a great room you can barely see across (*See also* **Alcove, Floor Plan**).

Location   **Are We There Yet?** Home is closer in . . . ; Be first to discover [*Brentwood*]; [*Brentwood*] **Trend-setter; Heart of** [*Brentwood*]; [*Brentwood*] [*$40,000*]; **Lowest** [*Brentwood*] **Price; Move Up to** [*Brentwood*]; in highly prized [*Brentwood*]; in sought-after [*Brentwood*]; in the small exclusive community of [*Brentwood*]; fashionable address; preferred address; **The Right Address;** an elegant address; **A Success Address;** estate-like area; fairy-tale setting; coveted location; very "in" area; Gold-Coast address; **The Bel Aire Of** [*Brentwood*]; **The Beverly Hills Of** [*Brentwood*]; exciting location; premier location; superb location; **Millionaires' Row;** community of fine homes; **On the Edge of** [*Brentwood*]; **Bordering** [*Brentwood*]; **Across From** [*Brentwood*]; **Adjoins** [*Brentwood*]; around the corner from . . . ; walk to . . . ; bike to . . . ; minutes to . . . ; [*Hillside*] **School District; Adjacent To** [*Brentwood*]; just steps to . . . ; short drive to . . . ; down the road from . . . ; nestled in the hills; knoll-top setting; majestically perched; in a [*Williamsburg*]-like setting; in a pleasantly secluded neighborhood of winding boulevards and intimate culs-de-sac; postcard setting; storybook setting; sited for excellence; in the coveted community of . . . ; the most prestigious street in . . . ; for the price of an ordinary home you can live in . . . ; the only available home in much-sought-after . . . ; on a private lane in . . . ; set in the estate area of . . . ; in the friendly community of . . . where neighbors still know each other by name; in the master-planned community of . . . ; a uniquely planned community; in the masterfully planned community of . . . ; on the best block of the most sought-after street in . . . ; **Location-Location** [*Brentwood*]; **Cut Your Commute**—just a short drive to . . . ; set in the pastoral seclusion of . . . ; set in a serene residential enclave; in a community of fine homes; **Sited for Excellence; A** [*Bel Air*] **Address** can be yours without a [*Bel Air*] price; [*Bel Air*] **Under** [*$400,000*]; **Can't Afford** [*Bel Air?*]; this . . . compares with [*Bel Air's*] finest at [*half*] the price; **The Address** you only dreamed of; if you could choose the most prestigious block of the most prestigious street for your dream home—this would be your choice; nestled in a quiet community of fine homes adjoining . . . ; **Almost** [*Bel Aire*]; [*Westwood*], where we put the privileged few in their place; **Be Among the First** to discover the pleasures of . . . ; offering small-town ambiance of long ago with all the metropolitan conveniences; **Meet the Neighbors** ask them why they chose

[*Clinton Gardens*]; **Go West to** [*Midvale*]; **Above the Smog; On the Greenbelt; The Weekends Start Earlier** in . . . ; **Walk to** [*Train*]; **Had Enough** of wasting your day commuting?; **Born to Shop**—this . . . is just [*minutes*] from the [*mall*]; conservancy-like area; strategically located [*near*] . . . ; [*Elm Grove's*] **Secret;** in unspoiled [*Suffolk County*]; on an historic street in . . . ; **Stop Commuting;** the address alone is worth the price of $; in the [*Newport*] tradition; the elegant ambiance of a [*French*] country village; **Come Home to** [*Middletown*]; nestled beneath the [*San Jacinto*] mountains; **Close to it All**—avoid the commuting nightmare with this . . . ; **Live Above It All; Stop Commuting—Enjoy!;** the address that spells success for just $; **Just** [*90 Steps*] **to the Beach; Near It All; Standin' on the Corner;** couched amidst [*giant boulders*]; [*Redlands*] **Schools; Follow Horace Greeley** west to . . . ; **Walk to Everything; Westside Story; Shop till You Drop;** you're just [*5 minutes*] from . . . ; **Country Quiet—City Close; On a Grassy Knoll;** a neighborhood where children grow and flourish; **Street Smart**—did you know that . . . is the most prestigious street in . . . ; **In a Country Village;** incredibly convenient; [*Sun City*] **Resale** (*See also* **Hills, Water-Related Property**).

Loft   Sleeping loft; Swiss loft; balcony sleeping area; **James Bond Loft; Loft With Light; Loft in Space;** balcony studio; artist's studio; library; loft apartment; bridge over the . . . ; **Loft-Lover's Loft; Skyloft;** lofty living for $; [*music*] loft commands a dramatic view of the living area; perfect studio home; Live/Work; would make the perfect [*home office*]; **Artist's Dream Loft; Lovers' Loft; Loft Lovers; Loft Suite;** [*16'*] **Ceilings;** [*Shoe Factory*] **Loft;** lofted music room; lofted den or [*4th*] bedroom (*See also* **Condominium**).

Lots   Tribe-sized; country-sized; estate-sized; double-sized; oversized; garden-size; orchard-sized; children-sized; huge lot; room for [*pool/tennis courts*]; wooded; corner; cul-de-sac; zoned for . . . ; approved for . . . ; possible lot split; blueprint-ready; building-ready; protected by restrictive covenants; water access; across from . . . ; walk to . . . ; [*M3*] zoning; owner will subordinate; [*5*]% down; ideal for [*sprawling ranch house*]; the steep grade lends itself to an imaginative buyer who wants the ultimate view site; feasibility study completed; all permits and approvals for . . . included; engineering completed for . . . ; tentative approval for . . . ; suitable for tri-level; **Buildable Now** [*$29,500*]; **Dirt Cheap; Dirt for Sale;** *The National Enquirer* never saw a choice piece of dirt like this . . . ; sewer and water in; [*Westwood*] [*$29,500*]; **Dream-House Ready—**[*$29,500*]; trilevel possible; **Your Piece of the Block;** ready to fulfill your dreams at [*$34,500*]; one look and you'll know where you want your dream home; bound to become the most sought-after area in . . . ; in a neighborhood of new, quality residences; awaits a very special home; **Zoned for** [*Mobile Homes*]; plans and approvals for [*34*] units; deed restricted homesite; sloping elevation; **No Flood Problem; Lots of Lots;** rock outcroppings; huge boulders; **Construction-Ready** (*See also* **Land, Undeveloped; Location; Trees; View**).

Maintenance   Well-maintained; meticulously maintained; **Restoration Not Needed** this . . . has been lovingly cared for; superbly maintained; exquisitely maintained; handsomely kept; reflects owner's pride; reflects caring owner; no deferred maintenance; up to code; **Needs Nothing; Impeccable** [*Colonial*] (*See also* **Clean**).

Management   Professionally managed; professional management available; management-free investment; EZ management; maintenance-free; tenant makes all repairs; almost management-free; **Tenant Does Everything.**

Manufactured Homes (Mobile Homes)   Double-Wide [*$29,500*]; **Super-Double-Wide; Triple-Wide [*$39,500*]; Wide-Wide;** [*24' × 50' Rollohome*]; **NADA Value [*$32,500*]—Sale Price [*$28,400*]; Park Model [*$32,500*]; [*1,420 Sq. Ft.*]; Less Than A Car [*$8,900*]; Heaven on Wheels?** Well not exactly—the wheels have been removed on this . . . ; screened and glassed [*Florida room*]; storage building; includes storage shed; move-in ready; park amenities include . . . ; [*Heath Estates*] **$39,500;** situated on the nicest street in the most sought after park; **[*5*]-Star Park; Rent-Controlled Park; [*$149*] Space Rent; Low Space Rent; Senior Park;** a park for the young at heart; **No Age Restrictions; Pets Welcome;** small pets allowed; a quiet park; walking-close to . . . ; with a view of . . . ; quiet streets for evening strolls; reasonable rent space lease available; [*10' × 40'*] covered deck; [*2-car*] carport; full skirting; ground-level entrance; paved parking; **No Park Rent** on your own lot in this . . . ; **Own Your Own Lot; You Own the Land; Why Pay** high space rent when you can own the land in this . . . ; **You Won't Believe** it really is a mobile home.

Marble   Italian; Carrara; Carrara—the sculptors' choice; Venetian; travertine; cultured; sheathed in [*travertine . . .*]; Grecian; [*Carrara*] marble enhances the . . . ; [*Carrara*] marble accents . . . ; extensive use of . . . ; real marble [*vanities*]; [*Vermont*] marble countertops.

Mobile Homes   (*See* **Manufactured Homes.**)

Negative Ads   **Small and Dreary** without a view; **You'll Hate It!; Low Self Esteem?** This . . . is too good for you; **Dirty Old House; Boring; Monotonous** just like every other house on the block; **Not for You; You Don't Need This** . . . ; **Don't Read This Ad; Procrastinators**—this is your chance to miss buying this . . . ; **Want To Be Sorry**—then fail to check on this . . . ; we can't figure out what to do with this . . . ; **Who Would Want It?** It's a regular home out of place in an estate area; **Poor Taste Abounds** in this . . . ; **Are You Eccentric?** If so; you might love this . . . ; if it were any uglier we would raise the price and call it a classic; **It's Just Too Big; You Don't Need [*5*] Bedrooms;** who would want to mow [*an acre*] of lawn; **Ugly,** this monstrosity proves that good taste and money are not synonymous; if it won't bother you to live in the least expensive home in [*Newport*] you might consider this . . . ; **It's Vulgar,** well, what do you expect for [*$69,500*]; no one ever accused the builder of originality; **Color Blind Decorator; Curly, Moe and Larry** were the decorators; **Bad Taste Abounds; Is Ugly Your Thing?** If so, you'll love this . . . ; **A Monument to Bad Taste;** (*See also* **Fixer-Upper**).

Warning: Never use a negative ad without the owner's permission to do so in writing.

Neighborhood   Friendly; on the prettiest street and the friendliest neighborhood in . . . ; sought-after; highly prized; desirable; family; neighborhood of fine homes and immaculate lawns; quiet; in the small community of . . . ; in a pleasantly secluded neighborhood; in the friendly community of . . . ; where neighbors still know each other by name and everyone knows the score of the latest Little League game; a neighborhood that retains a small-town ambiance; a neighborhood where pride of ownership is evidenced in the well-kept homes and impeccable lawns; there's still a place where children can run free and neighbors sit on front porches on warm summer evenings; where neighbors take pride in home and family; **Hopscotch** is still played on the sidewalks of the quiet tree-lined streets; an old fashioned community of well-cared-for homes and manicured lawns where neighbors lend a helping hand and watch over one another; a neighborhood where neighbors care about their homes and one another; neighbors who share your joys, hopes, and concerns; your chance to enjoy a friendly life for $; in a neighborhood that retains the best of the past (*See also* **Location**).

Occupancy   will be completed by . . . ; **Move Right In;** ready for occupancy within [*2 weeks*]; **Available Right Now; Buy Today** and move in tomorrow; [*owner financing*] will allow you almost immediate occupancy; vacant; **Move-in Ready.**

Office, Home   quiet home office; the home office has a private entrance; estate office . . . ; would make a great home office; **Combine Home and Office; Live and Work** at home; an opportunity to combine office and home; home office/music room; den/home office; **Commute from Home;** home computer center.

Open House   **Open for Admiration; Hey! Look Us Over!; Come and See; Come Visit; 1st Showing; 1st Offering; Premier Showing; First Opening; First Presentation; Open to Public; Open—Come Buy; Muddy-Shoes Preview; Come and Appreciate** this . . . ; **Don't Be a Drive-By; It's Bigger Than It Looks;** come inside—you'll be surprised; **Don't Drive By; Open To Sell; Open till Sold; Open House** [*1 P.M.*]–[*4 P.M.*]; **Sunday Open House Now!** Check www . . . ; **Open House Every Day** See property before it is advertised at www . . . ; **Open** [*1 P.M.*] **till Sold; Open Today— Will Be Sold By Tomorrow; Bring Your Boots**—the hammering has stopped, but the lawn and walks haven't been completed on this . . . ; take the Sunday drive that'll change your life; **Sneak Preview; Sneak Opening;** follow the signs from . . . ; better be first in line or be sorry; wait until you see what's inside this . . . ; you MAY want to see the rest, but you WILL want to see the best; your [*host*] [*John Jones*]; **Lookie Lous and Buyers Too.**

Owner or Former Owner   **Doctor's Home; Lumberyard Owner's Home;** [*Redheaded Sculptress*]; [*Lady Saxophone Player*]; **Millionaire's Hideaway; Millionaire's Home; Built By a Millionaire; Architect's Own Home; Architect-Owner; Artist-Owner; The** [*Jones*] **Estate; Owned By A Renowned** [*Pianist*]; built with care for [*his/her*] own family by a master builder; owner/builder designed and built this . . . for [*his/her*] own family; owner's pride shows throughout this . . . ; **Banker's Home; Physician's Home;** a meticulous builder crafted this . . . ; the owner's decision to sell provides a once-in-a-lifetime opportunity; owner says "sell"; former owner of this . . . [*won the lottery*]; **Lucky House**—we'll tell you why this home was lucky for the former owner; original owner has [*13*] children; the owner nearly gave up a promotion to stay in this . . . ; **Owner Relocated; Owner Ran Out;** because of unusual circumstances, the owner of this . . . must reluctantly sell.

Warning: Never include information about an owner, especially if it is a spoof, without the owner's prior permission.

Paneling   [*Cherry*] paneling; solid [*cherry*] paneling; tongue-and-groove paneling; mellow wood paneling; warm wood paneling; courtroom paneling; hardwood paneling; imported hardwood paneling; gleaming [*mahogany*] paneling; wainscoting; extensive wainscoting; solid [*walnut*] wainscoting (*See also* **Woodwork**).

Pantry   Walk-in pantry; butler's pantry; old-fashioned pantry; a real pantry.

Park   Almost in the park; around the corner from the park; borders [*National Park*]; **Walk to the [*Park*]** from this . . . ; **Bike to Park;** park view; a few hops, skips, and jumps to a park playground; **Swings and Things** are in the park just [*a block*] away.

Parking   Off-street parking; covered parking; protected parking; carport; double carport; indoor parking; indoor parking for 2 cars; gated parking; paved parking; secure underground parking; RV parking; room for your RV.

Patios   Brick patio; flagstone patio; tiled patio; family patio; inviting patio; picnic-perfect patio; flagstone terrace; expansive terrace; covered terrace; a terrace overflowing with flowers; courtyard terrace; enclosed patio; canopied patio; stone terrace; sun terrace; raised patio overlooks . . . ; covered patio; awning-covered patio; breakfast patio; dining patio; magnificent terrace enhanced with [*a secluded pool and spa*]; a delightful patio for intimate dining; enjoy your morning coffee on the flower-bedecked patio; fountain patio; rock-scaped patio; garden patio; sunbathers' patio; tree-shaded patio; the [*French doors*] open to a delightful dining patio; a private terrace for intimate sunbathing or dining alfresco (*See also* **Courtyard; Deck**).

Pets   **A Dog Door** leads to . . . ; **Puppy Paradise; Picture a Hound Dog** on the lazy day porch of this . . . ; **Attention Charlie Brown** Snoopy would love this . . . ; **For a Dog's Life; Fido Welcome; Dog House** is included with this . . . ; **Definitely Three Woofs; Friendly Dog** not included with his . . . ; **K-9 Heaven;** there's a [*poodle*] next door and a [*German shepherd*] down the block to welcome your dog to the neighborhood; a Great Dane-sized [*living room*]; chain-link dog run; there's room for a dozen kids and puppies in this . . . ; there's a dog door leading to the backyard with [*3*] oak trees waiting; there's even a fire plug [*on the corner*]; what more could your dog ask for?; carpeting Fido can't stain; bring Fido along to check out the accommodations; definitely not a dog—it's priced at $; a [*family room*] for rainy-day romping; flower beds that hold hundreds of bones; lots of trees for sniffing and squirrels for chasing; there's even a special door just for Rover;

a fireplace for Rover to curl up by; Rover will enjoy the quiet tree-lined streets when you go for walks; **The [*Collie*] Next Door** hopes the new owners of this . . . have a friendly dog to share trees with and to gossip through the back fence; a great place for a dog's life at $; **Cat People Special;** there are plenty of cats in this feline-friendly neighborhood; there are great woods to explore and trees to be climbed.

Planning   In the master-planned community of . . . ; in the masterfully planned community of . . . ; in the planned residential community of . . .

Porch

Enclosed   Screened and glassed porch; glassed-in porch; sunroom; California room; Arizona room; Florida room; garden room; conservatory; enclosed lanai; solarium; sun parlor; enclosed patio; summer room; sun gallery; sleeping porch; enclosed porch; glassed-in porch; jalousied porch; 4-season room; window-wrapped [*studio*]; sun-filled [*conservatory*].

General   **Front Porch Lovers;** Old-fashioned front porch; country porch; old-fashioned gallery; columned portico; fully screened porch; lanai; sleeping porch; wraparound porch; veranda; columned veranda; white-columned veranda; captain's porch; widow's walk; bring your rocking chair; rocking-chair-ready; just the place for your rocking chair or porch swing; **Rocking Chair Ready;** swing on the porch and lull your troubles away; you will love the large front porch of this . . . ; a screened porch just made for summer dreaming; lemonade-sipping front porch; pillared front porch; enjoy summer evenings on the veranda of this . . . ; the pillared front porch welcomes you to comfortable living; a [*huge screened*] porch for summer relaxation or entertaining; screened garden porch; the [*screened*] porch will be your favorite bird watching spot; lazy-day [*front*] porch; spindled porch; busybody front porch; gracious front porch (*See also* **Balcony, Deck, Patio**).

Price Closings   yours for the taking at $; proudly offered at $; impressive but not expensive at $; unpretentious luxury at $; the place for your future at $; everything about this home is impressive except the price $; available for your future at $; a proper residence at $; discerningly priced at $; for those who refuse to compromise on quality—this civilized residence is available at $; offered to you at $; the ultimate in civilized living at $; it's your opportunity to be lord of the manor at $; an investment in fine living $; a heritage for your family at $; you'll want it as your own for $; it's priced no more than an ordinary home at $; one look and we'll put up the Sold sign at $; an unparalleled residence at $; a one-of-a-kind masterpiece at $; this bold statement requires your action today at $; truly a spectacular residence at $; the living is easy at $; your opportunity to depart from the ordinary at $; over [*2,200*] feet of luxury living can be yours at $; priced for the very few at $; offering far more than any tract home at an affordable $; elegance beyond words can be yours for $; even the price is friendly at $; a private world for you at $; all this at a price that won't upset you—$; at $, enjoy; this is as good as it gets at $; the home you deserve at $; amazingly affordable at $; priced at an affordable $; the price is less than you expect at $; one look and you'll reach for your checkbook at $; and a price that won't break you $; the very finest at a conservative $; it's your future at $; it's waiting for you at $; no need to look further, as they don't get any better at $; it stands alone at $; our buy of the week at $; available for only $; you're not going to find a comparable home at $; your family's happiness priced at $; priced to move at $; lowered to $; priced at $ so to delay is to be sorry; priced to blow away the competition at $; priced well below appraisal at $; appraised at $, but priced to sell at $; all the amenities you desire for only $; priced far less than replacement cost at $; at $, you had better grab your checkbook and rush to . . . ; priced to avoid foreclosure at $; auction-priced at $; you would expect to pay far more than the $ price; it's a very special opportunity at $; a rare opportunity at $; call now—at $, it won't be available tomorrow; panic-priced at $; an opportunity unlikely to be repeated at $; definitely our best buy at $; your opportunity for an exceptional purchase at $; liquidation-priced at $; priced to sell quickly at $; priced for immediate sale at $; call now, as it won't last at $; an unusual opportunity to live in one of the most prestigious communities for only $; almost give-away priced at $; become the owner at $; a very special home at $; a home that definitely deserves your immediate attention at $; an exceptional offering at $; far above the rest but down-to-earth priced at $; priced to excite at $; a seldom available opportunity at $; the ultimate in quality of life at $; available at a very affordable $; not to be duplicated at $; it's yours at $; investment of a lifestyle at $; a truly exceptional value at $; for only $ you can have the lifestyle you deserve; even the price will delight you—$; to look is to own at $; you can take advantage of the market and be the owner for $; a very special home at $; an unusual opportunity at $; it's the ultimate in quality of life at $; priced no more than the ordinary at $; a home that deserves your investigation at $; you'll have to act fast at $; for the buyer who will not compromise it is priced at $; priced to sell this weekend at $; family-priced at $; an investment in your family—$; priced at FHA appraisal—$; old-fashioned priced at $; at $, it's your chance to create fond memories for the future; an investment in your peace of mind at $; a very special home at $; a home for joyous living at $; priced for you at $; priced at a pleasant $; a bargain is possible at $; priced thousands below appraisal at $; take it off our hands for $, please; a home for a lot of living at $; offered at a price that won't require you to sell the kids $; a city home that's country-priced at $; it's too perfect to last at $; a house to be envied, offered at $; realistically priced at $; you won't find another like it at $; at $, you need not settle for the ordinary; with a price of $; it's unlikely we'll repeat this ad; as much as you'll like this home, you'll like the price even better—$; it won't last at $; call and we'll prove that for $, you can have a home that knows no compromise; first one to the phone will be the winner at $; a rare offering at $; everything is impressive except the price—$; look and you're going to own at $; we think it's the best buy on the market at $; irresistibly priced at $; ten years from now your friends won't believe you only paid $; not as expensive as your friends will imagine at $; the only thing ordinary is the price—$; this one will be gone at $; definitely a "must-see" at $; your chance to own a bit of American history for $; everyone will think you paid much more than $; fairly priced at $; if you're not the first person in our office, you'll surely be disappointed since it's priced at $; offered on a first-come, first served basis at $; expect the best and you won't be disappointed at $; priced at an unusually affordable $; priced to like at $; a home offering the ultimate in lifestyle at a very affordable $; at $, there is no reason to hesitate; a fantastic opportunity at $; don't tell anyone you only paid $, they'll think you spent far more; if you want to spend more, then you'll have to go elsewhere—$; it's a lot more than you expected at $; about as close to perfection as you can get at $; priced to end your search at $; priced to enjoy at $; it doesn't get any better than this at $; the perfect home for your future is waiting for you at $; a home any family would love at an affordable $; at $, this fine home will not be available for long; first-come, first-served at $; at $, it will likely go to the first caller; there is no equal at $; a home to be proud of at $; the price is not a misprint—it's $; all this for only $; a bright future for $; keep in mind that others also are reading this ad, so at $, you'll want to call now; at $, you should stop reading and call; definitely not to be overlooked at $; honestly priced at $; available right now for only $; incidentally, the price is only $; it all awaits you at $; priced within your reach at $; more than a new home; at $, it's a whole new life; you can live your dream at $; happily priced at $; last one to call will be the loser at $; a home to be loved for $; the lowest priced home in [*Oakdale*] at $; your dreams are within reach at $; you'll proudly call it your home at $; priced for your pocketbook at $; you won't believe the price: only $; at $, your prompt action is advised; unusual circumstances allow us to offer this exceptional property at only $; ready for you at $; sorry, there's only one home at this price—$; please believe us when we say, "Call now or it will be too late" because it's priced at only $; down-to-earth priced at $; full price only $; priced for a very special few at $; an enviable estate at $; the impeccable taste of the [*builder*] [*owner*] is yours at $; available for the first time at $; proudly offered to qualified buyers at $; an estate for the civilized family at $; offered to the person who doesn't know the meaning of compromise at $; it looks far more expensive than $; available at $; conservatively priced at $; available for one fortunate family at $; the ultimate statement of your success at $; everything on your wish list for $; if you promised yourself the best in life, you can keep that promise at $; at $, it's truly incomparable; offering a new dimension in luxury living at $; presently available at $; a whole new lifestyle can be yours at $; not the least bit ordinary in size, quality or price—$; an opportunity that won't last at $; all yours for $; $ includes [*all appliances*]; it can't be duplicated at $; it's a home Currier would have traded Ives for and it's priced at only $; a fabulous find at $; would you believe $; join the neighborhood for $; with a price tag so low you'll be embarrassed to tell your friends $; at a surprisingly reasonable $; if ever there was a "must see"; this is it at $; waiting for you at $; and it's priced at no more than an ordinary home at $; with an old-fashioned price of $; a rare bit of Americana for only $; available for many tomorrows at $; an experience to be lived at $; for [*less than*] the price of a house you can own a real home $; the ideal place for your future at $; offered to the discriminating buyer at $; it will please even the most discriminating buyer at $; all yours for $; at $, it makes dollars and sense; personally priced at $; priced to excite at $; the problem is that at $, it won't last long; the payments will seem like rent at $; charm and dignity at a very affordable $; impressive but not ostentatious at $; make every day a vacation at $; an investment in yourself at $; unexcelled at $; your future at $; enjoy the lifestyle the rest of the world can only dream about for $; $ is a small price for happiness; a one-of-a-kind architectural masterpiece can be yours for $; yours forever at $;

modestly priced at $; budget-priced at $; unlikely to be excelled at $; extraordinary elegance at an uncommon value $; preconstruction-priced at $; all things bright and beautiful for only $; $ takes it; a penny pincher's paradise at $; elegant affordability at $; your home for all seasons at $; yours to enjoy for $; offered for the fortunate few at $; extraordinary elegance at an uncommon value—$; a home to be admired—proudly offered at $; gracious and spacious for $; call now or wish later $; out-of-the-world value at the down-to-earth price of $; value you can feel at $; at $, you had better call our toll-free number now [*1-800-555-8200*]; buy for the value of the land alone—$; a celebration of lifestyle at $; as spectacular as it is affordable at $; sophisticated city living for $; a lifestyle for a lifetime at $; if ever there was a "MUST SEE NOW" this is it—definitely a Best Buy at $; at $, a phone call can make your dreams a reality; the only thing modest is the price—$; favorably priced at $; extraordinary elegance at an uncommon value—$; let us put you in your place for $; priced to be sold tomorrow at $; the extras aren't extra at $; priced to make you smile at $; blowout priced at $; your chance to create fond memories at $; a bold statement as to what life is all about at a surprisingly modest $; priced within your means at $; circle-me priced at $; repo-priced at $; a delight to the senses at $; **It's See Worthy** at $; you can call it home at $; don't hold your horses—act now—$; don't hold your breath—act now—$; an offer you shouldn't refuse at $; priced for those who can't live without water—$; saddle-up priced at $; makes good cents at $; treat yourself—$; it's your chance to get your children into the . . . school district for only $; a great value at $; an obvious value at $; realistically priced at $; competitively priced at $; well-priced at $; priced right at $; rock-bottom-priced at $; action-priced at $; down-to-earth price of $; solid value at $; all this for only $; yours for only $; unmatchable at $; hard to believe at $; a tempting value at $; value-packed at $; packed with value; an uncommon find at $; an uncommonly fine home at $; the price is right at $; offered at an amazingly reasonable $; truly worth seeing and worth owning at $; hard to believe at only $.

Privacy   **Ultimate in Seclusion;** hideaway; escape; **Serene** hideaway; serenity; **End-of-the-Road Seclusion; A Private World; Sanctuary;** secluded; **Absolute Privacy; Close-In Seclusion; A Private World; Private Oasis; Oasis of Privacy; The Sound of Silence;** private road; secluded road; walled estate; in the private world of . . . ; in a very private corner of . . . ; very private pool; tucked away amidst the pines; on [*3*] very private acres; privacy garden; [*ancient oaks*] create a screen of privacy; a secluded place where there is time to ponder; privacy so complete one could swim in nature's garment; in a private wooded enclave; in a private wooded preserve; your own world of private elegance; cloistered behind high [*stone walls*]; scenic and secluded setting; providing pampered privacy; where the air is cleaner—water bluer and privacy still exists; one-way walls of glass; a most rare private setting; very private patio; a very private end unit; a very private sun porch; over [*3,000*] sq. ft. of privacy; in a hidden valley; offering seclusion without isolation; **In a Secluded Valley;** serene setting; **A Private Haven; Call for Directions**—while this secluded . . . is hard to find, your search will be rewarded; **Hushed Privacy [*$129,500*]; The Sound of Silence; Privately Yours; Privacy Is** this . . . ; hidden from the road and nestled in . . . ; natural seclusion; **Outlaws and in-Laws** will appreciate this secluded; **Want to**

be Alone?; Be a Hermit; Hermit's Choice; Love Your Privacy; Nudists' Delight privacy is absolute at this . . . ; **Disappear** to . . . ; **Desert Island** Well, it seems that way; **Behind the Gates** in . . . ; **An Hour to Nowhere.**

Recreational Vehicles   RV hookups; RV hookups for your traveling friends; room for your RV; RV parking; plenty of room for your RV; plenty of parking for your camper and boat; RV-park possibilities; zoned for RV park.

Redevelopment   Redevelopment area; redevelopment possibilities; redevelopment loans available; ripe for redevelopment.

Reduction   Down to your price; now at your price; reduced for action; price drastically reduced; price substantially reduced; substantial reduction; reduced $; second reduction; last reduction; final reduction; price reduced to $; **Price Slashed—[$84,500]; Price Massacre—[$42,500]; Catch a Falling Price [$239,500].**

Remodeled   Stunningly; completely rebuilt; better than new; with new everything; elegantly modernized; dramatically updated; thoughtfully updated to combine the best of the old with the new; updated systems; 19th-century elegance combined with 21st-century convenience; combines antique charm with today's conveniences; unobtrusive improvements include . . . ; offering the charm of yesteryear with the conveniences of tomorrow; it truly represents the grandeur of the past with all the modern conveniences of tomorrow; this classic offers a tour through yesteryear with the conveniences of tomorrow (*See also* **Homes, Old**).

Rental Property   (*See* **Investment Income Property.**)

Restored   Totally restored; superbly restored; exquisitely restored; charmingly restored; charming restoration; meticulously restored; faithfully restored; completely and beautifully restored; restored to combine old-fashioned elegance with up-to-date amenities; completely restored to capture the aura of yesteryear; tastefully restored; **Restored Nostalgia;** restored to its former splendor; lovingly restored; restored with the antique-lover in mind; [*90%*] restored; **Restored [*Colonial*];** restoration underway; partially restored; restored by . . . ; **Restorer's Treasure; Worthy of Restoration;** ready for restoration; a masterpiece in need of restoration; **Restorable [*Colonial*];** artistically restored to functional and aesthetic perfection; painstakingly restored; tastefully restored and updated to meet the living standards of the most discriminating; museum-quality restorations; restored with imagination and elegance; restored with integrity; has been transformed into an elegant showplace with all the conveniences of today; **Restoration Worthy;** restoration possible (*See also* **Homes, Old**).

River   **Tom Sawyer** would love this . . . ; **Tube Floatin', or Fishin';** meandering river; **Fish and Float;** clear mountain stream; lazy fish-filled stream; sparkling stream; babbling brook; a babbling brook runs merrily at your doorstep; the sound of rushing water; you'll fall asleep with the gentle sound of the babbling brook; rocky stream; your own waterfall (*See also* **Water-Related Property**).

Roads   (*See* **Streets and Roads.**)

Roof   Red tile roof; Spanish tile roof; mission tile roof; lifetime tile roof; slate roof; hand-split cedar shakes; gambrel roof; Dutch gambrel roof; Pennsylvania-Dutch gambrel roof; mansard roof; French mansard roof; multigabled roof; a real [*slate*] roof; newer roof; new roof; built-up roof; concrete tile roof; multicolored tile roof; **Nathaniel Hawthorne** would love the multigabled roof of this . . .

Rooms   Mammoth; Texas-sized; baronial-sized; manor-sized; tribe-sized; family-sized; magnificently proportioned; dramatically proportioned; castle-sized; rooms of grand proportions; [*16′*] × [*40′*] [*living room*].

Sauna   Finnish; Danish; Swedish; automatic gas; redwood; cedar; . . . for healthy relaxation; sauna room; sauna in fitness center; your own steam bath.

Schools   In the . . . school district; walking-close to schools and shopping; super schools are walking-close to this . . . ; late for school?—not from this . . . ; [*Wilson*] **School District;** it's your chance to get your children into the [*Wilson*] school district for only $; **Private Schools** not needed as you're in the . . . ; school district; **Even Little Legs** can walk to school from this . . .

Second Home   (*See* **Acreage, Homes, Vacation Homes, Water-Related Property.**)

Security   In the walled community of . . . ; guard gate; 24-hour guard gate; security gate; 24-hour doorman; **Behind the Gates;** high-rise security; **Behind Guarded Walls;** behind a gate-guarded entry; 24-hour security patrol; key-operated elevators; latest in electronic security; 24-hour parking attendants; underground security parking; smoke detectors; intercom security system; round-the-clock electronic surveillance; sonic alarm system; security cameras; ultrasonic security system for your peace of mind; alarm system on all windows and doors; central security system; police-connected alarm system; armed response alarm system; [*Honeywell*] alarm system; foyer security system; behind electronically controlled gates; state-of-the-art security; monitored security; video security; security gates open to reveal . . . ; full security system; sophisticated security system; security gates with intercom; behind a decorative wrought iron security gate; cloistered behind high walls; enclosed community; your sanctuary at $; gate house community of . . . ; premier-gated community; where neighbors seldom lock their doors; a place where you'll feel secure in mind and body; a place where children play and friends take evening strolls; security shutters.

Shed   Hobby building; storage shed for your . . . ; ideal as an artist's studio; would make an ideal [*workshop*]; could be converted to [*guest house*]; plenty of room for the collector; storage for your . . . ; potting shed; garden shed; English garden shed.

Shutters   Plantation shutters; colonial shutters; [*Blue*] **Shutters;** Bermuda shutters; privacy shutters; security shutters; French shutters; full shutters; New Orleans shutters; shutters that actually work; **Shutters and Brick.**

Soil Type   . . . acres silt loam; . . . acres productive silt loam; . . . acres deep loam; . . . acres rich loam; . . . acres productive bottom land; . . . acres fertile bottom land; rich deep soil; fertile lawn; garden-perfect soil.

Spa   Hydrotherapy spa; titillating hot spa; tantalizing hot spa; sumptuous hot spa; hot bubbly spa; sensuous hot spa; Jacuzzi; very private spa; therapeutic whirlpool spa for total relaxation; hot tub holds [*6 to 8*]; redwood hot tub; California hot tub; fantasy hot spa; [*double-size*] hot spa in [*master bath*].

Sprinklers   Underground sprinklers; automatic sprinklers; automatic sprinkler system; fully watered by automatic system.

Stairs   Angular staircase; dogleg staircase; center staircase; wide center staircase; grand staircase; curved staircase; **Graceful Curved Staircase;** gently curving staircase; dramatic curved staircase; spiral staircase; open staircase; closed staircase; circular staircase; the circular staircase spirals to . . . ; sweeping staircase; floating staircase; flamboyant floating staircase; dramatic floating staircase; mirrored staircase; cantilevered staircase; grand staircase; grand [*walnut*] staircase; **Gone-With-The-Wind** staircase; banistered staircase; solid cherry balustrade; intricately carved banisters; spindled staircase; handcarved banisters; intricately carved banisters; [*circular*] staircase of [*oak and cherry*].

Stone   River rock; orchard-stone; crab orchard stone; native stone exterior; solid stone construction; cut stone; solid granite; lannon stone; cut limestone; Tennessee stone; California driftwood; [*Limestone*] **Legend;** massive stone; split-rock; brick and stone; stone and cedar; glass and stone; **Set in Stone;** richly accented stone work (*See also* **Brick, Fireplace, Marble**).

Streets and Roads   All-weather road; improved road; paved road; county-maintained road; private road; **Down a Winding Road;** country lane; rustic lane; **On a Country Lane;** on a quiet country lane; a country lane weaves its way through this . . . ; tree-lined street; quiet tree-lined street; tree-canopied street; quiet no-through street; **End-of-the-Road Seclusion;** coach-lighted street; dead-end street; on a private lane in . . . ; no-traffic street; well-lighted quiet street; on a very special street in . . . ; the most prestigious street in . . . ; on the best block of the most-sought-after street in . . . ; [*Washington Blvd*] [*$94,500*]**;** on the prettiest street and the friendliest neighborhood in . . . ; in a pleasantly secluded neighborhood of winding boulevards and intimate culs-de-sac; tucked away on a quiet cul-de-sac; peaceful culs-de-sac; wooded cul-de-sac; shaded cul-de-sac; children-safe cul-de-sac; the right address; an elegant address; prestigious address; major highway frontage; [*200'*] *Highway* [*70*].

Studio   Artist's studio; skylit studio; sky studio; loft studio; balcony studio; attic studio; would make ideal artist's studio; a separate studio to appeal to the artist or writer; window-wrapped studio; sun-streaked studio; sun-drenched studio.

Sunlight   Sun-drenched; sun-filled; sun-streaked; filled with sunlight; light and bright; flooded with [*afternoon*] sunlight; bright with the [*morning*] sun; warm and sunny; [*18*] windows welcome the sun in this . . . ; sunset views; sunrise views.

Swimming Pools   Olympic-size pool; kidney-shaped pool; lap pool; oval pool; world-class pool; in-ground pool; Gunite pool; **Skinny-Dipping** pool; crystal-cool pool; dazzling pool; inviting pool; cool blue pool; shimmering pool; sparkling pool; heated pool; heated and filtered pool; private pool; secluded pool; solar-heated pool; glassed-in pool; caged pool; totally glassed pool; fully fenced pool; free-form pool; **Take the Plunge; a Summer Place;** [*secluded*] sparkling pool; **Attention Skinny-Dippers, Skinny Dipping Allowed; Splish! Splash!;** so private; you can swim in nature's garment; your chance to get in the swim at $; [*30′*] pool; fantasy pool; cool deck; your children will love the [*curved slide and diving board*] that come with the . . . ; you will **Vacation at Home** with our own delightful pool [*and spa*]; not only will your children never leave home, you can expect their friends as well with this . . . ; delightful dining patio overlooks the sparkling pool; **Dive In;** [*sensuous*] hot spa overflows into the sparkling pool; **Swimsuit Ready at $; Family with Swimsuits;** a tropical setting for the sparkling pool; your children and grandchildren will want to swim and frolic in your sparkling pool; **Buy Now—Swim Later; Cool Pool;** you'll save a fortune on vacations owning this . . . ; **California Lifestyle; The Pool Comes Free; Come Swimmin' Time,** you'll be ready with this . . .

Taxes   Low taxes; low-low taxes; taxes only [*$382*] in [*2003*]; benefit from [*Clearwater's*] low tax rate; the lowest tax rate in the county; **County Taxes; Country Ambiance and Taxes;** offering the sophistication of the city without city taxes; Escape City Taxes; taxes that make cents plus a lot more house for your money in . . .

Tennis   Night-lighted court; illuminated court; sunken tennis court; championship tennis court; world-class tennis court; close to courts; room for tennis court; **Love; Love in the Afternoon;** your own [*lighted*] tennis court; **Tennis Anyone?; Into Racquets?; Game, Set, Match; Tennis Anytime; Free Tennis**—the courts are yours as the owner of this . . . ; work on your backhand; not on your lawn.

Terms   (*See* **Assumable Loan, Financing.**)

Tile   Fully tiled; sleek ceramic tile; ceramic tile; stone tile; slate tile; Italian tile; Venetian tile; Mexican tile; Mission tile; Saltillo tile; Portuguese tile; travertine tile; **Tons of Tile** . . . (*See also* **Flooring, Tile**).

Time-share   Interval ownership; **Own Your Vacation;** special shared ownership plan; unique share-ownership plan; you want your [*cottage*] for [*2*] weeks—why pay for 52?; **Sample Paradise** each and every year as the owner of [*2 weeks*] . . . ; your own [*2*] weeks each and every year; vacation like a millionaire in your own . . . ; **Why Pay** for 52 weeks when you only have [*2*] weeks' vacation; you'll have all the amenities of a world-class resort at your beck and call; or trade your time at any of [*87*] worldwide resorts; **Two Weeks' Vacation**—why not own them?; offering a recreational ambiance rivaling the world's most exclusive resorts; almost limitless recreational opportunities; time-share development possibilities; **Buy the Beach** or 2 weeks of it; **Don't Rent Your Dream** (*See also* **Condominium, Vacation Homes, Water-Related Property**).

Trees   Your home in the woods; **Beneath Towering [*Pines*];** nestled beneath the towering trees; nestled in the forest; **Tall Timbers; Lofty [*Pines*]; Hardwood Haven; Wooded Wonderland; In the [*Oaks*];** sheltered by towering [*pines*]; shaded by a grove of native hardwoods; mature orchard; organic orchard; young orchard; producing orchard; mouth-watering family orchard; young orchard just coming into the most productive years; the backyard is enhanced with . . . ; the backyard is a tropical oasis of [*palms and citrus*]; many [*fruit and nut*] trees embellish this [*rolling*] parcel; maple trees for augering; your own maple syrup from the sugar maple in . . . ; there's a great place for a hammock between the [*elms*] in the pleasantly shaded backyard; lawn graced with shade and flowering trees; century-old [*oak*]; a tranquil wooded setting envelops this . . . ; a **Paul Bunyan-Size Forest;** rustic wooded; sprinkling of [*hickory and oak trees*] in the sunlit meadow; sprinkled with [*oak*] trees; cut your own Christmas tree in your family woods; **Virgin Timber;** mature hardwoods; marketable timber; timber cruised at an estimated $ per acre; no timber has been cut in over [*40*] years; your woodlot will keep you warm for many winters; **Peace and Pines; Home in the Woods; Bring Your Squirrels** there are [*7*] oak trees loaded with . . . ; ample wood lot for home heating; meandering drive through your scenic woodlot; captivating setting adorned by huge shade trees; tucked away in the trees; nestled on a large lot beneath mature shade trees; flanked by towering [*magnolias*] and graceful [*cedars*]; towering trees form a canopy over this . . . ; towering trees and flowering shrubs; [*100*]-year-old [*oaks*] shade this . . . ; tucked away on [*3*] enchanted wooded acres; set among huge and captivating hardwood trees; framed by flowering [*dogwoods*]; [*cherry blossoms*] and [*maples*] surround this . . . ; age-old trees and manicured lawns; flanked by ancient [*maples*]; nestled in a peaceful wooded setting; cloistered behind towering [*hemlocks*]; nestled in the [*pines*]; a tapestry of flowering shrubs and magnificent trees; a lush oasis of towering trees and flowering shrubs; hammock-ready trees; the perfect backyard spot to hang your hammock; specimen trees; specimen trees and shrubs; where the trees grow tall and the sun meets the sea; set in a sun-streaked wooded glen; woodlot is loaded with game; **Silent Woods;** a century-old [*chestnut*] tree shades this . . . ; a perfect branch to hang a swing; **Tall Trees** create a screen of privacy and soft cascades of light and shade add a timelessness where today, tomorrow, or next week need not mean urgency; a home as solid as the trees guarding it; **Amid the [*Apple*] Trees;** set in your own [*pecan*] orchard; century-old [*sugar maples ready for tapping*]; **Johnny Appleseed** must have come this way; **Apple Pie on Sunday** from your own apple trees; you'll have bushels of [*apples*] from your [*3*] trees that come with this . . . ; [*Apple*] **and** [*Peach*] **Blossoms** will bloom in the spring and there will be pie and preserves in the fall as the owner of this . . . ; conservancy-like area; a verdant canopy of [*whispering pines*]; **Birds, Bees, and [*Apple*] Trees; Nuts** and fruit trees come with this . . . ; [*Apple*], [*Pear*], [*Plum*]; **Beneath a Majestic [*Oak*]; Maple Syrup** from your own trees;

Guarded By a Giant [*Oak*]; **A Cathedral** of tall trees shelter this . . . ; ancient [*oaks*] and towering [*beech*]; set amidst peaceful woods and wild-flowers; bordered by a rustic tree-lined . . . ; [*Apple*]**-Picker's Dream;** ornamental trees; in a haven of [*oak*] and [*hickory*] trees; **Forest Primeval.**

Trim   (*See* **Woodwork.**)

Unfinished Areas   Bonus room; storage attic could be converted to [*studio or 4th bedroom*]; ideal spot for darkroom; ready for finishing to meet your needs; could be converted to guest facilities; expansion room in . . . ; a perfect playroom; would make a perfect . . . ; room for [*2*] bedrooms in the [*exposed*] basement; it awaits your imagination.

Urgency   Won't be around long at . . . ; can be yours today but it will be gone tomorrow; if you wait it will be too late; call now, for you are not the only one reading this ad; be first or be sorry; first one to view it will be the winner; call now because at $, it won't be available tomorrow; you'll have to act fast at $; priced to sell this weekend at $; with a price of $, it's unlikely that this ad will be repeated; the second caller is likely to be disap-pointed; **First-Come, First-Served;** an opportunity that won't knock again (*See also* **Price Closings**).

Utilities   City water and sewer; county . . . ; natural gas; economical natural gas; [*sewer and water*] to property; underground utilities; power to property; low-cost [*Middleton*] power; utilities in and paid.

Vacation Homes   **Attention Snowbirds;** Retreat; **Northwoods Retreat; Mountain Retreat; Corporate Retreat;** hideaway; **Artist's Hideaway; Country Escape;** escape the rat race; refuge; **Your Quiet Place; Getaway House;** chalet; **Northwoods Chalet;** for weekends or weeks on end; **Country Quiet;** lodge; **Mountain Lodge; Northwoods Lodge; Buy the Sun; Buy the Snow; Your Place in the Fun;** start a tradition with this extended family-size summer home; enjoy those lazy days of summer in this . . . ; every day will be a holiday at this . . . ; the place for your weekend getaway; where winter is just a memory; slow down the tempo of your life; the place for a relaxing country weekend; an experience with nature for weekends or a lifetime; loaded with peace and quiet; less than . . . from . . . ; you'll feel at peace with nature in this . . . ; located in a 4-season vacation-land; your escape-hatch from the city; **Your Retirement Plan; Paradise Found;** can be used as a vacation home or permanent residence; **Can't Retire Yet?** this . . . can be your vacation home now and your year-round home for your future; offering you a 365-day vacation; **Sol Searching**—this can be your place in the sun; a world of quiet pleasures and glorious sunsets; you'll revel in the warm sunny days; star-filled nights and crisp clean air; cradled by the beauty of . . . ; where the air is clean and the winds are calm; **Vacation Every Day; Lock in Your Future; Your Haven on Earth; Your Heaven On Earth** (*See also* **Homes, Water-Related Property, View**).

Value   (*See* **Price Closings.**)

View   Above the Eagles; Above the Lights; Sea of Lights; City Lights;
Above All; Ocean View; a view of the world; exhilarating view; incomparable view; million-dollar view; smashing view; cinemascope view; panoramic view; 360° view; sweeping view; mile-wide view; permanent view; guaranteed view; seductive view; incredible view; unparalleled vistas; bird's-eye view; eagle's-eye view; white-water view; river view; unreal vistas; awesome view; magical view; dazzling view; unsurpassed view; forever views; serene vistas; pastoral vistas; serene pastoral vistas; fairy-tale view; seventh heaven view; picture-book view; glorious view; commanding view; overlooks a variegated fairyland of lights; tranquil; unspoiled view; unobstructed view; breathtaking view; watch the [*sailboats*] from the deck of this . . . ; overlooking . . . ; sunrise view; sunset view; an almost fairy-tale diorama; surrounded by stunning vistas; celestial view; a vantage point overlooking . . . ; a breathtaking view at a breathe-easy price—$; unmatched vistas; unique view-site offers [*360°*] vistas; the views [*through the walls of glass*] stretch to the very edge of eternity; the magnificent vistas seem a part of the living space; woodland views; enjoy the inner peace of the [*sunrise*] [*sunset*] views from this . . . ; breathtaking view of . . . ; incomparable [*river*] view; you'll look down on the world from this . . . ; a practically-forever view; you'll glory in the magnificent vistas from . . . ; **Ansel Adams** loved these majestic mountains framed through the [*walls of glass*] of this . . . ; **Why Buy a Painting** when you can see the real thing from your easy chair through [*the walls of glass*] of this . . . ; **God Was the Decorator** who created the inspiring vistas that seem as one with this . . . ; **City Lights** will sparkle at your feet from this . . . ; **Eagles Nest;** let the rest of the world live in your shadow as the owner of this . . . ; **Afraid of Heights?** Then don't even consider this top-of-the-world . . . ; **Big Sky Views; A View of Nature** and not the neighbors; offering Ansel Adams vistas; fantastic vistas of [*city lights*] and sparkling stars; **King of the Hill**—you'll feel like royalty looking down from this . . . ; views unlikely to be excelled; **Own the City**—everything else is beneath you as the owner of this . . . ; **Everything Else Is Downhill** from this . . . ; **Sunrise, Sunset**—see it all from . . . ; designed to capture [*sunset*] vistas; Wide-Open Vistas; unobstructed [*ocean*] views; **Whitewater Views; Outrageous View;** sweeping [*mountain*] views; **See the World** from . . . ; **Touch the Stars** from the . . . ; captivating [*mountain*] vistas; all else will seem beneath you from this . . . ; a view that must be experienced; [*elevated site*] with commanding view; **The View Won't Quit**—It goes on forever; **Get High** above the city lights in this . . . ; **Drop-Dead Views; Killer Views; Knock-Your-Socks-Off** view of . . . ; **Twice the View** from this 2-story . . . ; awesome view; fairy-tale view; **360 Million $ View;** awe-inspiring view; **In the Treetops; Heaven Has a View; Sit and Watch** the [*changing shadows of the mountains*] from the . . . ; the quality is as clear as the view; views to dream about; postcard view; private garden view; enchanted garden view; vistas that can't be captured on canvas; protected vistas; a view that doesn't stop; **High on a Windy Hill; Overlooking the World; Watch the** [*Ships*] from this . . . ; **On a Clear Day** you can see forever from this . . . ; **Not Just the View** it's the vision of living; **Heaven Has a View.**

Wainscoting   [*Walnut*] wainscoting; solid [*walnut*] wainscoting.

Walkways Quiet walkways; flagstone walk; lighted walkways; shaded walks; covered walkways; quaint cobblestone paths; ancient stone path; a meandering walk.

Wall Coverings Imported wall covering; textured wall covering; decorator wall covering; designer wall covering; lavish use of . . . ; coordinated wall coverings; wall coverings you won't find in any store.

Warranty homebuyer warranty available; homebuyer [2]-year warranty is included; seller will pay for homebuyer protection plan; **Guaranteed House; We Warrant It.**

Water-Related Property **Creekfront Dazzler; Riverfront Sanctuary; Frog Paradise; A Big Fat Fish** was swimming by the dock when we put up our sign; **Beach Retreat; On the Waterfront; Lakefront Shangri-La; Beach House; A Place on the Beach;** white sand beach; spectacular white sand beach; wide sand beach; gradual sand beach; gentle wading beach; child-safe wading beach; stroll on the sand; miles of sand beach for barefoot walking; [200'] of choice sand frontage; a tranquil setting; the gentle sound of rushing water will lull you to sleep in this . . . ; the view of the sunset over the water is unsurpassed; pounding surf is at your front door; **Fish-Filled River; Fish off Your Own Dock; Spring-Fed Lake;** crystal-clear spring-fed lake; sparkling stream; **Swimmin', Fishin' Lake;** shimmering water; lake access; meandering stream; cool mountain stream; lazy fish-filled river; 30' dock; 30' dock with electric hoist; boat house with hoist; wet boat house; covered dock; permanent pier; deep-water dock; bulkheaded frontage; protected anchorage; on the perfect lake; at the water's edge; fish and float river; fish-filled creek; for the Tom Sawyer in you; sailboat water; **Walk to Beach;** stroll on the sand; stroll on the beach; **On the Sand;** blue water and white sails; **Beach Retreat; Buy the Sea;** commanding water-front site; practically in the water; for those who appreciate the beauty and serenity of waterside living; overlooking the tranquil waters of . . . ; babbling brook; a [*babbling brook*] runs merrily at your doorstep; you will go to sleep with the gentle sound of [*the babbling brook*]; only a short stroll to catch the waves; listen to the surf and watch the waves from this . . . ; sandy beaches await you at this . . . ; watch the reflections of the changing seasons in the tranquil waters of lake . . . ; enjoy the tranquility of wide waters and quiet beaches; promenade on a spectacular stretch of white sand beach; **Bike to Beach;** swim and fish in your own backyard; ice-cold flowing spring; clean mountain stream; beach privileges; private mooring; mooring rights; beach rights; **Steps from the Sand;** dock and davits; **Shh! Don't Tell** the relatives you purchased a . . . or they will bring their suitcases and friends; heavy-duty davits; beach access; dedicated beach access; seawalls; protective docking; private lake access; [*100'*] of Beach; [*100'*] on the Water; Lake [*Charles*] [*200'*] Frontage; the sparkling stream cascading through the property will fulfill a trout fisherman's fantasy; **Where the Sun Meets the Sea; Sand Between Your Toes; Steps to the Sand; Blue Water—White Sand;** enjoy the morning mist and the haunting cry of sea gulls; [*100*] **Footsteps To The Sand;** you'll want to take off your shoes and run barefoot through the sand; **Beach Cottage;** watch the fog roll in on wintry days; you'll take morning walks with your dog along hard packed sand—enjoying the sights, sounds, and smell of the sea; enjoy [*sunsets*] [*sunrises*] over the water; **Watch the Ships** from the [*deck*] of this . . . ; fishing from the [*dock*] is reported to be great; **Your own Private Beach;** fish-filled lake; spring-fed lake; crystal-clear lake; the haunting sound of loons over the water; [*100'*] **of Pristine Shoreline; Thoreau** wouldn't have wanted to leave this picturesque [*pond*] set amidst [*giant pines*]; **The Loon Calls** and a canoe glides across the gentle water of . . . ; **Tom Sawyer** would have loved this riverfront . . . ; overlooking the shimmering waters of . . . ; **Own the [*Lake*] [*River*];** you'll awaken to the sound of the surf and the cry of gulls; the relaxing sound of water gently lapping on the shore; **The Sound of Surf** will lull you into a sound sleep and the morning call of gulls will invite you to walk barefoot in the sand; **Reach Out—Touch the Surf;** there is nothing quite like the smell of sea air at your doorstep or the gentle sound of waves to lull you to sleep; **Fisherman's Dream;** on the sand in the solitude of your thoughts; breakfast on the [*terrace*] to the sound of waves caressing the shore; **Ocean Front; Water Front; Lake Front; Hear The Surf;** private bay; secluded bay; gently sloping frontage; [*200'*] of swimming frontage; **Wilderness Pond; Creek-Side Setting; Mariner Views;** coastal breezes; **See the Sea; Sand Between Your Toes; Ocean-Close; Home to the Sea;** your place to drop anchor at $.

Water, Well   Pure well water; sparkling well water; you will relish the cold pure water from your own well; water without the taste of chlorine; pure water from your own tap; chemical-free well water.

Wheelchair Access   (*See* **Handicapped.**)

Windows   Wall of glass; windowed wall; majestic wall of glass; 30' window wall; one-way walls of glass; knee-to-ceiling windows; one-way glass; Palladian windows; window-wrapped [*solarium*]; soaring window walls; [*Anderson*] window wall; greenhouse windows; picture windows; picture window overlooks . . . ; picture window frames [*a picturesque and private backyard*]; clerestory windows; mullioned windows; glassed-in; skylight; diamond-lite; glass-domed [*atrium*]; glass-enclosed [*atrium*]; the sliding glass doors open to . . . ; French doors; double glass doors; leaded glass; leaded-glass accents; fan light; vintage leaded glass; beveled glass; beveled and jeweled glass; etched glass; intricately etched glass; frosted glass; stained glass; oval glass; colorful window boxes; old-fashioned bay window; massive entryway framed by side lights; Thermopane; double-glazed; triple-glazed; solar bronze; self-storing storms and screens; wall-size picture windows; it's your window of opportunity at $; bathed in natural light; witness nature's treasures through walls of glass; windows that start at the knees and don't stop till they reach the ceiling; **Wrapped in Glass;** . . . meld the living area with nature . . . ; merge the indoor/outdoor areas together in perfect harmony; the [*vaulted ceiling*] blends well with the massive wall of windows to give a feeling of openness; flooded with natural light; expansive use of windows; windows that invite the outdoors in; **Bring the Outdoors Inside; Let There Be Light;** sun-filled elegance; sun-drenched rooms; **Windowful, [*12*] Windows;** outrageous view from every window; **Comfort and Glass** (*See also* **View**).

Woodwork   magnificent detailing; gleaming hardwood; richly paneled; fine wood detailing; intricate woodwork seldom seen in this country; old-world craftsmanship is evident in the [*intricate detailing*]; exceptional woodwork; massive [*oak*] beams; huge hewn beams; perfectly matched woodwork; finely crafted woodwork; lavish use of finely crafted hardwoods; [*maple*] woodwork with a special softness about it; the [*oak*] woodwork was matched as to grain and fitted with meticulous precision; exposed [*oak*] beams; tongue-and-groove paneling; crown moldings; dental moldings; hand-hewn logs; the warmth of [*cedar*]; lodge pole pine; generous use of wood trim; gleaming woodwork that reflects old-world craftsmanship; museum-quality woodwork; [*oak*] trim (*See also* **Kitchen Cabinetry, Paneling**).

Workshop   Separate workshop in . . . ; built-in workbench . . . ; would make ideal workshop; hobby shop; huge [*24'*] workshop; workshop area in . . . ; plenty of room in the [*dry basement*] for a hobby shop; studio/workshop; barn/workshop; garage/workshop; basement/workshop; perfect for making clever things and fixing what isn't even broken; heated workshop; **Are You a Fix-It?; Tinkerer?;** [*20' × 40' steel building*] would make a workshop to be envied; any hobbyist would envy this . . .

Zoning   Zoned [*C3*]; zoned for [*horses*]; rezoning possibilities; adjoining property zoned [*M3*]; [*M2*] **Zoning.**

Index

License Agreement

By breaking the sealed envelope, you agree to become bound by the terms of this license. If you do not agree to the terms of this license do not use the software and promptly return the unopened package within thirty (30) days to the place where you obtained it for a refund.

This Software is licensed, not sold to you by DEARBORN PUBLISHING, INC., owner of the product for use only under the terms of this License, and DEARBORN PUBLISHING, INC. reserves any rights not expressly granted to you.

1. LICENSE: This License allows you to:
   Use the Software only on a single microcomputer at a time, except the Software may be executed from a common disk shared by multiple CPUs provided that one authorized copy of the Software has been licensed from DEARBORN PUBLISHING, INC. for each CPU executing the Software. DEARBORN PUBLISHING, INC. does not, however, guarantee that the Software will function properly in your multiple CPU, multi-user environment. The Software may not be used with any gateways, bridges, modems, and/or network extenders that allow the software to be used on multiple CPUs unless one authorized copy of the Software has been licensed from DEARBORN PUBLISHING, INC. for each CPU executing the Software.

The Software can be loaded to the hard drive and the disk kept solely for backup purposes. The Software is protected by United States copyright law. You must reproduce on each copy the copyright notice and any other proprietary legends that were on the original copy supplied by DEARBORN PUBLISHING, INC.

Configure the Software for your own use by adding or removing fonts, desk accessories, and/or device drivers.

2. RESTRICTION: You may not distribute copies of the Software to others or electronically transfer the Software from one computer to another over a network and/or zone. The Software contains trade secrets and to protect them you may not de-compile, reverse engineer, disassemble, cross assemble or otherwise change and/or reduce the Software to any other form. You may not modify, adapt, translate, rent, lease, loan, resell for profit, distribute, network, or create derivative works based upon the Software or any part thereof.

3. TERMINATION: This License is effective unless terminated. This License will terminate immediately without notice from DEARBORN FINANCIAL PUBLISHING, INC. if you fail to comply with any provision of this License. Upon termination you must destroy the Software and all copies thereof. You may terminate the License at any time by destroying the Software and all copies thereof.

4. EXPORT LAW ASSURANCES: You agree that the Software will not be shipped, transferred, or exported into any country prohibited by the United States Export Administration Act and the regulations thereunder nor will be used for any purpose prohibited by the Act.

5. LIMITED WARRANTY, DISCLAIMER, LIMITATION OF REMEDIES AND DAMAGES: The information in this software (Materials) is sold with the understanding that the author, publisher, developer, and distributor are not engaged in rendering legal, accounting, banking, security, or other professional advice. If legal advice, accounting advice, security investment advice, bank or tax advice, or other expert professional assistance is required, the services of a competent professional with expertise in that field should be sought. These materials have been developed using ideas from experience and survey information from various research, lectures, and publications. The information contained in these materials is believed to be reliable only at the time of publication and it cannot be guaranteed as it is applied to any particular individual or situation. The author, publisher, developer, and distributor specifically disclaim any liability or risk, personal or otherwise, incurred directly or indirectly as a consequence of the use an application of the information contained in these materials or the live lectures that could accompany their distribution. In no event will the author, publisher, developer, or distributor be liable to the purchaser for any amount greater than the purchase price of these materials.

DEARBORN PUBLISHING, INC.'S warranty on the media, including any implied warranty of merchant ability or fitness for a particular purpose, is limited in duration to thirty (30) days from the date of the original retail. If a disk fails to work or if a disk becomes damaged, you may obtain a replacement disk by returning the original disk and a check or money order for $5.00, for each replacement disk, together with a brief explanation note and a dated sales receipt to:

DEARBORN PUBLISHING, INC.
30 SOUTH WACKER DRIVE, SUITE 2500
CHICAGO, IL 60606-1719

The replacement warranty set forth above is the sole and exclusive remedy against DEARBORN PUBLISHING, INC. for breach of warrant, express or implied for any default whatsoever relating to condition of the software. DEARBORN PUB-LISHING, INC. makes no other warranties or representation, either expressed or implied, with respect to this software or documentation, quality, merchantability performance, or fitness for a particular purpose as a result. This software is sold with only the limited warranty with respect to diskette replacement as provided above, and developers, directors, officers, employees, or affiliates be liable for direct, incidental, indirect, special, or consequential damages (including damages for loss of business profits, business interruption, loss of business information and the like) resulting from any defect in this software or its documentation or arising out of the use of or inability to use the software or accompanying documentation even if DEARBORN PUBLISHING, INC., an authorized DEARBORN PUB-LISHING, INC. representative, or a DEARBORN PUBLISHING, INC. affiliate has been advised of the possibility of such damage.

DEARBORN FINANCIAL PUBLISHING, INC. MAKES NO REPRE-SENTATION OR WARRANTY REGARDING THE RESULTS OBTAINABLE THROUGH USE OF THE SOFTWARE.

TECHNICAL SUPPORT IS NOT AVAILABLE ON THE ENCLOSED COMPUTER DISK. The software will auto install once the disk is inserted in your computer's CD-ROM drive. Please refer to the Software User Guide for instructions on how to use the software.

No oral or written information or advice given by DEARBORN FINANCIAL PUBLISHING, INC., its dealers, distributors, agents, affiliates, developers, officers, directors, or employees shall create a warranty or in any way increase the scope of this warranty.

Some states do not allow the exclusion or limitation of implied warranties or liabilities for incidental or consequential damages, so the above limitation or exclusion may not apply to you. This warranty gives you specific legal rights, and you may also have other rights which vary from state to state.

COPYRIGHT NOTICE: This software and accompanying manual are copyrighted with all rights reserved by DEARBORN FINANCIAL PUBLISHING, INC. Under United States copyright laws, the software and its accompanying documentation may not be copied in whole or in part except in normal use of the software or the reproduction of a backup copy for archival purposes only. Any other copying, selling, or otherwise distributing this software or manual is hereby expressly forbidden.